GEORGETOWN UNIVERSITY ROUND TABLE ON LANGUAGES AND LINGUISTICS 1994

Educational Linguistics, Crosscultural Communication, and Global Interdependence

James E. Alatis, *Editor*

Georgetown University Press, Washington, D.C.

Bibliographic notice

Since this series has been variously and confusingly cited as *Georgetown University Monograph Series on Languages and Linguistics, Monograph Series on Languages and Linguistics, Reports of the Annual Round Table Meeting on Linguistics and Language Study,* etc., beginning with the 1973 volume the title of the series was changed.

The new title of the series includes the year of a Round Table and omits both the monograph number and the meeting number, thus: *Georgetown University Round Table on Languages and Linguistics 1994*, with the regular abbreviation *GURT '94*. Full bibliographic references should show the form:

Kachru, Braj B. 1994. "The Speaking Tree: A medium of plural canons." In James E. Alatis (ed.), *Georgetown University Round Table on Languages and Linguistics 1994*. Washington, D.C.: Georgetown University Press. 6–22.

Printed in the United States of America

Library of Congress Catalog Number:
ISBN 0-87840-129-6
ISSN 0186-7207

To the memory of Francis P. Dinneen, s.j., Ph.d., 1923–1994

Contents

Welcoming remarks

James E. Alatis
Chair, Georgetown University Round Table on Languages and Linguistics

Good evening, ladies and gentlemen. My name is James E. Alatis, and I am Dean of the School of Languages and Linguistics and Chair of the Georgetown University Round Table on Languages and Linguistics.

Georgetown is an institution steeped in its traditions. One of those traditions, which has become particularly cherished and regularly recalled since I began chairing the Round Table, is that the Chair should make *very brief* remarks to leave sufficient time for the plenary speakers. So I shall honor that tradition this evening by restricting myself to words of welcome, words of thanks, and a few words of introduction.

First, the welcome. Welcome to Georgetown University, welcome to Gaston Hall and, most of all, welcome to the opening session of the Georgetown University Round Table on Languages and Linguistics 1994. Since that is such a mouthful, feel free to call our gathering GURT '94 for short. This, the forty-fifth annual Round Table, has as its theme "Educational Linguistics, Crosscultural Communication, and Global Interdependence."

Each year, the Round Table brings together senior college and university professors, program administrators, researchers, government professional staff, elementary and secondary school teachers, authors, and students of languages and linguistics. Here, they have the opportunity to listen, to discuss, and to learn from one another. Some have traveled great distances to be here: from Hong Kong, Singapore, Great Britain, the Ukraine, China, Israel, and Taiwan. Others have come all the way from the Intercultural Center, a good 100 yards from this room. No matter what the distance, we are delighted to have you join us and we hope you will consider the Round Table *your* conference.

Unlike a few other meetings and conferences that shall remain nameless—but their initials are MLA and TESOL—we have remained small and manageable enough that conversation is still possible. These conversations, through formal presentations, question-and-answer periods, and hallway and coffee break consultations, are a treasured characteristic of the Round Table, and one I am committed to maintain. I want to be sure that those who attend the Round Table are participants in the fullest sense of the word. I urge you to take advantage of the proximity of the most important voices in our field to ask questions or begin a scholarly debate. Please do not be shy. You will not ask the dumbest questions at the meeting: That is the prerogative of the conference Chair.

This year we have instituted a publishers' exhibition, which is being held in Copley Formal Lounge. Publishers will be displaying their books and taking orders, so please drop by, have a cup of coffee, and browse.

Before I move on, I would like to take a moment to recognize the organizers, speakers, and participants in the Round Table presessions. I am sure that those of you who had the opportunity to attend any of the presessions on Tuesday and Wednesday will agree that the themes, papers, and discussions were of a caliber that would be the envy of any major national or international scholarly meeting. I congratulate you on your hard work and your wonderful success. I am glad that the Round Table has been able to provide a venue for these presessions, and I hope that there will always be room at the Table for all studies in languages and linguistics.

A moment ago, I mentioned that a strength of the Round Table is its moderate size, and yet we do not wish to emulate the *first* Round Table, where lore has it that so few attended that everyone could be comfortably seated around a single round table. We need to achieve a certain critical mass, and that, believe me, does not just happen. It is a job that starts in July and keeps on going until the time to begin planning for the next meeting arrives again. Over the course of the semester, three fellows were assigned by the Linguistics Department. Their number was joined by a small army of some three dozen graduate and undergraduate student volunteers. And since I promised to leave at least a few minutes to our plenary speakers, rather than mentioning them all by name, let me suggest instead that we offer them all a round of applause.

I would be remiss, however, were I not to single out the individual who has directed the fellows and volunteers, kept the *S.S. GURT* on course, and generally made Cecil B. De Mille look like a rank amateur. That person is this year's conference Coordinator, Ms. Joan C. Cook. To get the word out, via journal listings, printed announcements, electronic bulletin boards, faxes, and telephone calls, is a monumental task. This year, the literally thousands of details that make up conference coordination were her responsibility, and her work has been nothing short of superb. Joan, who is working on her Ph.D. in sociolinguistics at Georgetown, has brought her considerable technical expertise to the Round Table. I am confident that through her use of the Internet and its countless lists—of which I am blissfully ignorant—we have been able to bring the word of the Round Table to more people than ever before. She has answered the same questions dozens of times and has resisted the temptation to tell us where we could find the answer in the written materials she has been sending us since July. And so, to Joan Cook, with thanks for all you have done and all I know you will be doing, please accept this bouquet of roses as a modest token of our gratitude.

In memory of the Rev. Francis P. Dinneen, S.J.

James E. Alatis
Chair, Georgetown University Round Table 1994

On Sunday, September 25, 1994, the Reverend Francis P. Dinneen, S.J., Professor Emeritus of Linguistics at Georgetown University, died from congestive heart failure in the Infirmary of the Jesuit Community at age 71. Father Dinneen was an important figure in the history of the School of Languages and Linguistics. He chaired the 1966 and 1974 Round Table conferences and edited the conference proceedings. Father Dinneen was also an influential figure behind the scenes of many other Round Tables, and in recognition of his many important contributions, the proceedings of this Round Table conference are dedicated in his memory.

When I learned of Father Dinneen's death I was, of course, deeply saddened and felt a great sense of loss—not just for me personally, but for the field of Linguistics and for Georgetown as well. His contributions to my life, to his discipline, and to this place and its people which and whom he loved, were profound and lasting. I think it appropriate to begin this volume by remembering the gifts he brought to each.

For me, Georgetown and Francis P. Dinneen were inextricably linked. In 1966, Dr. Lado hired me to come to Georgetown as his Associate Dean, then left for two years in Spain. Thus when I arrived on campus, I learned that Father Dinneen, as Acting Dean of the School of Languages and Linguistics, would be my "boss." I worked for him for the next two years and learned much from him about the Jesuits and their University. I also observed his leadership style, noting that he had high expectations, but that he trusted his colleagues and encouraged them to pursue their interests. Thus when he received a petition from some students to introduce Modern Greek into the curriculum, I told him that I would gladly teach it for "free." He told me that that was *exactly* the basis on which I would be doing it. It is an arrangement I have enjoyed for nearly thirty years.

Father Dinneen published what I believe to be the finest single volume on Linguistics ever published, called *An introduction to general linguistics*. Father generously permitted me to audit his course, "General Linguistics," in which he used his book, known by his students as "the catechism." I remember well his orderly way of introducing linguistics to some students for whom the abstract concepts did not come so easily. He would come striding into class, put on the blackboard the ten or so points he was going to cover, he would proceed to discuss them, and then he would return to the blackboard and tell us what it was we had covered. When he reviewed materials or answered questions, he knew each of his students by name, almost from the outset of the semester, no mean feat given the substantial enrollments in the basic graduate courses. He could do this because he took a photo of each one and linked the name with the face in the next day or two. His students never forgot him, either, and whenever and wherever I travelled, I would invariably run into his students, who would ask about him and share fond memories. Indeed, at the last SLL alumni reunion I hosted, I invited Father Dinneen as my guest. He received a warm and spontaneous standing ovation from his former students.

I also remember that before he taught his class, he left strict word with his redoubtable assistant, Mrs. Johansen, that he was not to be disturbed as he prepared for class. Mrs. Johansen was an excellent gatekeeper/protector and kept visitors at bay during this time. Once, in a rare moment of laxity, I managed to "penetrate the perimeter" and made my way into Father's office. I told him that I needed to see him about several matters at least as important as life and death. As he escorted me graciously, but swiftly, from his office, he reminded me that nothing at Georgetown was more important than teaching. That was a lesson I never forgot, and it has always been for me one of the defining characteristics of the University.

Father Dinneen was also a man who believed in the positive value of his field and of the power of a Georgetown education. I had written a successful proposal in 1968 to bring inner-city school teachers to campus to participate in our new Master of Arts in Teaching program. Many of the traditionalists on the faculty felt that these teachers would not benefit from our courses as they lacked the academic background to comprehend the lofty world of linguistics. These gentlemen resisted the new program and were not eager to teach in it. Father Dinneen, however, syllabus in hand, camera slung over his shoulder, and metaphysical "aviator scarf" flung around his neck, offered these new students his course in General Linguistics. The program was such a success, and his contributions to it so important, that he was the University's spokesman on a WETA program in the '60s talking about Georgetown's commitment to the city of Washington and its people.

Father Dinneen's service to Georgetown University is legendary, including decades of service on committees such as Campus Planning, Student Personnel Policy, Athletics, and Student Life. A long-time member of the Faculty Senate, he was also its President. I already mentioned his service as Acting Dean of SLL. When he completed that assignment, he got on the Nevils elevator, an act of faith in and of itself, and rode it down to the first floor to serve for a year as Acting Dean of the Graduate School.

Father Dinneen served his colleagues as Head of the Division of Theoretical Linguistics, and later he became the first Chair of the unified Linguistics

Department. As Chair, he was a strong leader and defender of Linguistics in all its aspects. His dedication was strongest to theoretical Linguistics, but he nevertheless was very supportive of applied linguistics—following the leadership of Dr. Lado—and he was most encouraging of sociolinguistics, both while the proposal for the program was being drafted and after the program was initiated here at Georgetown. It is thanks in large part to Father Dinneen that Georgetown enjoys such a prominent position in the many subfields of linguistics.

Today, when people refer to University service, they speak of committee work and terms as Chair. And to be sure, Father Dinneen's dossier is replete with examples of that kind of "service." But, as a lesson to younger colleagues, convinced perhaps of their own importance, he set an even greater example of "service." During his terms as either Chair or Acting Dean, following an evening session of the Georgetown University Round Table on Languages and Linguistics (GURT), he and Father O'Brien could be found sweeping the floors and otherwise tidying up the Hall of Nations for the morning meeting. When I asked him about this, he told me that the custodians would have had to stay late to do it and they should be getting home to their families.

He viewed all his work, including his high-level appointments, in the role of servant. Although surely a servant with strong views—views which he shared liberally—he sought no personal gain, no singular glory. He lived the motto of the Society, "*Ad Majorem Dei Gloriam*," and it was this humility, this utter lack of concern for self-aggrandizement that amazed and endeared him to so many of his students and colleagues whose cultural backgrounds had not prepared them for a man of his academic stature to be at the same time a man blessed with the "common touch."

So when that telephone call came on that Sunday afternoon telling me that Father Dinneen had passed away, I was saddened—not for him, but for all of us. I knew that, as a man of faith, rich in accomplishments and in friends, he was prepared for his passing from this life. For those of us whose lives he touched, we are left with our memories of Father Dinneen: a gentleman and a gentle man. We recall his incisive and infectious sense of humor and the twinkle in his eye as he delivered his punchline. We recall a friend, kinder and wiser than we had a right to expect, but for whose friendship we are forever grateful. As we say in Greek:

Αἰωνία ἡ μνήμη
Αἰωνία ἡ μνήμη
Αἰωνία αὐτοῦ ἡ μνήμη
Eternal the memory
Eternal the memory
May the memory of him be eternal.

The Speaking Tree: A medium of plural canons

Braj B. Kachru
University of Illinois at Urbana-Champaign

Introduction.[1] The Speaking Tree analogy in the title of this paper is relevant in more than one sense. The legend of the Speaking Tree has historical depth—it actually dates back at least four millennia—and has been mentioned with reference to Alexander the Great, who, we are told, was taken in India "to an oracular tree which could answer questions in the language of any [one] who addressed it." (Lannoy 1971: xxv).The trunk of the tree, it is claimed, was made of snakes and animal heads, and the branches "bore fruit like beautiful women, who sang the praises of the Sun and Moon" (xxv). In the Moghul miniature, following the Islamic tradition, the Waqwaq tree—the Speaking Tree—is viewed with both awe and attraction.[2]

The trunk of the English language—the Inner Circle[3]—evokes mixed responses, as did that of the Speaking Tree, but the branches are bearing delectable fruit. The linguistic Speaking Tree is blooming, for we believe it answers all our questions. The questions related to accessibility to knowledge, the questions of pragmatic functions, and those of creative functions. In short, we have a unique oracle with many faces.

And now, stretching the analogy a little further, I believe that the three dimensions of this year's theme of the Georgetown University Round Table—cross-cultural communication, global interdependence, and, indeed, educational linguistics—are again very closely related to the Speaking Tree of our times—the world Englishes. I shall, therefore, try to relate these three dimensions of the theme to world Englishes today.

The concept "world Englishes" demands that we begin with a distinction between English as a medium and English as a repertoire of cultural pluralism: one refers to the form of language, and the other to its function, its content. It is the medium that is designed and organized for multiple cultural—or

---

1. This paper is dedicated to James E. Alatis, whose own professional career represents active commitment to promoting the three dimensions of the 1994 theme of the Georgetown University Round Table on Languages and Linguistics (March 13-16, 1994).

2. There are versions of this legend in other cultures too.

3. See Kachru (1985) and later.

cross-cultural—conventions. It is in this sense that one understands the concepts "global," "pluralistic," and "multi-canons" with reference to the forms and functions of world Englishes. What we share as members of the international English-using speech community is the medium, that is, the vehicle for the transmission of the English language. The medium per se, however, has no constraints on what message—cultural or social—we transmit through it. And English is a paradigm example of medium in this sense.

When we call English a global medium, it means that those who use English across cultures have a shared code of communication. And the result of this shared competence is that, in spite of various types of crucial differences, we believe that we communicate with each other—one user of English with another, a Nigerian with an Indian, a Japanese with a German, and a Singaporean with an American. It is in this broad sense of interlocutors that we have *one* language and *many* voices. The Speaking Tree responds to our cultural specificity and moves us beyond.

It is this cross-cultural function in education, in business, in tourism, in personal interaction, and in literary creativity that has given English an unprecedented status as a global and cross-cultural code of communication. And the evidence for such unparalleled roles acquired by one language has been documented in several ways in numerous studies.[4] It is for this power that English is presented as an Aladdin's lamp for opening the doors to cultural and religious "enlightenment" as the "language for all seasons," a "universal language," a language with no national or regional frontiers and the language on which the sun never sets. Or, to use McArthur's (1994) term, "the organized Babel."

Medium vs. message. The cross-cultural functions and globalization of English have, however, come at a price. How high the price is depends on whom one talks to. The English language and literature have slowly ceased to be exclusively Eurocentric, Judeo-Christian, and Western.[5] There is, as it were, a diffusion of other traditionally unaccepted canons; it is not that other canons are as yet necessarily accepted or recognized—far from that. However, there is debate about such issues. Gates (1992: xvi) warns us,

4. For references, see, for example, Bailey and Görlach (ed.) (1982), Kachru (ed.) (1982[1992], and 1986[1990]) and McArthur (ed.) (1992).

5. I must hasten to add that I am aware of the hazards and oversimplification of using these broad cover terms, for example, combining the Judeo-Christian tradition, and considering the Western tradition as if it uniformly shares one tradition.

> Cultural pluralism is not, of course, everyone's cup of tea. Vulgar cultural nationalists—like Allan Bloom or Leonard Jeffries— correctly identify it as the enemy. These polemicists thrive on absolute partitions: between "civilization" and "barbarism," between "black" and "white," between a thousand versions of Us and Them. But they are whistling in the wind.

For some, Gates may sound too optimistic, it is, however, evident that the language and literary creativity in English have acquired many faces, of many colors, regions, and competencies.

And now, at least in some circles, the use of the term "English literature" is considered rather restricted and monocultural. Instead, the term "English literatures" is steadily gaining acceptance (See Quirk and Widdowson ed. 1985), and the term "Englishes" or "world Englishes" does not raise eyebrows in every circle. This terminological feud is not innocent; it is loaded with ideologies, economic interests, and strategies for power. And now a serious question is being asked about English: "Whose language is it, anyway?"[6]

By looking at English as a pluralistic language, we are actually focusing on its layer after layer of extended processes of convergence with other languages and cultures. And this convergence and contact is unique, since it has altered the traditional resources for contact, for example, French, German, Italian, and Scandinavian. The language has opened up itself, as it were, to convergence with the non-Western world: that part of the world that was traditionally not a resource for English. It is here that, for example, West Africa, East Africa, South Asia, West Asia, and the Philippines become relevant and have become contributors to and partners in the pluralism of the language.[7] The opening up of the language, and the multiculturalism expressed in the language, does not mean that these multi-strands, from the Inner Circle or the Outer Circle, have been accepted by the power elite. That has yet to happen. The canons in the Outer Circle, the African American, the Chicano, and the Asian American, continue to be "loose canons," as Gates appropriately characterizes them. And the result is "the culture wars."[8]

And now, coming back to our topic, by pluralism we mean the multiple identities that constitute a repertoire of cultures, linguistic experimentation and innovations, and literary traditions. And they come from a variety of sources.

---

6. For various perspectives on this debate from a linguistic perspective see relevant papers in Tickoo (ed.) (1991), especially papers by Honey, Quirk, and Kachru.

7. For an extended discussion and some examples see Kachru (1994a), and papers on this topic in *World Englishes in Contact and Convergence,* special issue of *World Englishes* 13.2. 1994.

8. For further discussion again, from a linguistic perspective, see, e.g., Dissanayake (1985), Kachru (1985,1986, and 1991) and Thumboo (1985 and 1992).

It is in this sense that English embodies multiculturalism. And it is in this sense that English is a global language. The input to this multiculturalism, then, comes from three types of users who constitute three Concentric Circles—the Inner Circle, the Outer Circle, and the Expanding Circle. This nomenclature has sociolinguistic, ideological, and pedagogical significance. It is again in this sense that the language represents "an organized Babel."[9]

Exponents of multiculturalism. The strands of multiculturalism in world Englishes are of several types, but all have one thing in common: they manifest the multilinguals' creativity. This creativity is not necessarily consistent with the traditionally accepted norms of English, particularly when the violation of the norm comes from the Outer Circle. The first strand is that of cultural identity of a variety—Nigerian, Indian, Singaporean—that is distinct from the Judeo-Christian identity of the language. An example is *The Serpent and the Rope* by Raja Rao of India, which essentially follows the Vedantic tradition. The Sanskritized style of the novel has an ideological and metaphysical context, e.g., "God is, and goodness is part of that is-ness." And for stylistic appreciation of G.V. Desani's *All About H. Hatterr* (1951), knowledge of Sanskrit compounding (*samāsa*) certainly facilitates interpreting constructions such as "Ruler of the firmament; Son of the mighty-bird," "... Thy sister my darling, thy name?" Naipaul believes that R. K. Narayan's novels are "... religious books ... and intensely Hindu" (Naipaul 1977: 13).

A recent excellent attempt in this direction is Shashi Tharoor's *The Great Indian Novel*: a contemporary story woven around the *Mahābhārata*, an epic of ancient India and the longest poem in the world, dating back to the fourth century B.C. We see the same types of strands in, for example, Gabriele Okara, T. M. Aluko, and Onuora Nzekwu in West Africa.

The second aspect brings in appropriate acculturation of the language, to mould it to function in the sociocultural, religious, and interactional context of Africa or Asia. We notice this in culture-specific personal interactions, in the news media, in matrimonial advertisements, in obituaries, and in letters of invitation. The matrimonial columns reflect African or Asian sensitivity and prejudices regarding color, caste hierarchy, regional attitudes, and family structure.

The third aspect relates to discourse strategies and speech acts. These are transcreated into English to approximate the Asian and African backgrounds, religious subgroups, and interactional contexts of a variety of African and Asian languages: They include culture-specific patterns of apologies, compliments, condolences, persuasion, politeness, and requests. These contextualized

9. See Kachru (1992) for discussion of the identities of English and innovations in creativity in the Outer Circle.

strategies are skillfully exploited by, for example, Mulk Raj Anand, Raja Rao, Ahmed Ali, and Anita Desai in South Asia and by Chinua Achebe, Wole Soyinka, and Nuruddin Farah in Africa.[10] It is this acculturation of English that raises the question: My language, your culture: whose communicative competence? (Nelson 1992).

This very significant question has yet to be answered. The reason is that our current paradigms of teaching continue to be based on monolingual and monocultural notions of creativity and canon formation or canon expansion. I will return to this point in the following section.

Canon expansion. When we talk of "canon expansion," it takes us to a complex question of what is meant by the concepts of canon and multi-canon. This, of course, is an elusive question, like defining the terms "standard" or "norm." "Standard," as Abercrombie (1951: 15) has warned us, provides "an accent bar," and "the accent bar is a little like color-bar to many people; on the right side of the bar, it appears eminently reasonable." And this is true of canon formation. As for norms and standards, one has to recognize "... the politics and ironies of canon formation," as Gates (1992: 32) clearly does, in defining the canon of African American literature. Following Kermode, one might say that

> canons are essentially strategic constructs by which societies maintain their own interests, since the canon allows control over the texts a culture takes seriously and over the methods of interpretation that establish the meaning "serious." (cited in Altieri 1990: 22)

In connection with canon formation, several questions come to mind. The first is, what are the defining characteristics of a canon? Now, keeping in mind what I said about the notions "standard" and "norm," canon is both a symbol of self-identification and of power. It is also a strategy for exclusion. However, canon does presuppose a cultural identity and tradition, a linguistic experimentation and innovation, and an extended period of creativity that makes it possible to compare creativity within a canon and across canons, in spite of the gatekeepers of canons. It is in this sense, then, that one talks of the "masterpieces," the "classics," and the "standard works." I used the words "self-identification" and "power." A good example of this is provided by Said (1993: 37) when he refers to the rather acrimonious debate on the curriculum changes at Stanford University.

10. For examples, see, Kachru 1982; Smith (ed.) (1987), and Y. Kachru (1991).

Bernard Lewis, a senior Orientalist—and, as Said says, "an authority on Islam"—entered the debate about changing the "Western canon." And commenting on Lewis's observation, Said writes:

> [Lewis] took the extreme position that "if Western culture does indeed go a number of things would go with it and others would come in their place." No one had said anything so ludicrous as "Western culture must go," but Lewis's argument, focussed on much grander matters than strict accuracy, lumbered forward with the remarkable proposition that since modifications in the reading list would be equivalent to the demise of Western culture, such subjects (he named them specifically) as the restoration of slavery, polygamy, and child marriage would ensue. To this amazing thesis Lewis added that "curiosity about other cultures," which he believes is unique to the West, would also come to an end.

This position of a distinguished Orientalist is not much different from William Bennett's call for "reclaiming our heritage" and my compatriot Dinesh D'Souza's alarm about multiculturalism.[11]

The question, however, becomes more complex when other dimensions are added to what is believed to be one medium and primarily one canon (the Western canon), ignoring the linguistic and cultural crossover of the language. What this attitude negates is:

- that English as a medium is used by two distinct types of speech communities, those that perceive themselves as monolingual and monocultural, and those that are multilingual and multicultural;
- that these speech communities represent distinct literary and/or oral traditions and mythologies; and
- that the norms of literary creativity and linguistic experimentation arc not necessarily shared.

A number of creative writers from Africa and Asia, and Chicano writers in the United States, have addressed this complex question. In 1965, Achebe asked the question, "Can an African ever learn English well enough to be able to use it effectively in creative writing?" His answer is "certainly yes." But then he adds: "if on the other hand you ask. 'Can he [an African] ever learn to use it like a native speaker?' I should say, 'I hope not.' It is neither necessary nor desirable for him to be able to do so" (1965: 222).

At another place—over two decades later—Achebe asserts the same position, much more forcefully (Jussawalla and Dasenbrock 1992: 16):

---

11. See D'Souza (1991).

> Most African writers write out of an African experience and of commitment to an African destiny. For them, that destiny does not include a future European identity for which the present is but an apprenticeship.

The second question is: What are the implications of canon expansion? I believe that canon expansion is an indicator of two processes: divergence and convergence. Divergence marks the differences between two or more varieties of English, and convergence indicates shared *Englishness* in world Englishes. It is the shared features that mark, for example, Nigerian English, Kenyan English, or Indian English as varieties of what we know as Englishes. In the Outer Circle, the divergence is conscious, as in, for example, Achebe, Rao, and Anand, and also a result of multilinguals' creativity. Ngũgĩ refers to this multilingual context when he says that in Kenya, there is Swahili as the lingua franca, and there are "nationality languages" such as Gikuyu and Luo. And "by playing with this language situation, you can get another level of meaning through the interaction of all three languages."[12]

Multi-canons as symbols and substance. We must view canon expansion as more than mere linguistic experimentation, since multi-canons in English have symbolic and substantive meaning: symbolic in the sense that one's identity is symbolic, and substantive in the way the identity is expressed, articulated, negotiated, and preserved in language.

How we respond to these symbols and articulation of identities is not just an issue of attitude toward another canon within world Englishes: It is more than that, it also becomes an issue of ideology and of power. And it is the ideological issues that reflect in the selection of paradigms of enquiry and models for research. These issues determine how one conceptualizes a speech community, how one constructs the barriers for US and THEM, for INSIDERS and OUTSIDERS. The issue has more serious implications when monolingualism, knowing only one language, is considered the norm for generalizations about the English-knowing speech community, for pedagogical models, for literary creativity, and, of course, for theory construction.[13]

And if we look at global language use, norms of language interaction, and literary creativity across societies—Asian, African, and European—it is evident that the majority of the world's population is either bi- or multilingual, or, at least, diglossic. The diglossic users of a language choose between a formal and

---

12. See Jussawalla and Desenbrock (eds.) (1992: 34); see also Kachru (1986 [1990], chapter 10).

13. In recent years this issue has been discussed in several studies, e.g., Phillipson (1992), Kachru (1994b).

colloquial variety of language, as do, for example, Arabic, Tamil, and Greek speakers.

And from a multilingual's perspective, even the concept *second* language learning is in reality somewhat restrictive and misleading. The concept *second* language learning and teaching does not have pragmatic validity in West Africa, East Africa, Southeast Asia, and South Asia. In these regions, as in many other regions, bilingualism or trilingualism is a part of daily interaction, and it is in such interactional contexts that English has emerged as yet another linguistic code interfacing in Nigeria, for example, with Yoruba, Hausa, and Igbo; in Singapore with Chinese, Malay, Tamil, and Panjabi; in Kenya with Swahili and several of "nationality languages"; and in India with at least eighteen major languages recognized by the Republic's constitution. It is in such culturally and linguistically pluralistic contexts that African English, South Asian English, and Philippine English have developed. I purposely used the modifiers *African*, *South Asian* and *Philippine* with English. The modifiers are markers of change and adaptation: change due to contact with languages and adaptation in terms of acculturation.

I have so far tried to unfold a dimension of English that looks at language variation, linguistic creativity, and linguistic identity within a pluralistic perspective. I believe that the global dimension of creativity in English, and its recognition in the classroom, in the curriculum, and in teacher training, has relevance to educational linguistics.

However, before we take that step we must seek liberation from consciously cultivated myths about world Englishes. These myths are the result of flawed hypotheses, a lack of empirical and sociolinguistic links with the contexts of language use, or deliberate myth-making. As examples, I shall consider here four such myths that are relevant to this topic.

The interlocutor myth: That across cultures English is functionally learned to interact with the native speakers of English, American, Australian, or British. Actually, most of the interaction in English takes place among and between its nonnative speakers: Indians with Sri Lankans, Germans with Singaporeans, Japanese with Malaysians, and so on.

The monoculture myth: That English is learned as a vehicle for learning American or British culture, or what has been labeled the Judeo-Christian tradition. This is only partially true. Actually, in what I have termed the Outer Circle, with ethnic and linguistic pluralism, English is used to impart native cultural values and historical traditions. An analysis of the textbooks, print media, and creative writing in India, Nigeria, Kenya, Pakistan, and Singapore provides excellent evidence for this claim. The roles English is assigned are primarily integrative in a national sense.

The interlanguage myth: That the nonnative institutionalized varieties are essentially "interlanguages" or "fossilized" varieties striving to achieve "native-like" character. It has already been shown that this conceptualization is of very limited merit (see e.g. Sridhar and Sridhar 1992; Nelson 1992; Y. Kachru 1993; B. Kachru 1994b).

The Cassandra myth. That the diversification and variation in English is an indicator of linguistic decay and that restricting the decay is the job of native speakers as teachers of English literature and language and of ESL professionals. This argument, of course, depends on how one views language codification, language dynamics, and sociolinguistic realities and pragmatism. I have addressed the Cassandra myth in detail in an earlier study (Kachru 1991).

This is only a partial list of the myths (see also Kachru 1990: 203–29, especially p. 224 for theoretical, methodological, formal, functional, and attitudinal fallacies).

World English literatures and transcultural canons. We have traditionally discussed literary creativity in English within the framework of monolingualism and the native tongue, monolingualism being the norm and literary creativity an artistic manifestation of it—in other words, within the impact of the above four myths. And the result of this monolingualism myth is that Conrad and Nabokov, for example, have been viewed as "exceptions" to this cherished norm (see e.g. Crystal cited in Paikeday 1985: 66–67; and Shils 1988: 560). These assumptions not only cloud our view of creativity in world Englishes but also distract us from the study of world Englishes as transcultural and multilingual canons. As a result, we have ignored the fact that this manifestation of literary creativity—more widespread than the monolingual's—reveals that bi- or multilingualism is normal activity and bilinguals' creativity is a normal manifestation of such linguistic competence.

This situation is well illustrated in Forster (1970), to give just one example. Forster traces multilingualism in European literatures through the Middle Ages and the Renaissance and illustrates it even with the writers of the twentieth century. He skillfully demonstrates (1970: 7) that "the idea of polyglot poets" is less strange than we believe. And he argues that it is due to the influence of the Romantics that:

> ... we have all been brought up to believe that each language has its mystery and its soul, and that these are very sacred things, in whose name indeed much blood has been shed in our own lifetime and is still being shed. ... [I]f we put sentiment aside, there are very many people and very many situations for which different languages are simply tools appropriate

> to certain definite purposes, analogous to the different stylistic levels within any one language.

In the global context, from the earliest period, elitist literary creativity has been carried on in nonnative languages. In Europe, we see such creativity in, for example, Latin and Greek, and in South Asia, in Sanskrit and Persian. In essentially monolingual contexts, or where the mother tongue has been the primary language for creativity, there generally are diglossic situations. In such situations, traditionally the High variety was used for literary creativity: *sādhu bhāśā* in Bengali; *granthikā* in Telugu; the formal variety in Tamil; Persianized or Sanskritized varieties in Kashmiri. The High varieties have always been distant from the common varieties used by the speakers of these languages. This much about the claims of Crystal and Shills.

In transcultural creativity in the *other tongue,* we have seen several distinctive characteristics. Such creativity entails formal "patterning"—conscious or unconscious from more than one language. However, there is one language that provides, as it were, the scaffolding and the raw formal apparatus for transcreation of the texts. In establishing such an equivalence, the creative writers obviously have to make several decisions. The writer can do what Mulk Raj Anand and Amos Tutuola have done in terms of equivalence: keep the text in English close to Punjabi and Yoruba, respectively.

A writer may take another track, that of Raja Rao. Rao does not establish equivalence at the lexical level or in terms of the speech functions only. He goes much beyond that; he recreates a distinct discourse. One type of strategy is evident in Rao's *Kanthapura* and another type in his *The Serpent and the Rope*: one representing the vernacular style of the mother tongue and the other, of Sanskritization. It is almost recreation (or transfer) of the diglossic situation into English. In such literary creation, much depends on how close the bilingual writer wants to remain to the formal patterning of the *other* language.

Does this, then, mean that in characterizing creativity in world Englishes, for example, in speech acts, we have three broad classes of writers, as D'souza (1991: 309) has proposed for Indian English: the Minimizers (e.g. Anita Desai, Amitav Ghosh, Kamala Markandaya, R. K. Narayan); the Nativizers (e.g. Mulk Raj Anand, Bhabani Bhattacharya, Khushwant Singh) and the Synthesizers (e.g. Meena Alexander, Upamanyu Chatterjee, Bharati Mukherjee)? At one level this categorization is insightful; but, then, once we discuss, for example, *Clear Light of Day* by Anita Desai, the Minimizer category creates problems in interpreting the vital functions of "the four-fold pattern" and the significance of the number four in the Indian tradition (Zimmer 1972: 13). At the lexico-grammatical level, Desai is a Minimizer, but not so at the higher level at which the text has a sociocultural meaning.

Perhaps as compared with Raja Rao's *The Serpent and the Rope,* Desai is less complex. Rao's *The Serpent and the Rope*, a metaphysical novel, is said to have four distinct voices. This requires contextualizing the text in the sociocultural and religious milieu of Vedanta and an understanding of the complexities of the Vedantic doctrine.

What we see, then, is that world English literatures raise a variety of theoretical, descriptive, and pedagogical issues concerning culture and its interpretation and comprehension of a text across cultures. One must ask, for example,

- How does one approach this totality?
- How does one approach the distinct parts of this totality?
- What is universal in such a body of creativity?
- What is specific?
- How does one apply the methodology of educational linguistics for teaching this body of culturally pluralistic creativity?

The above discussion brings to the forefront a string of broad points concerning transcultural literary creativity in English and the cultural component in such creativity, and issues related to interpretation.

I believe that there are other interconnected issues that deserve attention. One major point concerns the recognition of an unprecedented event of our times: the development of world Englishes as a vital multicultural resource. This resource has established itself as a multiplicity of canons, which incorporate several regional, sociocultural, linguistic, and literary identities. The process of canon formation is an ongoing one, an evolving one. In building this canon, in its distinctiveness, linguistic, discoursal, and stylistic, various linguistic processes, including that of translation, play a vital role. But this is only one part of canon building.

There is, as it were, "the interplay of diverse voices" (Dissanayake 1989: xvi): polyphony, multivocality, and heteroglossia. This view is precisely that of Bakhtin (1981: 262 cited in Dissanayake 1989). It is this process

> whereby the unified meaning of the whole is structured and revealed. In comprehension and interpretation of a text and the canon that it belongs to, the notion of intertextuality provides a good theoretical backdrop.[14]

---

14. Kristeva (1969:146) defines intertextuality as a "sum of knowledge that makes it possible for texts to have meaning: *meaning of text as dependent on other text that it absorbs and transforms*" (cited in Sareen 1989: 42).

One might ask: why is there a resistance to view literatures in world Englishes within this perspective? Is it, again, an extension of "monolingualization"? Lefevre (1990: 24) believes it is. In his view this attitude is

> another pernicious outgrowth of the "monolingualization" of literary history by Romantic historiographers intent on creating "national" literatures preferably as uncontaminated as possible by foreign influences.

The Romantic historiographers would certainly not approve of present "multilingualization" and extreme "contamination" of English from foreign influences.

World Englishes and educational linguistics. And now, let me turn to yet another dimension of the theme of the Round Table, that of "educational linguistics." In this brief discussion, I will not go into the controversies concerning this subfield but will instead accept the outline and boundaries of the subfield as presented in Stubbs (1986).

In the United States, multiculturalism as a societal or as a pedagogical concept has been perceived both as a divisive practice and as an enriching experience. It has been seen as a step toward national Balkanization and as a laboratory for mutual understanding. In literature and language, the variationist approaches have been applauded for social realism and attacked as "liberation linguistics," an offshoot of "liberation theology" (see Kachru 1991). However, we must agree with Hughes, who says that

> In society as in farming, monoculture works poorly. It exhausts the soil. The social richness of America, so striking to the foreigner, comes from the diversity of its tribes. Its capacity for cohesion, for some spirit of common agreement on what is to be done, comes from the willingness of those tribes not to elevate their cultural differences into impassable barriers and ramparts. (cited in Gates 1993: 115)

And commenting on this, Gates is right when he says that Hughes "...provides one of the most gruffly appealing defenses of genuine multiculturalism that we have" (1993: 115).

And now, let us take this vision of the United States beyond the United States and bring in Europe; the Middle East; South and East Asia; sub-Saharan Africa; the Philippines; and South America. That is almost the whole globe: that is the global vision. That abstract global vision, with its linguistic diversity, cultural interfaces, societal hierarchies, and conflicts, is captured in the various strands of world Englishes. The vision is Indian, Vedantic, and metaphysical in Raja Rao; it is Nigerian in Wole Soyinka and Chinua Achebe; it is East African in Ngũgĩ; and it is a Singaporean blend of Chinese and Malay in Catherine Lim. The architects of each tradition, each strand, and each variation have used the raw material of what is considered a Western medium, molded it, reshaped it, and redesigned it. And the resultant creativity reflects vitality, innovation, and cultural and linguistic mix. It is not the creativity of a monolingual and monocultural medium; it has redeemed the medium from "exhaustion."

That this literature is a product of multilingualism and of multiculturalism has yet to be seriously realized. The use of such literature(s) as a resource in the classroom has yet to be fully explored. The difficulties in doing so are not only that appropriate pedagogical resources are limited. That may be true, but that is only part of the problem. A more serious difficulty is that we have still not shaken off the "Romantic histographer's" view of the English language and literature—the legacy continues, as suggested by Lefevre.

What is more frustrating, we have marginalized such creativity and multicultural dimensions of English by using terms such as "commonwealth literature" or "Third World Literature." I will not elaborate on this point but will present an excerpt from Salman Rushdie (1991: 61). In this illuminating observation, Rushdie says,

> When I was invited to speak at the 1983 English Studies Seminar in Cambridge, the lady from the British Council offered me a few words of reassurance. 'It's all right,' I was told, 'for the purposes of our seminar, English studies are taken to include Commonwealth literature.' At all other times, one was forced to conclude, these two would be kept strictly apart, like squabbling children, or sexually incompatible pandas, or, perhaps, like unstable, fissile materials whose union might cause explosions.

And Rushdie continues,

> A few weeks later I was talking to a literature don—a specialist, I ought to say, in *English* literature—a friendly and perceptive man. 'As a Commonwealth writer,' he suggested, 'you probably find, don't you, that there's a kind of liberty, certain advantages, in occupying, as you do, a position on the periphery?' (1991: 61)

In reality, one doesn't have to quote Rushdie here: One sees this attitude about the African American canon and the Chicano canon. And not many years ago—just over half a century ago—the same attitude was expressed about American literature in Britain. The great pundit of the American language, H. L. Mencken, summarizes well the British attitude toward American English when he writes that "[t]his occasional tolerance for things American was never extended to the American language." This was in 1936.

Let me summarize the ways the preceding discussion relates to educational linguistics. I believe that literature in world Englishes and linguistic innovations from diverse cultural contexts provide refreshing texts for interdisciplinary debate and research. I have discussed these in detail elsewhere (Kachru 1992a, 1992b). These include

- crosscultural discourse
- the bilingual's creativity
- language contact and convergence
- language acquisition
- intelligibility
- lexicography
- language, ideology, and power

The teaching of world Englishes, then, entails a paradigm shift in several ways. The following points deserve attention for training professionals and for teaching advanced students:

- sociolinguistic profiles of the forms and functions of English;
- variety exposure and sensitivity
- functional validity of varieties within a variety (e.g., Nigerian Pidgin, Basilect, Bazaar English)
- range and depth of uses and users
- contrastive pragmatics
- multiculturalism in content and creativity

The application of educational linguistics for exploring the crosscultural dimensions of world Englishes entails three steps—actually three interrelated steps: i.e.,

- *Selection of a model,* that is, choosing a linguistic approach that is relevant to various dimensions of world Englishes. It has to be one of the models that provides a framework of socially realistic linguistics, e.g., Michael Halliday's and Dell Hymes's.
- *Identification of domains,* that is, demarcating the domains in which the distinctiveness of a canon is articulated and characterizing the innovations within a linguistic framework.
- *Development of materials,* that is, developing pedagogical and resource materials for the functions identified in the above two steps.

There is also a provocative ideological facet to English teaching: Why is English considered a language of power? What ideology does English represent? Why do, for example, Ngũgĩ—and some others—consider English a "culture-bomb," and, to quote Ngũgĩ again, "... probably the most racist of all human languages" (1981: 14)? Why does English evoke—or symbolize—positive or negative labels that range from "cultural-bomb" and "killer English" to language of "liberalism" and "universalism"?

Conclusion. These are some of the provocative and challenging questions for discussion related to one language in its various global incarnations, in its multicanons. I believe that we are depriving ourselves—as teachers and students—of an immense resource of cross-cultural perspectives and strategies of multilinguals' creativity if world Englishes are viewed exclusively from Judeo-Christian and monolingual perspectives.

By marginalizing the global uses of English, we are walling up an important world vision. And this reminds me of what an Indian pragmatist and wise man, Mohandas K. Gandhi (1864–1948) said so well in another context:

> I do not want my house to be walled in on all sides and my windows to be stuffed. I want the cultures of all lands to be blown about my house as freely as possible. But I refuse to be blown off my feet by any. I would have our young men and women with literary tastes to learn as much of English and other world languages as they like, and then expect them to give the benefits of their learning to India and to the world ... But I would not have a single Indian to forget, neglect or be ashamed of his mother tongue, or to feel that he or she cannot think or express the best thoughts in his or her own vernacular. Mine is not a religion of the prison-house. (1921, cited in Mesthrie 1993: 7)

The medium of English now provides that cross-cultural house. What is needed is a pluralistic vision to use this resource with sensitivity and understanding. And we must ask the right questions of the Speaking Tree to get appropriate answers for our linguistic, pragmatic, and pluralistic concerns and challenges. It means seeking answers for "curatorial" and "normative" functions of canon (Altieri 1990: 33). These are, then, the types of questions I have raised in this paper.

REFERENCES

Abercrombie, David. 1951. "R.P. and local accent." *The Listener* September 6, 1951. Reprinted in David Abercrombie (1965), *Studies in phonetics and linguistics*. London: Oxford University Press.

Achebe, Chinua. 1965. "English and the African writer." *Transition*, Kampala, April 18, 1995. Reproduced in Ali A. Mazrui, *The politics of the English language: An African Perspective*. The Hague: Mouton, 1973.

Altieri, Charles. 1990. *Canons and consequences: Reflections on the ethical force of imaginative ideals*. Evanston, Illinois: Northwestern University Press.

Bailey, Richard W. and Manfred Görlach (eds.). 1982. *English as a world language*. Ann Arbor: University of Michigan Press.

Bakhtin, Mikhail. 1981. *The dialogic imagination*. Austin: University of Texas Press.

D'Souza, Dinesh. 1991. *Illiberal education: The politics of race and sex on campus*. New York: The Free Press.

D'souza, Jean. 1991. "Speech acts in Indian English fiction." *World Englishes* 10(3): 307–316.

Desani, G.V. 1951. *All about H. Hatterr*. New York: Farrar, Straus and Young. Reprinted 1972, New York: Lancer Books.

Dissanayake, Wimal. 1985. "Towards a decolonized English: South Asian creativity in fiction." *World Englishes* 4(2): 233–242.

Dissanayake, Wimal. 1989. "Introduction: Literary history, narrative, and culture. Perplexities of meaning." In Wimal Dissanayake and S. Bradbury (eds.), *Literary history. Narrative and culture: Selected conference papers*. Honolulu: University of Hawaii Press.

Forster, Leonard. 1970. *The poet's tongues: Multilingualism in literature* (The de Carle Lectures at the University of Otago 1968). Cambridge, U.K.: Cambridge University Press (in association with University of Otago Press.)

Gandhi, Mohandas Karamchand. 1921. *Young India*.

Gates, Jr., Henry Louis. 1992. *Loose canons: Notes on the culture wars*. New York: Oxford University Press.

Gates, Jr., Henry Louis. 1993. "The weaning of America." *The New Yorker*. April 19, 112–117.

Hughes, Robert. 1993. *Culture of complaint: The fraying of America*. New York and Oxford: Oxford University Press.

Jussawalla, Feroza and Reed Way Dasenbrock (eds.). 1992. *Interviews with writers of the post-colonial world*. Jackson, Mississippi: University of Mississippi.

Kachru, Braj B. 1992. "Meaning in deviation." In Braj B. Kachru (ed.). 1982 [1992]. *The other tongue*. Urbana, Illinois: University of Illinois Press.

Kachru, Braj B. 1985. "Standards, codification and sociolinguistic realism: The English language in the outer circle." In R. Quirk and H.G. Widdowson (eds.), *English in the world: Teaching and learning the language and literatures*. Cambridge, U.K.: Cambridge University Press. 11–30.

Kachru, Braj B. 1986. "The power and politics of English." *World Englishes* 5(2–3): 121–140.

Kachru, Braj B. 1990. "World Englishes and applied linguistics." In *Learning: Keeping and using language* (Vol II). Edited by M.A.K. Halliday, John Gibbons, and Howard Nicholas. Amsterdam and Philadelphia: John Benjamins. Also in *World Englishes* 9(1): 3–20.

Kachru, Braj B. 1991. "Liberation linguistics and the Quirk concern." In Makhan L. Tickoo (ed.), *Languages and standards: Issues, attitudes, case studies* [Anthology Series 26]. Singapore: Regional Language Centre. First published in *English Today* 7(1): 1–13.

Kachru, Braj B. 1992. "The second diaspora of English." In T.W. Machan and Charles T. Scott (eds.), *English in the social contexts: Essays in historical sociolinguistics*. Oxford: Oxford University Press.

Kachru, Braj B. 1994a. "Englishization and contact linguistics." *World Englishes* 13(2): 135–154.

Kachru, Braj B. 1994b. "The paradigms of marginality." Plenary presentation at International TESOL, Baltimore, March 5–8, 1994.

Kachru, Braj B. (ed.). 1992. *The other tongue*. Urbana, Illinois: University of Illinois Press.

Kachru, Yamuna. 1991. "Speech acts in World Englishes: Toward a framework for research." *World Englishes* 10(3): 299–306.

Kachru, Yamuna. 1993. Review of *Rediscovering interlanguage* by Larry Selinker. *World Englishes* 12(2): 265–273.

Kermode, Frank. 1979. "Institutional control of interpretation." *Salmagundi* 43: 72–86.

Kristeva, Julia. 1969. *Semiotike.* Paris: Sevil.

Lannoy, Richard. 1971. *The speaking tree: A study of Indian culture and society.* New York: Oxford University Press.

Lefevre, Andrea. 1990. "Translation: Its genealogy in the west." In *Translation: History and culture.* London and New York: Pinter Publishers.

McArthur, Tom. 1994. "Organized babel: English as a global lingua franca." In James E. Alatis (ed.), *Educational linguistics, crosscultural communication, and global interdependence.* Georgetown University Round Table on Languages and Linguistics 1994. Washington, D.C.: Georgetown University Press.

McArthur, Tom (ed.). 1992. *The Oxford companion to the English language.* Oxford: Oxford University Press.

Mencken, H.L. 1936. *The American language, Fourth edition.* New York: Alfred A. Knopf.

Mesthrie, Rajend. 1993. "Gandhi and language politics." *Bua!* [Language Projects Review, Salt River, South Africa] 8(4): 4–7.

Naipaul, V.S. 1977. *India: A wounded civilization.* New York: Vintage.

Nelson, Cecil L. 1992. "My language, your culture: Whose communicative competence?" In Braj B. Kachru (ed.), *The other tongue.* Urbana, Illinois: University of Illinois Press. 327–339.

Ngũgĩ wa Thiong'o. 1981. *Writers in politics.* London and Exeter, N.H.: Heinemann.

Paikeday, Thomas M. 1985. *The native speaker is dead!* Toronto: Paikeday Publishing Inc.

Quirk, Randolph and Henry Widdowson (eds.). 1985. *English in the world: Teaching and learning the language and literatures.* Cambridge, U.K.: Cambridge University Press.

Rao, Raja. 1960. *The serpent and the rope.* London: Murray.

Rushdie, Salman. 1991. *Imaginary homelands: Essays and criticism.* New York: Viking.

Said, Edward W. 1993. *Culture and imperialism.* New York: Alfred A. Knopf.

Sareen, S.K. 1989. "The factor of intertextuality in translation." *International Journal of Translation* [New Delhi] 1(1): 41–48.

Shils, Edward. 1988. "Citizen of the world: Nirad C. Chaudhuri." *The American Scholar*, Autumn 1988: 549–573.

Smith, Larry E. and Cecil L. Nelson. 1985. "International intelligibility of English: Directions and resources." *World Englishes* 4(3): 333–342.

Smith, Larry E. (ed.). 1981. *English for cross-cultural communication.* London: Macmillan.

Smith, Larry E. (ed.). 1987. *Discourse across cultures: Strategies in World Englishes.* London: Prentice-Hall.

Sridhar, S.N. and Kamal K. Sridhar. 1986. "Bridging the paradigm gap: Second-language acquisition theory and indigenised varieties of English." *World Englishes* 5(1): 3–14. Also in Braj B. Kachru (ed.), 1992. *The other tongue.* Urbana, Illinois: University of Illinois Press.

Stubbs, Michael. 1986. *Educational linguistics.* Oxford: Basil Blackwell.

Tharoor, Shashi. 1989. *The great Indian novel.* New Delhi: Penguin.

Thumboo, Edwin. 1985. "Twin perspectives and multi-ecosystems: Traditions for a commonwealth writer." *World Englishes* 4(2): 213–222.

Thumboo, Edwin. 1992. "The literary dimension of the spread of English." In Braj B. Kachru (ed.), *The other tongue.* Urbana, Illinois: University of Illinois Press.

Tickoo, Makhan L. (ed.). 1991. *Languages and standards: Issues, attitudes, case studies* [Anthology Series 26] Singapore: Regional Language Centre.

Zimmer, Heinrich. 1972. *Myths and symbols in Indian art and civilization.* Joseph Campbell (ed.), The Bolinger Series VI. Princeton, N.J.: Princeton University Press.

The triumph of the yell

Deborah Tannen
Georgetown University

Deborah Tannen delivered a plenary address entitled "Beyond a culture of critique: The framing and reframing of academic discourse." Because Dr. Tannen spoke from notes rather than reading a written paper, we are including here an essay she wrote on the same topic which was published in the New York Times *on January 14, 1994. Her remarks at GURT made the same general points, with more emphasis on academic discourse.*

I put the question to a journalist who had written a vitriolic attack on a leading feminist researcher: "Why do you need to make others wrong for you to be right?" Her response: "It's an argument!"

That's the problem. More and more these days, journalists, politicians and academics treat public discourse as an argument—not in the sense of *making* an argument, but in the sense of *having* one, of having a fight.

When people have arguments in private life, they're not trying to understand what the other person is saying. They're listening for weaknesses in logic to leap on, points they can distort to make the other look bad. We all do this when we're angry, but is it the best model for public intellectual interchange? This breakdown of the boundary between public and private is contributing to what I have come to think of as a culture of critique.

Fights have winners and losers. If you're fighting to win, the temptation is great to deny facts that support your opponent's views and present only those facts that support your own.

At worst, there's a temptation to lie. We accept this style of arguing because we believe we can tell when someone is lying. But we can't. Paul Ekman, a psychologist at the University of California at San Francisco, has found that even when people are very sure they can tell whether or not someone is dissembling, their judgments are as likely as not to be wrong.

If public discourse is a fight, every issue must have two sides—no more, no less. And it's crucial to show "the other side," even if one has to scour the margins of science or the fringes of lunacy to find it.

The culture of critique is based on the belief that opposition leads to truth: when both sides argue, the truth will emerge. And because people are presumed to enjoy watching a fight, the most extreme views are presented, since they make the best show. But it is a myth that opposition leads to truth when truth does not reside on one side or the other but is rather a crystal of many sides. Truth is more likely to be found in the complex middle than in the simplified extremes, but the spectacles that result when extremes clash are thought to get higher ratings or larger readership.

Because the culture of critique encourages people to attack and often misrepresent others, those others must waste their creativity and time correcting the misrepresentations and defending themselves. Serious scholars have had to spend years of their lives writing books proving that the Holocaust happened, because a few fanatics who claim it didn't have been given a public forum. Those who provide the platform know that what these people say is, simply put, not true, but rationalize the dissemination of lies as showing "the other side." The determination to find another side can spread disinformation rather than lead to truth.

The culture of critique has given rise to the journalistic practice of confronting prominent people with criticism couched as others' views. Meanwhile, the interviewer has planted an accusation in readers' or viewers' minds. The theory seems to be that when provoked, people are spurred to eloquence and self-revelation. Perhaps some are. But others are unable to say what they know because they are hurt, and begin to sputter when their sense of fairness is outraged. In those cases, opposition is not the path to truth.

When people in power know that what they say will be scrutinized for weaknesses and probably be distorted, they become more guarded. As an acquaintance recently explained about himself, public figures who once gave long, free-wheeling press conferences now limit themselves to reading brief statements. When less information gets communicated opposition does not lead to truth.

Opposition also limits information when only those who are adept at verbal sparring take part in public discourse, and those who cannot handle it, or do not like it, decline to participate. This winnowing process is evident in graduate schools, where many talented students drop out because what they expected to be a community of intellectual inquiry turned out to be a ritual game of attack and counterattack.

One such casualty graduated from a small liberal arts college, where she "luxuriated in the endless discussions." At the urging of her professors, she decided to make academia her profession. But she changed her mind after a year in an art history program at a major university. She felt she had fallen into a "den of wolves." "I wasn't cut out for academia," she concluded. But does academia have to be so combative that it cuts people like her out?

In many university classrooms, "critical thinking" means reading someone's life work, then ripping it to shreds. Though critique is surely one form of critical thinking, so are integrating ideas from disparate fields and examining the context out of which they grew. Opposition does not lead to truth when we ask only "What's wrong with this argument?" and never "What can we use from this in building a new theory, and a new understanding?"

Several years ago I was on a television talk show with a representative of the men's movement. I didn't foresee any problem, since there is nothing in my work that is anti-male. But in the room where guests gather before the show I found a man wearing a shirt and tie and a floor-length skirt, with waist-length red hair. He politely introduced himself and told me he liked my book. Then he added: "When I get out there, I'm going to attack you. But don't take it personally. That's why they invite me on, so that's what I'm going to do."

When the show began, I spoke only a sentence or two before this man nearly jumped out of his chair, threw his arms before him in gestures of anger and began shrieking—first attacking me, but soon moving on to rail against women. The most disturbing thing about his hysterical ranting was what it sparked in the studio audience: they too became vicious, attacking not me (I hadn't had a chance to say anything) and not him (who wants to tangle with someone who will scream at you?), but the other guests: unsuspecting women who had agreed to come on the show to talk about their problems communicating with their spouses.

This is the most dangerous aspect of modeling intellectual interchange as a fight: it contributes to an atmosphere of animosity that spreads like a fever. In a society where people express their anger by shooting, the result of demonizing those with whom we disagree can be truly demonic.

I am not suggesting that journalists stop asking the tough questions necessary to get at the facts, even if those questions may appear challenging. And of course it is the responsibility of the media to represent serious opposition when it exists, and of intellectuals everywhere to explore potential weaknesses in others' arguments. But when opposition becomes the overwhelming avenue of inquiry, when the lust for opposition exalts extreme views and obscures complexity, when our eagerness to find weaknesses blinds us to strengths, when the atmosphere of animosity precludes respect and poisons our relations with one another, then the culture of critique is stifling us. If we could move beyond it, we would move closer to the truth.

Teaching culture in the language classroom: Toward a new philosophy

Rebecca L. Oxford
University of Alabama

The purpose of this article is to present a philosophy for teaching culture in the language classroom. This philosophy is growing and evolving daily, but it is solid enough to serve as a platform for discussion with colleagues and students throughout the language teaching field. Some elements are familiar, but many aspects of the philosophy are new to culture teaching. The philosophy relates to both *second language* situations, in which the language to be learned is used for daily communication by most people, and *foreign language* circumstances, in which the target language is not used as the everyday language of communication. Though many of my specific examples of books and materials relate to teaching culture in classes for English as a second language (ESL) and English as a foreign language (EFL), the basic principles apply just as readily to teaching culture in language classes devoted to French, Russian, Spanish, German, Arabic, Japanese, and so on.

Toward a new philosophy. Here are the components of the philosophy:

- Having clear goals for teaching culture;
- Understanding the meanings of culture;
- Linking culture learning and language learning through hands-on activities;
- Recognizing differences and similarities among cultures;
- Identifying the individual's steps in cultural awareness;
- Honoring multiple cultures, not just the target culture;
- Revealing the dark side of culture along with the light;
- Encouraging students to explore their own learning styles;
- Enhancing learning strategies to improve cultural awareness; and
- Using community resources and personal stories to teach culture.

Having clear goals for teaching culture. The teaching of culture in the language classroom can benefit from having clear goals. What should those goals be? They should clearly not involve merely imparting cultural trivia (Kramsch 1990), though that is what one might think when perusing many language textbooks. Instead, the goals should be more relevant and more important, and they should focus on *crossculturalism* (Banks 1994; Banks and Banks 1993; Batchelder and Warner 1977; Gaston 1984; Lee 1985; Luce and Smith 1987; Oxford forthcoming b; Putsch 1986; Seelye 1987; Weeks, Pedersen, and Brislin 1977). Here are some possible goals:

(1) For every student:
- to move beyond stereotypes and prejudice;
- to acquire at least a superficial understanding, but preferably a more in-depth understanding and appreciation, of the target culture in the context of other cultures;
- to develop a comprehension of differences and similarities across cultures;
- to recognize the essentiality of crosscultural tolerance, for "an understanding of the way of life [of other cultures] is important to survival in a world of conflicting value systems" (Seelye 1987: 14); and
- to create a desire to learn more about the culture.

(2) For students who plan to visit or live in the target culture:
- to develop all of the above attributes;
- to adjust as quickly as possible to being in the target culture;
- to use culture shock as a growth experience; and
- to come as close as possible to empathy with the target culture.

Cultural understanding is best viewed as a continuous, highly personal process (Galloway 1985; Seelye 1987; Crawford-Lange and Lange 1987) that can reach different levels in different individuals. Goals for culture teaching and learning thus depend on each student. Some students will settle for one level of awareness, and other students will seek higher levels. Some have the motivation and opportunity to live in the target culture, and others do not. The broad goals listed above are flexible enough to allow for differences among learners.

Understanding the meanings of culture. Language learners and their teachers need to understand what culture means. Culture is much more than just what the individual or group wears, eats, drinks, listens to, or smokes in certain situations. Herskovits (1948) defines culture as the human-made part of our environment. For Scovel (1991: 1), "Culture is the social cement of all human relationships; it is the medium in which we move and breathe and have our being." Behaviorists define culture in terms of observable behaviors, such as habits, customs, or traditions. Marriage and leisure customs are examples. Behaviorally inclined anthropologists and anthropological linguists sometimes say that culture is "all learned behavior which is socially acquired" (Nida 1954: 28).

Other definitions of culture include not only the behaviors, but also the inferable, not-always-obvious rules governing those behaviors. Such definitions also frequently mention attitudes. An example of this kind of definition comes from Brooks (1965: 218–221):

> Culture (relating to patterns of living) refers to the individual's role in the unending kaleidoscope of life situations of every kind and the rules or models for attitudes and conduct in them. By reference to these models, all human beings, from infancy onward, justify the world to themselves as best they can, associate with those around them, and relate to the social order to which they are attached ... What is important in culture ... is what one is expected to think, believe, say, do, eat, wear, pay, ensure, resent, honor, laugh at, fight for, and worship, in typical life situations ....

Cognitive anthropologists focus on how the individual perceives the culture. Similarly, symbolic anthropologists define culture as a system of symbols and meanings. Interpretations by the individual are the key aspect for both of these kinds of anthropologists, who believe that the individual can become competent in more than one culture.

Banks (1994: 82–84) gives a variety of historically well-known definitions of culture:

- Culture is that complex whole which includes knowledge, belief, art, morals, law, custom, and any other capabilities and habits acquired by man [or woman] as a member of society (Sir E.B. Taylor, 1871);
- The essential core of culture consists of traditional (i.e. historically derived and selected) ideas and especially attached values (Alfred L. Kroeber and Clyde Kluckhohn, 1952);
- Culture is the intangible symbols, rules, and values that people use to define themselves (M. Dimen-Schein, 1977); and
- Culture is a survival strategy (Brian M. Bullivant, 1984).

Regardless of the definition of culture, Banks (1991: 84) emphasizes that "Culture is dynamic, not static; any change in one aspect of a culture affects all its components."

Some writers distinguish between "everyday" culture and "sophisticated" culture (Oxford forthcoming b). Everyday culture involves the attitudes and behaviors of daily living, both the *why* and the *what* of eating, working, playing, talking, learning, teaching, timing, fighting, worshiping, loving, respecting, honoring, hating, celebrating, and grouping. Sophisticated culture involves personal refinement and fine arts: symphonies, sculptures, paintings, mosques, churches.

A famous image of culture is that of the iceberg (Hall 1969). Nine tenths of any iceberg is out of sight, below the water line. Likewise, nine tenths of culture is outside of conscious awareness. The *out-of-awareness* part is known as "deep culture" (sometimes "informal culture"). This part of culture is learned through imitating models. Once these behaviors and attitudes are learned, they are automatic and taken for granted. Anxiety results when the rules are broken. Examples include rules for gestures, facial expressions, eye contact, status behaviors, room sizes, child-rearing, modesty, beauty, physical distance, correct timing, cleanliness, work speed, friendship, and theories of sin, disease, death, god, sanity, self, justice, and mercy. These out-of-awareness aspects of culture cause the most crosscultural miscommunication problems simply because people do not think about them much.

The *in-awareness* part of the iceberg has two aspects: "technical culture" and"formal culture" (Hall 1969). At the technical level, which is easy to observe, rules are openly known and easily stated by members of the culture. Nobody is very upset if these rules are broken, because mistakes are easily corrected. Examples include health and educational practices, technical rules of business or government, and rules for introducing people, telling time, and participating in ceremonies. The formal level is also above the water line and within awareness. At this level, the rules are known but the reasons behind those rules might be unknown. People become emotionally involved when roles are violated. Examples are rituals, traditions (folk dancing, games, cooking, dress, music, drama, literature, art), etiquette, and the value of work.

The nature of culture (including both attitudes and behaviors) is captured in this poetic definition:

> Every human act—tipping your head, lowering or raising your eyes, smiling at someone you love, whispering a prayer, revving up a motorcycle, combing your hair in a certain way, greeting our friend, chatting with your family, accepting a suggestion from your boss or your teacher, exchanging money and goods at the market—is a cultural act. Culture is the dance of life of all humanity. (Oxford forthcoming b)

Culture is the loom, weaving the patterns of our lives. "We sleep, but the loom of life never stops, and the pattern which was weaving when the sun went down is weaving when it comes up tomorrow," said writer Henry Ward Beecher.

> Culture is the human face of mercy and the bloody act of war. Culture is anguished people praying for help and happy people laughing for joy. Culture is the shoulder against the plow, the arm carrying the water bucket, the hand with the baton leading the symphony. Culture is the sweetness of love and touch. It is also the bitter taste of hatred (Oxford forthcoming b).

Linking culture learning and language learning through hands-on activities. Language and culture are so close that they are sometimes considered synonymous (Scovel 1991). Language is one of the main symbol systems through which people interpret the world around them. Thus, language is one of the components of culture. It is an avenue for explaining or expressing culture. People's concept of the world is expressed through language, although this concept is also expressed nonverbally through gesture, touch, posture, music, dance, and many other media.

The Sapir-Whorf hypothesis underscores the uniqueness of each language and consequently the uniqueness of each culture's cognitive and perceptual patterning (Whorf 1956). However, a more recent perspective includes an understanding of the universality of fundamental aspects of language and culture (Scarcella and Oxford 1992; Scovel 1991). Both perspectives are correct: Languages and cultures have their unique aspects, but perhaps more importantly they also have some universal elements as well.

Culture is an excellent theme for any language class. Students are boundlessly interested in their own culture and other cultures if given the necessary exposure. If students are living or planning to live for awhile in a new culture, they especially want to understand the culture. Thus culture is a highly energizing and motivating theme. It provides unique content that captivates the attention of language learners of all ages.

Using culture as the main theme in a language class is an example of a major modern movement known as *content-based language learning* (Brinton, Snow, and Wesche 1989). In content-based language learning, the focus is on using language as a vehicle to understand and communicate about really meaningful content. Few content areas can be as meaningful as culture. "To study language without studying the culture of native speakers of the language is a lifeless endeavor," according to Crawford-Lange and Lange (1987). Teaching language without emphasizing culture can degenerate into discussion of disembodied forms and detached vocabulary; in short, it can become communicatively and culturally vapid. Culture vivifies language instruction for the majority of learners.

Culture gives learners something important to communicate about. Debates, role-plays, skits, simulations, "culture capsules," games, discussions, cultural attitude checklists, use of pictures and objects, stories, songs, poetry, cultural treasure hunts, projects, visits by native informants of many ages, and cultural style inventories—all these engage students in using the language interactively and communicatively for meaning. These activities, if handled correctly by the language teacher, can build up students' vocabularies, expand their grammatical accuracy, and develop their sociolinguistic, strategic, and discourse competence (Scarcella and Oxford 1992).

Increasing numbers of language books focus directly on culture as the main content theme. In the ESL/EFL field alone we find *Culture connection* (Wegman et al. 1994), *Journeys to cultural understanding* (Chan et al. 1994), *Patterns of cultural identity* (Oxford forthcoming b), *The international story: An anthology with guidelines for reading and writing about fiction* (Spack 1994), *Ourselves among others: Cross-cultural readings for writers* (Verburg 1994), *Common ground: Reading and writing about America's cultures* (Kirszner and Mandell 1994), *The American way: An introduction to American culture* (Kearney, Kearney, and Crandall 1984), *American ways: A guide for foreigners in the United States* (Athern 1988), and many others.

Use of literature is common in the teaching of many languages. Literature can be a key to understanding culture, especially as seen in the authentic tales of a person or a set of people. Sometimes best sellers are among the most exciting and culturally informative works. Consider the following literary "hits" (novels, diaries, stories, biographies, or autobiographies that have been best sellers in the United States or elsewhere): *The Joy Luck Club* (Tan 1989), *Zlata's diary: A child's life in Sarajevo* (Filipovic 1994), *Kitchen* (Yoshimoto 1993), *Lost in translation: A life in a new language* (Hoffman 1990), *The exile: Cuba in the heart of Miami* (Reiff 1993), *Blue highways: A journey into America* (Least Heat Moon 1982), *The woman warrior: Memories of a girlhood among ghosts* (Hong Kingston 1976), and *Life and death in Shanghai* (Cheng 1987). Think about the potentially tremendous cultural value of these works to the ESL/EFL classroom. Books by small, less widely known publishers can also be culturally powerful in the language classroom, as witnessed by JoAn Criddle's (1992) most recent book about Cambodian refugees forging a new life in California. Science fiction has a fascinating role in helping language students develop cultural awareness (see for example Sheri Tepper's 1993 novel, *Sideshow*). Cartoon books (for instance Berke Breathed's 1983 *Bloom County: Loose tails*) can also shed light on current culture, and their cultural humor usually demands considerable discussion, which is good for a language class. Though my examples are for ESL/EFL, almost every language (classical or modern) has enticing literature to offer, through which students can readily understand key aspects of the culture.

The "civilization" courses faced by language majors are sometimes taught in the traditional and deadly way, as a lecture-and-textbook-based collection of dates. However, it is far better to teach such courses by imparting cultural texture through literature, art, music, and a multitude of other hands-on modes.

Recognizing differences and similarities across cultures. The teaching of culture in language classes (and elsewhere) usually focuses on *differences* between the native culture and the target culture. Differences are usually framed in very tangible, superficial terms. For instance, Jules's father wears a beret and pedals a bike to work while Sally's mother wears a suit and carries a briefcase on the subway; teenage Ilka drinks beer with the family while her transatlantic peer Mary drinks diet soda at home; or Jorge plays soccer while Bill plays football. These differences might have some significance, but they are likely not to be the most important concepts. Deeper aspects of cultural differences—attitudes about religion, work, play, family—are more interesting and more profoundly meaningful. For dozens of examples, see Argyle (1975, 1976), Braganti and Devine (1992), Condon (1985), Geertz (1973), Hall (1969, 1973), Hall and Hall (1990), and Luce and Smith (1987).

In addition to cultural differences, we must also consider cultural similarities (Kirszner and Mandell 1994; Scovel 1991). Here are two enlightening statements that encourage us to think about similarities:

> Walk together,
> Talk together
> All ye peoples of the earth.
>
> Then and only then
> Shall ye have peace.
>
> —Sanskrit saying

> We are all the leaves of one tree,
> The drops of one ocean,
> The flowers of one garden.
>
> —from Ba'hai writings

The two statements above demonstrate that, despite our fragmentation into disparate cultures and races, humanity is nevertheless one. These statements imply that people must learn to understand each other's *similarities* as well as differences if world peace is to prevail. Understanding similarities across cultures does not mean just knowing that people in Mexico eat tacos and that people in the United States go to Taco Bell. Understanding crosscultural likenesses does not mean simply grasping that many Europeans and North Americans decorate Christmas trees. Comprehending intercultural similarities does not mean merely recognizing that heavy metal rock music has touched the young people of many nations, such as Russia, England, and the United States. These are surface features of culture. Instead, comprehending crosscultural similarities involves deeper aspects of culture, such as concepts of time, personal space, body language, worship, relationships, hatred, prejudice, love, and respect.

Identifying the individual's steps in cultural awareness. Learning and teaching about culture in the language classroom must involve some degree of self-assessment of each student's own cultural awareness. Building on Hanvey (1992) and Gaston (1984), I have designed a self-assessment framework with five steps. A summary of that framework is shown below; see Oxford (forthcoming b) for more details.

Steps in cultural awareness.

(1) No understanding—does not know anyone from the culture, knows few if any facts.
(2) Superficial understanding—knows some superficial facts and stereotypes.
(3) Growing awareness and possible conflict—is aware of more subtle traits but may experience cultural conflict (perhaps real culture shock); typically believes own culture is superior.
(4) Greater intellectual awareness—understands culture intellectually but not emotionally.
(5) True empathy and respect—understands the culture both intellectually and emotionally; can feel what the people in the culture feel; can only reach this level through living in the culture.

Here I shall discuss only levels two and three, the stages most relevant to most language learners. Level two is where most language students are located, I sadly assert. This level consists of awareness of superficial aspects of culture, frequently very negative aspects. At this stage, the person knows a few basic facts, which serve as the basis of stereotypes—common cultural myths, frequently containing a grain of truth but typically exaggerated. Stereotypes of United States mainstream culture abound: rich, friendly but shallow, uncaring about family and old people, loud, rude, aggressive, opinionated, hurried, driven by money, competitive, future-oriented, active, spendthrift, direct, open, immature, geographically ignorant, ethnocentric, prejudiced, promiscuous, risk-taking, and so on. Likewise, every other culture is tarred with stereotypes that might be partly true but are certainly blown out of proportion. One German student stated,

> Well, I didn't like the fact that people's first impressions of me were always mostly stereotypes of a foreigner. People would immediately recognize that I wasn't "from around here" and ask where I was from. And then ask how I liked it in America. I got very tired of that same conversation over and over ... Looking around me in the media or in commercials, I discovered that Germany was iconified to the Bavarian image. That irked me because

> I thought, well, that wasn't my part of Germany, and I never really cared much for Bavaria. Certainly not all the stuff that seemed to catch people's eyes over here anyhow. The um-pah bands and the clothes (lederhosen), the beer steins, etc. To me that stuff was always redneck or rather rural. Not the Germany of today. (Hans Kaufman, personal communication, 1993)

Language teachers cannot afford to let their students relax at level two. Through constant cultural activities (viewed as part of the content of the language class, not as a frill), language teachers can move their students beyond this very comfortable but highly dangerous level.

At level three, however, students often encounter greater discomfort and (particularly if foreign travel is involved) sometimes even culture shock. Culture shock is anxiety resulting from the loss of commonly understood cultural signs and symbols. People feel culture shock when the familiar hints are stripped away. The *disease view* of culture shock shows the individual as a helpless victim who is lost, isolated, and unable to function. In this view, culture-shocked people become frustrated, angry, resentful, and rejecting of the new culture, which they consider ridiculous or stupid. They may begin to glorify the home culture, fear contact with people from the new culture, and exhibit symptoms of illness or "reduced personality." There is little or no benefit to culture shock in this view. The *growth view*, on the other hand, holds that culture shock can be part of a positive learning experience involving self-awareness. This view contends that culture shock can lead from one cultural frame of reference to another, force the person into serious self-examination, and cause the individual to try new attitudes and behaviors (Adler 1987).

Language teachers, particularly those who lead students in study abroad programs, can be sensitive to the symptoms of culture shock and can help learners identify, label, and understand their own culture shock in the most positive way. Language teachers can thus enable students to adopt the growth view of culture shock, rather than the disease view.

Honoring multiple cultures, not just the target culture. The target culture should be viewed in the context of other cultures. Comparisons and contrasts are valuable and should be encouraged, along with deeper probing for the similarities among cultures. In the teaching of French, it is crucial to deal with francophone Africa, Quebec, and other French-speaking parts of the world, not just with France; and these cultures should be understood in the context of students' own home cultures. Insofar as possible, learners of ESL/EFL should grow to understand the many cultures of English-speaking countries, even if one country is seen as central to learners at a given time.

Language teachers should allow ample time for students to express their own cultural views and see how close or how far those views are from the concepts typically found in the target culture(s). By this means, students build upon their personal *schemata* (mental frameworks), adapting and accommodating those frameworks as needed. Students construct their own meaningful understandings of culture and any other subject, according to the learning theory called "constructivism" that pervades educational psychology today (Oxford forthcoming a). Unless teachers help students to use what they already know, starting with their own cultures and moving outward, new cultural information will have nothing to "hook into" and cannot take root.

Students in multicultural language classrooms—classrooms that include representatives of many different cultures or subcultures—have a distinct advantage. These students have a ready-made United Nations in which they can bring up cultural issues and find expert explanations. Language teachers should take advantage of such circumstances, using students as cultural informants whenever possible.

Revealing the dark side of culture along with the light. Culture learning is not incessantly happy and cheerful, though this "light side" of culture is important (see for example Axtell 1993; Barry 1991; Fulghum 1989). Culture learning does not always involve trying out folk dances, tasting quiche, and having a good laugh at oneself and others. In fact, a great deal of culture learning can and should consist of coming to grips with what I call the "dark side" of culture.

In my new language book for students of EFL and ESL, *Patterns of Cultural Identity* (Oxford forthcoming b), there is certainly plenty of wholehearted cheer and cultural humor—the light side. Yet I also depict the dark side. For example, fear of the unknown appears to be a fixture in most cultures, and this fear translates into prejudice and discrimination. In my book, there are true personal stories of prejudice and discrimination around the world.

Even in a mostly upbeat chapter about families as the bedrock of culture, I included the following authentic family stories: three generations of single mothers, a father–son clash in a new country, abuse of spouses and children, sex role skirmishes, and contrasting views of divorce. Cultural stories about families and about women and men are not necessarily lighthearted (see Aries 1962; Herman 1992; Kornblum 1988; LeGuin 1989; Skolnik and Skolnik 1991; Stone 1988), though they are sometimes so.

In dealing with time and physical aspects of culture (space, gesture, posture, touch, and gaze), the personal stories in the *Patterns* book cause readers to stop and think. Authentic stories of culture shock and linguistic trauma are also included. These realistic topics are eye-opening to students, especially those who are at the lower levels of cultural awareness.

The lighter side of culture makes students learn while laughing, but informal pilot tests of the *Patterns* book reveal that the more serious element has an even deeper impact on many students. For instance, a graduate language student from Chile was all dressed up and ready for a big Saturday night party. He became so engrossed in reading the chapters about families and about prejudice that he kept on reading throughout the night. "I forgot all about going to the party, but I'm not sorry. Reading these chapters touched my heart like nothing else. It shocked me into a better understanding of culture and human motivations," he wrote in his journal (Eduardo Saenz, personal communication, 1994). This response to serious cultural themes is more typical than not, in my experience. Language students are more eager to face cultural realities than they have been given credit for in the past.

Authentic personal tales, often told with the first-person "I," are essential for conveying both the dark side and the light side of culture. Students can relate especially well to actual events in the lives of real people, particularly people their own age and individuals who remind them of relatives or friends.

Encouraging students to explore their own learning styles. Most students want to understand themselves better, and they love to find out about their own learning styles (Oxford, Ehrman, and Lavine 1991). Years of research and learner training in the area of style convince me that one of the best ways to teach culture is to link culture with learning style. Some initial linkages between culture and learning style are described by Oxford, Hollaway, and Horton-Murillo (1992) and Reid (1987). Gudykunst, Ting-Toomey, and Chua (1988) discuss relationships between culture and what they sometimes call communication style, which appears closely linked with learning style. Harshbarger et al. (1986) present learning styles of ESL students from different cultures.

There is a serious danger of falling into stereotypes when linking culture and learning style. Students must be aware that not everyone in a given culture has the same learning style. However, many cultures help shape a certain "ideal style" that is readily observable.

As Harshbarger et al. (1986) point out, many Hispanic students are more global than analytic in learning style. They are relatively field-dependent and feeling-oriented, basing judgments on feelings and on personal relationships. In contrast, many Asian students like highly structured, deductive classes with a focus on small details and on logic, indicating an analytic and thinking-oriented style.

Arabic-speaking and Hispanic students are often gregarious, overtly verbal, and interested in a whole-class, extroverted mode of instruction (Harshbarger et al. 1986; Willing 1988). In comparison, Japanese and Korean students are often quiet, shy, and reticent in language classrooms, indicating a reserve that is the hallmark of introverts. Asians often have a traditional cultural focus on group membership, face-saving, and solidarity (Hofstede 1986).

Concrete–sequential learning styles (rather than intuitive–random styles) appear to be encouraged by cultures, such as Asian and Arab, that stress memorization (Harshbarger et al. 1986). Arabic speakers are particularly prone to rote memorization of long passages. Some language teachers call this plagiarism, but it is not considered such in Arab countries (Oxford et al. 1992).

Many Asian and Arab students have a closure-oriented style. For instance, Korean students insist that the teacher be the authority figure who provides a single correct answer; Japanese students frequently want quick and constant correction; and Arabic-speaking students often see things in black/white, right/wrong terms (Harshbarger et al. 1986). In comparison, Hispanic students are more concerned with social harmony, negotiation, and flexibility, which relate closely to the open learning style.

Even sensory learning styles (visual, auditory, kinesthetic, and tactile) are culturally related. Reid (1987) shows that Korean students are the most visual of all, significantly more so than American and Japanese students. Arab and Chinese students are also strongly visual. Strongly auditory students were Arab, Chinese, Malay, Thai, and Spanish. The most highly kinesthetic (movement-oriented) students were Arab, Spanish, Chinese, Korean, and Thai. Most nonnative speakers of English were highly tactile (touch-oriented) in their learning style.

Cultural "style wars" between teachers and students are important (Oxford, Ehrman, and Lavine 1991). Wallace and Oxford (1992) found that ESL students at a university English-language institute were significantly more extroverted and feeling-oriented than their teachers in that particular sample. The teachers thus had a different style from their students. When such style differences occurred, they often resulted in significantly lower course grades for students, the researchers found.

Teachers can use learning-style assessment as a springboard to communicative language activities. Many learning style instruments exist (see Wallace and Oxford 1992). One inventory is the *Style analysis survey* (Oxford 1994), which covers five dimensions: "How you use your physical senses for study and work" (visual, auditory, hands-on), "How you deal with other people" (extrovert vs. introvert), "How you handle possibilities" (intuitive–random vs. concrete–sequential), "How you approach tasks" (closure-oriented vs. open), and "How you deal with ideas" (global vs. analytic). To date, students of French, Spanish, EFL, and ESL in the United States, Canada, and Turkey have used the *Style analysis survey* in their language classes. Frequently the use of this survey has led to small-group and whole-class style comparisons, "style charting" on the board, style skits, and other activities revealing crosscultural style differences (and of course crosscultural style similarities in some instances).

Enhancing learning strategies to improve cultural awareness. Learning strategies are specific behaviors used by students to enhance their own learning (Oxford 1990, 1993; Oxford and Crookall 1989). These strategies are not innate in the student but instead can be learned with the help of the teacher or the textbook author. Many of the most recent language textbooks for French, Spanish, German, and ESL/EFL published by major houses now include specific learning strategies for students to apply. The entire *Tapestry program* of over forty ESL/EFL books weaves in learning strategies throughout each book, with activities that show students how to apply and transfer the strategies. Each of the *Tapestry* volumes contains dozens of useful learning strategies for language learners.

Language students who are learning culture (and what language student is not?) can benefit from a variety of learning strategies. The following are some directly from a draft of my own book, *Patterns of cultural identity* (Oxford forthcoming b); but many books available, particularly in the *Tapestry program*, might provide similar illustrations. Remember that the strategies shown are not fully useful without activities by which to practice them.

(1) Testing Hypotheses:
- Before you listen to a cultural story, predict what might be coming.
- Search for evidence to test your cultural hypotheses, and revise those hypotheses if necessary.

(2) Forming Concepts:
- Make a concept map of culture to help you understand ideas more rapidly and more easily.
- Compare different definitions of culture to gain an expanded understanding.
- Find stereotypes to help you understand others and avoid crosscultural conflicts.

(3) Overcoming Limitations:
- Guess meanings from the context to help yourself get the idea quickly and strengthen your knowledge.
- Carefully consider the things that make you uncomfortable. Things you would ordinarily choose to ignore can help you learn to accept your culture and other cultures.

(4) Understanding and Using Emotions:
- Delve into the motivations behind actions if you want to understand people and cultures.
- Avoid immediately condemning people who show prejudice or discrimination; instead, realize that we all have negative biases (intentional or unintentional) against others.

(5) Remembering New Material:
- List cultural topics to help yourself remember them and also expand your understanding.
- Label words as culturally "negative" or "positive" concepts to help yourself remember those words.

(6) Managing Your Learning:
- Assess your own cultural abilities to help yourself know what you need to learn.
- Observe more closely to increase your cultural awareness.
- Check yourself to see if you are right whenever you make a cultural prediction.

(7) Personalizing:
- Listen for personal details to help yourself understand the other person and her culture.
- Express your preferences often to help yourself clarify your own cultural influences.

Notice that these examples cluster into the following groups of strategies: Testing hypotheses (cognitive), forming concepts (cognitive), overcoming limitations (compensation), understanding and using emotions (affective), remembering new material (memory/cognitive), managing your learning (metacognitive), and personalizing (affective/social/cognitive).

These are just a few illustrations of learning strategies useful for culture learning. To enable students to use strategies optimally, teachers should say the strategy aloud, making sure students know the explicit strategy terms; give a quick demonstration of the strategy ("modeling"); ask if there are any questions about the strategy; and ask students to apply the strategy in a specific activity. Strategies are never discussed in a vacuum. They are always linked to a communicative task and arise from a need created by that task, because strategies are for solving learning problems and making progress.

Later the teacher asks students if the strategy helped in the given activity, and if so, how. The same strategy can be recycled until students are completely familiar with it, can transfer it to various related tasks, and can use it more or less automatically. In addition, new strategies are introduced during the same time frame, depending on the needs generated by the language/culture activities. There are many ways to assess students' use of learning strategies: diaries, interviews, class discussions, "think-aloud" procedures (students telling their strategies aloud while doing a task), observation, and questionnaires. The value of each technique is explained by Oxford (1990, 1993). The "Strategy Inventory for Language Learning" (in Oxford 1990) is a quick, comprehensive strategy questionnaire that is available in ten languages, has high reliability and predictive validity, and has been used by approximately 8,000 to 9,000 students to date in different parts of the world. Strategy assessment of any type provides a sound basis for teaching strategies to enhance cultural awareness. Moreover, strategy assessment helps students to examine their own strategies and often motivates them to try new strategies that might be useful.

Using community resources and personal stories to teach culture. In a second language situation, in which the language is used for daily living, the teacher has virtually unlimited access to the target culture and language. Examples are learning Hebrew in Jerusalem and learning English in London or Chicago. Here are some suggestions for capitalizing on this rich environment:

- The teacher can invite native speakers of the target language who are specialists on time, space, families, prejudice, or any other cultural subject. Or visitors can simply be invited to tell their own personal stories, which inevitably intersect with the general culture. These visits will create a personal bond between the community and the students, as well as an institutional bond between the community and the language instruction institution. Community members are honored to serve as cultural experts.
- Conversely, teachers can send students out into the community to conduct surveys, interviews, discussions, or searches for cultural objects. Students can serve as participant observers of culture—ethnographers in their own cultural setting (see Chan et al. 1994 for excellent examples of ethnographic activities for ESL students). Teachers must make sure students are well prepared for out-of-class activities. These tasks help students know the community better while learning about the overall culture.
- Teachers can make cultural assignments to watch the local television news or certain network programs that reflect aspects of the target culture.
- Teachers can make cultural assignments involving students watching target language movies at local theaters. Students should create their own list of film options.

In a foreign language situation, in which the language is *not* used for daily survival and communication, there are fewer language and cultural resources. Examples are learning Swedish in Orlando or learning Russian in Edinburgh. Nevertheless, even in such a setting at least some resources are typically available. For instance:

- Teachers can invite native speakers (there are almost always a few around, even in isolated communities) to talk about specific aspects of culture, to tell their personal stories, or to lead cultural activities in class.

- Teachers can send out students, possibly in groups rather than individually, to conduct interviews, surveys, etc. among the native speakers in the community, even though there might be fewer native speakers to locate than in a second language environment.
- Teachers can make cultural assignments involving television, movies, or radio (for example, British Broadcasting Corporation or Voice of America programs). Because of the limited resources caused by the foreign language environment, teachers must provide as many "leads" or suggestions as possible for students. Teachers can also bring cultural media (particularly video and audio) into the classroom frequently, rather than expecting students to track down these scarce resources in the community.

The personal stories that real people—including the students themselves—bring to the classroom are crucial for developing cultural awareness. Experiencing the feelings and attitudes of actual people from different countries makes culture come alive. It helps students reflect on their own personal experience. Personalizing is known as one of the most effective learning strategies (Schmeck 1988; Oxford and Cohen 1992), and the use of personal stories for learning culture can strengthen the use of that strategy. Personal stories are also found in print as well as in the community. Many of the culture books mentioned earlier contain richly textured stories, sometimes hilarious and sometimes agonizing, but always informative.

Conclusions. In this paper I have shared the rudiments of a developing philosophy for teaching culture in the language classroom. This instructional philosophy has clear cultural goals, imparts varied meanings of culture, links culture learning and language learning through hands-on activities, and highlights both differences and similarities among cultures. This philosophy also helps students identify their own levels of cultural awareness, reveres multiple cultures, reveals the dark side of culture along with the light, encourages students to explore their own learning styles, enhances learning strategies, and uses community resources and personal stories to enliven instruction. The net result of this evolving philosophy is the ongoing growth of a personal awareness of culture on the part of every language student. With the help of such an instructional philosophy, all people can (as Seelye 1987 said) learn to survive in a world of conflicting value systems. The philosophy is not simply a grab bag of techniques or methods. Instead, it is rooted in a deep sense of what it means to become fully human in a pluralistic world. I am currently implementing this philosophy in my own classes and books, but I want to see it develop further through exchanges with colleagues and students around the world.

REFERENCES

Adler, Peter. 1987. "Culture shock and the cross-cultural learning experience." In Louise F. Luce and Elise C. Smith (eds.), *Toward internationalism: Readings in cross-cultural communication, Second edition*. New York: Newbury House/Harper and Row. 24–35.

Aries, Phillippe. 1962. *Centuries of childhood: A social history of family life*. New York: Vintage.

Athern, Gary. 1988. *American ways: A guide for foreigners in the United States*. Yarmouth, Maine: Intercultural Press.

Argyle, Michael. 1975. *Bodily communication*. New York: International Universities Press.

Argyle, Michael. 1976. *Gaze and mutual gaze*. Cambridge, U.K.: Cambridge University Press.

Axtell, Roger. 1993. *Do's and taboos around the world, Third edition*. New York: Wiley.

Banks, James A. 1994. *Multiethnic education: Theory and practice, Third edition*. Boston: Allyn and Bacon.

Banks, James A. and Cherry A. McGee Banks. 1993. *Multicultural education: Issues and perspectives, Second edition*. Boston: Allyn and Bacon.

Barnlund, Dean D. 1975. *Public and private self in Japan and the United States*. Tokyo: Simul Press.

Barry, Dave. 1991. *Dave Barry's only travel guide you'll ever need*. New York: Fawcett Columbine.

Batchelder, Donald and Elizabeth G. Warner. 1977. *Beyond experience: The experiential approach to cross-cultural education*. Brattleboro, Vermont: Experiment in International Living.

Braganti, Nancy L. and Elizabeth Devine. 1992. *European customs and manners*. New York: Simon and Schuster.

Breathed, Berke. 1983. *Bloom County: Loose tails*. Boston: Little, Brown.

Brinton, Donna, M. Ann Snow, and Mari Wesche. 1989. *Content-based second language instruction*. New York: Newbury House/Harper and Row.

Brooks, Nelson. 1965. "Teaching culture in the foreign language classroom." *Foreign Language Annals* 1(3): 204–217.

Chan, Debra, Judith Kaplan-Weinger, and Deborah Sandstrom. 1994. *Journeys to cultural understanding*. Boston: Heinle and Heinle.

Cheng, Nien. 1987. *Life and death in Shanghai*. Boston: Grove Press.

Condon, John C. 1985. *Good neighbors: Communicating with the Mexicans*. Yarmouth, Maine: Intercultural Press.

Crawford-Lange, L.M. and Dale Lange. 1987. "Doing the unthinkable in the second-language classroom: A process for integration of language and culture." In Ted Higgs (ed.), *Teaching for proficiency, the organizing principle*. Lincolnwood, Illinois: National Textbook Co. 139–179.

Criddle, JoAn D. 1992. *Bamboo and butterflies: From refugee to citizen*. Dixon, California: East/West BRIDGE Publishing House.

David M. Kennedy Center. 1992. *Culturgrams*. Provo, Utah: Brigham Young University.

Fast, Julius. 1970. *Body language*. New York: Pocket Books.

Filipovic, Zlata. 1994. *Zlata's diary: A child's life in Sarajevo*. New York: Viking.

Fulghum, Robert. 1989. *It was on fire when I lay down on it*. New York: Ivy/Ballentine.

Galloway, Vicki. 1985. *A design for the improvement of the teaching of culture in foreign language classrooms*. Hastings-on-Hudson, New York: American Council on the Teaching of Foreign Languages.

Gaston, Jan. 1984. *Cultural awareness teaching techniques*. Brattleboro, Vermont: Pro Lingua Associates.

Geertz, Clifford. 1973. *The interpretation of cultures*. New York: Basic Books.

Gudykunst, William B., Stella Ting-Toomey, with Elizabeth Chua. 1988. *Culture and interpersonal communication*. Newbury Park, California: Sage.

Hall, Edward T. 1969. *The hidden dimension*. Garden City, New York: Doubleday/Anchor.

Hall, Edward T. 1973. *The silent language*. Garden City, New York: Doubleday/Anchor.

Hall, Edward T. and Mildred Reed Hall. 1990. *Understanding cultural differences*. Yarmouth, Maine: Intercultural Press.

Hanvey, Robert G. 1992. "Cross-cultural awareness." In Louise F. Luce (ed.), *The Spanishspeaking world: An anthology of cross-cultural perspectives*. Lincolnwood, Illinois: National Textbook Co. 22–33.

Harshbarger, B., Theresa Ross, Seija Tafoya, and Judith Via. 1986. "Dealing with multiple learning styles in the ESL classroom." Symposium presented at the annual meeting of Teachers of English to Speakers of Other Languages, Anaheim, CA.

Herman, Judith Lewis. 1992. *Trauma and recovery: The aftermath of violence—from domestic abuse to political terror*. New York: Basic Books.

Herskovits, Melville. 1948. *Man and his works*. New York: Knopf.

Hoffman, Eva. 1990. *Lost in translation: A life in a new language*. New York: Penguin.

Hofstede, Geert. 1986. "Cultural differences in teaching and learning." *International Journal of Intercultural Relations* 10(3): 301–320.

Hong Kingston, Maxine. 1976. *The woman warrior: Memories of a girlhood among ghosts*. New York: Knopf.

Jung, Carl. 1964. *Man and his symbols*. New York: Doubleday.

Kaufman, Hans. 1993. Personal communication through an interview with Catherine Callender.

Kearney, Edward N., Mary Ann Kearney, and JoAnn Crandall. 1984. *The American way: An introduction to American culture*. Englewood Cliffs, N.J.: Prentice-Hall.

Kirszner, Laurie G. and Steven R. Mandell. 1994. *Common ground: Reading and writing about America's cultures*. New York: St. Martin's Press.

Kornblum, William. 1988. *Sociology in a changing world*. New York: Holt, Rinehart and Winston.

Kramsch, Claire. 1990. "Discourse and culture." Keynote presentation at the annual meeting of the Alabama Association of Foreign Language Teachers, Birmingham.

Least Heat Moon, William. 1982. *Blue highways: A journey into America*. New York: Fawcett Crest.

LeGuin, Ursula K. 1989. *Dancing at the edge of the world: Thoughts on words, women, places*. New York: Harper and Row.

Lee, Enid. 1985. *Letters to Marcia: A teacher's guide to anti-racist education*. Toronto: Crosscultural Communication Center.

Luce, Louise F. and Elise C. Smith (eds.). 1987. *Toward internationalism: Readings in cross-cultural communication*. Cambridge, Massachusetts: Newbury House/Harper and Row.

Nida, E. 1954. *Customs and cultures*. New York: Harper and Row.

Oxford, Rebecca L. 1990. *Language learning strategies: What every teacher should know*. Boston: Heinle and Heinle.

Oxford, Rebecca L. 1993. "Research on second language learning strategies." *Annual Review of Applied Linguistics* 13: 175–187.

Oxford, Rebecca L. 1994. *Style analysis survey, Revised edition*. Tuscaloosa, Alabama: University of Alabama.

Oxford, Rebecca L. forthcoming a. "Toward a unified metatheory of language learning strategies: Implications of information processing theory, individual differences theory, self-efficacy and attribution theory, and constructivism." In progress.

Oxford, Rebecca L. forthcoming b. *Patterns of cultural identity*. Boston: Heinle and Heinle .

Oxford, Rebecca L. and Andrew D. Cohen. 1992. "Language learning strategies: Crucial issues of concept and definition." *Applied Language Learning* 3(2): 1–35.

Oxford, Rebecca L. and David Crookall. 1989. "Language learning strategies: Methods, findings, and instructional implications." *Modern Language Journal* 73(4): 404–419.

Oxford, Rebecca L., Madeline E. Ehrman, and Roberta Z. Lavine. 1991. "Style wars: Teacher-student conflicts in the language classroom." In Sally Sieloff Magnan (ed.), *Challenges in the 1990s for college foreign language programs*. Boston: Heinle and Heinle. 1-25.

Oxford, Rebecca L., Mary Evelyn Hollaway, and Diana Horton-Murillo. 1992. "Language learning styles: Research and practical considerations for teaching in the multicultural tertiary ESL/EFL classroom." *System* 20(4): 439–456.

Putsch, Margaret D. (ed.). 1986. *Multicultural education: A cross-cultural training approach*. Yarmouth, Maine: Intercultural Press.

Reid, Joy, 1987. "The learning style preferences of ESL students." *TESOL Quarterly* 21(1): 87–111.

Reiff, David. 1993. *The exile: Cuba in the heart of Miami*. New York: Simon and Schuster.

Saenz, Eduardo. 1994. Personal communication.

Scarcella, Robin. 1990. *Teaching the language minority student in the multicultural classroom*. Englewood Cliffs, N.J.: Prentice-Hall.

Scarcella, Robin and Rebecca Oxford. 1992. *The tapestry of language learning: The individual in the communicative classroom*. Boston: Heinle and Heinle.

Schmeck, Ronald R. 1988. "Individual differences and learning strategies." In Claire Weinstein, Ernest Goetz, and Patricia Alexander (eds.), *Learning and study strategies: Issues in assessment, instruction, and evaluation*. New York: Academic. 171–191.

Scovel, Thomas. 1991. *The role of culture in second language pedagogy* (Commissioned manuscript). Boston: Heinle and Heinle.

Seelye, H. Ned. 1987. *Teaching culture: Strategies for intercultural communication*. Lincolnwood, Illinois: National Textbook Co.

Skolnik, Arlene and Jerome Skolnik. 1991. *Family in transition, Seventh edition*. Boston: Little, Brown.

Spack, Ruth. 1994. *The international story: An anthology with guidelines for reading and writing about fiction*. New York: St. Martin's Press.

Stewart, Edward C. and Milton J. Bennett. 1991. *American cultural patterns, Revised edition*. Yarmouth, Maine: Intercultural Press.

Stone, Elizabeth. 1988. *Black sheep and kissing cousins: How our family stories shape us*. New York: Penguin.

Tan, Amy. 1989. *The Joy Luck Club*. New York: Ivy.

Tepper, Sheri S. 1993. *Sideshow*. New York: Bantam.

Verburg, Carol. 1994. *Ourselves among others: Cross-cultural readings for writers, Third edition*. Boston: Bedford/St. Martin's.

Wallace, Bill and Rebecca L. Oxford. 1992. "Disparity in learning styles and teaching styles in the ESL classroom: Does this mean war?" *AMTESOL Journal* 1(1): 45–68.

Weeks, William H., Paul B. Pedersen, and Richard W. Brislin (eds.). 1977. *A manual of structured experiences for cross-cultural learning*. Yarmouth, Maine: Intercultural Press.

Wegman, Brenda, Miki Knezevic, and Patti Werner. 1994. *Culture connection*. Boston: Heinle and Heinle.

Whorf, Benjamin. 1956. *Language, thought, and reality*. Cambridge, Massachusetts: MIT Press.

Willing, Ken. 1988. *Learning styles in adult migrant education*. Adelaide, Australia: National Curriculum Resource Center.

Yetman, Norman R. (ed.). 1991. *Majority and minority: The dynamics of race and ethnicity in American life, Fifth edition*. Boston: Allyn and Bacon.

Yoshimoto, Banana. 1993. *Kitchen*. New York: Washington Square Press.

Toward an acquisition-oriented syllabus

Gen-yuan Zhuang
Hangzhou University

Introduction. This paper is a work-in-progress report on a second language acquisition research project in Hangzhou, China. For more than three years, I have been experimenting with college and high school students in the use of authentic auditory input for the teaching of English. The original purpose of our research project was to carry out experiments to test and provide empirical data to support Krashen's second language acquisition theory, especially his input hypothesis (Krashen 1982, 1985). Basically, our research focuses on providing a great amount of comprehensible *auditory* language input to students of English, especially in a nontarget language environment such as China.

The LAD. Why do we emphasize *auditory*? Let me begin with Chomsky. Chomsky has proposed a hypothetical language acquisition device (LAD) to account for "the child's innate predisposition to learn a language" (Chomsky 1965: 25). He states that "on the basis of observation of what we may call *primary linguistic data*, a child who has learned a language has developed an internal representation of a system of rules that determine how sentences are to be formed, used and understood" (1965: 25; italics in original). Chomsky regards acquisition of language as a special case of "the acquisition of knowledge" (1965: 47) and clearly favors the rationalist approach to the problem of knowledge acquisition.[1] According to Chomsky, "there are innate ideas and principles of various kinds that determine the form of the acquired knowledge." He points out that "a condition for innate mechanisms to become activated is that appropriate stimulation be presented" (1965: 48). I think that even though language acquisition is much more complicated than a transfer of knowledge, this last statement of his is correct, and evidence provided by our research supports his hypothesis of a language acquisition device.

If I could describe the relationship among the language acquisition device, primary linguistic data, and language acquisition in very, some might fear simplistic, mathematical terms, it would look like an equation:

---

1. Recent neurolinguistic and psycholinguistic research findings suggest that language acquisition is not just a transfer of knowledge, but also involves the perfection of procedures (see Paradis 1992).

LAD + primary linguistic data = language acquisition

A child acquiring his or her native language possesses a language acquisition device and is provided primary linguistic data, hence the result is language acquisition. But for an adult or adolescent learning a second or foreign language, especially in a nontarget language context, why is language acquisition so difficult to accomplish?

If we take a look at the equation, there may be a few possible explanations. For example, we may say that the language acquisition device has ceased to work in an adult learning a second or foreign language, with or without the linguistic data. Therefore language acquisition will not be achieved. Or we may say that the adult learner has not been given the linguistic data, so even though we assume theoretically that the language acquisition device may still work in a person past puberty, it is not activated because of the lack of the linguistic data. As a result, language acquisition cannot be achieved. In other words, if we suppose that the language acquisition device still works for adult learners of a second or especially foreign language, then lack or deficiency, both qualitative and quantitative, of what Chomsky terms "primary linguistic data" is the condition that can be held accountable for the fact that language acquisition does not happen in the adult learner.

As a matter of fact, one cannot do much about the language acquisition device. Whether or not it is still there is well beyond the learner's direct control because it is built into the brain. So linguistic data is the only area that we can focus our attention on to move toward the goal of acquisition.

The input hypothesis. Here I think Krashen's second language acquisition theory fits right in, especially his input hypothesis. I was fascinated by his hypothesis because in many ways his theory was the closest approximation of my own experience and processes of learning and acquiring English as a second or foreign language.

Despite opposition to and criticism of his *formulation* of the input hypothesis, even people who have argued against the hypothesis agree that "second language acquisition theory should indeed include an input hypothesis" (White 1987) and that

> Krashen's emphasis on the input hypothesis has been useful in drawing our attention to the role of input, and to the degree to which acquisition is dependent on the learner. It would be a pity to discard the hypothesis because of its shortcomings; rather, we should aim at a far more precise characterization of the possible interactions between learner and input. (White 1987)

I believed at the time we started the research project, and I still believe now, that Krashen's idea of optimal input is the heart and soul of his input hypothesis. Since optimal input is the most important contributing factor in language acquisition, the first task we faced when we began our work was trying to determine what optimal input was. I maintain that the optimal input for language acquisition should indeed be what Chomsky calls "primary linguistic data."

What, then, qualifies as optimal language input, or what are the characteristics of "primary linguistic data"? As is well known, human languages have been handed down from generation to generation for nobody knows how long before writing systems were invented, and there are still many languages in the world today without written forms. More specifically, a child acquires his or her native language before learning to read and write. All this is enough evidence to prove that language acquisition does not necessarily require one to learn to read and write. Speech is of prime importance in language acquisition.

This realization has enabled me to take a new look at Krashen's input hypothesis, and it seems to me that two fundamental features of the optimal language input need to be emphasized for the purpose of language acquisition: oral and natural. I hypothesize that the language acquisition device is, and perhaps can only be, triggered by speech rather than the writing system. In order to activate the language acquisition device, the optimal input for the language acquirer needs to be, first of all, oral. I believe that exposure as early as possible to this oral language context is crucial to language acquisition, whether first or second. I speculate that it has something to do with the resonant nature of the sound of speech, which, when perceived by the hearer, triggers the reverberation of language process mechanisms in the brain. The resonance of the human voice, therefore, is a fundamental difference between auditory language input and visual language input in terms of their roles in language acquisition.

By "natural" I mean "authentic." The language input can be very simple to begin with. But this does not mean that beginning or intermediate level language input needs to be simplified. Preschool children receive an abundance of comprehensible auditory language input. But they also get a good deal of less-comprehensible input. They make use of context clues in the spoken discourse to understand messages that contain incomprehensible input. They learn to ignore the irrelevant and at the same time try to understand the relevant by asking questions or resorting to other means. So the most important thing for language teachers is to plunge their students into the sea of the spoken language to initiate the language acquisition process.

However, with very few exceptions throughout the history of second or foreign language teaching and learning, teachers and students alike have relied too much on the written text. This is understandable, though, because providing students with a natural language environment, especially in a nontarget language situation was, and maybe still is, easier said than done. Nevertheless, the ready availability of VCRs, TVs, videotapes, and TV programs has, both technologically and financially, made the reproduction of a simulated language environment possible in the language classroom.

Auditory language input. So, in essence, what we have been trying to do in our project is to provide a large quantity of auditory language input to enable the learner/acquirer to simulate the language acquisition process. The auditory input is provided through watching TV programs and playing videotapes for an *extended* period of time.

It is true that language teachers have been using tape recorders in the language laboratory ever since they were commercially manufactured. But there are very important differences between this kind of use of tape recording and our use of TV programs and movie videos. First of all, playing a video film or tuning in to a TV program in the classroom encourages active participation on the part of the students, while listening to an audiotape or the radio is a much more passive activity. Secondly, the soundtrack of a TV program or movie provides much more authentic (though, to some extent, scripted) language input than commercially available audiotapes, which are by and large recorded readings of simplified and manipulated written texts. Last but not least, watching TV is far more interesting than listening to a tape. In the English classroom, there is hardly anything that is more enjoyable than this.

Students get tired easily in a language laboratory. But they are hooked on the screen as long as they are getting increasingly comprehensible input. The auditory language input we provide the students with does not have to be 100% comprehensible. But in the meantime, students are finding the input more and more comprehensible by getting more and more comprehensible input in the simulated language environment. Because the input is enjoyable, it is possible to provide students with a large quantity of auditory language input for a long period of time.

However effortlessly the language acquisition process of children may seem, "five-year olds have," according to McGill University neurolinguistics professor Michel Paradis, "invested about 10,000 hours of practice in the acquisition of their native language" (Paradis 1992).[2] And they have managed to do so mostly on their own through listening, with indeed very limited speaking, when we scrutinize the language behavior of preschool children.

In order to provide our students with the auditory language input that they need for the purpose of acquisition, we have screened TV programs and collected movie videos to show in the classroom. We have found that for our university English majors who have had six years of high school English instruction, movies and TV programs that center on family themes, especially where

2. Morley cites Asher (1977) to give a slightly different figure (see Alatis 1990: 318).

children are involved, appear to be the most desirable. Situation comedies, for example, contain lots of structurally simple, yet sensible and meaningful, everyday conversations that, when used appropriately, are largely comprehensible to the students. A teacher helps them with the transition in the auditory language input from incomprehensible to comprehensible and as a result facilitates the acquisition process. When the stories are about family life, the scenes are very much like the language environment where a child picks up his or her first language. The family setting controls the language naturally. Therefore, this kind of auditory language input meets all the requirements set forth by Krashen for optimal input for language acquisition: comprehensibility (with the help of a teacher), interest/relevance, nongrammatical sequencing, and sufficient quantity (Krashen 1982).

The research project. Initial attempts were made in the fall of 1990 when I was teaching English composition to five classes of more than one hundred junior English majors at the University of Hangzhou. The immediate reason I started playing some TV programs for them was that I did not like the way my students wrote their compositions. Most of them seemed to be doing translation from their Chinese sentences rather than writing original English ones. This was because, I figured, they had to internalize the structure of English, especially the acoustic rhythmic patterns of the language, before they could be expected to produce native-sounding sentences, paragraphs, and essays. Exposure to this (simulated) real-life English would help them toward building up a store of retrievable auditory language components for later use either in writing or speech.

To the surprise of most of my colleagues, feedback from students was so overwhelmingly positive that we seriously considered launching the project. Meanwhile, we tried to do a feasibility study. In the spring of 1991, we decided to recruit some volunteers from the two-year teacher training program for an experiment. Of the seventy-three students who were in their second year of studying English at the University, sixty volunteered. This shows the popularity of the project, even in its infancy. Since I could not handle such a large group, I only picked the fourteen students whose grades had been the lowest in their listening comprehension course. My thinking at the time was that they were normal human beings and were born with a language acquisition device. If the experiment worked well with them, it would certainly work well with their peers. On the other hand, if the experiment should turn out to be a complete failure, these students would suffer the least damage.

In addition to their regular classes, these fourteen students met twice a week with me for a two-hour class period each time, watching TV programs like "Growing pains" and "The Cosby show." I explained in English and in great detail phrases and sentences from the script with which I would expect them to have difficulty. Later, however, I only needed to repeat the sentences for them to understand what had been said. In the following years, especially when I worked with the freshmen, I found myself sometimes going into more detail, adopting almost a line-by-line approach for the first few days.

After four weeks, it happened to be time for the midterm examination. I did not give any test myself. However, I analyzed the test results of a listening comprehension class that was taught by a colleague of mine. In order to ensure the objectivity of the test results, I did not inform him of my intention until after the midterm. If the average score of the seventy-three students for listening comprehension were taken as an adjusted score of 100, the average score of the fourteen students rose from 67.03 for the final examination of the previous semester to 79.05 for the midterm. After the midterm, other students joined them in the experiment until the end of the semester. The average score of the fourteen students for the final examination of the semester dropped a little from 79.05 for the midterm to 76.13 for the final. I concluded that this was due to the fact that the other students improved their grades after joining the slower students.

Beginning with the 1991–1992 school year, we continued our project with the sophomores (one year earlier) in a more systematic way. They started to watch American (and some British, depending on availability) TV programs on a more regular basis with a teacher. Since our project switched from the third-year students in the previous (1990–1991) school year to the second-year students in the 1991–1992 school year, we skipped the then-juniors who were enrolled in the year of 1989. That is to say, they were not exposed to such simulated language input. After one semester we designed a test made up of fifty multiple-choice questions based on a twenty-minute-long children's movie. Both the second- and third-year students watched the movie twice. The first time they just watched it all the way through to the end. Then they were given the test questions and the movie was played in four segments with a two-minute pause in between. The results of the test were that the second-year students did better than the third-year students: Out of the fifty questions, the average raw score for the second-year students was 33.29 whereas the third-year students only scored an average of 28.66.

Since we started the project, national test scores for students who have participated in the experiments have improved remarkably. For example, within one year, the average score for TEM 4 (a national test for English majors throughout the country in their second year) rose from 63.18 in 1992 to 68.79 in 1993, and the percentage of the number of students who passed TEM 4 increased from 69.32% in 1992 (sixty-one out of eighty-eight) to 92.19% in 1993 (sixty-one out of sixty-four). This is a significant increase. The main reason is that the eighty-eight students in the class of 1992 begin to watch TV programs in their second year whereas the sixty-four students in the class of 1993 started watching TV programs as soon as they entered the University. In other words, they received one year more of this kind of auditory language input, which translated into a difference of about eighty hours of authentic auditory language input in the classroom.

Assessment, evaluation, and the definition of language acquisition. Valid and reliable as these objective test scores are, assessment and evaluation remain a problem for our acquisition-oriented research project. For example, how do we find out that one student has acquired English while another has only learned it? Personally, sometimes I like to have my students transcribe fairly long passages from TV programs or movies like *Father of the bride*, or even write down the lyrics of popular songs, such as Michael Jackson's "Gone too soon." I think I can have a much better picture of their degree of acquisition, but it is time-consuming work, especially when you have hundreds of students.

In a way, the question of assessment and evaluation boils down to the definition of language acquisition, first as well as second. A lot of the terms related to language acquisition are really not accurately defined. First of all, we need to define "acquisition" and "learning." To the best of my knowledge, linguists have not reached a consensus on "what it means to have acquired a language."[3] People seem to use the term "acquisition" very freely. For example, I do not think it is appropriate to talk about the "acquisition of writing," because writing skills are learned at school with conscious effort, even for native speakers. Good writers are indeed good readers; but as in mathematics the reverse may not always be true. It takes much more than reading alone for anyone to become a writer, let alone a good one.

Most people would agree that language acquisition refers to the phenomenon that a child picks up his or her native language in a matter of two to three years in the language environment without formal instruction and subconsciously, that is to say, without learning grammatical rules and without conscious effort.[4] When we consider the situation of adults learning a second or foreign language, difficulty in definition may arise because conscious effort is often present and the language environment is not easily available even if grammar is not taught. Therefore, the distinction between acquisition and learning is not clear cut.

Although I have not come across better definitions for "acquisition" and "learning," I have noticed that one difference between them lies in the fact that synchronization of comprehension and verbal message intake, either oral or written, is realized in language acquisition, while language learning results in

3. See Asher (1994: 1905).

4. See Malmkjaer (1991) in which she states that "Language acquisition or first language acquisition is the term most commonly used to describe the process whereby children become speakers of their native language or languages."

delayed comprehension. This delay allows the learner time to decode the perceived verbal message. The process of speech production, on the other hand, is more complicated than comprehension. On certain occasions, even native speakers need time to think before they speak. But messages are understood the moment they are received if they are comprehensible. This means that the question of what is often referred to as language or linguistic competence should be examined more carefully.

Competence. In this section I would like to clarify a few things regarding language/linguistic competence, drawing on recent findings in neuropsychological research. As can be seen from the last section, a distinction needs to be made between language comprehension competence and language production competence. In addition, within the category of comprehension competence, we ought to further distinguish between auditory (listening) comprehension competence and visual (reading) comprehension competence.

It is common knowledge that a child's listening comprehension competence begins to develop long before his or her speech production competence.[5] In addition, there is far less discrepancy in the listening comprehension competence than the speech production competence among native speakers who are said to have acquired a language. Good speakers are in fact good listeners; however, great variation exists among native speakers as far as their speech production competence and performance are concerned. How many Americans, for instance, would have aspired to succeed Johnny Carson as host of the Tonight Show?

Moreover, neuropsychology has shed some light on the nature and role of implicit competence as it is derived from implicit memory[6] in language acquisition. "This competence is acquired incidentally, stored implicitly and used automatically" and "incidental acquisition ... leads to an implicit competence that is used automatically and that remains opaque to introspection" (Paradis 1992). According to Paradis, "the advantage of incidental acquisition is that it leads to implicit internalization and automatic use," whereas "explicit knowledge about the structure of the language is within the purview of declarative memory, and ... can be recalled to consciousness on demand, but cannot be incorporated in the automatic use of language" (1992).

---

5. Eimas et al. (1971) have proved that one-month-old babies can already discriminate syllables, and Mehler et al. (1985) have pointed out that infants are also sensitive to acoustic variations and recognize voices. See also Asher (1994).

6. Graf and Schacter (1985) define "implicit memory" as the "form of memory revealed when performance on a task is facilitated in the absence of conscious recollection; [whereas] explicit memory is revealed when performance on a task requires conscious recollection of previous experiences." See also Dunn and Kirsner (1989).

The acquisition-oriented syllabus. Therefore, our acquisition-oriented syllabus is more concerned with the process, rather than the end product, of language acquisition. It concentrates on building up the comprehension competence of the students by making maximum use of their implicit memory and aims at achieving the synchronization of comprehension with verbal message intake. I would like to draw a parallel between language learners trained by more traditional teaching methods that rely too much on written texts and patients with auditory (acoustic) agnosia. They hear a sequence of sounds, but they fail to make the connection between the sequence of sounds and meaning right away. Our project has demonstrated, however, that extensive exposure to auditory language input can correct this problem.

In the past three years, we have been exposing the English majors at our university to such a simulated language environment through TV programs. As I explained earlier in this paper, we started with the third-year students and then moved down to the second-year students and then the first-year students. Last year, I went one step further. I spent one semester with the eleventh graders of one high school and a second semester with the eleventh graders of another high school in Hangzhou. Feedback from the students has also been encouraging. I have even succeeded in getting the English teachers of the second high school interested and involved in the experiment. We have started a retraining program for the teachers at the school.

English majors in China spend four years studying English. So far, we have only scheduled an additional two hours every week for their exposure to this kind of auditory language input. In four years, they will have received about 400 hours of such input in the classroom alone, not counting the time the students watch rented movie videos on their own. We don't know yet how many hours of exposure to the simulated language environment would result in language acquisition. However, only 200 hours of such exposure has brought remarkable results. In 1992, our students watched the American presidential debates with great interest and relative ease. This would have been unthinkable in the past.

Conclusion. Thus far, our second language acquisition research project seems to indicate that in the past we may have greatly underestimated the potential of the human brain for mastering a second language, that the LAD may still function just as well for adolescent and adult language learners, that for them the goal of language acquisition is attainable once they are given the real or simulated language environment, and that comprehensible auditory language input plays the crucial role in triggering the language acquisition process.

ACKNOWLEDGMENTS

I am grateful to Dr. William Slager and Dr. Adrian Palmer of the University of Utah for their lectures on methodology and second language acquisition theory in Hangzhou, China, in the spring of 1982.

I am indebted to the Canadian Studies Association of Canada for funding my research tour in Canadian universities during the summer of 1992.

I would like to thank my colleague and Language Laboratory Director, Professor Ye Zhihong, for his unreserved support throughout all these years.

REFERENCES

Adamson, Hugh Douglas. 1988. *Variation theory and second language acquisition*. Washington, D.C.: Georgetown University Press.

Alatis, James E. 1990. *Linguistics, language teaching and language acquisition: The interdependence of theory, practice and research*. The Georgetown University Round Table on Languages and Linguistics 1990. Washington, D.C.: Georgetown University Press.

Asher, R.E. (ed.) 1994. *The encyclopedia of language and linguistics*. Oxford: Pergamon Press.

Barasch, Ronald M. and C. Vaughan James. 1994. *Beyond the Monitor Model*. Boston: Heinle and Heinle Publishers.

Brown, J. Marvin and Adrian S. Palmer. 1988. *The listening approach*. London: Longman.

Caplan, David. 1987. *Neurolinguistics and linguistic aphasiology: An introduction*. Cambridge Studies in Speech Science and Communication. Cambridge, U.K.: Cambridge University Press.

Chomsky, Noam. 1965. *Aspects of the theory of syntax*. Cambridge, Massachusetts: MIT Press.

Cook, Vivian J. 1991. *Second language and language teaching*. London: Edward Arnold.

Cook, Vivian J. 1992. "Evidence for multicompetence." *Language Learning* 42(4): 557–591.

Dunn, John C. and Kim Kirsner. 1989. "Implicit memory: Task or process?" In Stephan Lewandowsky, John C. Dunn, and Kim Kirsner (eds.), *Implicit memory: Theoretical issues*. Hillsdale, N.J.: Lawrence Erlbaum Associates, Inc.

Durkin, Kevin. 1989. "Implicit memory and language acquisition." In Lewandowsky et. al. (1989).

Eimas, Peter D., Siqueland, E.R., Jusczuk, P., and Vigorito, J. 1971. "Speech perception in infants." *Science* 17(1): 303-306.

Ellis, Rod. 1985. *Understanding second language acquisition*. Oxford, U.K.: Oxford University Press.

Ellis, Rod. 1990. *Instructed second language acquisition: Learning in the classroom*. Oxford, UK. and Cambridge, Massachusetts: Blackwell.

Ellis, Rod. 1992. *Second language acquisition and language pedagogy*. Clevedon, U.K. and Philadelphia: Multilingual Matters.

Graf, Peter and Daniel L. Schacter. 1985. "Implicit and explicit memory for new associations in normal and amnesic subjects." *Journal of Experimental Psychology* 11: 501–518

Krashen, Stephen D. 1982. *Principles and practice in second language acquisition*. Oxford, U.K.: Pergamon.

Lewandowsky, Stephan, John C. Dunn, and Kim Kirsner. 1989. *Implicit memory: Theoretical issues*. Hillsdale, N.J.: Lawrence Erlbaum Associates, Inc.

Malmkjaer, Kristen (ed.). 1991. *The linguistics encyclopedia*. London and New York: Routledge.

Mehler, Jacques. 1985. "Language related dispositions in early infancy." In Jacques Mehler and Robert Fox (eds.), *Neonate cognition*. Hillsdale, N.J.: Erlbaum.

Morley, Joan. 1990. "Trends and developments in listening comprehension: Theory and practice." In James E. Alatis (ed.), *Linguistics, language teaching and language acquisition: The interdependence of theory, practice and research*. Georgetown University Round Table on Languages and Linguistics 1990. Washington, D.C.: Georgetown University Press.

Paradis, Michel. 1992. "Differential cerebral involvement in language learmng as a consequence of various teaching methods." Paper presented at Second Language Acquisition and Teacher Education Conference, University of Illinois at Urbana-Champaign.

Pinker, Steven. 1994. *The language instinct*. New York: William Morrow and Co.

Scarcella, Robin C. and Stephen D. Krashen. 1980. *Research in second language acquisition: Selected papers of the Los Angeles Second Language Acquisition Research Forum*. Rowley, Massachusetts: Newbury House.

Schneiderman, Eta I. 1988. "A neuropsychological substrate for talent in second language acquisition." In L. Obler and D. Fein (eds.), *The exceptional brain*. New York: The Gal Press.

Scovel, Thomas. 1981. "The effects of neurological age on nonprimary language acquisition." In Roger W. Andersen (ed.), *New dimensions in second language acquisition research*. Rowley, Massachusetts: Newbury House.

White, Lydia. 1987. "Against comprehensible input: The input hypothesis and the development of second-language competence." *Applied Linguistics* 8(2): 95–110.

White, Lydia. 1989. *Universal grammar and second language acquisition*. Amsterdam and Philadelphia: John Benjamins.

The use of language tests for power and control[1]

Elana Shohamy
Tel Aviv University

Introduction. Tests are used for a variety of purposes—to measure students' knowledge in relation to future tasks which they are expected to perform, to place students in appropriate levels of classes, to grant certificates, to determine whether students can continue in future studies, to select those who are most suitable for higher education institutions, to obtain jobs, and to accept candidates to different programs. Thus results obtained from tests have a strong impact on the lives of many individuals. The Irish novelist McGahern (quoted in Madaus 1991) describes, in the following poem, the impact of tests—taken to an extreme—on a child who is about to take a test:

Please God may I not fail
Please God may I get over sixty per cent
Please God may I get a high place
Please God may all those likely to beat
me get killed in road accidents and
may they die roaring.

This strong impact of tests on test takers has turned tests into powerful and authoritative devices which are capable of changing and prescribing the behavior of those who are affected by their results. A phenomenon that can be observed as a result is the exercise of power and control through tests. This can be observed in a variety of settings and contexts. Tests are used by policy makers in central agencies as tools to manipulate the educational system, to control curricula, and to impose the introduction of new textbooks and new teaching methods. Principals use tests to prompt teachers to teach, and teachers use tests to force students to study. On the national level power is exercised by bureaucrats through nation-wide tests such as matriculation examinations and national assessment surveys; on the school level control is exercised by principals and administrators through school-wide exams; and in the classroom

1. This is a revised version of a paper presented at the AILA Conference in Amsterdam, August, 1992. Another version of this paper was published in the Carleton Papers of Applied Linguistics and in the East West Proceedings, Jyvaskyla, 1992.

power is exercised by teachers through tests, quizzes, and grades. The power and authority of tests turns them into tools for enforcing educational goals especially in situations when actual education has failed. This phenomenon can be observed in all levels of education—national, school, and classroom.

Madaus (1991) states that tests represent a social technology deeply embedded in education, government and business, and as such they provide the mechanism for enforcing power and control. Foucault (1979), in *Discipline and punish: The birth of the prison*, views the examination as the most efficient tool through which society imposes discipline, as it contains all the features needed for power and control:

> The examination combines the technique of an observing hierarchy and those of normalizing judgement. It is a normalizing gaze, a surveillance that makes it possible to quantify, to classify and to punish. It establishes over individuals a visibility through which one differentiates them and judges them. That is why, in all the mechanisms of discipline, the examination is highly ritualized. In it are combined the ceremony of power and the form of the experiment, the deployment of force and the establishment of truth. At the heart of the procedures of disciplines, it manifests the subjection of those who are perceived as objects and objectification of those who are subjected. (1979: 184)

This paper will bring evidence from testing discourse to show how tests are used for power and control, specifically for observation, surveillance, quantification, classification, normalization, judgement, and punishment. Evidence will be reported from two main sources: (1) Rhetorical and discourse devices used in tests and testing; and (2) the gap existing between the discourse and intentions of decision makers regarding tests and the specific actions observed in actual test use.

Rhetorical devices

The channel of communication. The first rhetorical device indicative of the power and control of tests relates to the channel of communication. Most tests used today are written examinations. Madaus (1991) claims that it was not until the latter part of the eighteenth century, when paper was more readily available, that written tests were systematically introduced into European schools, replacing the traditional oral mode of testing. Foucault (1979) contends that written examinations mark the beginning of scientific pedagogy. The written test defines what is expected and forces students to reveal periodically how their learning is progressing. It has "guaranteed the movement of knowledge from the teacher to the pupil, but it extracted from the pupil a knowledge destined and reserved for the teacher, thus becoming a mechanism for exercising power over the pupil" (1979: 187).

Earlier tests which employed the oral mode left room for a dialogue between a tester and a test taker—the student had the opportunity to ask questions, to elaborate on what s/he had learned, and to demand clarification. The written test introduced a form of discourse which altered the act of communication from a dialogue to a one way channel of communication focusing on what the teacher had taught without considering the test taker's views and interpretations. Thus, while the oral mode is characterized by negotiation, elaboration, expansion of ideas, use of contextual clues, correction, argument, revision, debate, the reading of facial clues, etc., the written mode is one-sided; information flows in one direction as the test taker writes what s/he knows in response to his/her interpretations of a written stimulus.

The power of the language of numbers. Another rhetorical device which contributes to the power and control of tests is the language of numbers through which test results are disseminated. Numbers are powerful since they allow quantification, classification, normalization, and judgment. Much has been written about the use of numbers and statistics as effective devices for power and control, and about the fact that they speak more than words (McLouan 1983). Bureaucrats, principals, and teachers use numbers to classify, punish, reward, place, accept, and reject.

Those who work with statistics and numbers know how unreliable numbers are, but those affected by numbers have trust in their power and authority. The power of numbers also lies in the fact that they can be challenged only if one has numbers which counter them. In testing, however, the tester has the numbers while the test taker does not, and the only numbers s/he can refer to are those provided by the tester who "owns" the numbers.

The power of numbers also lies in the impression that they are objective and therefore represent the "truth"; they are not open to discussion and challenge. Numbers are powerful also because they allow classification and standardization on the same scale, and thus enable all test takers to be judged according to the same yardstick. Thus the language of numbers as a device for disseminating test results provides decision makers with power, authority, control, and the legitimacy for decisions and sanctions.

The power of the language of science. The language of science is viewed as a tool for power and control. The fact that testing is perceived to be a scientific and empirical discipline grants testing authority and status. Testing is powerful because it is believed to be scientific, experimental, statistical, and therefore objective and true.

The "objective" and "empirical" information gleaned from tests is then used by bureaucrats to support their beliefs. MacIntyre (1984) states that since the aim of the bureaucrat is to adjust means to ends in the most economical and efficient way, s/he will deploy scientific knowledge organized in terms of, and comprising a set of, universal law-like generalizations to help him. Schwandt (1989) elaborates on this phenomenon and claims that bureaucratic managerial expertise in both the public and the private sectors rests on this assumption of scientifically based practice. Evaluators, policy analysts, researchers, and consultants enhance bureaucratic expertise by acting as scientific resources. "As masters of the tools of scientific analysis, these experts generate empirical evidence—scientifically based knowledge—that managers use to enhance their authority and control" (Schwandt 1989: 12).

Although testers know that they are unable to generate accurate generalizations concerning human behavior in view of the constraints imposed by real-world problems on methods of scientific investigation, the belief in the role of the evaluator as an expert who provides scientifically derived knowledge for managers and policy makers remains essentially intact.

The power of written documentation. Results obtained from tests are documented. Foucault (1979) claims that the examination which places individuals in an area of surveillance also situates them in a network of writing; it generates a whole mass of documents to capture and fix them. Thus the power of writing constitutes an essential part in the mechanism of disciplines. Specifically he states that not only is the aptitude of each individual assessed, but the procedure of writing also situates these abilities and indicates the possible use that might be made of them.

The procedure of writing made it possible to integrate individual data into cumulative systems in such a way that they were not lost, and to arrange things so that an individual could be located in the general register and, conversely, each datum of the individual examination might affect overall calculations. Thanks to the whole apparatus of writing that accompanied it, the examination opened up two correlative possibilities. First, the individual was redefined as a describable, analyzable object. This happened not in order to reduce the individual to "specific" features, as did the naturalists in relation to living beings, but in order to maintain him in his/her individual features, in his/her particular ovulation, and in his own aptitude or abilities, under the gaze of a permanent corpus of knowledge. Secondly, a comparative system was constituted that made possible the measurement of overall phenomenon, the description of groups, the characterization of collective facts, the calculation of the gaps between individuals, and their distribution in a given "population" (Foucault 1979: 191).

Combining the tests with documentation implies that what happens on a test is recorded, will remain, and will provide those who are interested in the information with evidence for possible sanctions against test takers. Thus the documentation allows the transfer of the procedure of writing and registration into the formation of a mechanism for discipline.

The power of the objective test format. Test format relates to the genre in which test questions are posed. Most tests used by testing agencies employ "objective" items such as multiple choice and true false. The assumption underlying these procedures (and the reason they are called "objective") is that there is one correct answer, i.e. one "truth," one interpretation. Furthermore, that "truth" is owned by the tester and the test taker has to try to find out what it is. Objective testing controls knowledge by creating one "truth" with no deviation and no alternatives; it provides power and control through the format of the test. The "truth" is absolute and determined in advance by the tester who wrote the test and selected all the alternatives. It does not ask the test taker to present his interpretation or any other possible interpretation of the truth. This is especially problematic in the testing of reading comprehension where there may be many interpretations of a similar text, as readers construct meaning differently depending on their background, age, views, etc.

Thus, an "objective" format means control since the information is in the hands of the tester who writes the item, selects the correct answer according to his/her interpretation, and allows no deviation from it. Since comprehension is subjective, the "objective" format of testing demands a type of knowledge which is an inaccurate reflection of "truth."

The next part of the paper will describe the gap that exists between how decision makers "talk" about tests and the actual uses made of tests for power and control.

The gap between words and action. The comparison between the stated intention of the tests and their actual use provides evidence to support the claim that tests are used for power and control. Tests are described by decision makers as useful, educational, beneficial, and significant for the advancement and improvement of education; yet in examining their actual use there is ample evidence to show that what is said is not what is done, and what is said often hides a different message, that of power and control. Specifically tests are used for observation, surveillance, quantification, classification, normalization, judgment, and punishment. A specific case of a national test administered in reading comprehension and math for fifth and sixth grades in Israel will be used to exemplify this point. This test is typical of other national tests given in many countries for monitoring achievement, especially in countries which have centralized educational systems, e.g. a national curriculum and national exams for different age groups. This specific national test was administered to 160,000 students, in 6,000 classes, in 1,600 schools, and employed 6,000 external proctors. Prior to the administration of the test the educational system (the Ministry of Education) sent the following letter to the parents of the students who were to be tested:

> Dear Parent:
>
> The Ministry of Education and Culture is about to administer tests in Math and Reading Comprehension to all the students. The results of the test will enable us to find out about the level of achievement of children in these important subjects. The tests will help the school plan its work for the next academic year. The results will be used by the Ministry only for pedagogical purposes, for tracking, for research and for establishing policy. There will not be any use of the results for purpose of selection. The data will be kept in the data base of the Ministry of Education in accordance with the Privacy law (1981). The detailed results will be sent to the school after the beginning of the next academic year.

This is clearly a very "educational" document. Yet, in the next sections, the consequences of the test mentioned above in terms of power and control will be analyzed and described.

Using tests for surveillance. The first indication of the use of tests for power is using them for surveillance. The reading comprehension test was admittedly an act of surveillance by the educational system. The educational system follows the progress of all the children of the country. It can, without asking permission of parents, students or teachers, compel them to be tested; it can enter the classrooms and demand that all the children in the country take a test and show the system what they know in a certain subject according to the educational system's criteria. If in fact the system did not intend to use the results of the test for the selection of individuals, why were students asked to write their names? Why were the scores released to schools by students' names? In administering the tests the educational system did not have to prove that the tests are not "harmful" to the students or that these tests are of such high quality that they provide accurate scores. Students or parents have no right, and in most cases no tools, to examine the quality of the test beforehand. All students are obligated to participate, and if they refuse, they or their teachers may be punished. The performance of each of these students is then recorded in the form of a number which is classified as pass or fail. The educational system now has records on each of its pupils (including most immigrants for whom the language of the tests is still foreign).

The information that the educational system can obtain from this surveillance cannot be of very high quality, since the decision on who failed and who passed was based on a limited number of questions. The results do not take into consideration the relevance of the texts to the background of the students, their social and ethnic environment, their home culture—especially the environment of the immigrant population, nor whether the student had a good or bad day when doing the test.

But not only are students surveyed, so too are teachers and schools. The documented, recorded, and classified information related to teachers as well, as if it depended only upon the teachers whether their students succeeded in or failed the reading comprehension test.

Using tests for *quantification*. Students and teachers are now recorded in the data base of the educational system in the form of quantification, i.e. their identity is now described, defined, and summarized in terms of "percentage of correct answers" on a limited number of test questions and texts.

Using tests to classify people. In addition to the ability to test anybody, anytime, and to quantify them, another aspect of power and control is the classification of students as successes or failures, as good or bad. Thus it is possible for the authoritative group to classify students, teachers, and schools into categories. Often the students, schools, and teachers are not even aware that they have been classified as successes or failures.

Using tests for judgments and sanctions (Punishments). Once the information is available (observed, documented, quantified, and classified), there is legitimacy for imposing sanctions. Examples of sanctions are forbidding students from entering certain class levels, demanding that they repeat grades, and withdrawing from upgrading programs.

Even if the educational system claims not to use this information for selection, the availability of the information implies that it will be used. Schwandt (1989) claims that bureaucrats are looking for such information in order to justify their actions and will therefore make use of it. There are many examples of situations where teachers arrive at decisions based on test results which were meant for entirely different purposes. In some schools, teachers were fired, textbooks were changed, and students were placed in low level groups based on tests which were initially intended only to evaluate the level of the schools (Shohamy 1991).

The difference between description and judgment is relevant in this context; while tests give descriptive information, decision makers often use the results for judgment, i.e. punishment or reward.

It is hard to believe that a single test score can result in major decisions and consequences for people's lives. Madaus (1991) claims that rarely do we find a single device that is so powerful that it can dictate so many decisions as a single standardized test score that can independently trigger automatic admission, promotion, placement, or graduation decisions. These decisions are non-negotiable even in the face of contradictory judgements from educators about what a student knows or can do. Such reliance on a single test score is a process vulnerable to simple error. In the area of policy, a test is a social technique which yields information that can be used to direct people in different directions. Thus, using a single test score can put children at risk.

Using tests for scaling and standardizing the population. While each of the students tested on the reading comprehension test was an individual case before the test, after the test s/he was judged in relation to all the other students of his/her age in the country. It is important to mention that the norm for a country is determined, in most cases, by how the rest of the country does on the very same reading comprehension questions, as the same test is given throughout the country. Thus the test has the power to straighten the level of deviation in the country. Whereas this year there may have been some deviations as a result of different backgrounds, different teachers, different learning contexts, and different ways of constructing meaning, the effect of this test will ensure that this will not happen again and that students around the country will construct meaning in the same way, ending up with exactly the same knowledge. In countries which have centralized educational systems this is a well known phenomenon, since any national test ensures that all students will arrive at the same knowledge. The test, therefore, plays a major role in this standardizing and norming effort. This phenomenon of standardizing knowledge throughout the country based on the same test questions is exemplified in Figure 1, taken from Foucault's book *Discipline and punishment* (1979).

Although the above phenomenon has long been typical of countries with centralized educational systems, in the past few years there has been a similar trend even in countries with decentralized educational systems (Shohamy 1991). Thus in the U.S., the ACTFL guidelines, often referred to as a "common yardstick," were introduced to define the core of knowledge to be acquired and tested by all foreign language learners as part of the effort to upgrade the proficiency level in foreign language learning. These guidelines imply one type of foreign language knowledge; deviations from it need to be corrected. This is an act of control and power as people are being controlled and standardized according to a single scale. While it is clear from language learning theories that there are many routes to acquiring a foreign language; the common yardstick concept implies standardization to one single path. It is interesting to note that when such an act occurs in countries with decentralized systems based on free-

Figure 1. Taken from *Discipline and punishment*, Foucault (1979).

10 N. Andry, *L'orthopédie ou l'art de prévenir et de corriger dans les enfants les difformités du corps* (Orthopaedics or the art of preventing and correcting deformities of the body in children). 1749.

dom of education, scales are often used to circumvent that underlying assumption.

Using tests to demonstrate authority (Who is in charge). Tests are often used for the purpose of declaring where authority lies; this is especially true in centralized systems. In many developed countries responsibility and authority are shared by one body. In some countries there is a clear distinction between authority and responsibility.

The tension between the authority and those who are responsible for introducing the change is clear in the case of the national reading comprehension test. One wonders whether teachers (those responsible for change) will be willing to cooperate with the centralized educational system (those in authority) in the future. The teachers were humiliated by the system, which viewed them as potential cheaters and not trustworthy, when they were forced out of their own classrooms during the test and not briefed on what their students were expected to know. One also wonders what kind of message is delivered to students about their teachers. It is, after all, the teachers who will be asked to cooperate in "correcting" the various reading comprehension problems detected on the tests.

Another strategy to demonstrate who is in control is a mark, called often a "defense mark," which is used in a number of countries as part of the matriculation examinations administered at the end of secondary school. The defense mark, assigned by the students' teacher, is one component of the matriculation score. The students' final score consists of the average of the external matriculation examination and the "defense mark." The term "defense mark" already implies that the student needs to be "protected" from the educational system, from the authorities. But if the school deviates from the external score, it receives a warning from the authorities based on the assumption that the external score (of a once in a lifetime test) is "the correct score," and that the Ministry of Education which administers the external test provides the most valid assessment, while all other grades, especially those assigned by the teacher (who may have known the student for a number of years and in a variety of contexts), are not valid and the teacher must conform to the external scale. Thus if gaps occur between the two scores, the school receives a warning that the school does not assign valid grades, as the Ministry owns the "truth."

It is often the case that tests are conducted by the educational systems when they feel that their authority has been threatened, or when they feel that they are losing control; the use of the test helps bring the authority back to power. The administration of national tests of any kind is often aimed at indicating who is in charge. The reading comprehension test discussed above was administered by the educational system to a large extent as a reaction to complaints that innovations and new programs in reading comprehension were not being introduced into the system. Similarly, the introduction of the ACTFL guidelines in the U.S. was a reaction to criticism that there were no new programs in foreign language teaching and that children were not performing as expected. Though no new programs have been introduced recently, the administration of the test is an indication to the public that something is being done.

Using tests to frighten or deter. Using tests to frighten or deter is related to the use of tests by the authoritative agencies to stimulate the system. It usually occurs when there is a failure in learning. Thus the current proposals to introduce national tests in the U.S. are a result of the low scores that American children obtain on international tests (Madaus 1991). There are a number of cases where educational systems introduce tests in order to "shake up" the instructional system. It is interesting to note that this goal of shaking the system is not done through the introduction of new curriculum but through tests. This is a result of the power of tests and the fear that students and teachers have of failing.

There are various techniques the Ministry employs to enhance that fear and make it more effective. Before the administration of the national reading comprehension test, the Ministry of Education used the strategy of not making information available to teachers and students; it refused to release any information about the test, the format, the questions, or its purpose. Withholding information, not unexpectedly, created tension, anger, and anxiety. One reason that teachers were asked to leave the classrooms was not to reveal the questions, so that the same test could be used the following year. Keeping information from the public is the same strategy often used by teachers, who try to avoid releasing information about tests to students and thus to exercise power and control. The element of mystery is strongly enhanced and is related to the ritual phenomenon, mentioned by Foucault (1979), that is typical of thc usc of disciplinary tools.

Absence of information about the tests is a device testers use to impose power and control. By withholding information from the public at large and the test takers in particular, the situation created is that of the tester owning the knowledge which the test taker lacks. That knowledge gives the tester extreme power and leaves the test taker with no power.

However, newspaper reports indicated that in spite of the Ministry of Education's intention, students spent long hours preparing for the test; some poor students were removed from classes in fear that they would lower the school average, good students were not excused from school even if they had a previous, engagement.

Using tests to control learning. Testers claim that the nation-wide test assesses what the students have learned. However, it turns out that the testers dictate what will be tested and consequently what will be learned. Shepard (1991) claims that testers view tests as synonymous to curriculum and to learning. Nation-wide tests are often based on material that not all schools were exposed to.

A decision to include a certain language skill (e.g. speaking) or, alternatively, not to include another area (e.g. grammar) on a high school matriculation exam, will result in students and teachers practicing speaking and not being motivated to practice grammar. Thus tests control the knowledge of students by determining that they learn the topics considered important by testers.

Consider the example of a national supervisor of language who felt that students graduating from high school lack proficiency in reading comprehension and writing. In order to "cure" this problem he decided to change the national exam at the end of high school by adding reading comprehension and writing components. As a result, teachers demanded more hours to teach the content, new textbooks were commercially produced, children were tutored in these skills, and a major effort was put into the study of areas which had not been taught before, all in preparation for the important test. Interestingly, reading and writing had always been included on the national curriculum, but since they had never been tested on a national exam they apparently had not been taken seriously by teachers and students.

Is the use of tests for power and control effective? Since the use of tests for the purpose of power and control has become such a wide-spread phenomenon in many countries, questions have been raised not only regarding the ethics of using tests for these purposes but also regarding whether using tests in such a way can advance and improve learning in a meaningful way. A number of studies have shown that prescribing behavior is not an effective way to upgrade the level of learning (Stake in press; Smith 1991). This leads to skepticism about the extent to which the introduction of tests, per se, can bring about meaningful improvement in learning and teaching. Consequently, there are serious doubts whether it is at all beneficial to rely on the power and authority of tests to create change in the behavior of teachers and students.

Stake (in press) and others studied the effect of introducing tests as devices for upgrading achievement, and they found that although the tests did make teachers more focused in their teaching, the tests resulted in narrowing the scope of the subject matter because teachers were teaching primarily for the test.

Similarly, Shohamy (1993) examined the effect of the introduction of a new EFL (English as a Foreign Language) oral test as part of the nation-wide high school matriculation exam on the level of English proficiency and found the impact to be that of teaching "test language," that is, only those language tasks and skills likely to appear on the tests were taught in English classes. Furthermore, teachers tended to shift their teaching from the means and procedures that facilitated learning to the goals of learning. Some teachers admitted returning to "normal" teaching right after the administration of the test; they clearly viewed the test as an external, irrelevant act in relation to their routine teaching.

Such findings should not come as a surprise. After all when there is exclusive reliance on tests to create change; when the emphasis is not on what takes place in the classroom as part of the learning process; when tests are introduced as authoritative tools, are judgmental, prescriptive, and dictated from above; when the tests do not involve those who are expected to carry out the change—the teachers; and when the information provided by tests is not detailed and specific, and does not contain meaningful feedback and diagnosis that can be used for repair, it is difficult to expect tests to lead to meaningful improvement in learning. Tests, after all, comprise only one component in the educational process.

Incorporating tests into the educational system. Creating change through tests can be effective, however, since schools will usually strive to meet external standards and will alter teaching and learning habits to attempt to improve performance on tests. At present, however, curricular change does not result; only the performance of the students on these tests is emphasized. The effect of this is to narrow the curricula in ways which are inconsistent with real learning and real needs.

The main question is, therefore, how the device of testing can be utilized so as to create positive effects on learning. One solution offered is to maximize the role of tests as a means for obtaining information which is relevant to the improvement of learning while minimizing their role in power and control. The real power of tests lies not in their authority and prestige, but rather in their ability to provide meaningful information which can be incorporated into the educational system. Thus there is a need to rely less on the power of tests and more on the useful information that tests can provide for the improvement of teaching and learning. It is possible, for example, to use tests to supply decision makers (students, teachers, and administrators) with valuable information and insights on teaching and learning. The information obtained from tests, when it is relevant and innovative, can provide evidence of teachers' performance, of students' ability over a whole range of skills, subskills and dimensions, and of students' achievement and proficiency on a continuous basis and in a detailed and diagnostic manner. According to Nitko (1989) information that is innovative and meaningful can lead to utilization. Such information can be useful for judging students in relation to the expectations outlined in the curriculum, to determine whether the school as a whole is performing well in relation to other schools that share the same curricula, to determine whether the teaching methods and textbooks used are effective tools for achieving those goals, and to determine whether the goals are realistic and appropriate. It is the information obtained from tests and its utilization which should make them valuable and powerful. When decision makers realize the value of the information tests provide, improvement can result. Information can be utilized properly especially when teachers, who are expected to carry out the changes, are involved in the assessment process. Once conclusions are reached based on this information, it is possible to align the curriculum with the information and to implement changes in goals, teaching methods, and textbooks. These changes can then be monitored through repeated administration of tests in an ongoing basis.

Fredriksen and Collins (1989) contend that information obtained from tests can contribute to improved learning when tests are connected to the learning that takes place in the classroom. They introduce the notion of "systemic validity" to refer to the introduction of tests together with a whole set of variables which are part of the learning and instructional system. Accordingly, the introduction of tests is a dynamic process in which changes in the educational system take place according to feedback obtained from tests. In systemic models, a valid test is one that brings about, or induces, an improvement in the tested skills after a test has been in the educational system for a period of time. Fredriksen and Collins contend that high systemic validity can only be achieved when a whole set of assessment activities foster it. They identify such activities as the use of direct tests, practicing self assessment procedures, repeated testing, feedback on test performance, and multiple levels of success. They claim that the efficiency of current testing practices is greatly outweighed by the cost of using a system that has low systemic validity—one that has a negative impact on learning and teaching, since the goal of testing has to be to support the improvement of learning and teaching. Thus tests that are used for the purpose of improving learning can be effective when they are connected to, and integrated into, other elements which are part of the educational system, but not when used in isolation.

Testers must begin to examine the consequences of the tests they develop. Testers often feel they have completed their job after obtaining a high reliability and validity, and do not find it necessary to observe the actual use of the test. It has been claimed (Messick 1989) that it is the responsibility and obligation of the testers to examine the uses, misuses, and abuses of tests in the real world. The testers' role is to warrant against such misuses as described in this paper, and to show that in spite of the educational purposes of tests, they may actually be used for power and control.

It is essential that testers cooperate with experts not involved in testing and acquaint all those concerned with tests and their use with the vocabulary of testing, so that they can enter the discourse without being dismissed as naive, thus improving communication between groups and having more people outside the testing community address the social and technical values of testing.

Tests can be used effectively by integrating them with learning, by having testers examine the use of tests in the real world, by placing the responsibility for guarding the moral aspects of tests, and by involving nontesting groups in the discourse of testing. There is a need for greater awareness of and increased responsibility for uses and misuses of the devices which testers so naively develop. A move towards a meaningful dialogue (as opposed to inspection) may be one step in that direction. Freire calls for:

> Evaluation, that is, and not inspection. Through inspection, educators just become objects of vigilance by a central organization. Through evaluation, everyone is a subject along with the central organization in the act of criticism and establishing distance from the work. In understanding the process in this way, evaluation is not an act by which educator A evaluates educator B. It's an act by which educators A and B together evaluate an experience, its development, and the obstacles one confronts along with any mistakes or errors. Thus, evaluation has a dialectical character.
>
> It's essential that members of the evaluating organization deeply believe that they have as much to learn from educators directly linked to popular bases as those who study at the bases. Without this attitude, the evaluators from an external organization will never admit to any gap between their view of reality and reality.
>
> By believing they possess the truth, the evaluators act out their infallibility. And with such a hypothesis, when they evaluate, they inspect.
>
> Accordingly, the more bureaucratic the evaluators are, not just from an administrative point of view but above all from an intellectual view, the narrower and more inspection like the evaluators from outside will be. Conversely, the more open and accessible to creativity they are, the more anti-dogmatic, and the more evaluative (in the sense here described) they will be. (Freire 1985: 23–24).

REFERENCES

Foucault, Michel. 1979. *Discipline and punish*. New York: Vintage Books.

Fredriksen, John and Allen Collins. 1989. "A system approach to educational testing." *Educational Researcher* 18(9): 27–32.

Freire, Paulo. 1985. *The politics of education*. South Hadley, Massachusetts: Bergin and Gravey Publishers, Inc.

Madaus, George. 1991. "Testing as a social technology." Paper presented at the conference "Testing and evaluation: Feedback strategies for improvement of foreign language learning," February 4–5, Washington, D.C., the National Foreign Language Center.

MacIntyre, Alasdair C. 1984. *After virtue, second edition.* Notre Dame, Indiana: University of Notre Dame Press.

McLuhan, Marshall. 1962. *The Gutenberg galaxy: The making of typographic man.* Toronto: University of Toronto Press.

Nitko, Robert. 1989. "Designing tests that are integrated with instruction." In R. Linn (ed.), *Educational measurement.* New York: Macmillan Publishing Company.

Schwandt, Thomas. 1989. "Recapturing moral discourse in evaluation." *Educational Researcher* 18(8): 11–16.

Shepard, Lorrie. 1991. "Psychometricians' beliefs about learning." *Educational Researcher* 20(7): 2–9.

Shohamy, Elana. 1993. "The Power of Tests: A Study of the Impact of Language Tests on Teaching and Learning." NFLC Occasional Papers. Washington, D.C.: National Foreign Language Center.

Stake, Robert. (in press). *Effects of changes in assessment policy.* Greenwich, Connecticut: JAI Press.

The impact of college entrance examinatons on high school ESL/EFL writing

Chen-ching Li
Taipei Economic and Cultural Representative Office in the United States

1. **Introduction**. After the two-decade debate of whether or not essay writing should be implemented in the English component of the Joint College Entrance Examination (henceforth CEE) in Taiwan, a compelling body of evidence has accumulated recently supporting the positive impact of testing ESL/EFL writing for better learning of English as a second or foreign language. It has been observed that this educational innovation has prompted the integration of English grammar instruction and communicative language use in general, and efficient English writing in particular. Results gathered through my research in the English essay writing and Chinese-English translation in CEE between 1981 and 1990 has been compatible with the study of Sandra S. Fotos (1994: 323) manifested in her observation of grammar consciousness-raising tasks. It is noted that mistakes in ESL/EFL writing which are natural and even necessary aspects of language learning (Brown 1991: 108) have been converted into a positive channel for enhancing the learning of efficient writing. This argument has been supported by the analytical data that I gathered from the CEE, and justified by the cognitive argument that Krashen (1983) maintained.

Indeed, the teaching and learning of English as a second or foreign language has been widely regarded as one of the most challenging educational endeavors in Taiwan. Due to the demands of traditional academic pursuits—both at home and abroad—as well as to the everexpanding professional needs of an increasingly global market, the study of English as a second or foreign language is no longer just a fashion, it has become a practical necessity. To meet these needs, educational programs of all sorts have focused their curricula to include a greater emphasis on acquiring all of the four language skills needed to communicate competently in English: listening, speaking, reading, and writing.

A crucial question in Taiwan is how well both teachers and students are respectively performing their missions of teaching and learning the four language skills. The question is quite controversial due to the role that the CEE plays in the whole process of English education in Taiwan. In the three decades of debate on the most effective ways to teach English as a second or foreign language, many different methods have been suggested to Taiwan's English teachers at different stages. In 1981, however, new light was shed on this problem. The catalyst for the approach that began to develop at this time was the restoration of translation and English composition categories to the CEE. This landmark change in education policy has redefined the course of the ESL/EFL profession in Taiwan. It has presented teachers and students with the formidable challenge of improving students' English language composition skills.

Statistics tabulated by the CEE Committee indicates that this challenge was a source of much frustration for both high school students and their English teachers during the early 1980s. However, there is hope. Positive feedback to my research focusing on the connections between reading, writing, and English composition instruction skills has surfaced among teachers participating in the summer programs of In-Service English Teachers of the Department of English, National Taiwan Normal University, 1982–1989.

I agree with Kroll (1990) that "becoming a writer is a complex and ongoing process, and becoming a writing teacher is no less complex." Kroll's timely and straightforward comment serves as a footnote to my recent research on the impact of the CEE on high school ESL/EFL writing in Taiwan. Evidence manifested through error analysis will be applied to argue for the present case study of ESL/EFL writing in Taiwan's secondary schools.

2. Joint College Entrance Examination in Taiwan. Three major factors should be expounded so as to better appreciate the durability of the CEE in Taiwan for more than thirty-five years (1958–1994). The creation of the CEE is historically and socially significant in relation to the national education policy which has been held for its accountability the whole time. With the steady increase in large enrollments for the nation-wide CEE, a new breakthrough in ESL/EFL has been found in different settings.

2.1 Historical and social perspective. Historically, the Chinese are people that espouse the examination system, considering it as the most justifiable and impartial evaluation system with which to screen the most talented candidates for official positions. The CEE has adopted the same format since 1954, and has been considered the most impartial way of testing all students, regardless of their social and family background. Despite the drawbacks of the CEE system, the format has survived, and there is not yet any better alternative for it.

Different schools of linguists have various opinions on CEE English essay writing. Some have argued that the grading of students' English essays can never be fair to all due to the individual readers' views. As a result, a computerized multiple choice format was designed for the English portion of the CEE in the 1980s. This practice led all high school students to prepare for the challenge of the English portion of the CEE by randomly choosing fragmentary segments of the English language, without acquiring any rightful ability of correlating the four language skills of English, as divided by Robinett (1978: 175) into receptive skills and productive skills.

The computerized multiple choice format led students to learn English in an abnormal manner, and created an unpredicted situation among the young secondary school students in Taiwan: They could comprehend the isolated vocabulary words, but failed to comprehend the language data when it was presented in a context.

2.2. Breakthrough and challenge of ESL/EFL writing initiated by the CEE. In 1981, however, there was finally a great breakthrough in the English portion of the examination: English composition and translation were added under the active campaign of many English professors, including this writer. Positive feedback is now considerable.

Initially, however, this addition sent a powerful shock wave throughout the nation. A large majority of high school graduates failed the exam miserably, for they had no idea what to write. In the first and second years after the addition of English composition and translation to the exam, over one third of the examinees received zero on this section. English teachers then suddenly found that their teaching burden had become much heavier. Frustration and disappointment confounded most of the teachers in Taiwan between 1982 and 1985.

An important impact that the restoration of English composition and translation had was that, due to this thought-provoking and innovative method of testing, the Republic of China's high school students finally embarked upon the appropriate road for learning practical English, focusing primarily on reading and writing skills. Figure 1 shows a gradual decline of the percentage of students who scored zero points on the English composition section of the CEE between 1982 and 1991. These statistics show that high school students have been cured, at least partially, of their original "English-phobia." This first step toward writing skill development in the teaching of English as a second or foreign language is of remarkable significance.

Figure 1 clearly indicates that high school graduates who participated in the 1982–1984 CEEs were essentially helpless when it came to writing English compositions, whether doing "guided writing" or "free writing." Thus, in the 1982 and 1984 CEEs, 26.46% and 24.66% (respectively) of the total examinees who received zero scores. Their failure can be attributed to their inefficiency in learning to write English compositions and to their English teachers' inability to appreciate the relationship of theory, research, and practice in second language instruction (Silva 1990: 19; Li 1991: 83–84).

What is particularly significant in Figure 1 is that a shocking 42.36% of the students participating in the 1983 JUEE CEE received zero points scores. This is because the topic designated for that year's English composition was "A taxi

Figure 1. Percentage of zero scores in English composition (1982–1993).

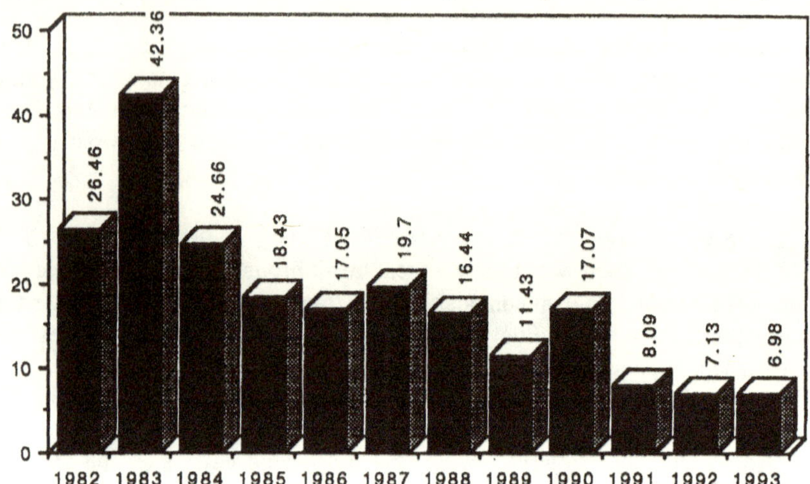

ride." In the process of evaluating the high school students' JUEE CEE English compositions, I found that most of the students mistook "A taxi ride" for "A taxi driver." Consequently, a very high percentage of the students failed to grasp the topic. Instead, most of them concentrated on describing the education and social responsibilities of taxi drivers. One student must have memorized a lot of model compositions and articles, as he quoted former President John F. Kennedy's inauguration address to describe his views on taxi drivers of today: "A taxi ride should not ask what his country can do for him. Instead, he should ask what he can do for his country."

Similar responses were found in many compositions, making 1983 one of the most discouraging years for testing English writing skills. These statistics (shown in Figure 1) indicate an inability on the part of students to adopt practical strategies for learning English writing skills. Likewise, they indicate that high school English teachers and educational administrators need to assume more responsibility in applying proper teaching methodologies and providing suitable educational materials for enhancing students' skills of ESL/EFL writing.

Fortunately, right after 1982, the instruction of English composition in high schools improved dramatically through the joint efforts of administrators of the Ministry of Education, scholars from the Department of English at National Taiwan Normal University, and high school teachers from Taiwan and the two offshore islands of Kin-men and Ma-tsu. A new consensus about the proper methods for teaching high school English had begun to form among these experts. As part of this process many applied linguists, including myself, were invited to assist inservice English instructors in teaching English composition to their students.

Although no significant progress in CEE English compositions was visible between 1983 and 1985, improvement in basic writing skills was obvious after 1986. In Figure 1 we can see that the percentage of zero scores has declined drastically and distinctively. In Figure 2, however, we notice that the percentage of four-point scores remained rather stable, whereas the percentage of three-, two- and one-point scores gradually declined.

Figure 2. Contrastive percentages of four- to one-point scores in CEE English compositions, 1982–1991.

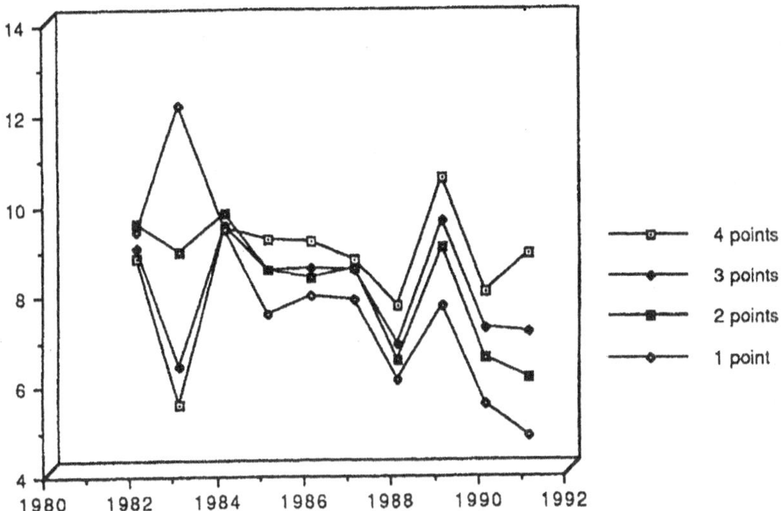

The statistics as shown in Figure 2 indicate that high school students are gradually acquiring fundamental English writing skills, thanks to the improvements made in Taiwan's innovative approach to preparing test formats and to training secondary school English teachers through diversified measures. Also it is essential to remember that mistakes, as Brown (1991: 108) argues, are a natural and even necessary aspect of language learning. Mistakes are often the only way to get feedback from other people on one's linguistic progress. Bearing this concept in mind, learners (high school students in this case) can be persuaded to boldly and freely practice ESL/EFL writing under the guidance of their English teachers. This preliminary step of ESL/EFL writing is essential to not only senior high school students, but to students of all levels interested in nurturing and upgrading their writing skills. Further evidence of this can be seen in Figure 3 which shows a gradual increase in higher scores of 9, 8 and 7 points, in striking contrast with the drastic decline of undesirable scores such as four to zero points shown in Figure 1 and Figure 2.

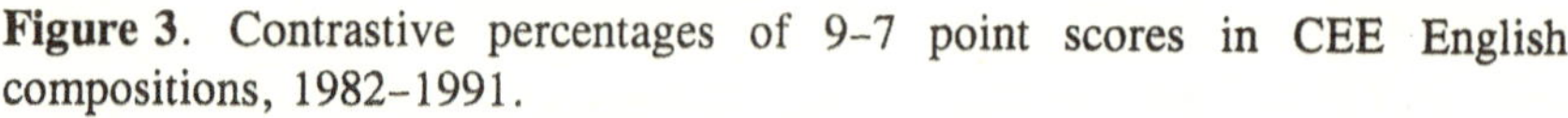

Figure 3. Contrastive percentages of 9–7 point scores in CEE English compositions, 1982–1991.

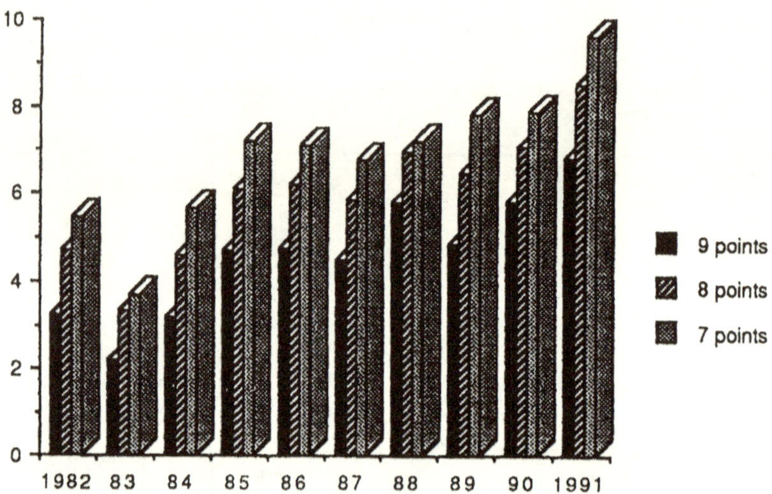

In this conjunction, it is important that students should be aware that: "By taking control of one's own learning, students should be successful language learners." (Brown 1991: 5) In beginning to write, students should not worry too much about possible mistakes in their English compositions. It is believed that in addition to constant writing practice, the first steps toward learning English as a second or foreign language (ESL/EFL) should emphasize instilling self-confidence in the students, in addition to focusing on composition writing. "Self-confidence is a key to successful language learning." (Brown 1991: viii) The contrastive scores shown in Figures 1 to 3 have clearly justified this argument.

In reviewing the contrast of the rising percentage of high scores and the declining percentage of low scores—indicated in Figure 4—we get a glimpse of the significant progress in ESL/EFL writing by high schools students, made possible through the implementation of English essay writing in the CEE in 1982.

The progress in ESL/EFL writing demonstrated by high school students participating in the CEEs is not limited to scores between nine and twelve as indicated in Figure 4. As a matter of fact, students did well year after year. Figure 5 shows the results of their progress and steady improvement in ESL/EFL writing. This stark reality has justified the conviction of Taiwanese policy makers and educators about the direct impact of CEE on high school ESL/EFL writing along the lines of optimal teaching and learning strategies.

Figure 4. Declining vs. rising percentages of low and high scores in CEE English compositions, 1982–1993.

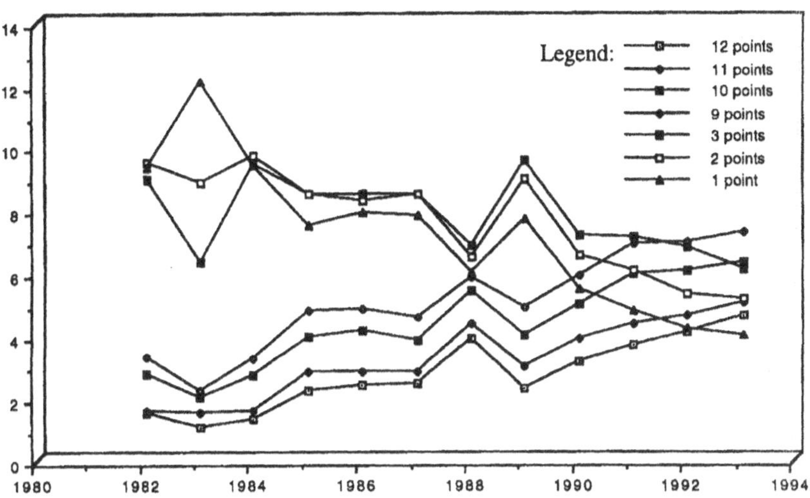

Figure 5. Rising high scores in CEE English compositions, 1982–1993.

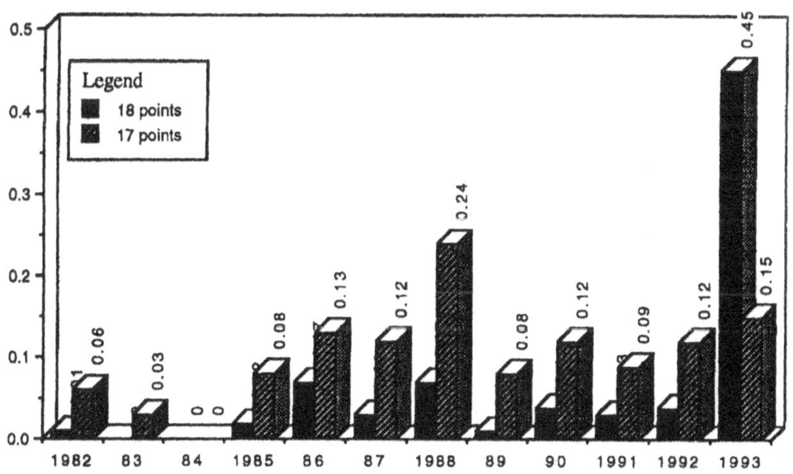

Correlation between reading and writing has thus been further justified as well.

Taken altogether, Figures 1, 2, 3, 4, and 5 show that the teaching and learning of English writing in Taiwan has made noticeable progress since the early 1980s. Students no longer suffer the composition-phobia that afflicted past generations.

As time passed, a new consensus on teaching English in high school began to build among educational policy makers, scholars, and English teachers. Many applied linguists from National Taiwan Normal University, including myself, have been invited to assist inservice English teachers to teach English composition to their students. Our joint efforts gradually paid off. Although no dramatic progress was visible between 1983 and 1985, an improvement in basic writing skills was obvious.

By further analyzing the progress accomplished in ESL/EFL writing in the CEE by singling out the twelve-, eleven-, ten- and nine-point scores, in contrast with four-, three-, two-, and one-point scores as indicated in Figure 4, the high school students' progress in writing CEE English compositions becomes salient. Both the graphics and values reflected in Figure 4 have assured us that high school students are indeed demonstrating more confidence in their performance of ESL/EFL writing as a whole. With the input of English teachers' innovative pedagogical strategies for ESL/EFL writing in high school, students are certain to score better in the annual CEE. Changing the test format by adopting the English essay writing format has successfully motivated both high school students and English teachers to follow the justifiable path of teaching and learning English more productively.

In recalling the large percentage of students scoring zero points in English compositions in 1982 (26.46%) and 1983 (42.36%), we are certainly pleased to find that on average, students are now able to score eleven points or more in the CEE English composition. Not too many of the high school students appear to be "plagued" by English-composition-phobia any more. The steadily rising percentage of upper–medium scores, namely ten to fourteen points in CEE English composition writing, has revitalized our confidence in implementing more similarly innovative testing devices so as to complement more desirable teaching strategies of English in high schools. This finding can also be generalized to the even higher scores, namely thirteen to eighteen points. (Twenty points is the highest mark for both English essay writing and Chinese–English translation.) Although the percentage of students scoring eighteen and seventeen points was not high enough, one can predict that the teaching of English in high school and junior high schools has a rosy picture ahead, as long as we continue with this test format.

Many educators have been opposed to the direct testing of English writing, because human evaluators are employed and therefore the possibility of human error exists (Kroll 1990: 78). These educators tend to believe that having evaluators read and grade each short English essay written by students will create biases. However, the small discrepancies incurred by human grading is not as serious as the larger discrepancy created by the computerized testing of items that can hardly interpret the genuine potential of students' English writing skill.

3. Impact and prospect of required ESL/EFL writing in high schools. The statistics demonstrating gradual progress in high school students' CEE English composition writing have inspired both English teachers and students to be more confident in teaching and learning English as a second/foreign language in the Republic of China on Taiwan. As I have stated above, this first step toward ESL/EFL writing is essential. However, this step is by no means easy to initiate. It takes diversified challenges to foster the skills of English composition and translation, both of which have been the major areas of CEE English testing since 1982. For young learners of English, the series of challenges are not liabilities. Instead they can be proven to be assets that high school students can employ to nurture their English writing skills.

One of the best ways to learn English well is to make good use of what one has gradually acquired linguistically under the guidance of a competent teacher who employs precise and efficient methods for teaching English as a second or foreign language. In this manner, students of English can expect to make progress in the process of language learning, and thereby build a solid foundation for developing practical communication skills. In the end, the student will learn the four language skills of listening, speaking, reading and writing, with each complementing the other. By so doing, not only will students lay the ground work for English language learning, but as they become used to expressing themselves in English (by means of speaking and writing) and become able to absorb English (by means of listening and reading), they will progress in big strides. Eventually they will begin getting high scores on the English composition, translation, reading comprehension, and the other sections on the English portion of the CEE that measure the students' synthesis of language skills. This is not just a pipe dream, but a reality on which the theoretical foundations of this study are based.

Scores on the English portion of the CEE, especially those for composition and translation, diagnose a high school student's English language proficiency, study techniques, and even their high school English teachers' instructional methodologies. Although current CEE English testing methods are still controversial due to grading techniques, English composition and translation are undeniably quite effective measures for determining high school students' English proficiency. Such English language proficiency not only determines students' performance on the college entrance examination, it also has a decisive impact on future study both at home and abroad, and on future professional and personal development.

Most senior and junior high school students feel that English classes are frightening and frustrating. This being the case, students find the classes uninteresting and are quite anxious during examinations. When they finally come face to face with the "fate-determining" college entrance examination, many feel upset and even stupefied. As a result, we have no choice but to face three unpleasant realities.

First, because the study methods used by students preparing for the English composition and translation sections of the CEE are often undesirable, the result in examination performance is far from satisfactory. Though the English composition and translation sections of the the exam total forty points (twenty points each), some students may get a total of only about ten to fifteen points. Other students taking the examination may get twenty-eight to thirty points total because they have a knack for studying, and have developed more solid language skills. These students may achieve scores two or more times higher than other students. In addition to this difference in performance, some colleges weigh CEE English more heavily than others do. Also, the impact of other related test items (such as reading comprehension and the combination test), make the difference between English scores even greater. Consequently, some examinees can achieve quite different scores than other, equally bright and studious examinees, simply because their English study methods are superior.

Secondly, once in college, the strength of the students' English skills often determines their level of success in the academic performance. This is because books used in colleges are often in English, and the role that English plays—be it listening, speaking, writing, or reading—is extremely important to every freshman's education and growth process. Furthermore, once a student graduates from a university or a three-year junior college, English remains a tool that, if well used, increases his professional and other opportunities. Thus, taking advantage of the gradual and proper procedures for learning English, as offered by the complete and multifaceted method introduced by English teachers, students will ultimately benefit more than "hanging onto the Buddha's feet" (making a last ditch effort) simply to pass the CEE. By using the methods exemplified in *Breaking the barrier of ESL writing* (Li 1992), students will be able to strengthen and improve their English language as a "tool," through the multitude of effective study methods it offers.

Thirdly, since 1987, when the Ministry of Education of the Republic of China announced a new policy that allowed high school graduates to study overseas, young Taiwanese students faced great hardships in English-speaking nations because of their insufficient English language skills. This, too, was a result of their unsatisfactory English study habits. The teaching of English in high schools used to consist primarily of boring memorization and recitation exercises, with no emphasis on practical application. Even though such high school graduates can afford to study abroad, how can they possibly hope to survive with such undesirable preparation? How will these students survive in a foreign learning environment fraught with the challenge of adapting to a new culture, a new language, and school work?

Solving the very real problems mentioned above is not actually that difficult. It can be done by following the the wisdom of the saying, "to climb to the greatest height, one must start from the lowest level." If one makes the effort, English can become a tool to enjoy and benefit from throughout one's life no matter where one goes.

4. Interaction between reading and writing: An essential step to ESL/EFL writing. Reading and listening as receptive skills are contributive to writing and speaking, the productive skills (Robinett 1978: 175). To be specific, ESL/EFL writing (output) should never be alienated from reading (input). Reading and writing are indeed complementary to each other in educational functions.

The development of good writing is not an instantaneous skill. Writing is a unique, accumulated art composed of diverse variables. Good writing exceeds the scope of any individual language skill of listening, reading, speaking and writing. It takes the integration of all of the four basic skills combined in order to produce ideal writing in general, and presentable ESL/EFL writing in particular. In light of the research I have presented above, it is understandable that Chinese high school students produce a large quantity of ungrammatical English sentences as listed in Appendix. As a matter of fact, this problem of English writing is partially attributed to insufficient general knowledge of ESL/EFL writing. Consequently, high school students and English teachers in Taiwan are at loss, not knowing just how to write acceptable English compositions. This is one of the major reasons why most of the earlier statistics presented in this paper were so shocking. Barbara Kroll's argument in her book *Second language writing* should always be remembered:

> Becoming a writer is a complex and ongoing process, and becoming a writing teacher is no less complex. A teacher's journey toward understanding the complexity of both writing and teaching often begins with a look to the past, for scholarship originates from the ability to synthesize past insight and apply them in the pursuit of continued inquiry. (Kroll 1990: 1)

Examining the state of the art of teaching English as a foreign or second language in relation to CEE, it is imperative that both high school English teachers and students devote more time and energy to learning how to read and write through an analytical approach. Indeed the process of integrating reading and writing is an indispensable shortcut to linguistic success and to high school students' development of English writing. There are abundant facts and experiences to justify this hypothesis. The data gathered from the annual CEEs are invaluable as well in persuading both students and teachers what is the right path to successful ESL/EFL writing.

In her 1990 book *Writing as thinking: A guided process approach*, Marcella Frank stresses the absolute correlation between reading and writing. She regards English composition, accomplished after reading, thinking and discussion, as a top priority. Frank's proposition justifies my series of arguments that students should be encouraged to incorporate ideas or support from various ESL/EFL readings (Li 1986, 1986a, 1987, 1987a, 1987b, 1989, 1990, 1991; Robinett 1978: 175; Robinett 1992 personal communication). Chinese high school students have demonstrated various English writing skills through the CEE English composition performance. It is my argument that an ability to sustain the correlation between reading and writing, be it on the part of the teachers' methods of instruction or on the part of the students' own learning strategies, is crucial to ensure desirable performance in the English composition and Chinese-English translation sections of the CEE—sections which total 40% of the entire English scores.

It is my belief that my findings and analyses based on the college entrance examination on high school ESL/EFL writing are also significant to students of all linguistic backgrounds, native speakers of English included.

REFERENCES

Aboderin, Yemi. 1986. "Integrating reading and writing." *English Teaching Forum* 24(1): 38–40.

Adams, W. Royce. 1989. *Developing reading versatility, Fifth edition*. Chicago: Holt, Rinehart and Winston, Inc.

Arapoff, Nancy. 1967. "Writing: A thinking process." *TESOL Quarterly* 1(2): 33–39.

Baskoff, Florence. 1981. "A new look at guided writing." *English Teaching Forum* 19(3):2–6.

Brown, H. Douglas. 1991. *Breaking the language barrier*. Yarmouth, Maine: Intercultural Press, Inc.

Burt, Marina K. and Carol Kiparsky. 1972. *The gooficon: A repair manual for English*. Rowley, Massachusetts: Newbury House.

Carr, Donna H. 1967. "A second look at teaching reading and composition." *English Teaching Forum* 1(1): 30–31.

Chiang, Tai-hui. 1981. *Error analysis: A study of errors made by Chinese learners*. Taipei: Crane.

Dixon, Duncan. 1986. "Teaching composition to large classes." *English Teaching Forum* 24(3): 2–5.

Fotos, Sandra S. 1994. "Integrating grammar instruction and communicative language use through grammar: Consciousness-raising tasks." *TESOL Quarterly* 28(2): 323–351.

Frank, Marcella. 1990. *Writing as thinking: A guided process approach*. Englewood Cliffs, N.J.: Prentice Hall Regents.

Hamp-Lyons, Liz. 1990. "Second language writing assessment issues." In Barbara Kroll (ed.), *Second language writing*. New York: Cambridge University Press.

Jacobs, Suzanne E. 1982. *Composing and coherence*. Washington, D.C.: Center for Applied Linguistics.

Krashen, Stephen. 1983. "The din in the head: Input and the language acquisition device." In John W. Oller and Patricia A. Richard-Amato (eds.), *Methods that work*. Rowley, Massachusetts: Newbury House.

Kroll, Barbara (ed.). 1990. *Second language writing*. New York: Cambridge University Press.

LePan, Don and George Kirkpatrick. 1988. *The Broadview book of common errors in English*. Peterborough, Canada: Broadview Press.

Li, Chen-ching. 1986. *A communicative approach to teaching English as a foreign language*. Taipei: Mason Publishing Co.

Li, Chen-ching. 1987a. "The application of the input-intake approach to teaching language arts." *Papers from the fourth conference on English teaching and learning, R.O.C.* Taipei: The Crane. 183-195.

Li, Chen-ching. 1987b. "New light on ESL writing as derived from the Joint College Entrance Examination." *English Teaching Journal* 12(1): 29-36. (in Chinese)

Li, Chen-ching. 1987c. "Innovations for teaching English through the impact of the Joint College Entrance Examination." *Ladder English Journal* 10(7): 53-58. (in Chinese)

Li, Chen-ching. 1989. "Interaction between reading and writing and its impact on the method of teaching English." *English Teaching Journal* 13(3): 3-10. (in Chinese)

Li, Chen-ching. 1991. "Translation and interpretation for CSL class: Strategies to employ." Paper presented to the 1992 Chinese Language Teachers Association (CLTA) Annual Meeting, Washington D.C.

Li, Chen-ching. 1992. *Breaking the barrier of ESL writing*. Taipei: Crane Publication.

Moody, K.W. 1965. "Controlled composition frames." *English Language Teaching* 19(4): 146-155.

Newsweek. March 15, 1982. "English, English everywhere."

Oller, John W., Jr. and Patricia A. Richard-Amato. 1983. *Methods that work*. Rowley, Massachusetts: Newbury House.

Richards, Jack C. (ed.). 1974. *Error analysis: Perspectives on second language acquisition*. London: Longman.

Rivers, Wilga M. 1989. *Communicating naturally in a second language: Theory and practice in language teaching*. Cambridge, Massachusetts: Harvard University Press.

Robinett, Betty W. 1978. *Teaching English to speakers of other languages*. Minneapolis, Minnesota: University of Minnesota Press.

Rybowski, Tadeusz. 1986. "Ways to English: Some remarks on teaching practical grammar." *English Teaching Forum* 24(1): 24-28.

Salvatori, Mariolina. 1983. "Reading and writing a text: Correlations between reading and writing patterns." *College English* 45(7): 657-666.

San Francisco Chronicle. May 13, 1992. "One in eleven have trouble speaking California's official language."

Schumann, John H. and Nancy Stenson (eds.). 1976. *New frontiers in second language learning*. Rowley, Massachusetts: Newbury House.

Silva, Tony. 1990. "Second language composition instruction: Developments, issues, and directions in ESL." second language writing." In Barbara Kroll (ed.), *Second Language Writing*. New York: Cambridge University Press.

Taffe, Juliane and Gary W. Wolek. 1992. "Journalling in composition conferences: A whole language experience." Paper presented to the 1992 NAFSA annual conference, Chicago, May 24-27, 1992.

Taylor, Barry P. 1976. "Teaching composition to low-level ESL students." *TESOL Quarterly* 10(3): 309-319.

APPENDIX

Typical errors and mistakes made by Chinese students in their CEE English compositions, 1982-1993. The following unacceptable sentences contain typical errors and mistakes in English grammatical structures, vocabulary usage, idiomatic expressions, logic, rhetoric, etc. All major errors are printed in bold letters. Read them carefully and then try to practice correcting and improving these sentences.

1. *English is so popular that Americans **does** not need to learn the second language.
2. ***Can** you sure that he never **have said** a lie?
3. *I thought I **must to** take a rest.
4. *But **a few taxi ride** is not good.
5. *We may see the taxi **in** everywhere.
6. *I was very **fear**.
7. *Mother **very like** her.
8. *It is better rich and polite than poor and not **polishing up**.

9. *I really don't **feel like to take** a taxi.
10. ***I like ride** a taxi.
11. *I told the driver **hurrier**.
12. *He said that he's glad to see the education in Taiwan **had made** great **gress**.
13. *Now, I like ride taxi **very well**, I thought, when I was **a old** man, I would lie down the taxi **for die**.
14. ***I had been rided** a taxi several years ago.
15. *I had better **went** to school in a hurry.
16. *I **runned** into the school gate.
17. *Five men and ... **are hijacked an airplane**.
18. ***Do you can** be never lie?
19. *When we were were enjoying the nice feeling, we **were arrived**.
20. *The **most of taxi ride** is good.
21. *We **can't to go** home, So we take a taxi.
22. *It is **rain** because people **was** wet.
23. ***We not** to be jamped.
24. *If you often walk, you will **be health**.
25. *I **was luck** that I got **a good drivers** last time.
26. *I **am very like** to ride a taxie.
27. *Because **of late**, I got off **hurrioed** and forgot my bag.
28. *We must **be respect** the older.
29. ***Can** you sure he never **tell** lies.
30. ***Will you sure** that he never **tell** lie?
31. *I **am after** that he'll object our project.
32. *Can you make sure that he never **teels** a lie?
33. *Many people **are also like** a taxi ride.
34. *Many people **are also like taxi ride**.
35. *Taxi is **more smaller** than bus, and more convenienter than bus.
36. *When I was a child, I **very like taxi**.
37. *When I was a little child, I **take** a taxi ride with my family.
38. *He **everyday** can see **very much people**, car...
39. *Taxi can **halp** we go to the we go a place and take **we** home.
40. *In this taxi ride I **talled** to myself. "There are many people **need** help."
41. *My father **drived** our car to take me to the exam today.
42. *If the drives ran through red and **drave** fast would **caused to** many traffic **publems**.
43. *Are you sure that he has never **telled** a lie?
44. *Then a taxi **drived to me near**. I told the **drier** that I **got missing**. Then my teacher **brought** me home.
45. *My father is a **taxi ride**.
46. *That taxi **ride** is a lady. She is very beautiful.
47. *If I were a taxi **ride**, I will stop to see the red light.
48. *If I were a taxi **ride**, I **will** help others. A taxi **ride** can do many things for many people. Most taxi **ride** are good men.
49. *Being a taxi **rider**, he must know clearly every ways of the city.
50. *The national flag **代表** our country.
51. ***Are sure** that he has never **tell** a lie?
52. *Are you sure that he has never **tells** a lie?
53. *Are you sure that he never **tell** a lie?
54. ***Can** you sure that he never **tell** a lie?
55. *We must **go to** by taxi for the time, because time is **powr** so **we by** taxi.
56. *In Taiwan the car is too **much**.
57. *I called a taxi **today** morning.
58. *Some people think that a free man is a man who can do what **we** can, so to **do** a taxi ride is a good work.
59. *I have got a **teach** of the taxi ride.
60. *The five men and a woman hijacked an airplane **in order tofreedom**.

Sample articles written by high school students during the Joint College Entrance Examinations.

Sample 1 (1994 CEE English Composition):

Most people confuse "house" with "home." In fact, they are different words and have different meanings. However, they sometimes mean the same thing. A family live in a house, so this house is the home of the family. In this case, "house" and "home" are similar.

Nevertheless, a house is not always a home. It is a home only when there is in it a family sharing their happiness and sadness together. Take my own home for example, there are five people in my family. My families all treat me very well, and they are my best partners in my life. When we get together, our house is full of joy. In a home, we can cure our pain of our hearts, but can 掐 get any warmth from a house. Even though we don't have a luxurious house, we still can live happy lives in our home. (18 out of 20 points have been awarded.)

Sample 2 (1993 CEE English Composition)

Near-sightedness is a serious problem among the youth of our country. Many students in primary schools have become nearsighted. needless to say, students in high schools have even more serious problems. The problem results from more and more homework and the watching of TV. Another reason is that children in the city can' t see many green trees. As a result, it is unusual to find a student not wearing glasses.

I have some suggestions for solving this problem. First, don' t put so much pressure on students. Second, let children do other activities instead of becoming couch potatoes. Then make the city greener. Children are the hope of the country, so we ought to protect them against any harm, such as nearsightedness. (19 out of 20 points have been awarded.)

The beginnings of language testing as a profession

Bernard Spolsky
Bar-Ilan University

Professionalization. The inclusion of the term *educational linguistics* in the theme for a Round Table is surely a major step in the recognition of a professional and academic field for which I have been arguing for some time (Spolsky 1974, 1978, 1985). It seems appropriate in this paper to reciprocate in kind by recounting some contributions of Georgetown and the Round Table, some forty years or more ago, to the development of one key subfield of educational linguistics, that of language testing.

To be considered a profession, a calling needs to have a number of attributes, such as professional associations, textbooks, training programs, journals, conferences, and certification. Perhaps language testing is still not a distinct profession in these terms. The first association specifically for language testers (the International Language Testing Association) was founded only in 1992, and there are still no certification or formal training programs expressly for language testers. The first textbook was published in 1961, a journal is now ten years old, and this 1994 GURT comes just over forty years after the first major session on language testing at a Round Table. In fact, I think it is not unreasonable to consider the early 1950s as the beginning of the professional status of our field.

The training of language testers. Up until forty years ago, language testing had been the work of people trained either as testers or as language educators. The Ph.D. dissertation completed by Villareal in 1947 is probably the first in which someone was trained to bridge the disciplines. There had been earlier doctoral dissertations on language testing. The earliest, dealing with prognosis or aptitude testing, was probably that earned at Stanford by Walter Kaulfers (1933). While it is true that Kaulfers published a good deal on aptitude testing, and wrote an unappreciated but seminal paper on oral–aural testing in 1944, his main professional work was as a foreign language educator. Another early dissertation was one written at Wisconsin by Ficken (1937) that showed that the correlations between the various parts of the Cooperative French Test varied according to the kind of teaching program: Vocabulary and reading generally correlated at about 0.80, but less than 0.70 when there was an oral emphasis and less also in schools that stressed reading, where the highest correlation for reading was with vocabulary. The incipient professionalization of these three early doctorates became even more marked with the writing of a dissertation by

Robert Lado, who, a decade later, was to make an equally crucial contribution to the process by publishing the first textbook in the field.

Lado had earned an M.A. degree at the University of Texas, where Professor Herschel T. Manuel had introduced him to testing. Herschel Truman Manuel was Professor of educational psychology at the University of Texas in 1930, when, in a book on the problems of the education of Spanish-speaking children in Texas, he called attention to their linguistic problems and to the need for measures of their intelligence that would reflect this (Manuel 1930). He was a regional director for the Army–Navy Qualifying Tests in 1944. He argued strongly over the years for tests that would be "fair" (Manuel 1965: 70), and he led the team that constructed the Inter-American Series of Tests of General Ability and Tests of Reading (with parallel Spanish versions) that were published by Educational Testing Service in 1950. Lado dedicated his book on language testing to him. Another of Manuel's students was Sydney Sako, who received his doctorate from the University of Texas some years later and was to make his career in language testing at Lackland Air Force Base.

Lado's M.A. thesis looked at aspects of the Inter-American tests of Spanish and English written by Manuel and used in Texas, Puerto Rico, and Latin America. His M.A. completed, Lado went to Michigan in 1945, where, under the direction of Professor Charles Fries, his interest in language testing continued to grow.

He soon wrote a paper on aural comprehension testing (Lado 1946) and developed three forms of the Test of Aural Comprehension in English as a Foreign Language, published by the English Language Institute at the University of Michigan in 1946–1947. Following the philosophy that Lado enunciated in his thesis (Lado 1949) and developed in his book (Lado 1957), the items in the test had been chosen on the basis of contrastive analysis to include features that would give special difficulty to foreign learners.

This test was still in demand ten years later, when a manual for use was printed. It was reviewed in *The fifth mental measurements yearbook* (1959: 261) by Lado's former teacher, Herschel T. Manuel. In the review, Manuel pointed out how it differed from the test with a similar goal that had been written by A. L. Davis (see below), who had chosen to concentrate his attention on idioms. He found the format good and the scoring straightforward. The internal reliabilities of 0.87 were satisfactory, but they were low enough to suggest more than one form should be used before making decisions in the case of individual students. He hoped that Lado himself would go on to develop more tests.

Lado did. Two of the next tests that Lado wrote focused on contrastive problems in phonology. The Test of Aural Perception in English for Latin American Students (Buros 1975: 262) by Robert Lado was first prepared in 1947 and revised in 1957 and distributed by George Wahr Publishing Company. The Test of Aural Perception in English for Japanese Students (Buros 1975:

362), written by Robert Lado and R.D. Andrade, appeared in 1950. Though originally intended for research use only, it was distributed through Follett's Book Store. Another test constructed at this time under Lado's leadership was the Examination in Structure (English as a foreign language) (Buros 1975: 260).

While preparing these practical tests, Lado was also working on his dissertation, which set out the theoretical background. In it, Lado reviewed the few attempts that had been made to test aural comprehension and oral production. While he rejected some of these tests because they lumped all learners of English into a single undifferentiated set, he found points of interest in many. His own starting point in test construction was structural phonological theory, as he sought to identify the minimal significant problems a foreign learner would face. His task was to test the aural comprehension not of a native speaker but of a learner. If a native speaker did not score 100 per cent on the test, then something outside its scope was being measured.

Lado concentrated on testing the sounds and the structures. In assessing aural perception, some of his early tests used a phonemic alphabet. The difficulties caused by this approach were overcome when he adopted a suggestion that he credited to Lloyd Swift, one of his colleagues at the English Language Institute. Swift proposed a technique of reading two words or sentences to the candidate and having him or her indicate whether the two were the same or different. This, it will be noted, was the technique proposed by structural linguists to identify phonemic differences in a language: In other words, the language learner was being asked to do what a native speaker is assumed to be able to do. Each item in a test, he argued, must measure one thing at a time; items of high frequency were preferable. Aural comprehension passages should be complete utterances. Pictures were useful stimuli. Responses should be multiple choice.

The English Language Test for Foreign Students (Buros 1975: 234, 257) (usually called the Lado test) was published in 1951 and consisted of 134 items, 54 of them concerned essentially with phonemic contrast. The student was required to match the identical sounds in words spelled in different ways (e.g. build, reindeer, kicked). Both the pronunciation and structure sections concentrated on such phonemic problems, with items provided for various linguistic contrasts (e.g. /l/ and /r/ for Japanese speakers, /b/ and /v/ for Spanish speakers). The third section covered vocabulary, with several cases of two-word verbs.

The Lado test was reviewed in *The fourth mental measurements yearbook* (1953) by Clarence Turner and in *The fifth mental measurements yearbook* (1959) by John Cox. Turner remarked that considerable "careful linguistic analysis and testing ingenuity" had gone into the test, which he thought to be useful and easily administered, requiring no special equipment. While he was uncomfortable with some items, he thought the test as a whole to be "an unusually sound and practical one." Cox (a psychologist who was responsible for the tests developed at Lackland Air Force base) was not so easily charmed. While on the face of it, it appeared to be "a satisfactory instrument for measuring proficiency in the comprehension of written English," he was unforgiving about the absence of reliability and validity data and norms. He refused to be reassured by the author's claim to have pretested until he saw the results of these pretests.

In retrospect, Lado's significant contribution in this work was to attempt to combine a theoretically based structural linguistics and a psychometrically based testing method in the process of constructing language tests. For the first time, he claimed that each of these disciplines should have its say in the development of tests. While there were later arguments both with the theories themselves and with Lado's implementations, his explicit appeal to theory was a crucial step in the professionalization of the field. The structuralist psychometric test that Lado constructed was a model for finding an objective method of measuring aspects of human language proficiency. With Lado, and with the students and colleagues he gathered at Michigan like Harris and Palmer and Upshur, the language testing profession had taken a major first step, to become even more evident when the three of them moved to Georgetown in the early 1960s. But that story I will tell elsewhere.

Jobs for language testers. The early 1950s also marked the beginning of professional employment for language testers. The significant sites were Ann Arbor, Michigan (already mentioned), San Antonio, Texas (where John Cox wrote the first form of the Mutual Defense Assistance Pact English Proficiency Examination in 1953 and was joined a few years later by Sidney Sako), Princeton, New Jersey, and Washington, D.C.

Princeton had become an important site for testing when the College Entrance Examination Board moved its test development and research there in the 1930s. In 1948, the Board, with support from the Carnegie Foundation and the American Council of Education, granted independence to these activities with the establishment of the nonprofit corporation, Educational Testing Service. This is not the place to tell the story of the development of that giant testing agency, but simply to make the point that it provided a place where language testers could work. One simply needs to mention names like John Carroll, David Harris, Leslie Palmer, John Clark, and Grant Henning—who all spent time there—to make clear its significance.

Two important government-related initiatives in the 1950s also made Washington, D.C. the important center it has become for language testing. One important battery of tests was associated with the American Language Center in Washington. The earliest version of these appears to have been the Diagnostic Test for Students of English as a Second Language (Buros 1975: 255) published in 1953 by Educational Services and written by A.L. Davis at the American Language Center of American University. The Davis test was far from satisfactory. It contained 150 multiple-choice items where the candidate was required to choose the best of three words or phrases—for example, "They meet (at) (to) (on) eight o'clock." The emphasis was on idioms. There was no formal pretesting. Reliability was claimed to be very high, and norms had been established on the basis of experience with many students at the Center. In a review in *The fifth mental measurements yearbook* (1959), Nelson Brooks said he would have invalidated about a third of the items, which contained impossible forms like "severals" and "gooder" or impossible collocations like "can to write." He believed a more systematically prepared test would do the job much better. A second review was written by Herschel Manuel, who characterized the test as "the type of measuring instrument which is developed to meet a need in a particular situation and then made available to other users without sufficient descriptive material on which the new user can base an independent judgment of its value." He noted the absence of a comparative linguistic basis such as that provided by his one-time student, Robert Lado. He concluded by saying that while the test might well have served its original purpose satisfactorily, it is not clear what it measures nor how idiom knowledge relates to other aspects of language ability.

The test was improved some years later when David Harris, in Florida after his time at Michigan and after a spell at Educational Testing Service, was invited to come to Washington to work with A.L. Davis. By the time he arrived, however, Davis had left, so Harris took charge of the test development work that followed. The Center, which in 1960 moved to Georgetown University, later prepared tests for two U.S. government agencies, the International Cooperation Administration (which became the Agency for International Development (AID) about 1961) and the Department of State Bureau of Cultural Affairs, to be used for overseas screening of applicants for their various programs (Harris 1961).

The second important testing unit was at the State Department. What is now officially known (to those who are being cautiously bureaucratic) as the Federal Interagency Language Roundtable scale is more familiar as the FSI scale, in recognition of its creation by the Foreign Service Institute of the United States Department of State in 1957. The Foreign Service Institute was established in 1946. Dr. Henry Lee Smith, Jr., was Dean of the School of Languages from 1946 until 1955, during which time it expanded its range of languages taught to thirty-five. He was succeeded as Dean by Howard E. Sollenberger, who served until 1966, and was in his turn replaced by James R. Frith.

The scale's genesis was the intensification of the Cold War in 1952 leading to concern over the language proficiency of government officials. Although the first attempt to use a test to encourage civil service knowledge of foreign languages failed, a beginning was made on specifying criteria for such a test. Sollenberger (1978), who was present at the creation, reported that in 1952, the Civil Service Commission was instructed, in accordance with the National Mobilization and Manpower Act, to establish a register of government officials with skills or background knowledge and experience in foreign areas and languages. As member of an interagency committee charged with devising procedures for this, Henry Lee Smith argued for differentiating between levels of knowledge rather than just labeling people simply "fair/good/fluent/bilingual." Smith and Sollenberger proposed the use of a test, but in the face of what some people thought was interference with the affairs of the agencies and a threat to individuals who had reported themselves on job applications as "fluent," the committee agreed to allow each agency to conduct its own survey using common criteria (but not testing procedures). With the ending of the Korean war and the change of administrations, the Civil Service Commission lost interest in the whole matter. The Foreign Service Institute, however, continued to work on developing the scale and a related method of structured oral interview testing.

The matter was not allowed to drop, and in 1955, Loy Henderson, then deputy undersecretary, decided that a survey should be conducted of language skills in foreign service employees and insisted, in the face of opposition, that the survey be supported by testing. Foreign language proficiency would become a criterion for promotion in the foreign service, and the Foreign Service Institute, where U.S. diplomats received their training, was instructed to design and conduct the requisite tests.

As Sollenberger (1978) remarked, this made the whole process "serious business" for foreign service officials and for the Institute. Some 200 officers were immediately tested and graded in accordance with the 1952 scale, but it became clear that differentiation between speaking and reading was needed. Over 4,000 officers received a self-report scale to complete, but fewer than half reported themselves to be at or above the L-4 or R-3 level in French, German, or Spanish, which was then considered the level of proficiency that was "useful to the service." Upset by these results, the Secretary of State announced on November 2, 1956, a new language policy, which stated that because language proficiency was an essential skill for foreign affairs, every foreign service officer would be "encouraged to acquire a 'useful' knowledge of two (2) foreign languages, as well as sufficient command of the language of each post or assignment to be able to use greetings, ordinary social expressions and numbers; to ask simple questions and give simple directions; and to recognize proper names, street signs and office and shop designations." An officer's level of proficiency was to be determined by tests conducted by the Foreign Service Institute. To overcome problems remaining before mandatory testing began in 1957, Frank A. Rice was appointed to head an independent testing unit, and Claudia Wilds became his assistant, later succeeding him.

During the 1950s, then, the first employment opportunities for language testers started to suggest that it would be a possible profession, with the opening up of a handful of jobs at Ann Arbor, San Antonio, Princeton, and Washington. More were to develop as other government agencies established testing units and as university departments added testing as a key course in educational and applied linguistics.

Meetings. A vital factor in the growth of the language testing profession was the provision of regular opportunities for personal contacts between testers. When Carroll (1961) opened the 1961 Washington conference that led to TOEFL with the words "This is not the first conference ever called on language testing, nor will it be the last one," he was probably referring to a second meeting he had been invited to that same month on foreign language testing. There had been earlier meetings.

The 1951 summer seminar in psychology and linguistics at Cornell University (Carroll 1951) had a much wider scope than just testing, its outcome being the formal creation of the new field of psycholinguistics. Agard's presentation on second language learning discussed the work of the Investigation of the Teaching of a Second language at Chicago, which had revealed the need for psychological experimental study of language learning. Three categories of research looked worthwhile. First was the development and testing of measures of individual aptitude for second language learning. Second was controlled experimental testing, in laboratory conditions, of the various methodological approaches. The third was language proficiency, Carroll's special interest at the time. The report says:

> Objective tests of auditory comprehension, reading ability and grammar exist at present, but we are not certain that each constitutes a valid measure of the particular skill involved. We have no data on the reliability of the (as yet unstandardized) auditory comprehension tests which are now in use, and we have no objective tests of oral production at all. It seems probable, however, that only in the light of long experience gained in the measurement of second-language aptitude and in the experimental evaluation of instructional methods, can we expect to success in devising proficiency tests of proven validity and reliability for all the skills. (Carroll 1951: 42–43).

One of the results of this seminar was to establish language testing as a relevant concern for psycholinguists and applied linguists and to move it out of the unchallenged domain of psychometrists and language teachers working alone or in tandem. This was an important step in the burgeoning semi-independence of the field of language testing.

The territorialization was confirmed at the fourth annual Georgetown Round Table on Languages and Linguistics in 1953, organized by Archibald Hill. Hill (1953), who was at that time Vice Director of the Institute of Languages and Linguistics at Georgetown, organized a day-and-a-half program that brought together an interesting amalgam of theoretical and applied linguists. The luncheon speaker on the first day was Bernard Bloch, who presented in a brief talk his view of a unified theory of linguistic structure and linguistic analysis. On the second day it was Norman Torrey, who presented a number of anecdotes adding up to an argument for foreign language learning.

While there had been many earlier practical meetings and even some more theoretically inclined ones, the 1953 Georgetown Round Table seems to have been one of the first with a session devoted specifically to language testing. The next major language testing meeting after Georgetown with published results was the 1961 Center for Applied Linguistics meeting. A broken series commenced in 1967 at the National Association for Foreign Student Affairs annual meeting (Wigglesworth 1967), followed by a meeting at Ann Arbor, Michigan (Upshur 1968), Idlewild (Brière 1969), Hasselt in Belgium in 1973, and at the TESOL Conference in Puerto Rico in 1973 (Palmer and Spolsky 1975). A third meeting in 1973 was the Washington Language Testing Symposium, held at the Georgetown Round Table (Jones and Spolsky 1975). Out of these meetings later grew the Language Testing Research Colloquium, which first met at TESOL at Boston in 1979. Thus, the 1953 session may be considered the forerunner of a developing series.

The session, chaired by John Carroll (then at Harvard) consisted of five papers. Carroll (1953) himself opened by noting that language testing brought together two groups of people: "psychometricians" and "linguisticians," although he preferred the terms applied psychologists and applied linguists. Language teaching, he said, involved interesting problems of testing and measuring both aptitude and achievement, which were closely related, for the traits that were characteristic of a speaker were carried from one language to another. In a first language, there were a number of "fundamentally independent dimensions of individual differences" that would show up in different performances or as "factors" in tests. Carroll's life's work has been focused on this issue of isolating, as far as scientifically possible, the primary factors that make up human cognitive abilities; his book, with that title, has just appeared. One factor, Carroll guessed, was vocabulary, probably including "grammar" (putting sentences together grammatically, however, Carroll suspected was separate). Other factors that he identified covered skill in doing anagrams, in free associations, and in naming colors. There were differences to be found, too, in "the ability to emit language spontaneously and effectively in various situations," and in speech rate and care of articulation. While Carroll expected that these same dimensions would be found in second language achievement, he cautioned against "clever" methods of language testing that might turn out to measure unimportant traits. In this remark, he foreshadowed his later suspicions about the cloze technique (Carroll, Carton, and Wilds 1959).

Believing as he did that second language performance was based on first language competence, Carroll argued that among the best predictors of success in learning a second language would be measures of proficiency in the first. A person who could not carry on a conversation in his first language would be unlikely to be able to do so in a second. Finally, he noted that the work of Henmon and his colleagues (1929) showing that measures of general intelligence, reasoning, and inductive capacity were the best predictors for learning a second language in the grammar-translation method, but he believed that for an approach emphasizing aural-oral skills, different traits might be relevant. He mentioned one technique that he later tried out in the Modern Language Aptitude Test, namely, the ability to imitate the phonetic or phonemic structure of an utterance. But what these traits were, he was unwilling at this time to list.

The next two papers in the session also focused on studies of prediction and prognosis. James Frith (1953), then with the U.S. Air Force Institute of Technology and later Dean of the School of Languages at the Foreign Service Institute, described trial courses used by the Air Force before sending airmen to study languages. Earlier, on the basis of scores on general intelligence and technical aptitude tests, possession of a high school diploma and a desire to study the language, airmen had been sent to university to learn Mandarin Chinese. Because half of the candidates dropped out by the end of the first three weeks, a trial course was set up that used the materials from the first few days of the regular training course, was taught by the same instructors, and met for six hours a day (four hours with live instructors and two hours of drill). The course started in high gear, with no time for review, and with frequent tests. After an initial trial run of eight days, it was reduced to four. In fact, 70% of the decisions could be made in two days, but for the rest the extra two were needed. As a result of using the trial courses, the attrition rate in training courses dropped from 50% to 14%, each run of the trial thus saving the Air Force over $10,000.

William J. Morgan (1953), a psychologist, also described aptitude testing to select students for a course in Russian he had done for an unnamed government agency. One can surmise it was the Central Intelligence Agency, referred to in the linguistics literature of the day as the Department of Agriculture—note the listing for Jacob Ornstein in the register for the fourth Round Table (Hill 1953: 112). Morgan persuaded his fellow consultant, Leon E. Dostert, Director of the Institute for Languages and Linguistics at Georgetown University, who had proposed a two-week trial course like the one described by Frith, also to give the first batch of thirteen students a battery of tests, including a projective "written interview questionnaire" and a personality inventory. After careful study (at least an hour in each case) of these data, Morgan made his own predictions of the rank ordering of the students in their course, which proved to be correct in all but one case. The various tests did have some predictive power—the Iowa Foreign Language Aptitude Examination could have made a pass–fail prediction for 80% of the students, while his own clinical predictions were about 0.92. But only the clinical approach could consider the extra traits—attitudes, motivation, age, energy, perseverance, adaptability, or rigidity—that predicted language learning success. He was not convinced that there was such a thing as "language aptitude"; rather, there were "intellectual and personality traits and work habits" that in certain circumstances make it possible for individuals to learn a new language. To understand this better, it would make sense to "breed" a new kind of psychologist "equipped to work in the field of linguistic science." In answer to a question by Frith, Morgan said that the army was experimenting with pencil-and-paper tests of pronunciation, but standardization had not been achieved because of many complex variables. He reported also that Dostert had suggested using tape stimuli and recording student responses, but this had not yet been done. Dostert expanded on this, reporting that the Institute of Languages and Linguistics had prepared four Language Achievement Tests for the army and was engaged in testing employees of the World Health Organization for proficiency in English and Spanish. These tests included oral as well as written skills, but they had not been systematized. He also pointed out the potential of using a tape recorder with a double recording head to develop imitation tests.

Henry Lee Smith, Jr., at the Foreign Service Institute of the Department of State, raised questions about Morgan's presentation by recounting a wartime experience. He and William Moulton (later at Princeton) were given an afternoon to devise a test to grade a group of German prisoners of war who were about to start an intensive course in English. The test that they developed consisted of true–false questions in English based on passages taken from the Army Manual of Spoken German and two anecdotes in English. The results of these tests, which took only half an hour to administer, correlated very highly with a skilled interviewer's judgment in dividing students into four groups. They were followed by interviews. In grading 450 men, there was only one occasion when a grade had to be changed. The predictions of the test were also valid for success in non-linguistic parts of the test and in subsequent employment of the individual in military government. Smith asked why a test of half an hour and a five minute interview worked so well. Carroll, who responded, linked his answer to Morgan's:

> Competency in language and in learning languages is a very central part of the G factor, or general intelligence. What you were really testing was this factor, measured by how much English the prisoners had learned in their previous experience. (Hill 1953: 38)

The next two papers dealt with achievement tests. The first was a seldom-cited but very significant report by Paula Thibault (1953). A tester at Educational Testing Service, she raised questions that Stevenson (1981) and others would ask about language tests a quarter of a century later: Why are there such high correlations between different tests? Thibault wanted to sum up "a few of the things that the Educational Testing Service has learned about foreign language testing." Her summary included all tests for language administered by Educational Testing Service, but the College Board modern language tests provided the clearest evidence. Basically, she noted that "we seem to know how to put together impeccable tests ... but we do not know why it is that they work" (Hill 1953: 22). Rather than setting out the results of studies that had been published or describing the "commonsense" basis for the "knack" of item-writing, she planned to present some questions whose answers were not known.

The first of these questions concerned the homogeneity of items in language tests. Language tests, she reported, produced biserial 7Js "that are the envy and admiration of my colleagues in other subject-matter areas." (Hill 1953: 22) The good side of this was the absence of the ambiguities in the items that produced low rs. But there was a puzzle to be solved in the implication that "people who can do one kind of linguistic task can do other kinds as well." (Hill 1953: 23) Thibault found this hard to believe. She noted that even when the proportion of vocabulary was reduced, or when items using more colloquial language were introduced, the measures of internal consistency remained high. Changes in comprehension items from word to sentence-level items produced no change, and English-to-foreign vocabulary items provided the same information as foreign-to-English items, and both were much the same as the grammar and reading sections.

The main business of the College Board's language committees at the time was developing ways to assess oral-aural achievement. For practical reasons, it was not possible to add spoken tests to the batteries. In the meantime, she could be satisfied by finding items that looked like the skills taught in oral-aural skills but that did not have the normal high correlations with reading skills. But there seemed to be no way to achieve this:

> The trouble must be, since one can not believe the apparent implications of those high biserial 7Js, that our statistical techniques are too crude to allow us to draw any conclusion other than that we have highly homogeneous tests. What seems to be needed before we can make significant improvements in our tests in the way of weighting various aspects of language learning in an equitable way, is a series of detailed factorial studies that would tell us what aspects are differentiable, and would give us a clearer

> idea of the common factor that obscures everything by bringing about uniformly high *r*'s. (Hill 1953: 25)

Lacking a solution to this problem, Thibault went on to discuss other issues more amenable to solution, such as better face validity and better methods of selecting distracters. Commenting on Thibault's paper, Morgan wondered if the high 7Js might not correlate the "rather mysterious entity" of "abstract intelligence" referred to in British psychological literature. "If language aptitude testing is to be significantly improved, it will have to go beyond paper-and-pencil tests, beyond personality tests, and be based on a systematization of the findings of linguistic scientists and language teachers." (Hill 1953: 33) Thibault expressed some concern about the use of isolated words in the pronunciation test. A quite different approach was taken by Robert Lado (1953), who presented a strong claim for the objectivity that could be achieved by what he called testing the language, independently of the situations in which it occurred. He supported this claim, which he based on Bloomfield's (1933) distinction between the finite language system and the infinite situations preceding and following speech, by pointing out the problem in the opposite (functional or situational) approach: "it is often possible to by-pass language in grasping a situation" (Hill 1953: 30). Applying this principle permitted him to answer a good proportion (from 54% to 80%) of the items in the English test for the Investigation of the Teaching of a Second Language (Agard and Dunkel 1948) without listening to the four long aural comprehension passages on which they were based. He attacked other aspects of the "situation" approach: its failure to be specific, its preoccupation with voices rather than phonemes, its concentration on content to the detriment of form.

His technique for testing pronunciation on a pencil-and-paper test was not the essential part of his work in developing the Test of Aural Comprehension in English (Lado 1946); what was important was the fact that he was testing "the structural elements of the language" and in particular those elements that contrastive analysis had shown would be most difficult. He went on to present some of the results of the use of the test, which he said correlated highly with teachers' judgments. It produced a good range of results. It correlated well (0.85) with a test of actual pronunciation. It also correlated highly with other English tests, including direct listening tests. His paper concluded with the perhaps over-enthusiastic claim that "Pronunciation, which seemed the most difficult of the linguistic situations to test, is now perhaps the simplest" (Hill 1953: 32).

The discussions at the Round Table session on testing showed a high standard of sophistication, with the interchange between psycholinguists, psychometricians, applied linguists, and language teachers that was to come to define the burgeoning professional field of language testing. These were small beginnings, but it is noticeable that language testing already was proving useful employment for a number of the small group (Parker 1954 estimated that in 1954 there were two or three hundred) of American structural linguists.

REFERENCES

Agard, F.B. and H.B. Dunkel. 1948. *An investigation of second language teaching*. Boston: Ginn.

Bloomfield, Leonard. 1933. *Language*. New York: Holt.

Brière, Eugène. 1969. "Current trends in second language testing." *TESOL Quarterly* 3(4): 333-340.

Buros, O.K. (ed.) 1975. *Foreign language tests and reviews*. Highland Park, N.J.: Gryphon Press.

Carroll, John B. 1951. *Report and recommendations of the interdisciplinary summer seminar in psychology and linguistics: Cornell University, June 18 through August 10, 1951*. Ithaca, N.Y.: Cornell University Press.

Carroll, John B. 1953. "Some principles of language testing". In Archibald A. Hill (ed.), *Report of the fourth annual round table meeting on linguistics and language teaching*. Washington, D.C.: Institute of Languages and Linguistics, Georgetown University. 6-10.

Carroll, John B. 1961. "Fundamental considerations in testing for English language proficiency of foreign students." In *Testing the English proficiency of foreign students*. Washington, D.C.: Center for Applied Linguistics.

Carroll, John B., A.S. Carton, and Claudia Wilds. 1959. *An investigation of "cloze" items in the measurement of achievement in foreign languages*. Cambridge, Massachusetts: Laboratory for Research in Instruction, Graduate School of Education, Harvard University.

Ficken, Clarence Edward. 1937. *Intercorrelations of part scores in foreign language tests*. Unpublished Ph.D. dissertation, University of Wisconsin.

Frith, James R. 1953. "Selection for language training by a trial course." In Archibald A. Hill (ed.), *Report of the fourth annual roundtable meeting on linguistics and language teaching*. Washington, D.C.: Institute of Languages and Linguistics, Georgetown University.

Harris, David P. 1961. "The American University Language Center Testing Program." In *Testing the English proficiency of foreign students*. Washington, D.C.: Center for Applied Linguistics.

Henmon, V.A.C., et al. (eds.) 1929. *Prognosis tests in the modern foreign languages: Reports prepared for the Modern Foreign Language Study and the Canadian Committee on Modern Languages*. Publications of the American and Canadian Committees on Modern Languages. New York: Macmillan.

Hill, Archibald A. (ed.). 1953. *Report of the fourth annual round table meeting on linguistics and language teaching*. Washington D.C.: Georgetown University Press.

Jones, Randall and Bernard Spolsky (eds.). 1975. *Testing language proficiency*. Washington, D.C.: Center for Applied Linguistics.

Kaulfers, Walter Vincent. 1933. *Forecasting efficiency of current bases for prognosis*. Ph.D. dissertation. Stanford University.

Lado, Robert. 1946. *Test of aural comprehension in English*. Ann Arbor, Michigan: English Language Institute, University of Michigan.

Lado, Robert. 1949. *Measurement in English as a foreign language*. Unpublished Ph.D. dissertation. University of Michigan.

Lado, Robert. 1953. "Test the language." In Archibald A. Hill (ed.), *Report of the fourth annual roundtable meeting on linguistics and language teaching*. Washington, D.C.: Institute of Languages and Linguistics, Georgetown University.

Lado, Robert. 1957. *Linguistics across cultures: Applied linguistics for language teachers*. Ann Arbor, Michigan: University of Michigan Press.

Manuel, Herschel T. 1930. *The Education of Mexican and Spanish-speaking children in Texas*. Austin: The Fund for Research in the Social Sciences, The University of Texas.

Manuel, Herschel T. 1965. *Spanish-speaking children of the Southwest*. Austin: University of Texas Press.

Morgan, William J. 1953. "A clinical approach to foreign language achievement." In Archibald A. Hill (ed.), *Report of the fourth annual roundtable meeting on linguistics and language teaching*. Washington, D.C.: Institute of Languages and Linguistics, Georgetown University.

Palmer, Leslie and Bernard Spolsky (eds.). 1975. *Papers in language testing 1967–74*. Washington D.C.: TESOL.

Parker, W.R. 1954. *The national interest and foreign languages*. Washington D.C.: U.S. Government Printing Office.

Sollenberger, H.E. 1978. "Development and current use of the FSI Oral Interview Test." In J.L.D. Clark (ed.), *Direct testing of speaking proficiency: Theory and application*. Princeton, N.J.: Educational Testing Service.

Spolsky, Bernard. 1974. "The Navajo Reading Study: An illustration of the scope and nature of educational linguistics." In J. Qvistgaard, H. Schwarz, and H. Spang-Hanssen (eds.), *Applied linguistics: Problems and solutions*. Proceedings of the Third Congress on Applied Linguistics, Copenhagen, 1972. Heidelberg:

Julius Gros Verlag.

Spolsky, Bernard. 1978. *Educational linguistics: An introduction*. Rowley, Massachusetts: Newbury House Publishers.

Spolsky, Bernard. 1985. "Educational linguistics." In T. Husen and T.N. Postlethwaite (eds.), *The international encyclopedia of education*. Oxford: Pergamon.

Stevenson, Douglas P. 1981. "Beyond faith and face validity: The multitrait–multimethod matrix and the convergent and discriminant validity of oral proficiency tests." In A.S. Palmer, P.J.M. Groot, and G.A. Trosper (eds.), *The construct validation of tests of communicative competence*. Washington, D.C.: TESOL.

Thibault, Paula. 1953. "Implications of experience with College Board language tests." In Archibald A. Hill (ed.), *Report of the fourth annual roundtable meeting on linguistics and language teaching*. Washington, D.C.: Institute of Languages and Linguistics, Georgetown University.

Upshur, John A. and Julia Fata (eds.) 1968. "Problems in foreign language testing." *Language Learning*. Special issue no. 3.

Villareal, J.J. 1947. *A test of the aural comprehension of English for native speakers of Spanish*. Unpublished Ph.D. dissertation, Northwestern University.

Wigglesworth, David C. (ed.). 1967. *Selected Conference Papers of the Association of Teachers of English as a Second Language*. Washington, D.C.: NAFSA.

Retooling for communication: Hungary reorients its FL teaching

Katalin Nyikos
Georgetown University

Political and economic changes in Eastern Europe have brought with them an urgency to change the focus and method of foreign language teaching to develop communicatively competent speakers. As the opportunities for scholastic, cultural, and business exchange and cooperation have expanded, the call for excellence in the teaching of foreign languages has become increasingly strong.

This has been particularly true in Hungary, which presently has an unusually high dependence on foreign trade, and which views trade with Western Europe and North America as the primary avenue for future economic growth. But in a departure from the decades-old complacency of many students who were resigned to gaining a reading knowledge of a foreign language (usually Russian) with minimal productive capability, many now can choose from among several foreign languages and set their goals much higher. The last few years have witnessed ambitious plans to expand the options open to students and to revitalize foreign language teaching.

The most essential task facing foreign language pedagogy in Hungary is the need to change or augment the linguistic capabilities of teachers who have taught languages different from those students now wish to study. Furthermore, many do not have the expertise or skill to engender the acquisition of a more active, productive linguistic competency in their students. Yet this is precisely what is demanded by the marketplace.

This paper will briefly summarize the teaching of foreign languages since World War II and the fundamental changes being undertaken now to retool for communication. At issue is the reconceptualization of teachers' roles as learning facilitators rather than as conduits of knowledge. The conceptual shift from a transmission model to a communicative one is complex and should not be underestimated. Since the majority of foreign language teachers in Hungary taught Russian, with varying capabilities in a second foreign language, the changes demanded of them are daunting.

The teaching of Russian in Hungary for the last four decades under Russian occupation and communist rule was an abysmal failure. The minimal goal of Russian language studies was to develop passive language understanding. From the age of ten through high school and into the university years, Russian was mandatory, but very few learned it.

The underlying reasons were political, social, and cultural as well as pedagogical. University entrance requirements were lower for those wishing to teach Russian than for other foreign languages for the simple reason that there were more slots to fill and competition was not as keen. Since there was little motivation and a general negative attitude among learners, a great many Russian teachers became at first disheartened, later burned out, and finally cynical.

The law abolishing Russian as a compulsory subject was enacted in 1989. It was obvious even by then that few students would elect to continue studying Russian, and thus the oversupply of Russian teachers would have to be channeled into the suddenly tremendously increased need for teachers of other foreign languages, particularly German and English.

After some pilot projects, the general framework took shape. The Ministry of Education established the requirements for the retraining of Russian teachers to teach other languages. Teachers were required to take 800 to 1,000 hours of instruction, which was stretched over six semesters. The hope was that this retraining would constitute a thorough grounding in the Western language.

By academic year 1990–1991, a nationwide retraining program was set up by English, German, French, and Spanish departments of colleges and universities. Teachers of Russian were encouraged to switch rather than face the eventual possibility of unemployment. The greatly diminished demand for the teaching of Russian and the concomitant clamor for languages *other* than Russian was very strongly felt almost immediately—from Budapest to the smallest villages of Hungary.

Those who volunteered for retraining were given reduced teaching loads and an increase in salary for the duration of the retraining programs. Nevertheless, it constituted a very real hardship and *pedagogical reorientation* for midcareer Russian teachers, who were often in their forties and fifties. The majority were accustomed to a predominantly transmission model of foreign language teaching. The challenges they faced included learning not only a new language but also new teaching methodologies that were often *incompatible* with their accustomed teaching paradigms.

The need was so great and the pressure so strong that in 1990 the English Language Teachers' Association of Hungary held separate courses that were designated for "qualified teachers of English" and another for "*unqualified* teachers" in the elementary and secondary schools. A circular that they put out in 1991 declared unequivocally, "Nearly all the Russian teachers have become unwelcome persons in our schools." In the same 1991 circular, they reported a shortage of 15,000 foreign language teachers in Hungary.

By academic year 1992–1993, there were a little over 900 Russian teachers regularly attending the English retraining programs nationwide, close to 1,000 retraining to be German teachers, and a little over 100 in French and fewer than 100 each for Italian and Spanish.

Accurate, official statistics from the Hungarian Ministry of Education (1994) were available only for 1991–1993 as to the significant changes in the number of foreign language learners in the elementary and high schools. By academic year 1991–1992, the percentage of students of Russian had shrunk from 100% to 35% in the upper four grades of elementary school. In the following school year, 1992–1993, they numbered a mere 18%. The combined statistics for academic and vocational high schools show 26% of their students taking Russian in 1991–1992 and less than half that, 12%, the following school year.

This dramatic *decrease* becomes even more significant in light of the *increases* in the number of students choosing English and German, respectively. In the upper four elementary grades, 25% took English in 1991–1992, but that number jumped to 32% in 1992–1993. In 1991–1992, 36% took German and in 1992–1993, 45% did. High school students (in academic as well as vocational high schools) preferred English over German. In 1992–1993, 35% took German, while 40% opted for English.

In a recent scientific survey of Budapest residents (Petzold 1994), favorable attitudes toward English learning and the American culture are very pronounced. Of those surveyed in 1992–1993, 79% felt that "all Hungarian children should learn English." The importance of this finding is further emphasized by the fact that 92% of the respondents felt that English or another Western foreign language should be learned even if one's job did not require it at all. Furthermore, 63% felt that "Knowing English improves a Hungarian's quality of life."

This very favorable orientation was already apparent in 1991, when I was invited by the English Language Teachers' Association of Hungary and the Soros Foundation to teach in an intensive enrichment and retraining course. It was designed to provide active, productive training in both the use of English and its pedagogical presentation. Emphasis was placed on practical, inclass applications of both materials and methods of teaching.

Our entire approach was based on the premise that as teachers, we ourselves should model the teaching behavior that we felt to be most productive and successful. The goal was to achieve active and maximal involvement on the part of all participants in the course. To this end, the teachers participated in role plays and group problem-solving and in learning partnerships. Teachers were asked to reflect in a very critical way on their experiences and to discuss applications to their own classrooms. We elicited information from the teachers regarding their own theoretical frameworks and the educational philosophies that informed their teaching. While the teachers were aware of much of the L2 acquisition research data, it seemed to have had little direct effect upon their classroom instructional practices.

The most difficult conceptual shift for teachers was in changing their roles to one of *facilitation* rather than *control* in all aspects of the classroom environment. The realization of what it meant to place the responsibility for learning into students' hands by consistently requiring *very active* participation from them was initially met with skepticism. We continually illustrated the fundamental difference between delivery of information that results in passive intake on the part of students versus the active, inner-directed activity of students who have taken responsibility for their own learning.

During this course we also kept in mind that the American and Hungarian education systems are quite different and that ultimately Hungarians would have to develop *their* methodologies in engendering communicative competence in their students. Hungarian pedagogy has traditionally been one of accuracy and exactitude. This begins in the earliest grades when the orthography of Hungarian permits children to enter literacy at an early age.

In foreign language classes that begin in the fifth grade at the age of ten, lessons are expected to be learned in detail, and precision is stressed from the beginning. Teachers participating in our course stated quite strongly that they were not willing to sacrifice accuracy for fluency.

Our own experience showed us that teachers were extremely frustrated when their verbal mistakes were not corrected. They repeatedly demanded that we interrupt them in midsentence to correct mistakes of every kind—be they semantic, phonological, grammatical, or suprasegmental (intonation being one of their major difficulties).

The bottom line is that the communicative capabilities of students can be developed by teachers who themselves are confident in their language expertise. In order to develop communicative competence on the part of students, teachers themselves must possess this competence. The greatest challenge for the majority of teachers in Hungary today is to bring their language skills and teaching methodologies to that level. There is also a deeply felt wish to achieve communicative competence without suffering a decline in exactitude. Teachers in our course expressed the need to develop teaching methodologies that will not make accuracy and fluency mutually exclusive.

One of the most promising initiatives undertaken in the last few years has been the founding of dual language academic high schools. Mainly a product of Hungarian eagerness to make up for the last 40 years, which were lost under Soviet-Russian occupation and culture, they are designed to make their students fully bilingual upon graduation from high school.

There are two curricular models, and competition for acceptance is extremely high for both. For those who acquire a sufficient level of proficiency in their chosen foreign language by the end of elementary school, schooling lasts four years. For those who have never learned that language and for those whose proficiency is found inadequate, an additional school year is added. This addition is their first year in the dual language high school, and it is considered—as well as called—"grade zero."

During grade zero, the chosen foreign language is taught intensively for twenty class periods a week, i.e. four daily classes. Hungarian, music, art, and physical education are additionally taught, but in Hungarian. The goal is to attain adequate proficiency for studying all subjects—except the ones just listed—in English throughout the next four academic high school years.

In Budapest there are five dual language high schools for each of the major Western languages: English, French, German, Italian, and Spanish. There is one such dual language high school in nine other cities as well. The teachers often comprise an assortment of Hungarian and imported native speakers of the language taught.

Lofty aims, sincere commitment, and strenuous work are hampered by a long list of problems. For example, poorly translated textbooks often acquired even more errors when they were typed by secretaries who were less than proficient in English. Even these textbooks have been in short supply and are sometimes based on outdated Western and Hungarian texts that lack pedagogical value.

The question of quality in this hasty and perhaps overambitious retooling of foreign language teachers is a concern that arises again and again. In the last few years, increasing numbers of freshly graduated college students with backgrounds in many academic fields have gone to Hungary from English-speaking countries. They have various degrees of preparation and experience in teaching English to nonnative speakers—many have none at all. A picture is worth a thousand words. This note was composed by such a volunteer addressed to the mother of one of his Hungarian pupils:

> Hello Im your sons teaching just moved here from N.Y. your son is a fine student. I live here know with my girlfriend engaged actualy. I would very much like to meet you and learn how you came about Hungary and what you do here. and some other questions. I seem to have a small problem. I have lots of bills from home I must pay But they say I can not make forent's into dollors . What to do if you could help it would be great. looking forward to meeting you.
>
> Thankyou
>
> PS. We are not with the peace core. this is what we chose

This is a typed version of this American volunteer "teacher's" exact words, spelling, and punctuation. I was relieved to hear that this individual taught "conversation" rather than composition.

Turning back to the question of Hungary's own teacher retraining, the question of quality again comes up. How effective is it? Obviously it depends on the efficiency of the retraining program, on the expertise and skill of the master teachers who conduct the classes, and on the talents, age, flexibility, and circumstances of the participants. A recent comprehensive progress report of the Ministry of Education (1994) advises caution regarding the relative value of retraining as compared to the actual full master's degree earned by those who have majored in foreign languages. As the Ministry's ongoing study continues, the evaluation of programs and the resultant learning will yield valuable information on the needs and products of Hungarian foreign language teaching. The need for more teachers is great, but the need for well-trained teachers with superb academic preparation and communicative skills is even greater.

Before communist rule, educated Hungarians were generally admired for their multilinguality. But the "mandatory Russian" generations who were raised in relative linguistic isolation have a challenging road ahead of them. Of the former Eastern Bloc, Hungary already has the highest per capita level of international trade and scientific and cultural exchange. Hence, it has a particularly pressing need for effective foreign language teaching. As Budapest prepares to host the 1996 World Exposition, it can serve as a model for the rest of Eastern Europe in promoting excellence in foreign language pedagogy.

REFERENCES

Hungarian Ministry of Education. 1994. "Interim report: Statistical data on retraining foreign language teachers."

Petzold, R. 1994. *English in Hungary: The negative reaction.* Manuscript.

Language choices for West Africa in the global village

Jerry Cline-Bailey
Xavier University (Cincinnati)

Introduction. The recent signing of the NAFTA agreement and the closer economic ties in Europe as a result of actions taken recently or planned by the European Community (E.C.), together with the implementation of initial plans for a global information superhighway, have given new meaning to the term "global village." This paper examines the language choices facing West African countries in light of the rapidly growing importance of regional economic affiliations and radical advances in world communications technology. The study is based partly on assumptions reached in work done by François Grin (1993) on the effects of European integration on language use and in the work of, among others, Myers-Scotton (1993) and Bamgbose (1991) on the language situation in sub-Saharan Africa. It attempts to integrate these into a functional analysis of language policy options facing West African countries today.

At present, and for the foreseeable future, most West African countries do and will continue to depend heavily on trade with former European colonial powers. When African countries gained political independence approximately three decades ago, economic factors significantly influenced the decisions of these countries to retain the use of European languages as exolects. Even colonialism, which radically affected the spread of European languages in West Africa, had an economic impulse as its main driving force. Language issues such as high illiteracy rates can be causally linked to hard economic times in many African countries today. It is thus clear, even to the casual observer, that economic policy decisions frequently affect language maintenance, spread, shift, and vice versa.

Economics and language: The case of the European Community. Increased economic benefits are the main reason why E.C. governments are moving toward the harmonization of policies on, among other things, trade and industry. It is estimated that the consequent greater specialization in trade and industry should result in a 4–7% increase in the Community's gross national product within a short period.[1]

---

1. See Antille, Calevero, and Schmitt (1990).

Grin (1993) relies on an international trade model to illustrate a connection between economics and language by showing how the use of a common language between trading partners reduces transaction costs. In the new, closer E.C., it does not seem likely that the choice of a common language will be negotiated between each set of trading partners, but rather a European lingua franca is likely to emerge. Presently, English seems to be the most likely to fill that position because of its economic and political influence within Europe, together with its recognition by trading partners outside of the E.C..

With English emerging as a European lingua franca, pundits (Grin 1993) expect the use of such European majority languages as Danish, Dutch, Greek and Italian to suffer while that of French and Spanish would be contingent on their performance as regional lingua francas. Add to the expected preeminence of English in Europe, the increased importance of an English-dominated economic block in NAFTA, and one can begin to envisage a growing role for and use of English, perhaps to the detriment of other languages. In fact, English, Spanish, and French seem set to assume increasing importance as world or regional lingua francas.

Internet and the information superhighway. Envisioned as the culmination of the convergence of hardware, software and networking technologies, the superhighway started as the National Research and Educational Network (NREN), a U.S. federal computer networking initiative designed to knit together existing U.S. federal networks as the core of a national research and education infrastructure. The NREN initiative is really an attempt to enhance U.S. portions of Internet, the global network of over a million computers, spanning all seven continents and providing an estimated ten to twenty million or more users with electronic mail, file transfer, data retrieval, and other applications. It is a system of interconnected networks which appears to its users as a seamless network, though its pieces vary tremendously in size. Given the global nature of Internet and the steady erosion of physical borders by new information technologies, one expects interesting consequences for language use. Thomas E. Weber ("Global Villagers" in *The Wall Street Journal*, November 15, 1993) asserts that the effect of chat line interaction by average users of Internet is the "equivalent of meeting a group of regular friends at the neighborhood bar." Richard Hudson ("Incommunicado," *The Wall Street Journal*, November 15, 1993) sees Europe as a backwater with regard to the use of bulletin boards, data bases, networks, and online computer services. He estimates that the U.S. is three to five years ahead of Europe in the use of Internet facilities and blames Europe's slowness to catch up on two factors: (1) high telephone charges, and (2) language differences which fragment the market. These could be applied to the situation in most of sub-Saharan Africa to an even greater extent.

In light of the fact that the E.C.'s Impact Program includes plans for Europe to become an integral part of the U.S. Information Superhighway, English and French appear set to be the main beneficiaries in Europe. France's Minitel[2] is at the cutting edge of this type of technology, and English is the language in which most of the data to be made available is stored. In commerce and industry, decision-making suffers in the absence of ready access to information. An increasing number of people who want access to information stored in these networks will need English. The power of the marketplace seems likely to propel English and, to a lesser extent, French to a place of unprecedented importance in the global village.

Problems for the application of Internet technology in West Africa include: (1) The large number of languages, (2) the lack of basic infrastructure, (3) high telephone costs, (4) high illiteracy rates, and (5) the fact that ASCII codes used in internet technology are not friendly to some African languages. It is significant that three out of these five factors are directly or indirectly connected to language use. Given the fact that Africa has a much lower ratio of computers to people than either Europe or the U.S., and that most Africans have little or no access to such technology, it is reasonable to ask if this technology is essential for, or even attainable by, Africa's developing nations in the near future. Some might view such technology as benefiting only the elite in Africa and, therefore, not essential. The most important question to be addressed in this regard, however, is whether the information available through Internet is, in fact, useful or essential for the development of West African countries. While not essential, given the fact that Africa has survived without this technology up to this point, one must not forget that it gives governments and businesses the potential to transfer important information relatively cheaply and with greater efficiency than other methods used at present. If the only benefit of Internet for African countries is that it can cut down on government expenses and transaction costs, then it may be considered an important investment for the future. In addition, the main trading partners of West African countries are the E.C. and NAFTA countries who are already on, or about to get on, the information superhighway. This should facilitate quicker and, therefore, more profitable trade with these regions.

The example of the economic success of Japan over the last twenty years has been used to support the view that language is not an important factor affecting international trade or a country's economic prosperity. The point being made is that Japan competes favorably with other world economic powers despite the fact that the Japanese language is not widely used outside of Japan or by its major trading partners. However, one major difference between Japan

2. Minitel is a communications technology company with major interests in France's telephone system.

and either individual West African countries or the region as a whole is the existence of multilingualism.

Multilingualism in West Africa. The region of West Africa and the Economic Community of West African States (ECOWAS) is made up of sixteen countries of varying size and prosperity, but with similar sociolinguistic problems. Most of the countries have a three-tiered multilingual situation in which the exolects or official languages are those inherited from the colonial period. In ten of these countries French is the official language, while five others retain English for the same purpose. Portuguese is the official language in only one country within the region. In addition to the exolects, each country has a number of endolects which could be divided into two groups: Those indigenous languages spoken widely enough to be considered regional or provincial lingua francas, and those minority languages which serve for intra-ethnic communication only.

In West Africa the use of English, like that of French, functions as a status symbol for urban dwellers and students or graduates of advanced educational institutions who make up the elite. Myers-Scotton (1993) argues that the educated elite in sub-Saharan Africa use official language policies and non-formalized language usage patterns to limit the access of non-elite groups to positions of political power and socioeconomic advancement. She further asserts that wide gaps between educated elites and the masses are maintained by: (1) The use, for important functions, of European languages which are not made accessible to the masses; and (2) the masses' support for maintaining this status quo. Citing work done by Djite (1985) in Côte d'Ivoire and a parable from Butembo in the Kivu province of Zaire, Myers-Scotton asserts that the traditional view in much of sub-Saharan Africa is that knowledge of a standard variety of an exolect is less important than the ability to make money, and that the two are not often seen as connected. This seems rather surprising given the obvious social and economic benefits which a command of the exolect can provide for individuals.

The fact that an estimated 20% or less of the populations of Francophone countries are functional in French (Bokamba 1984), and a slightly higher percentage is estimated for English in Anglophone West African countries, is a cause for concern among West African governments. Those not functional in the official language(s) of their country cannot be expected to participate fully in national development. They form a large underclass whose potential will not be fully harnessed until the majority of the nation's work force is functional in the language of the state. Thus there is a good case for changing the language of the state, or for ensuring that competence in non-indigenous languages performing this role be made a realistically achievable goal for all sectors of the population.

Language and international trade in West Africa. ECOWAS[3] was formed in the mid-1970's to facilitate increased economic activity among the states of the region. After almost twenty years, the volume of intracommunity trade has not changed significantly, and the overwhelming volume of trade is still between ECOWAS members and their former European colonial powers. The little intracommunity trade which takes place now is apparently also influenced by language-based affiliations. There is much more trade, for example, between countries using the same exolect.[4] This is even more significant when one considers the fact that most English-speaking West African countries are completely surrounded by French-speaking ones. Nigeria is surrounded by Niger, Benin, and Cameroun,[5] Ghana by Burkina Faso, Togo, and Côte d'Ivoire, the Gambia by Senegal, and so on. Here, the lack of a widely used common language appears to act as a barrier to trade between immediate neighbors. This situation also highlights the importance of language for international trade and, as we have seen, international trade is expected to become increasingly important in the global village.

Language planning in West Africa. Language planning usually entails a change in the linguistic behavior of the target community. It sometimes requires the acquisition by some people of new languages or varieties in addition to, or in place of, their natural speech patterns. Old speech habits are difficult to change, and studies have shown that most people learn new languages only if they are perceived as useful for personal advancement or necessary for participation in a culturally or economically richer life. In short, for a language to be voluntarily learned it should serve a participatory function for the learner. It is desirable then that any language chosen as an official or national language perform a unifying function.

Very few African countries have made such a basic decision as choosing a national language. For the majority of West African countries, language planning will have to start at the level of policy formulation, because even in countries where some policy decisions have been made, there is still no clear allocation of the domains of usage for the national language vis-à-vis the other indigenous languages and exolects. One reason for this may be that it is potentially a volatile political issue on which governments are unwilling to act

---

3. The ECOWAS countries are: Benin, Burkina Faso, Côte d'Ivoire, the Gambia, Ghana, Guinea, Guinea-Bissau, Liberia, Mali, Mauritania, Niger, Nigeria, Senegal, Sierra Leone, and Togo. Cape Verde joined two years after the establishment of ECOWAS in 1975.

4. Source: *Britannica World Data*, 1992

5. Note that Cameroun is not Francophone, but recognizes both English and French as official languages.

decisively. For instance in Togo and the Central African Republic, the national language has not been assigned any significant function. Even in Tanzania, the African country with the most rigorously implemented language policy, there is still no consensus as to the desired functions to be performed by Swahili. Clearly, then, a most relevant aspect of language planning to West African countries is policy formulation. Because of high levels of multilingualism, policy formulation raises quite a number of questions, some of which are addressed below.

The expressive function of language is important, because language is an embodiment of a people's culture and is expressive of their experiences and world view. In the West African context, the unmodified exolects cannot, in the view of many, satisfactorily capture all those experiences which are peculiarly African. One solution to this problem may be to develop the use, for official functions, of one, some, or all the indigenous languages within each West African country. Objections will arise no matter which language is taught in the school system, partly because historical ethnic antagonisms are still very strong in many parts of West Africa. The cost of implementing a policy of using all indigenous languages as media of instruction in each country's educational system would be too difficult for these already overburdened economies to handle. Nearly 100,000 primary school students in Oyo, one of Nigeria's twenty-one states, are being taught mostly in Yoruba, one of the country's three major indigenous languages. Nine other Nigerian states, with two million students are in various stages of adopting the mother tongue program. At the same time, the federal government has embarked upon an intensive effort to translate school textbooks now written in English into Yoruba, Hausa, Ibo, Nupe, and other Nigerian languages (Kenneth B. Noble in *The New York Times*, May 23, 1991: pg. A7). The crusade to adopt all the country's four hundred mother tongues within the educational system enraged much of Nigeria's establishment, who fear that this will create a bureaucratic nightmare. Noble quotes one concerned Nigerian who, in response to these efforts, wrote the following in the *Daily Times* published in Lagos: "The least luxury we can afford in the last decade of the twentieth century is an idealistic experiment in linguistic nationalism which could cut our children off from the main current of human development." Such concerns constitute a major problem facing language policy makers and planners in West Africa. This has become an even more urgent problem with the increasing importance of global computer communications links and the proposed information superhighway. Education in languages like English and French will be important for participation in these aspects of the global village. This will continue to be so until African languages develop the necessary terminology and capabilities to perform functions essential in the modern, technologically advanced society.

In contrast to the inward-looking separatist function of language, the participatory function is outward looking. The participatory function is performed with varying degrees of effectiveness by all modernized languages. However, English, French, and sometimes German are still used in scientific reports, for example, by scholars from such countries as Poland and Holland, which already possess highly standardized/modernized languages of their own. This is because the need for communication with a worldwide audience can not as yet be fulfilled satisfactorily by Polish and Dutch. The same is true for indigenous West African languages, and precludes them from performing the participatory function in the global sense. Even Ethiopia, one of only two modern African states that were never colonized by a European nation, has found it necessary to adopt English, in addition to Amharic, for official purposes both internally and externally. The participatory function requires that language policy formulators order national priorities with respect to the people with whom participation is desired. In West Africa, the desire to identify itself as part of the Arab world contributed to Mauritania's adoption of Arabic in addition to French as its official language. A similar case also occurred in Sudan, where Arabic replaced English. In making a decision about a national or official language, West African governments must consider the fact that English and French are important for trade not only with the E.C. but also globally, and at present no West African language is likely to be able to achieve equal or similar importance soon.

Language choices for West Africa. Language choices for West Africa depend on answers to the following questions: (1) Are the countries within the region going to be inward or outward looking? (2) Should community languages be promoted, or will the forces of the marketplace be allowed to dictate which languages survive? and (3) Will minority languages be protected?

With regard to the first question, regardless of the choice, international languages must be given maximum attention. English and French as second and foreign languages in the respective countries' educational systems is very important for both intra- and interregional trade and communication. One concern about this issue is the fear that lack of opportunities to speak English or French as foreign languages would prevent West African university and teacher training college students from becoming effective teachers of English and French as spoken languages (Bamgbose 1991). However, in the global village a reading knowledge of the language in question would suffice for most functions, especially on the information superhighway.

Regarding whether community languages should be promoted or whether the forces of the marketplace should be allowed to dictate which of the indigenous languages survive, it would seem most probable that the languages with large numbers of speakers would be the most likely to survive, although this is not necessarily so. Languages which fall into this group, especially those which are spoken in more than one country (such as Ewe, Hausa, Mandinka, Yoruba and Wolof), are important to interethnic and international communication between West African countries. Here, the coordination of efforts in the countries concerned is essential to ensure a harmonization of standards, in terms of orthography for example. Non-standard or creolized varieties of European languages have been largely ignored for adult literacy (for example Krio in the Gambia and Sierra Leone, pidgin English in Nigeria and Cameroun, and popular French in Senegal and Côte d'Ivoire). In the absence of common exolects, regional lingua francas used across political boundaries can enhance opportunities both for trade and for a culturally richer or more diverse life.

On the question of whether minority languages should be protected, it should be noted that language shift and death are natural phenomena which will occur regardless of the amount of planning. Witness, for example, the case of the increasing use of Mende and Temne adversely affecting the use of Sherbro (Sengova 1987) in Sierra Leone. The increased use of some languages will often adversely affect the use of others. Since planning cannot guarantee the survival of lesser-used languages, all that can be done is to give them a chance to survive. One way to do this is to give them a role in the education system. The major problem with this solution is that there are too many of these lesser-used languages and too few people with the expertise to develop quality educational programs in them. Should West African governments assume that the task of ensuring the survival of the lesser-used languages in the near future is almost impossible and, therefore, devote their efforts to the widely-used languages? This is an option which, though reasonable from one perspective, will not be acceptable in the current circumstances to native speakers of the lesser-used or minority languages, and it may affect the nature of the multilingualism which has always added color to life in the region.

In the global village where the ability to communicate with larger and larger groups of people worldwide is increasing in importance, conditions seem ripe for a world lingua franca to emerge. For West African countries to avoid being outcasts in the village, candidates for that role such as English and French may have to be embraced with renewed vigor in the various educational systems. Having said that, though, it is important to keep in mind that this need not distract from efforts to modernize, standardize, promote, and/or protect indigenous languages.

REFERENCES

Antille, Gabrielle, Fabrizio Calevero, and Nicolas Schmitt. 1990. "Europe 1992 and beyond: Towards a quantitive general equilibrium assessment for Switzerland." *Revue Suisse d'économie, politique et de statistique* 126: 193–213.

Bamgboṣe, Ayọ. 1978. "Models of communication in multilingual states" *Journal of the language association of East Africa* 4(1): 5–18.

Bamgboṣe, Ayọ. 1991. *Language and the nation: The language question in sub-Saharan Africa*. Edinburgh: Edinburgh University Press.

Bokamba, Eyamba. 1984. "French colonial policy in Africa and its Legacies." *Studies in Linguistic Sciences* 14: 1–22.

Dalby, T. David. 1981. *The republic of Sierra Leone: national languages in education*. Paris: UNESCO Technical Report 1/514/03. 1979–1988.

Djite, Pauline 1985. *Language attitudes in Abidjan: Implications for language planning in the Ivory Coast*. Unpublished Ph.D. dissertation, Georgetown University.

Fishman, Joshua A. 1988. *Language and ethnicity in minority sociolinguistic perspective*. Philadelphia: Multilingual Matters Ltd.

Grin, François. 1993. "European economic integration and the fate of lesser used languages." *Language Problems and Language Planning* 17(2): 101–116.

Heine, Bernd. 1990. "Language policy in Africa." In B. Weinstein (ed.), *Language Policy and Political Development*. Norwood, N.J.: Ablex Publishing Company. 167–184.

Hudson, T. 1993. "Incommunicado" *The Wall Street Journal*, November 15, 1993. pg. R19.

Mann, Michael and David Dalby. 1988. *A Thesaurus of African Languages*. London and New York: Hans Zell Publishers.

Myers-Scotton, Carol. 1990. "Elite closure as boundary maintenance: The case of Africa." In Brian Weinstein (ed.), *Language policy and political development*. Norwood, N.J.: Ablex Publishing Company. 25–42.

Myers-Scotton, Carol. 1993. "Elite closure as a powerful language strategy: The African case" *International Journal of the Sociology of Language* 103: 149–163.

Noble, Kenneth B. 1991. "Nigerian plan: Adopt (250) mother tongues," in *The New York Times*, May 23, 1991, pg. A7.

Organization of African Unity. 1985. "The Linguistic Plan of Action for Africa." Mimeo of report from meeting of linguistic experts in Kampala, Uganda.

Richmond, Edmund B. 1986. *A Comparative Survey of Seven Adult Functional Literacy Problems in sub-Saharan Africa*. Lanham: University Press of America.

Sengova, Joko. 1987. "The national languages of Sierra Leone: A decade of policy experimentation". *Africa* 57(4): 519–530.

Tollefson, James. 1990. *Planning language planning inequality*. London and New York: Longman.

Weber, Thomas E. 1993. "Global Villagers," in *The Wall Street Journal*, November 15, 1993, pg. R12.

Politeness across cultures: Implications for second language teaching

Ayọ Bamgboṣe
University of Ibadan and University of Illinois at Urbana-Champaign

Knowing a language well, it is generally agreed, is not only knowing the correct forms of expression in the language but also knowing the appropriate situations in which to use such expressions. This knowledge of appropriate language use in communication in different sociocultural contexts or, to use the conventional term coined for it by Hymes (1972), *communicative competence,* has come to be accepted as a legitimate goal of second language learning (Paulston 1974). In some approaches (Canale and Swain 1980; Canale 1983), communicative competence is viewed as a complex of competencies, including grammatical, sociolinguistic, discourse, and strategic. However, for our purposes in this paper, the relevant aspect is sociolinguistic competence, which embraces sociocultural rules of language use.

Culture and second language teaching. Basic to a proper understanding of rules of communication is an awareness of the cultural underpinning of language expressions. In fact, in the foreign language teaching model proposed by Byram (1989: 136–147), language awareness and cultural awareness, which involve a comparison of the culture of the target language with that of the learner's language, serve as a complement to language learning and cultural experience in the target language. An essential component of language teaching is seen as cultural competence, which comprises monocultural and intercultural competence.

The immediate question that arises from the cultural basis of communication is: Whose culture is to be represented in the model presented for teaching a second language? Is it that of the native speaker or that of the second language user? The traditional English Language Teaching (ELT) approach is that no matter how much we are aware of English as a Second Language (ESL) culture, the ultimate goal is to make the learner familiar with English as a Native Language (ENL) culture and the sociocultural implications of expressions in that variety. ENL usage is held out as the norm, and cases in which ESL usage differs from native usage are considered "inappropriate." Similarly, and perhaps more appropriately, in foreign language teaching, teachers are advised that

> direct experience of the foreign culture needs to be structured in such a way that it gives learners insight into the culture from the native speaker's viewpoint ... Learners need to be prepared for experience of the daily rhythm of the foreign culture, of the behaviors which are different and those which are the same but have a different significance. Such phenomena are verbal and nonverbal, and learners need both the skills of fluency and accuracy in the language and the awareness of the cultural significance of their utterances. (Byram 1989: 145)

Underlying this concern for the language learner to conform to the socio-cultural norms of the native speaker is the assumption that such learners will need to communicate with native speakers. While this assumption may be true in the case of English as a Foreign Language (EFL), it is certainly not true of ESL countries as Kachru (1987: 250) has correctly pointed out:

> There is little recognition of the fact that current communicative contexts of English break the conventionally held paradigms of research. These paradigms presuppose that every interactional context in the Outer Circle [i.e. ESL countries] involves a native speaker and a non-native speaker (NS–NNS). This myth results in a wrong assumption, namely that the pragmatic success of an interaction must be judged within that context.

To substantiate the above claim, Kachru (1990: 110) draws attention to the fact that, in India, only "a minimal fraction of the English-speaking Indian literate population has any interaction with native speakers of English." Proof of this is that, in a survey of faculty members of English departments in a sample of Indian universities and colleges, 62.64% are reported to have only occasional interaction with native speakers of English, and 11.79% have no interaction at all with such speakers. The implication of this for ELT is that communicative competence in an ESL situation has to look more in the direction of an ESL model with its cultural associations.

In order to explore the importance of ESL culture in language learning, it is useful to consider politeness across cultures as an example of culture-induced communicative acts. Crosscultural studies on politeness have generally been of two types. The first type is an examination of politeness strategies in different cultures with a typology of universals. Brown and Levinson (1978) is the first detailed study of this kind with its useful framework of strategies for doing or not doing face-threatening acts and their implications for different types of politeness.

The second type of crosscultural studies on politeness concentrates on the cultural differences underlying expressions of politeness, drawing attention to the culture-specific realizations of what may be considered polite behavior (Coulmas 1981; Matsumoto 1988, 1989; Janney and Arndt 1992, 1993). In an extensive review of the two approaches, Janney and Arndt (1992: 38), who see *tact* as a major component of polite behavior, conclude that

> cultural differences in communicative styles and strategies are embedded in, and supported by, unquestioned cultural assumptions that are difficult to change. Such assumptions are relatively nonnegotiable: behavior that contradicts them simply tends to be interpreted as abnormal. For this reason, people from different cultures often remain something of a mystery to each other, especially at the emotive level, where differences in cultural assumptions may make it difficult to predict each other's reactions. .... Ultimately, it may well be that tact in the intercultural sense is simply impossible in many intercultural situations.

In both the universal and the culture-specific approaches to the study of politeness, practices in different languages are compared with one another. From an ESL perspective, what is of interest to us is the way politeness practices in learners' languages are transferred into nonnative varieties of English and how such practices resemble or differ from those of the native varieties of the language. For this purpose, our examples will be drawn mainly from Nigerian English.

It is a reasonable assumption that in an ESL situation, learners transfer the cultural norms of their first language into the variety of English they speak. It does not follow from this, however, that the verbalization of such norms will always be considered acceptable even in the ESL situation. Consider, for example, deference in reference to persons that, in many Nigerian languages, is expressed by second and third person plural pronouns. Transferred into English, it means that a student says "They are calling you" in reference to the school principal, instead of "He is calling you." Because of the conflict in number and the consequent potential misinterpretation, the culture-induced transfer in this case is not considered acceptable in educated Nigerian English. Those who use this expression as a basilectal or transitional form can easily be distinguished from educated users of the language. In the discussion of culture-induced expressions of politeness, such nonacceptable forms will be excluded.

Politeness in Nigerian English. Culture-laden verbal interaction involving politeness may be observed in several activities, including modes of address, greetings, apologies, requests, expressions of gratitude, etc. These activities will be examined in this paper, and for the purpose of highlighting the more interesting polite behavior, we shall concentrate on communication between persons of unequal age or rank. Previous studies of politeness in Nigerian English include Afolayan (1974), Akere (1978), Adetugbo (1979a), and Adegbija (1989).

Modes of address are of two types: *vocatives* used in calling someone's attention, and *labels* used in reference to someone who may or may not be present at the scene of the communicative act. For vocatives, the main strategy employed is avoidance of names. This strategy is reported in other varieties of English e.g. South Asian varieties (D'souza 1988: 166). There is also a distinction between formal and informal vocatives. Those employed to express formality include *Sir, Madam,* or a title such as *Professor, General, Chief, Doctor*, etc. For informality, there are such terms as *Oga* ("Master"), *Daddy, Uncle, Mommy* (written as *Mummy*), *Auntie*, the last two pairs of which can be used in addressing any adult male or female, respectively, who is not in the least bit related to the speaker.

Labels for referring to persons superior in rank or age need not involve avoidance of names, provided such names are appropriately adorned with a title. In this connection, it must be noted that it is unacceptable to use a plain *Mr., Mrs., or Ms.* for someone who is known to possess a professional or honorific title, except that, in the case of a married female title holder, *Mrs.* may be used along with a title. This is the origin of the proliferation of professional titles such as *Architect, Surveyor, Engineer, Lawyer, Barrister, Evangelist*, etc. The practice is similar to the labelling of persons in American English as *Dean X, Passenger Y, Associate Director A,* although such labels refer to roles rather than professions and the motivation for their use may be the avoidance of gender-specific terms. More and more, there is an avoidance of titles as labels in American English, particularly in written communication. In contrast to this, nonuse of titles is frowned upon in Nigerian English. A Nigerian newspaper, *The Guardian*, which tried to abolish labels in titles a few years ago by referring to everyone as plain *Mr., Mrs.*, or *Miss,* failed miserably under pressure of protests by aggrieved title holders.

Under the influence of nationalism, people are now proud of being labelled with their names, including their first names, even by persons younger or subordinate to them. Hence, expressions such as "May I request Chief Dr. (Mrs.) Olubunmi Johnson to declare the conference open?" "The Chairman of the Committee, Architect Alaba Bada," and "The Honorable Minister of Education, Professor Okon Eyo" are not considered insolent, even though they contain the referent's full names. A variant of such expressions in the northern Nigerian variety of English is the use of a referent's first name instead of either both names or the last name. This may well be because last names are considered sacred, since they belong to the progenitor or because many last names are identical, since they coincide with place of birth. It is, therefore, common to refer to someone named "Abubakar Funtua" as "Alhaji Abubakar" (with the last name left out and the title Alhaji indicating that the referent has been on pilgrimage to Mecca) rather than "Alhaji Abubakar Funtua."

There are obviously some similarities in modes of address between ENL and Nigerian English practices. If we compare the scheme of rules of address in Ervin-Tripp (1969) with those discussed above, the striking differences include:

a. avoidance of names in vocatives
b. formality–informality vocatives for superiors
c. avoidance of any label that does not reflect the possession of a professional or honorific title
d. title with first name used as a label
e. multiple titles, all of which refer to the same person (e.g. *Alhaji Chief Honorable Dr.* Musa Abdul).

The closest thing to (e) that I know of in European languages is the German use of multiple academic titles such as *Herr Professor Doktor Doktor* ("(Mr.) Professor Dr. Dr.") Klaus Schmidt.

Greetings occupy a central place in the culture of all ethnic groups in Nigeria. For practically all imaginable situations, there is a suitable greeting. Apart from greetings for time of day, which occur in most languages, there are greetings for being at work, being at home, standing, sitting, walking, eating, or even just doing nothing. The same is true of happenings such as a birth, illness, death, appointment, loss of a job, promotion, housewarming, purchase of any valuable asset, etc. It is not just that one has to greet those involved in these situations, there are specific formulas appropriate for each situation.

In order to make English perform the cultural role normally performed by the indigenous languages, it is part of the nativization process to transfer some of these formulas into the nonnative varieties of English spoken in the country. The result is that, compared with ENL varieties, greetings in Nigerian English are characterized by three features: First, they are extensive and include such expressions as *Well done* (meaning "I greet you as you are working"), *Sorry* (used, for instance, as a greeting to someone sneezing or who has just knocked his or her foot against a stone), *Don't be late* (meaning "See you soon"), *I am coming* (meaning "Won't be a minute" or "See you later"), *You meet me well* (meaning "I am eating and I invite you to join me"), *Till tomorrow* (meaning "Goodnight"), and *Peace be unto this house*! (a survival of an archaic biblical expression). Second, the greetings are formal with the addition of such deference markers as *sir, ma* (for "ma'am"), or any appropriate title. Third, greetings in Nigerian English are elaborate, including enquiry about the entire household. It is not unusual for a "good morning" or a "welcome" greeting to be followed by *How are the children? How is Madam? How is Papa? What of Mamma? How is work?* and to these enquiries, the respondent, in a ritualistic manner, answers with the formulas: *They are well, She is well, He is well, She is well, It is fine.*

A brusque *Good morning* not followed by one or two of these ritual enquiries tends to convey an impression of distance or unfriendliness.

Apologies in Nigerian English are expressed by *Sorry*, usually followed by a deference marker. But, as shown above, the use of this expression also extends to sympathy for an unpleasant event as well as a harmless activity such as sneezing. Borkin and Reinhart (1978), in a discussion of the uses of *Excuse me* and *I am sorry* in American English, point out that the former is a formula to remedy a past or impending breach of etiquette, while the latter is an expression of regret at some unpleasantness suffered by one or the other or both of the interlocutors. For example, *Excuse me* is more appropriately used when two people are about to bump into each other, while both expressions are suitable after they have actually done so.

In Nigerian English, *Excuse me* or, just simply, *Excuse* is also used to remedy an impending breach of etiquette, but *Sorry* can also be used. Once the breach has occurred, the only acceptable apology is *Sorry*. In going up and down the elevator or walking down crowded corridors in this country, I still find it strange when someone says *Excuse me* after she or he has bumped into me. Somehow, I feel that this is not right and that I deserve *Sorry* instead. In Nigerian English, *Excuse me* is more typically used for calling someone's attention or seeking permission to perform an action.

Requests in Nigerian English are expressed with an interrogative or an imperative sentence accompanied by *please* or a deference marker (such as *sir* or *ma*) or a combination of the two. In addition, an imperative sentence prefixed with *kindly* may be used as a request. For instance, all the following expressions are acceptable requests: *Can I take the book, please? Please ma, may I go? Give it to me, sir! Please give it to me, sir! Kindly help me, (ma).*

House (1989: 97) quotes Stubbs (1983) as saying that in ENL, *please* is unacceptable in assertions, promises, offers, invitations, etc. Hence, the following sentences are unacceptable: **He ate more pudding please.* **Would you like more pudding please?* **Do you want to come to my party please?* With the probable exception of the first of these three sentences, the use of *please* in the other two sentences is acceptable in Nigerian English.

Another difference between ENL and Nigerian English is the incidence of simple imperatives in requests. As long as *please* or *kindly* is used to tone down the force of an imperative, requests in an imperative form are perfectly acceptable in Nigerian English. In fact, as pointed out in Bamgboṣe (1994), *please* is an overworked marker of respect which is often used in ESL situations as a hypercorrect form e.g. "Can I please see you?" "May I please talk to you?"

Gratitude in Nigerian English is expressed with such utterances as "Thank you," "I am grateful," with the addition of appropriate deference markers. However, the difference between ENL and Nigerian English in this regard is that the expression of thanks is not limited to the immediate situation but goes on till any subsequent meeting. Hence, it is not unusual to say "Thank you for yesterday" in gratitude for a favor done to one the previous day. An expression of gratitude may also be flowery, e.g. "May God bless you abundantly!" "God bless you, sir!" "May you live long!" "May your pocket never run dry!" In practically all cases, expressions of gratitude are accompanied by nonverbal gestures such as a female going on her knees or a male prostrating himself.

The interactional activities examined above show differences in usage between ENL and ESL varieties. There are considerable differences in the weighting attached to age, status, role, situation, and shared norms of behavior. There are also differences in nonverbal expressions of politeness ranging from appropriate bowing of the head or knee to full prostration on the floor, depending on the interactional activity involved, the occasion, and the age, status, or rank gap between the interlocutors.

Cultural basis of politeness and ESL. Studies of politeness across cultures, particularly in non-Western cultures, indicate more and more that the phenomenon is perhaps more culture-specific than previously thought and that putative universals of *face* need to be re-examined. Politeness is socially motivated and one needs to be familiar with sociocultural patterns in order to produce polite behavior (Matsumoto 1988: 421). Hence, politeness is perceived and manifested in different culture-bound ways. As Nwoye (1992: 228) aptly puts it with a pun on "face": "Face is usually found to wear different cultural faces."

In the ESL context, a speaker's mother tongue and the sociocultural conventions associated with it represent the basis for politeness strategies in a nonnative variety of English (Sridhar 1989: 115), and it is the notion of appropriateness that determines choice of strategy leading to the choice of structures rooted in the conventions of the learner's culture (Pandharipande 1992: 242).

What the above crosscultural studies of politeness have in common is the emphasis on the culture that lies behind the communicative competence of speakers. The role of culture in politeness is best summed up in the words of Ferguson:

> The point to be made here is the old familiar anthropological and linguistic one that although a particular phenomenon is universal in human societies—in this instance the phenomenon of politeness formulas—the structures and the incidence of use are so culture-specific and tied to the cultural history of the particular society or group that the structural and functional universals must be sought at other levels. (Ferguson 1981: 26)

Given the overwhelming importance of cultural behavioral norms, the differences in the verbal expression of politeness noted above may lead to a conflict between the rules and assumptions of second language use and second language reality. For instance, the use in an ENL situation of a greeting that is only culturally relevant in an ESL situation may lead to miscommunication and a negative reaction (cf. Wolfson 1983: 62). Similarly, the use of a mode of address that is appropriate in an ENL, but inappropriate in an ESL, situation is bound to cause offense. An example I am fond of quoting in this regard is Quirk's letter writing rule for British English which stipulates that letters that begin with "Dear Mr. Jones" must end with "Yours sincerely," while those that begin with "Dear Sir" must end with "Yours faithfully" and that mixing these formulas is evidence of poor education (Quirk 1962: 217). The fact is that norms of politeness in Nigerian English preclude naming an older person in the opening of a letter! Hence what is appropriate in this variety of English is to open a letter with "Dear Sir" and end it with "Yours sincerely."

Implications for ELT. What are the implications for ELT of the pull between ENL cultural norms and practices and ESL realities? Which usages should the learner be exposed to: those of ENL or those of ESL? There are three possible solutions to this problem: teach the norms of ENL, teach the norms of ESL, or teach the norms of both ENL and ESL.

The argument for teaching the norms of ENL is that English is a language of wider communication (LWC) and that to know it is to be able to take advantage of its use as an international language. This, in turn, means that international intelligibility must be one of the goals of whatever model of English is taught to a learner of the language. Such an argument, however, ignores three important considerations: first, that English in ESL countries is required more and more for internal communication between speakers who share a common non-Anglo-American culture; second, that ESL varieties have become institutionalized with their own dynamics of development through various processes of nativization; and third, that this development is rooted in the culture into which English has been transplanted. Thus, in an ESL context, communicative competence, as D'souza (1988) puts it, must be seen as "a fit between grammar of language and grammar of culture," and since it is the indigenous culture that is involved, the use of an exonormative model or standard in ELT is bound to lead to a mismatch between language and culture (D'souza 1988: 169).

The case for teaching the norms of ESL usage derives from its primary use for internal communication. In order to function effectively in an ESL context, one needs to be familiar with such norms. In fact, such are the sociolinguistic pressures that even those who have native-speaker-like competence need to conform to the behavioral norms of ESL usage. To that extent, one can say that knowledge of such norms constitutes a crucial aspect of the second language user's communicative competence. The argument in support of this position is forcefully put by Adetugbo (1979b: 181):

> [I]t appears that the goal of English language teaching in Nigeria should be communicative competence in the language within the Nigerian socio-cultural context, that this competence cannot be equated with linguistic competence in any native English idiom and that because Nigerian English must of necessity be different from any other dialect of English, mutual intelligibility and acceptability in the Nigerian situation must take precedence over international acceptability or intelligibility.

Those who need English to function in an ENL situation may well need to undergo supplementary instruction or learn through experience to become bidialectal in a nonnative and a native variety of English. In any case, it must be remembered that interaction between native speakers and nonnative speakers is usually characterized by accommodation, which calls for some adjustment on the part of both sets of interlocutors.

The option of teaching both ENL and ESL norms appears to be a reasonable compromise. However, unless the scope of such teaching is strictly specified, it may lead to a lot of wasted effort in teaching ENL norms to ESL users of English who may never need them. It seems to me that the first thing to do is separate two kinds of ESL situations: ESL teaching in an ENL context and ESL teaching in an ESL context.

In teaching English as a second language in an ENL country, it seems fairly obvious that the goal must be to enable learners to function maximally in all relevant sociocultural interactions in that society. It is, therefore, important that they be taught the behavioral norms appropriate in such interactions. This means that it is the knowledge of ENL usage that is primarily required. It is, of course, legitimate to contrast such usage with norms and practices in the learner's own language in order to draw attention to similarities and differences, thereby encouraging mutual understanding of, and respect for, both cultures.

In an ESL country, on the other hand, the primary goal of teaching English must be to enable learners to function in an ESL context. Thus, instruction should be based on ESL norms and usage. However, while teaching these, it is also useful to draw attention to similarities and differences between ESL and ENL norms. The purpose of this is not to make ENL norms a standard or point of reference, but only to create an awareness of them, particularly at higher levels of instruction and proficiency in English.

Conclusion. In making a case for an ESL-based communicative competence, this paper has used politeness, which is deeply rooted in culture, as an example of what knowledge of a language entails. It may well be that in ESL countries, there are individuals who, by virtue of greater exposure or proficiency, have learned to move freely between ENL and ESL norms. This notwithstanding, the point is that, even for such persons, knowledge of ENL norms is certainly not enough, since the primary goal is to produce speakers who can function maximally in the ESL sociocultural context. The pedagogic implication of this is that all aspects of ELT, including curriculum design, preparation of materials, and teacher training, must pay more attention to the crucial role of culture.

REFERENCES

Adegbija, Efurosibina. 1989. "A comparative study of politeness phenomenon in Nigerian English, Yoruba and Ogori." *Multilingua* 8(1): 57–80.

Adetugbo, Abiodun. 1979a. "Appropriateness and Nigerian English." In Ubahakwe (ed.) 1979, 137–166.

Adetugbo, Abiodun. 1979b. "Nigerian English and communicative competence." In Ubahakwe (ed.) 1979, 167–183.

Afolayan, Adebisi. 1974. "Politeness in English." *Journal of the Nigerian English Studies Association* 6(1): 65–76.

Akere, Funso. 1978. "Sociocultural constraints and the emergence of Standard Nigerian English." *Anthropological Linguistics* 20: 407–421. Reprinted in John Pride (ed.). 1982. *New Englishes*. Rowley, Mass: Newbury House Publishers. 85–99.

Bamgboṣe, Ayọ. 1994. "Language and cross-cultural communication." In Martin Putz (ed.), *Language in contact and conflict situations*. Amsterdam: Benjamins. Also available in preprint edition L.A.U.D. Paper No. 233, Duisburg: L.A.U.D. 1992.

Borkin, Ann and Susan M. Reinhart. 1978. "Excuse me and I'm Sorry." *TESOL Quarterly* 12(1): 57–69.

Brown, Penelope and Stephen Levinson. 1978. "Universals in language usage: Politeness phenomena." In Esther N. Goody (ed.), *Questions and politeness*. Cambridge, U.K.: Cambridge University Press.

Byram, Michael. 1989. *Cultural studies in foreign language education*. Clevedon, U.K.: Multilingual Matters Ltd.

Canale, Michael. 1983. "From communicative competence to communicative language pedagogy." In Richards and Schmidt (eds.) 1983, 2–27.

Canale, Michael, and Swain, Merrill. 1980. "Theoretical bases of communicative approaches to second language teaching and testing." *Applied Linguistics* 1(1), 1–47.

Coulmas, Florian (ed.). 1981. *Conversational routine: Explorations in standardized communication situations and pre-patterned speech*. The Hague: Mouton de Gruyter.

D'souza, Jean. 1988. "Interactional strategies in South Asian languages: Their implications for teaching English internationally." *World Englishes* 7(2): 159–171.

Ervin-Tripp, Susan. 1969. "Sociolinguistic rules of address." In L. Berkowitz (ed.), *Advances in experimental social psychology*. Reprinted in Pride and Holmes (eds.) 1972, 225–240.

Ferguson, Charles. 1981. "The structure and use of politeness formulas." In Coulmas (ed.) 1981, 135–151.

House, Juliane. 1989. "Politeness in English and German: The functions of *please* and *bitte*." In Shoshana Blum Kulka, Juliane House, and Gabriele Kasper (eds.), *Cross-cultural pragmatics: Requests and apologies*. Norwood, N.J.: Ablex Publishing Corporation.

Hymes, Dell. 1972. "On communicative competence." In Pride and Holmes (eds.) 1972, 269–293.

Janney, Richard and Horst Arndt. 1992. "Intracultural tact versus intercultural tact." In Richard J. Watts, Sachico Ide, and Konrad Ehlich (eds), *Politeness in language*. Berlin: Mouton de Gruyter. 21-41.

Janney, Richard and Horst Arndt. 1993. "Universality and relativity in cross-cultural politeness research: A historical perspective." *Multilingua* 12(1): 13–50.

Kachru, Braj B. 1987. "The past and prejudice: Toward de-mythologizing the English canon." In Ross Steele and Terry Treadgold (eds.) *Essays in honour of Michael Halliday*. Amsterdam: John Benjamins Publishing Co. 245–256.

Kachru, Braj B. 1990. *The alchemy of English*. Urbana and Chicago: University of Illinois Press (Originally published in 1986 by Pergamon Press).

Matsumoto, Y. 1988. "Re-examination of the universality of face: Politeness phenomenon in Japanese." *Journal of Pragmatics* 12: 403–426.

Matsumoto, Y. 1989. "Politeness and conversational universals from Japanese." *Multilingua* 8: 207-221.

Nwoye, Onuigbo G. 1992. "Linguistic politeness and sociocultural variations of the notion face." *Journal of Pragmatics* 18(4): 309–328.

Pandharipande, Rajeshwari. 1992. "Defining politeness in Indian English." *World Englishes* 11(2/3): 241-256.

Paulston, Christina Bratt. 1974. "Linguistic and communicative competence." *TESOL Quarterly* 8(4): 347-362.

Pride, J.B. and Janet Holmes (eds.). 1972. *Sociolinguistics*. Harmondsworth, Middlesex: Penguin.

Quirk, Randolph. 1962. *The use of English*. London: Longmans.

Richards, Jack C. and Richard W. Schmidt (eds.). 1983. *Language and communication*. London and New York: Longman.

Sridhar, Kamal K. 1989. *English in Indian Bilingualism*. New Delhi: Ramesh Jain Manohar Publications.

Stubbs, M. 1983. *Discourse analysis: The sociolinguistic analysis of natural language*. London: Blackwell.

Ubahakwe, Ebo (ed.). 1979. *Varieties and functions of English in Nigeria*. Ibadan: African Universities Press.

Wolfson, Nessa. 1983. "Rules of speaking." In Richards and Schmidt (eds.) 1983, 61–87.

What do "Yes" and "No" really mean in Chinese?

Yu-hwei E. Lii-Shih
National Taiwan Normal University

Introduction. Foreigners are often confused by Chinese ways of acceptance and refusal. When a Chinese says "yes" he could mean "no," and when he says "no," he might mean "yes." What is even worse, after a sequence of give-and-take negotiations, the invitation or request initiator might still be at a loss as to what the speaker's real intention is. This has resulted in many instances of cross-cultural miscommunication. Chinese native speakers sometimes may have difficulties in grasping the exact meaning too, but most of the time they can capture the meaning easily from verbal or nonverbal clues, or at least they know how to clarify and how far they can go in the negotiation exchanges to clarify, if not solve, the puzzles.

The objectives of this study are: (1) to present and discuss the patterns of acceptance and refusal in invitations, gift-giving, offers, and requests in Mandarin Chinese; (2) to propose a theoretical framework to account for language politeness in general as well as the patterns of acceptance and refusal in Mandarin Chinese,[1] and (3) to help foreigners understand the meanings of "yes" and "no" in Chinese social interactions and thus promote intercultural communication.

Data and methodology. Invitations, gift-giving, offers, and requests were chosen as the subjects of this research for the reason that the first three are what I call hearer-beneficial face satisfying acts (FSAs), and the last, requests, is a hearer-cost face threatening act (FTA). In this paper I will discuss and compare the general speech differences between FSAs and FTAs.

The data used for the analysis comes mainly from 282 realistic conversations collected from September 1992 to December 1993. They include thirty recorded telephone conversations, forty-nine conversations based on participant observation, thirty-eight conversations recorded from TV programs, and 165 realistic written conversations.[2] The realistic written conversations were

---

1. "Mandarin Chinese" here refers to the Mandarin used in Taiwan, because the data used for this study were collected in Taiwan.

2. The recorded telephone conversations were collected by my brother, two of my friends, and myself. The speakers have all given permission for conversations to be used in this research.

provided by subjects of different social backgrounds. They were asked to write down conversations embodying invitations, gift-giving, offers, or requests that they had actually engaged in and record them as realistically and truthfully as possible. Relevant background information about the interlocutors and the social settings was also provided. By using these composite realistic conversations I was able to obtain enough data for the analysis of the patterns of acceptance and refusal.

In order to get deeper insight into the concept of politeness and the usage and meanings of "yes" and "no," I also interviewed thirty native speakers of Chinese to ask about their concept of politeness and their experiences and viewpoints concerning the acceptance and refusal of speech acts. In addition, I also asked thirty-eight undergraduates and twelve graduate students each to write a two to three page report about the above-mentioned speech acts, to be given as guidelines to help foreigners visiting or living in Taiwan to communicate well in social interactions. These reports have revealed interesting and valuable viewpoints concerning the norms implicit in these forms of discourse, although they might be somewhat subjective or prescriptive.

Theoretical framework. Since Brown and Levinson (B&L) published their article in 1978, many studies have been devoted to language politeness (see references). Fraser (1990) classifies them into four approaches: the social norm view, the conversational maxim view, the face-saving view, and the conversational contract view. Among them, B&L's face-saving approach was evaluated to be a more fully articulated version (Fraser 1990), and it is the most widely cited and followed model. However, it has difficulties in explaining some politeness phenomena, especially in the non-Western languages, and it has been one of the theories frequently challenged (cf. Kasper 1990; Matsumoto 1988; Gu 1990; Janney 1993). In this paper I am going to point out some of the drawbacks of B&L's model and propose a revised version of it.

The theoretical framework adopted here is primarily based on Brown and Levinson's model (1978, 1987), with a redefinition of "positive politeness" and an addition of the concept of face satisfying act (FSA) on a par with their original face threatening act (FTA). B&L's face-saving view may be suitable for the more individualism-oriented Western cultures, where interactants' territory, privacy, and freedom of actions are highly valued, but it is not adequate to account for such situation-centered oriented cultures as Chinese and Japanese (Kasper 1990: 195). It is suggested here that the face-satisfying concept be incorporated into the model to compensate for the biased face-saving view and thus make it a more balanced, and hopefully more full-fledged politeness framework.[3]

According to B&L, communication is seen as a fundamentally dangerous and antagonistic endeavor (Kasper 1990). Schmidt (1980) criticizes Brown and Levinson's theory as representing too pessimistic and paranoid a view. This is mainly due to the fact that B&L regard all interactions as (potentially) face-threatening, and acts of politeness are strategies redressing FTAs as shown in Figure 1.

Figure 1. Strategies for doing FTAs proposed by Brown and Levinson (1978, 1987)

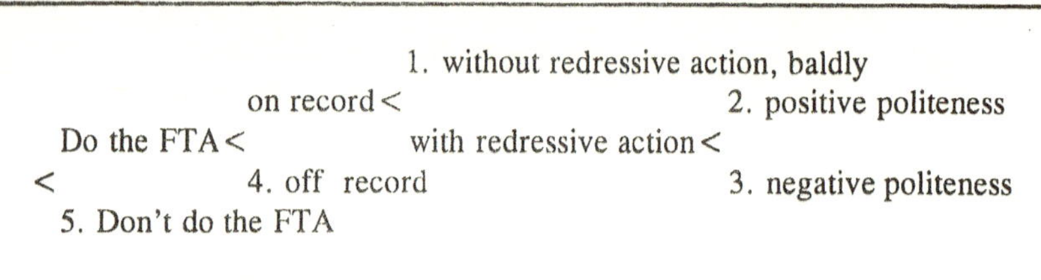

Positive politeness strategies are strategies for doing FTAs on record plus redress to the hearer's (H's) "positive face" (i.e. the want of every member that his or her wants be desirable to at least some others), and negative politeness strategies are strategies for doing FTAs on record plus redress to H's "negative face" (i.e. the want of every "competent adult member" that his or her actions be unimpeded by others) (B&L 1987: 60–62). It is understandable that negative politeness strategies are treated as redressive actions to counterbalance the force of FTAs. However, it is hard to understand why positively polite acts, such as thanks, invitations, greetings, compliments, and gift-giving, are viewed as redressive acts for softening some threatening force. For Chinese these are addressee-beneficial or addressee-desirable acts. They express friendship and appreciation, and should be treated as face satisfying acts. B&L do not offer satisfactory explanations as to why all social interactions are (potential) FTAs. For example, when explaining the strategies of "welcomings," "farewells," and "offers" as potential FTAs, their reasons are that those acts are inviting H to impinge on the speaker's (S's) preserve and there is a risk that H may not wish

3. The concept of FSA can be viewed as a universal concept, although in this article I only argue that it is an important concept for dealing with the Cinese politeness phenomenon. In the future I would like to look into more data in other languages to test the validity of the concept of FSA and to verify whether the framework proposed here can serve as a general politeness model for analyzing politeness phenomena in all languages.

to receive such acts (1987: 99). These kinds of explanations are far from convincing and are counterintuitive to Chinese concept of politeness.[4] For a Chinese, inviting, greeting, welcoming, or thanking is a sign of showing friendship, goodwill, or gratitude, which has little to do with face-threatening force. One of the major functions of speech is to establish and strengthen social relationships. Politeness, therefore, should not be viewed merely as a conflict avoidance strategy, but also positively as a harmony and friendship enforcement strategy.

"Face" is one's dignity, one's self-esteem, or one's socially given self-image. "Face wants," the constituents of "face," are the wants or the positive social values that every member of the society likes or wants to claim for him- or herself with the approval of others in a sociocultural context. These include values such as deference, modesty, intimacy, agreement, praise, appreciation, acceptance, care, respect of privacy, unimpediment, truthfulness, and sincerity (Lii-Shih 1986). The exact constituents of "face wants" are culturally determined, and the relative importance of face wants may vary from culture to culture. For example, in one culture, deference is valued more highly than intimacy, while in another it may be the opposite. On the whole, face wants that are valued as important are quite similar among people within the same culture, and they are by and large the cultural values that are highly respected by the majority of the people within the culture. Knowing cultural values is, therefore, essential in sending and interpreting messages. The face wants for each person within the same cultural group may differ somewhat, and they may vary according to the social contexts, too. Therefore, to be polite, one has to be first aware of which face wants are generally valued highly in the culture. The choice of the face wants for a particular speech act and the proper linguistic strategies to fulfill the face wants is then in turn determined by social variables, such as the social distance and the power relationship between the interlocutors, the formality of the social setting, etc. The rules (R's) of politeness for the present study are formulated as follows:

R1: Do the FSA sincerely.
R2: Don't do the FTA.
R3: If one has to do an FTA, minimize it with redressive actions.

4. According to the research I did in 1986, the present survey, and my student's term paper (D. Huang 1994), Chinese people value mutual care and interdependence. The Chinese concept of politeness is best characterized by sincerity, solidarity, considerateness, empathy, modesty, deference, not offending others, and not making others lose face. To make others feel happy, cared for, and respected is far more important than respecting others' privacy and keeping a distance from each other. Japanese have a similar concept of politeness, which puts a great emphasis on showing solidarity, interdependency, deference, and empathy (Clancy 1986; Matsumoto 1988; Ide et al. 1992).

An FSA is an act satisfying one's face wants, while an FTA is one threatening one's face wants. If one fulfills R1, one is observing positive politeness, and if one fulfills R2 and R3, one is observing negative politeness. Since R2 uses no linguistic behavior, it has received little attention in the study of linguistic politeness and it will not be dealt with here, either.

Strategies for positive politeness include:

(1) using appropriate address forms,
(2) using appropriate speech style,
(3) showing agreement or approval,
(4) complimenting,
(5) using expressions of gratitude,
(6) using humble expressions,
(7) using in-group language,
(8) being clear and direct, and
(9) joking or teasing.

Strategies for negative politeness include:

(1) using an interrogative sentence,
(2) using a hedge,
(3) giving hints,
(4) showing hesitation,
(5) giving excuses and reasons,
(6) apologizing, and
(7) impersonalizing S or H (Lii-Shih 1986).

The exact linguistic expressions used for each strategy are mostly language-specific, and many of them are conventional, ritualized expressions. This model can account for the politeness phenomena in the Chinese language more adequately, and it should also be a good model for crosscultural comparison, for it can take into account the general politeness rules and the culture and language-specific politeness phenomena (Lii-Shih 1986).

The positive politeness defined here is different from B&L's in that it includes not just the acts showing solidarity or asserting common ground but any speech acts that can give or satisfy the addressee's face wants in the given situation. The face want(s) desired may vary according to the interlocutor and the social context. For example, in Chinese culture, addressing a close friend by a nickname in a casual occasion is an act of positive politeness. However, in a formal situation addressing someone by a nickname may not be assumed to be a positively polite act, because it does not satisfy the addressee's want of being treated with respect in the given situation. It is a violation of R1 and therefore is regarded as improper behavior.

An FSA is beneficial or desirable to H, but an FTA is costly or threatening to H. If an act is assumed to be an FSA to H, the speaker usually feels free to do it directly, at least for Chinese. On the contrary, if a speech act is assumed to be an FTA to H, the speaker usually tries to avoid it, or performs it tactfully and indirectly so as to mitigate the force of the FTA. In the cases of extending invitations, giving gifts, and offering food or help, Chinese speakers are often quite direct and sometimes even appear pushy and imposing, because they regard those as addressee-beneficial acts. The imposition here signals sincerity and/or hospitality on the part of the initiator. Refusal of an invitation, a gift, an offer, or a request is an FTA, and therefore it is usually performed indirectly and tactfully. If no distinction is made between FSAs and FTAs, and if inviting, gift-giving, and offering are not treated as FSAs, it will be hard to explain why Chinese are so direct and pushy in inviting, giving gifts, and offering, but so indirect when it comes to acts like making requests or refusals.

Considerable research has been done on the aspect of speech acts of the FTA type, especially requests/directives and refusals. Not much has been devoted to acts of the FSA type.[5] In this study I will focus on FSAs, including invitations, gift-giving, and offers. I will only discuss one type of FTA, requests, for the purpose of comparing the difference between FSA and FTA speech behavior.

Extending an invitation is an FSA. So is accepting an invitation, because it attends to the inviter's face wants of "being accepted and being appreciated." However, the speech act of accepting an invitation, though an FSA, is not straightforward. As Gu (1990: 252) comments, "In Chinese, it is rare that a successful performance of inviting is realized in a single utterance. It more often than not takes several talk exchanges." The recipient often declines the invitation more than once, and the inviter has to repeat the invitation again and again. The same goes for gift-giving and offering food or help. What is the cause of this behavior?

The main reason for it is that Chinese is a debt-sensitive culture. To be generous and empathetic toward others, and to be modest and not greedy oneself, are highly regarded social values and the primary guidelines in the social interactions of inviting, gift-giving, and offering. On receiving an invitation, the invitee may incur a psychological cost–benefit imbalance. The invitee becomes the benefit receiver and puts the inviter in the adverse position of spending money or doing the extra work of preparing a meal. Accepting the invitation causes the invitee to appear greedy and to become indebted to the inviter, but refusing the invitation causes the invitee to commit an FTA, namely,

5. Gu (1990) and Mao (1992) have dealt with invitations in Chinese. Gu analyzed them from the conversational maxim view and Mao discussed them mainly within B&L's framework. In this study they are treated as FSAs and are analyzed by using the proposed new model of politeness.

turning down the inviter's "friendship." In order to get out of this dilemma, the recipient first has to evaluate which is more important: to observe the positive politeness and accept the offer, or to reject the offer in order not to be indebted. Usually people want both. The way to accomplish both is to accept the offer but try to be reserved at first and make some polite decline, trying to reduce the cost–benefit imbalance before the final acceptance. One can maintain a cost–benefit balance through the give-and-take of verbal exchanges, or by returning an invitation in the future, or by giving a gift in return. This strategy confirms the Chinese concept of *bu-qian ren-qing* "not to be indebted," or *li-shang-wang-huan* "to be reciprocal."

Patterns of acceptance and refusal in invitations, gift-giving, and offers.[6] The consideration of FSA/FTA, the cost–benefit balance, and other social variables result in the following patterns of acceptance and refusal in invitations, gift-giving, and offers. In the following discussion, "offer" is used to represent a gift or an offer of food or help. The parts in bold type are the common or ritualized expressions of acceptance and refusal.[7]

Pattern A: to accept an [FSA <+CB>] invitation/offer directly and clearly. For example:

(1) S is H's elder sister. S's daughter has just come back from the United States.

S: *Xiao-fen hui lai le. Ming-tian wan-shang ni-men yao-bu-yao guo-lai gen wo-men yi-qi chi-fan?*
Xiao-fen is back. Would you like to come over and join us for dinner tomorrow night?
H: ***Hao a**, ji-dian?*
Okay, what time?

Pattern A usually happens between close friends or within families, where no formality is required, or to a superior where a refusal is regarded as impolite behavior. In (1), S invites her brother and his family over for dinner. According

6. Most of the data collected are long, authentic conversations. Yet, for the sake of space, the pre-invitation talk, after-invitation talk, and question and talk not directly relevant to the patterns discussed are omitted from the examples given in this paper.

7. The following abbreviations are used: S represents the speaker or the initiator of the speech act; H represents the hearer/addressee or the recipient of the speech act; [FSA<+>CB>] represents an FSA that may cause a psychological cost–benefit imbalance for H.

to S's report, her brother seldom rejects her invitation, but instead he often brings a gift when he comes. As a matter of fact, this is a quite commonly practiced strategy. Pattern A is also common among high school and college students, who often regard polite declining as the formality of the adults' world. The common expressions for accepting an invitation, a gift or an offer are: *hao a* "okay," and *xie-xie* "thank you." Sometimes *bu-hao-yi-si* "feeling embarrassed" is added at the end to acknowledge the cost or inconvenience caused to S.

Pattern B: to decline an [FSA <+CB>] invitation/offer more than once before accepting it, as in example (2).

(2) S and H are two male high school English teachers. They got acquainted with each other during a three-week inservice Teachers Training Program at National Taiwan Normal University. The following dialogue occurred during the second week.

S: *Wo-men dao na-li chi-fan?*
Where should we go for lunch?
H: *Sui-bian.*
Any place will be fine for me.
S: *Na wo-men qu Lailai hao le. Jin-tian wo qing-ke.*
Then let's go to the Lailai restaurant. It's my treat today.
H: ***Wei-shen-me? Bu-yong la!***
Why? You don't have to.
S: *You shen-me guan-xi? Zuei-jin rang ni bang le hen-duo mang ne.*
Why not? You have been helping me a lot recently.
H: *Na-li-de hua.* ***Zhen-de bu-yong la! zhe-yang tai puo-fei le.***
It's nothing. **Really, you don't have to! This will cost you a lot.**
S: *Gan-ma na-me ke-qi? Zhi-shi chi ge bian-can er-yi.*
Why being so polite? It's just a simple lunch.
H: ***Hao ba! Na zhe-hui ni qing, xia-hui huan wo qing.***
Well, okay. Then you treat this time, but next time it should be my turn.
S: *Hao, na jiu zhe-yang. Zou ba!*
Okay, let's do it that way. Let's go!

In example (2), it takes three conversational exchanges to complete the invitational discourse. The invitee tried to decline twice, and the third time he even made a suggestion that it should be his turn to treat the next time in order to maintain a cost-benefit balance. The inviter, on the other hand, kept persuading H to accept the invitation by using various kinds of strategies, including indicating his previous debt to H, downgrading the cost of the meal, and accepting H's final suggestions, in order to make H feel that he does not owe too much to S. Although H declines twice, he does not give explicit and valid reasons for not being able to go, so the inviter, according to the Chinese cultural conventions and conversational implicature, could interpret this to mean that H does not really mean to reject and his declining is out of politeness. Ueda (1974) calls polite declines like these internal "yes," external "no" strategies.

Example (3) illustrates offering something to drink when a guest visits one's home:

(3) S and H are old friends.

S: *Yao-bu-yao he-dian she-me?*
Would you like to have something to drink?'

H: ***Bu-yong ma-fan le. Wo bu-ke.*** *Gang-gang cai he-guo.*
Don't bother. I'm not thirsty. I just had a drink.

S: *Bu-hui ma-fan de. Fan-zheng wo yie yao he. Ni yao cha huo-shi ka-fei?*
It's no trouble at all. Anyway, I want to have something, too. Would you like tea or coffee?'

H: *Dou hao. Shen-me fang-bian jiu he shen-me.* ***Bu-hao-yi-si gei ni ma-fang.***
Either will be fine. Whatever is convenient for you. **It's embarrassing to bother you.**

A guest normally would decline an offer of drink once or twice, as in Example (3). Another common Chinese way of offering something to drink is for the host to serve a drink without asking whether the guest wants it or not. In this circumstance, the guest would follow Pattern A and accept it and say *xie-xie* "thank you." If the guest does not want to drink anything he or she does not have to refuse, but leaves it there. But given a "yes" or "no" option, the guest usually would choose "no" to indicate reluctance to be bothersome. Therefore, if one wants to show one's kindness by giving options to the guest, one usually asks an A-or-B (or A-or-B-or-C) question instead of a yes-or-no question, such as "Would you like to have coffee, tea, or soda?"

A native speaker can infer the real intention of H from the nonverbal expressions and from the hints given by conventional ritualized declining expressions, such as *bu-yong la* or *bu-bi la* "you don't have to," *bu hao la* "it's not good for you to ...," *ni tai ke-qi le* "you are too polite," *bu yong ma-fan* "don't bother," *zhe-yang tai ma-fan le* "it's too much trouble," *bu-hao-yi-si* "feeling embarrassed," *rang ni tai puo-fei le* "make you spend too much money on it," etc. Among these expressions, *bu-yong la* and *bu-hao-yi-si* are the most commonly used.

The collected data revealed that the exchange sequence for Pattern B ranges from two to five turn exchanges. One turn exchange means an S–H pair, i.e. S's question/talk plus H's response. In this pattern, conversations with two or three declining exchanges are very common (see Table 1). An inviter would usually repeat an invitation at least once after an invitee's initial decline. If the inviter takes the initial decline at face value and stops inviting, he or she may be blamed for being insincere. Gift-giving and offers share the same transactional pattern. The recipient usually declines a gift or an offer two or three times before the final acceptance. Example (4) below shows gift-giving:

(4) S and H are two women working in the same company. They have a close relationship. S just got back from a tour to Europe, and paid a visit to H.

S: *Hao-jiu bu jian. Zhe-shi wo cong Ying-Guo dai-hui-lai-de yi-ge xiao ji-nian-pin, song-gei ni.*
Long time no see. Here is a small souvenir I brought back from England for you.

H: ***Ren lai jiu hao le, hai dai shen-me li-wu? Chang-chang na ni-de dong-xi. Zhen-me hao-yi-si? Zhe-ge wo kan ni hai-shi liu-zhe zi-ji yong ba!***
It's wonderful that you came, but why do you have to bring a gift? I've often received gifts from you. How can I feel right about it? I think you'd better keep this for yourself!

S: *Bie na-me ke-qi ma! Wo jia-li yie hai-you.*
You don't need to be so polite. I've got some at home too.

H: ***Na ni liu-zhe song bie-ren hao le.***
Then keep it for someone else.

S: *Ni zai gen wo ke-qi, jiu jian-wai le.*
If you keep being so polite [if you don't want to accept it], it seems that we're getting too distant.

H: ***Hao ba, na wo jiu bu ke-qi shou-xia le. Xie-xie.***
Okay, then I'll take it. Thank you.

From the exchanges between S and H it sounds like neither of them wants the souvenir, because H asks S to keep it for herself or someone else, and S says that she still has some at home. Chinese often depreciate their gifts by saying *yi-ge xiao li-wu* "a small gift," *yi-dian xiao dong-xi* "a small thing," *bu-cheng jing-yi* "not worth showing respect," or even *jia-li hai-you* "still got some at home" or *bang-mang xiao-yi-xiao* "help consume it" for the purpose of reducing the value of the gift and making H not feel indebted. People seldom reject a gift (except one with a special intention), because having a gift rejected is a great

FTA to the giver. The best way to maintain the cost–benefit balance is to reciprocate a favor or a gift in the future.

Pattern C: to reject an [FSA <+CB>] invitation/offer with explicit or good reasons, as in example (5).

(5) S and H are next-door neighbors, and good friends.

S: *Mei-li, ming-tian yao-bu-yao wo song ni qu ji-chang?*
Mei-li, do you want me to give you a ride to the airport?
H: ***Bu-yong le, xie-xie.*** *Wo ge-ge yao song wo qu.*
No, thank you. My brother is going to take me there.
S: *Hao, na yi-hou ru-guo you xu-yao wo bang-mang, qing bu-yong ke-qi.*
Okay, in case you need any help in the future, please do not hesitate to ask me.

This kind of refusal, with explicit reasons, is different from the polite decline of Pattern B. The inviter can tell the difference, and usually would not repeat the invitation or the offer again. Besides the explicit reasons, the recipient often uses the expressions of *xie-xie* "thank you" or *dui-bu-qi* "sorry". This is more similar to the American style, in which a "no" means "refusal."

Pattern D: to decline an [FSA <+CB>] invitation/offer vaguely or indirectly once or more than once, as in example (6).

(6) H is a college professor. His students, the seniors, are graduating, and they are going to hold a farewell party to thank their teachers in the college. S is one of the seniors.

S: *Lao-shi, xing-qi-tian-de xie-shi-yan qing nin wu-bi shang-guang.*
Sir, we sincerely hope that you may come to the thank-teacher farewell party next Sunday.
H: ***Xie-xie, wo xian-zai bu-neng que-ding na-tian you-mei-you kong.***
Thank you, but right now I cannot be sure whether I will be free then.
S: *Lao-shi yi-ding yao lai o. Dao-shi wo-men hui qu jie nin.*
Sir, you must come. We will go and pick you up then.
H: ***Bu-yong le.*** *Jia-ru wo neng qu wo hui zi-ji qu.*
You don't have to. If I can go, I'll go by myself.
S: *Na wo-men jiu deng lao-shi lai le cai kai-dong.*
Then we won't start until you come.

H: ***Bu-yong deng wo**, yin-wei na-tian you wei peng-you yue hao yao lai zhao wo. Wo bu zhi-dao ta ji-shi hui li-kai, suo-yi ni-men bu-yong deng wo. **Xie-xie ni-men-de yao-qing**, ye **xie-xie nin-men-de hao-yi.***
You don't have to wait for me, because a friend of mine is coming to see me, and I don't know when he will leave. So you don't have to wait for me. **Thank you for inviting me**, and **thank you for your kindness**.

Here H gave two vague responses, but S kept offering an even more sincere alternative. The commonly used vague refusal expressions for this pattern are: *xian-zai bu-neng que-ding* "it can not be decided now," *kong-pa mei-kong* "I'm afraid I won"t have time," *kong-pa bu-fang-bian* "may not be convenient," *xian-zai hai bu-gan que-ding* "I can't be sure now." The last utterance in example (6) implies a refusal, because at the end H thanks them for their invitation and their kindness. The inviter may conclude the invitation there. However, it could imply uncertainty, too; therefore, the inviter may try again before the party to make sure whether the invitee can come or not, and in addition to show the inviter's sincerity and hospitality.

Patterns A through D share a common feature: They are FSAs, but they may lead to a psychological cost–benefit imbalance for the recipient. In order to reduce the degree of cost to S and keep a psychological cost–benefit balance, H may repeat the polite decline one or more times, and S will repeat the invitation to show sincerity. These four patterns may be diagrammed as in Figure 2.

Figure 2. H's options for responding to an invitation, gift-giving, or offer that may lead to a psychological cost–benefit imbalance for H

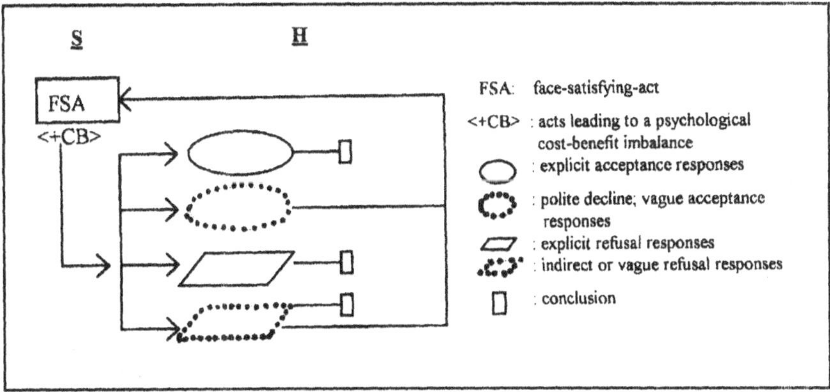

In Figure 2, the solid line figures represent genuine responses, and the dotted ones represent the vague, indirect, or ambiguous responses. Some of the responses represented in the dotted oval figure are the internal "yes," external

"no" responses, while some of the responses represented in the dotted parallelogram figure are the external "yes," internal "no" responses.

Below are two other patterns of invitation, which involve no psychological cost–benefit imbalance for H. They include invitations for things like getting together, a class reunion, or going to a movie together, where each party pays his or her own expenses. These patterns also go for wedding party and birthday party invitations. On these ceremonious occasions, the invitee is not supposed to show modesty and make polite declines, because they are important occasions for the inviter to celebrate. In addition, according to the tradition, the invitee has to give a gift or a *hong-bao* (a red envelope with money inside), so there is no psychological cost–benefit imbalance on the invitee. If H can accept the invitation, H gives S face, so H usually accepts it directly. On the other hand, rejecting the invitation is an FTA, for it may imply rejecting the inviter's friendship. If H cannot go to the party, H usually follows the negative politeness strategies by apologizing and giving good explanations, sometimes even expressing a willingness to try very hard to go. Whether H accepts the invitation or not, it is customary to send a gift or *hong-bao*.

Pattern E: to accept an [FSA <-CB>] invitation directly or definitely, e.g. example (7).

(7) S and H were high school classmates and have been keeping in touch.

S: *Lao-zhang a, san-yue liu hao you-mei-you kong a? Wo da er-zi jie-huen, yao qing ni he xi-jiu.*
Old-Chang, will you be free on March 6th? My eldest son is getting married. We would like to invite you to the wedding party.

H: *Gong-xi, gong-xi.* ***Dang-ran qu. Zai-mang yie-yao qu.***
Congratulations! Congratulations! **Of course I will go. Even if I am very busy I still want to go.**

S: *Xie-xie. Wo hui zai ji tie-zi gei ni.*
Thank you. I will send you the invitation card.

Pattern F: to reject an [FSA <-CB>] invitation with explicit reasons, e.g. example (8).

(8) S and H are colleagues working in the same institute.

S: *Lin-zhu-ren, yue-di wo-men you wu liou-ge ren yao dao Tai-ping-shan qu. Yao- bu- yao gen wo-men qu?*

Director Lin, there are five or six of us going to Mt. Tai-Ping at the end of this month. Would you like to join us?

H: ***Xiang-shi-xiang, bu-guo*** *zai gan yi-pian bao-gao.* ***Kong-pa mei shi-jian qu.***
I'd like to go, but I am working on a report. **I'm afraid I don't have time to go.**

S: *Dao-shi jia-ru ni gan-wan-le, hai-shi huan-ying ni lai can-jia.*
If you finish it by then, you're welcome to join us.

In example (8), after the invitee gives his reason for not being able to go, the inviter usually stops inviting, but he may still give an option to the invitee in case he can make it. This shows S's sincerity in wanting H's company and friendship.

Pattern G: to reject an [FSA <-CB>] invitation vaguely or indirectly, e.g. example (9).

(9) S and H were high school classmates.

S: *Mei-qing, xia li-bai-tian zhong-wu wo-men ban yao kai gao-zhong tong-xue huei. Ni neng-bu-neng lai?*
Mei-qing, we are going to have a high school class reunion next Sunday noon. Can you come?

H: ***Bu-zhi-dao ne,*** *yin-wei wo sian-sheng chu-guo le. Xiao-hai mei ren dai.*
I don't know, because my husband is out of the country. There is nobody taking care of the child.

S: *Ba er-zi yi-qi dai lai ma. Fan-zheng dou shi zi-ji tong-xue, mei guan-xi la.*
Bring your son along. We are all classmates. It's okay.

H: *Dai xiao-hai ding bu fang-bian de.* ***Zai kan-kan hao le. Xie la.***
It's very inconvenient to take a child along. **I'll think about it. Thanks anyway.**

In example (9) the invitee does not give a direct "no" or a direct "yes" in both turns, yet her response at the end implies that she cannot go. Patterns F and G are quite similar except that the explanation in Pattern G is not as explicit or convincing, and therefore it can be interpreted as a rejection. The inviter in this pattern may stop inviting after the fist decline or try one more time as in example (9) to show sincerity. So Pattern G may either end with one exchange or extend to a second exchange to clarify H's exact response. After S's repetition of the invitation, H usually would give a more definite response but may still give an indecisive response, if he or she can't make a final decision then. Patterns E through G can be diagrammed as Figure 3.

Figure 3. H's options for responding to an invitation that does not involve a psychological cost-benefit imbalance for H

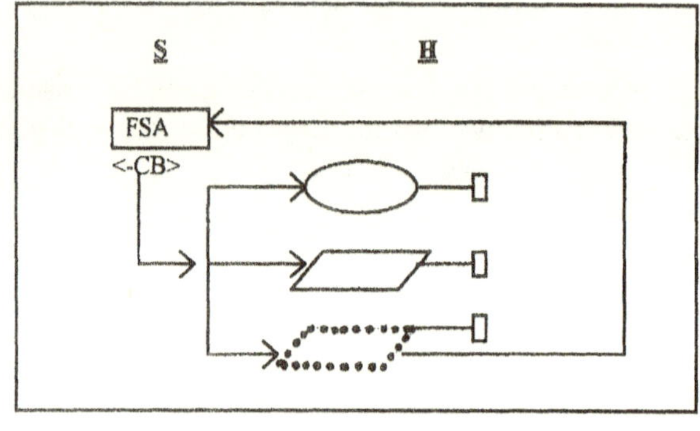

The major differences between Patterns A through D and Patterns E through G are that the addressee in the former cases has to consider how to maintain the psychological cost-benefit balance through some ritualized declines, while in the latter cases H does not have to go through the roundabout give-and-take negotiation because there is no problem of cost-benefit balance. The occasional recurrence of S's invitation in Pattern G clarifies and reinforces S's sincerity and friendly attitude toward H.

Following the flow charts of Figure 2 and Figure 3, we can derive several patterns of turn exchange combinations. The turn exchanges of Patterns A through G can be summarized by Figure 4.

Pattern B may range from two up to five or six exchanges, but two to three turn exchanges are most common. Pattern D may occasionally end up with an acceptance because of S's sincere insistence or H's fear of offending S. Patterns C and F are usually completed with only one turn exchange, since they are clear and true refusals and the inviter may not impose too far. Patterns D and G usually will not go beyond two exchanges, since the responses have a strong implication of "no," though they are not as explicit as those in Patterns C and F. Of course, the dialogues in Pattern D and G may also end up with indecisive responses, if the addressee has made no definite final decision then. S's reiteration of the invitation serves, on the other hand, to emphasize sincerity and friendship. Besides those mentioned, other kinds of combinations are also possible. For example, S may stop after H's initial polite decline in Pattern B, but this is marked as insincere. We are not going to exhaust all the possible combinations. The seven acceptance/refusal patterns plus the two flow charts show the general pattern of turn exchanges in [FSA <+CB>] and [FSA <-CB>] types of social interactions.

Table 1 displays the frequency of one to five turn exchanges per conversation for different types of responses to the FSA speech acts we have discussed so far: invitations, gift-giving, and offers. It also displays the contrast between

Figure 4. The turn-exchanges of Patterns A through G

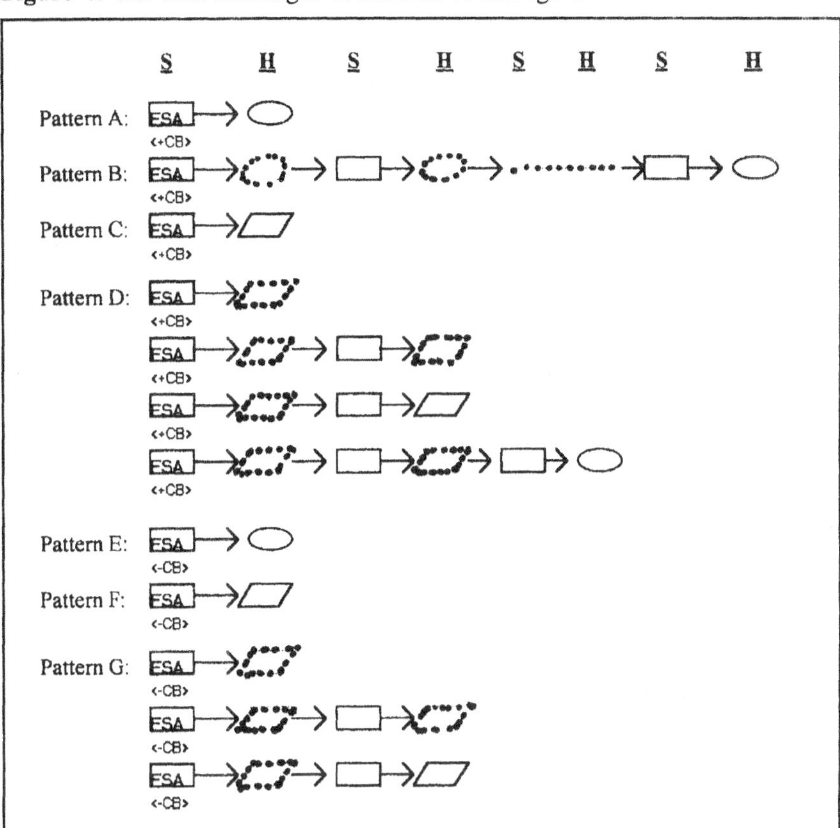

responses to <+CB> and <-CB> types of acts.

Table 1 indicates that most of the conversations embodying invitations, gift-giving, and offers take more than one turn exchange to complete. Overall, conversations with two or three turn exchanges are the most common. In Table 1, if we divide the one-turn exchange dialogues from the more-than-one-turn exchange dialogues, we find for accepting invitations <-CB> conversations of only one turn exchange are the most frequent (81.8%). But for accepting invitations of the <+CB> type only 23.3% of the conversations needed just one turn exchange. Refusal to invitations <-CB> in one-turn exchange also has a pretty high percentage (42.1%). This indicates that Chinese are quite direct in responding to an FSA <-CB>. They are indirect and vague in responding to FSA <+CB>. This explains why the consideration of the cost–benefit balance is an important factor in the acceptance and refusal behavior.

Table 1. The frequency of turn-exchanges per conversation for different types of responses to FSAs: Invitations, gift-giving and offers.

Types of responses to FSAs	Frequency of turn-exchanges per conversation					Total
	1	2	3	4	5	
Acceptance						
invitations <+CB>	14	17	18	10	1	60
	(23.3%)		(76.7%)			
gift-giving <+CB>	10	29	22	5	1	67
	(14.9%)		(85.1%)			
offers of food/help <+CB>	10	14	8	0	0	32
	(31.2%)		(68.9%)			
invitations <-CB>	18	3	1	0	0	22
	(81.8%)		(18.2%)			
Refusal						
invitations <+CB>	4	18	4	0	0	26
	(15.4%)		(84.6%)			
gift-giving <+CB>	1	2	1	1	0	5
	(20.0%)		(80.0%)			
offers of food/help <+CB>	7	11	9	0	0	27
	(25.9%)		(74.1%)			
invitations <-CB>	8	9	2	0	0	19
	(42.1%)		(57.9%)			

Patterns of acceptance and refusal in requests. Making a request is an FTA because it threatens the face want of "unimpediment." So is rejecting a request, since it violates S's want of "being accepted" or "being helped in times of need." On the contrary, accepting a request is an FSA because it is beneficial to the requester. As mentioned previously, if it is an FSA it can be performed directly, but if it is an FTA, it is best avoided or be performed with negative politeness strategies. Below are the patterns of acceptance and refusal in requests.

Pattern H: to accept a request directly and clearly, e.g. example (10).

(10) H was S's former student in college.

S: *Lao-shi, wo yao chu-guo jin-xiu. Nin neng-bu-neng bang wo xie-feng jie-shao xin?*
Sir, I'm going abroad to study. Could you write a recommendation letter for me?

H: ***Hao de, mei wen-ti.***
Sure, no problem

Pattern I: to turn down a request directly with little redressive action, e.g. example (11).

(11) S and H are boss and employee in a small trading firm.

S: *Lao-ban, wo ming-tian ke-bu-ke-yi qing-jia? Yin-wei jia-li you shi.*
Boss, can I take a day off tomorrow? There is something I have to take care of at home.

H: ***Bu-xing.*** *Ni zui-jin qing tai duo jia le.*
No. You have taken too many days off recently.

Pattern J: to turn down a request directly but with an apology and explicit explanations, e.g. example (12).

(12) S and H are colleagues and close friends.

S: *Lao-wang, ke-bu-ke-yi jie-yong yi-xia ni-de che-zi?*
Old Wang, can I borrow your car for a while?

H: ***Dui-bu-qi,*** *wo-de chi-zi huai le. Song-qu xiu-li, hai-mei na-hui-lai.*
Sorry. My car broke down, and it's [in the garage] getting fixed. I haven't gotten it back yet.

Pattern K: to turn down a request indirectly with various strategies, e.g. example (13).

(13) S and H are business acquaintances, not very close.

S: *Wo-men gong-si dao-bi, wo xian-zai shi-yie le. Ni-men gong-si zui-jin you-mei- you que-ren?*
Our company went bankrupt, and I'm out of job. Does your company have a vacancy now?

H: ***Hao-xiang mei ting-shuo you zhi-que ne.***
It seems that I haven't heard of any vacancy.

S: *Na ni ke-bu-ke-yi bang wo wen-wen kan?*
Then can you check for me?

H: ***Zui-jin lao-ban chang-chang chu-chai. Hen nan zhao-dao ta, bu-guo wo hui bang ni wen-wen kan.***
Our boss is often out of town recently. It's very hard to find him, but I'll try to check for you.

S: *Xie-xie. Na jiu bai-tuo ni le.*
Thank you. Then I'll have to rely on you for help.

Figure 5. H's options for responding to a request

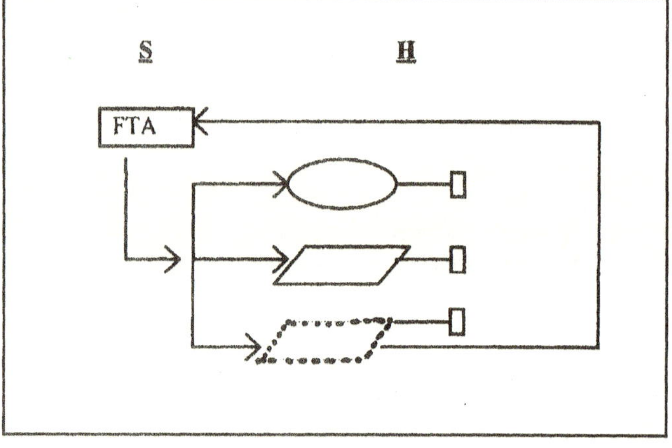

Pattern H, an acceptance to a request, involves an FSA. It can be easily performed in one turn exchange. Patterns I–J involve FTAs. According to the rules of politeness, they are best avoided, or performed indirectly or tactfully. Consequently, a direct response with little redressive action like Pattern I is seldom used. It is used only in an emergency or between a superior and a subordinate in special cases. Pattern J, like Pattern I, is usually completed in one turn exchange. However, it contains an apology and a good explanation and is, therefore, more polite than Pattern I. According to B&L, Pattern I is a bald on record strategy, and Pattern J is an on-record- with-redressive action strategy, i.e. negative politeness (cf. Figure 1). Patterns H through K can be diagrammed by the flowchart in Figure 5 and the turn exchange sequences in Figure 6.

Making a request is difficult, but declining a request is even more difficult. The degree of difficulty varies with the weight of the FTA, and the weight of an FTA is in proportion to the social dis-tance, the power rela-tionship between S and H, and the cost of the requested act, etc. According to Lii-Shih (1986), among the seven strategies for requesting, Chinese prefer more indirect

Figure 6. The turn-exchanges of Patterns H through J

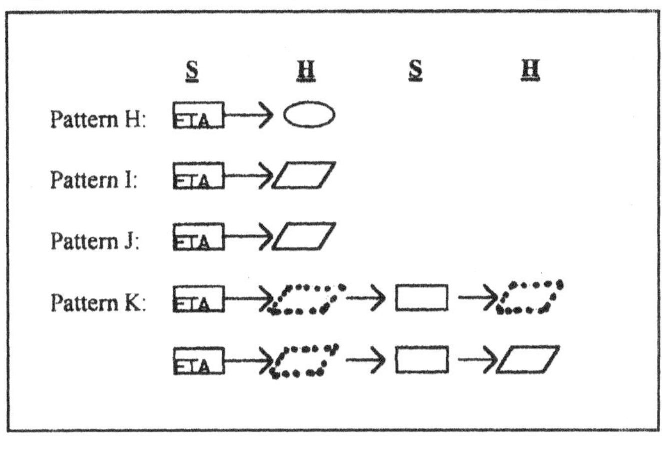

strategies, including hints. As for refusing requests, there are more than fifteen strategies in Mandarin Chinese (Liao and Lii-Shih 1993), and most of them are so vague or indirect that foreigners often have difficulty in understanding the real intention of the recipient. However, a Chinese, based on communicative competence, knows that a response without explicit "yes" has a high degree of negative implication, and if one wants to be sure of the real meaning, one needs to infer it from the context, linguistic or nonlinguistic.

Conclusion. Eleven patterns of acceptance and refusal have been presented and discussed in this paper. It has been found that many of the patterns take more than one turn exchange to complete the act. Very often, acceptance and refusal strategies in Mandarin Chinese proceed like a negotiation. Through the process of give-and-take negotiation in the discourse of invitations, gift-giving, and offers, the initiator indicates sincerity and friendship and the recipient shows considerateness of the cost and inconvenience caused to the initiator, and they may thus strengthen their social ties.

We have introduced in this paper the new concept of the face satisfying act (FSA), which together with the face threatening act (FTA) makes the whole politeness framework more balanced. It makes it easier to explain the use of direct and indirect politeness strategies, and it explains why Chinese are sometimes so direct and pushy in inviting, giving a gift, or offering food or help and why they are so indirect and vague in issuing or rejecting a request. In this paper we have also introduced the concept of psychological cost–benefit imbalance. This is an important concept for taking account of the different kinds of responses to invitations to a dinner, as opposed to invitations to a wedding feast, a birthday party, a reunion, a get-together, or a go-dutch dinner. Most importantly, it explains why a Chinese has to decline an invitation, an offer, or a gift several times before finally accepting it.

The similarities among the expressions used in genuine acceptance, genuine refusal, polite decline, and indirect, vague refusal have made acceptance and refusal complex and ambiguous behaviors, and they have also made it difficult for foreigners to figure out the real meanings of "yes" and "no" in Chinese. In order to help foreigners communicate well and comprehend the real message of "yes" and "no" in Chinese, the Chinese concept of politeness, Chinese rules of politeness, and patterns of acceptance and refusal, along with the ritualized formulaic expressions used in these patterns, have to be made known to them through textbooks or other means of instruction. However, a preliminary survey of the Mandarin textbooks used in Taiwan reveals that few of them include explicit explanations and authentic dialogues concerning these kinds of speech acts. It is hoped that this study may make some contribution to the understanding of language politeness behavior with regard to acceptance and refusal in Mandarin Chinese, and may also shed some light on the theory of language politeness in general.

REFERENCES

Beebe, Leslie, Tomoka Takahashi, and Robin Uliss-Weltz. 1990. "Pragmatic transfer in ESL refusals." In Robin Scarcella, Stephen D. Krashen and Elaine Andersen (eds.), *On the development of communicative competence in a second language*. Cambridge, Massachusetts: Newbury House. 55–73.

Blum-Kulka, Shoshana, Juliane House, and Gabriele Kasper. 1989. *Cross-cultural pragmatics: Requests and apologies*. Norwood, N.J.: Ablex Publishing Corporation.

Brown, Penelope and Stephen Levinson. 1978. "Politeness phenomena." In Esther N. Goody (ed.), *Questions and politeness: Strategies in social interaction*. Cambridge, U.K.: Cambridge University Press. 56–299

Brown, Penelope, and Stephen Levinson. 1987. *Politeness: Some universals in language usage*. Cambridge, U.K.: Cambridge University Press.

Clancy, Patricia M. 1986. "The acquisition of communicative style in Japanese." In Bambi Schieffelin and Elinor Ochs (eds.), *Language socialization across cultures*. New York: Cambridge University Press. 213–250.

Ervin-Tripp, Susan, Jiansheng Guo, and Martin Lampert. 1990. "Politeness and persuasion in children's control acts." *Journal of Pragmatics* 14(2): 307–331.

Fraser, Bruce. 1990. "Perspectives on politeness." *Journal of Pragmatics* 14(2): 219–236.

Gu, Yueguo. 1990. "Politeness phenomena in modern Chinese." *Journal of Pragmatics* 14(2): 237–257.

Huang, Doris. 1994. "The concept of politeness: An empirical study of Chinese and English." Unpublished term paper. Graduate Institute of English, National Taiwan Normal University.

Ide, Sachiko. 1982. "Japanese sociolinguistics: Politeness and women's language." *Lingua* 57(2–4): 357–385.

Ide, Sachiko, Beverly Hill, Yukiko M. Cranes, and Tsunao Ogino. 1992. "The concept of politeness: An empirical study of American English and Japanese." In Richard J. Watts et al. (eds.), *Politeness in language: Studies in its history, theory and practice*. New York: Mouton de Gruyter.

Janney, Richard W. 1993. "The problems of other minds: In cross-cultural politeness research." Paper presented at 4th International Pragmatics Conference, Kobe, Japan, July 1993.

Kasper, Gabriele. 1990. "Linguistic politeness: Current research issues." *Journal of Pragmatics* 14(2): 193–218.

Liao, Chao-chih and Yu-hwei E. Lii-Shih. 1993. "Refusal in Mandarin Chinese." Paper presented at the 4th International Pragmatics Conference, Kobe, Japan, July, 1993.

Liao, Chao-chih. 1994. "A study on the strategies, maxims, and development of refusal in Mandarin Chinese." Doctoral dissertation. The Graduate Institute of English, National Taiwan Normal University.

Lii-Shih, Yu-hwei E. 1986. *Conversational politeness and foreign language teaching*. Taipei: The Crane Publishing Co.

Mao, LuMing. 1993. "Invitational discourse and Chinese identity." *Journal of Asian Pacific Communication* 3(1): 79–96.

Matsumoto, Yoshiko. 1988. "Reexamination of the universality of face: Politeness phenomena in Japanese." *Journal of Pragmatics* 12(4): 403–426.

Rubin, Joan. 1983. "How to tell when someone is saying 'no' revisited." In Nessa Wolfson and Elliott Judd (eds.), *Sociolinguistics and language acquisition*. London: Newbury House Publishers.

Saville-Troike, Muriel. 1989. *The ethnography of communication: An introduction* (2nd edition). New York: Basil Blackwell.

Schmidt, Richards W. 1980. "Review of Questions and Politeness in Social Interaction." *RELC* 11(2): 100–114.

Ueda, Keiko. 1974. "Sixteen ways to avoid saying 'No' in Japan." In John C. Condon and Mitsuko Saito (eds.), *Intercultural encounters with Japan*. Tokyo: Simul Press.

Watt, Richard J., Sachiko Ide, and Konrad Ehlich. 1992. *Politeness in language: Studies in its history, theory and practice*. New York: Mouton de Gruyer.

Culture, discourse, and choice of structure

Ren Shaozeng
Hangzhou University

Introduction. In English as well as in Chinese (putonghua) there are two ways of expressing the same proposition that can be logically represented as F(x). For instance, the proposition "Rose (red)" can be represented as "The rose is red" and "a red rose" in English and as *meigui shi hongde* ("rose be red") and *hong meigui* ("red rose") in Chinese. Grammarians have tried to account for the relationship between the two structures from different perspectives: Chomsky (1957: 72) in terms of transformation, H.A. Gleason, Jr. (1965: 128) in terms of agnation, and M.A.K. Halliday (1985: 327) in terms of grammatical metaphor. Jespersen (1924) approaches this phenomenon in his own way, regarding the two structures as two different ways of joining a primary to a secondary, and using the terminology "junction" and "nexus". What he calls a junction is in fact a noun phrase consisting of a head plus a modifier, and the grammatical function underlying this structure is modification. On the other hand a nexus is usually a clause consisting of a subject and a predicate, which in the case of English, is made up of a copula and a subject complement. The grammatical function underlying a nexus is complementation. The difference between the two can perhaps be appreciated by Jespersen's comparisons:

- "A junction is like a picture, a nexus is like a drama or process." (1933: 95)
- "Junction is static, nexus dynamic." (1937: 121)
- "A junction serves to make what we are talking about more definite or precise, while a nexus tells us something by placing two (or more) definite ideas in relation to each other." (1937: 121)
- "In a nexus something new is added to the conception contained in the primary." (1933: 95) or "to what has already been named" (1933: 96).

In spite of the differences, the fact remains that both structures may express the same propositional meaning. The term nexus also has a wider application, for it can be used to refer to what he calls inner structure such as "him (happy)" in "The baby made him happy."

As modification and complementation are two of the major syntactic functions in language, they naturally find expression in the two languages under investigation in this article, English and Chinese. In English, alongside "a pretty girl" we find "The girl is pretty." Their corresponding equivalents in Chinese are *haokande nuhai* ("pretty girl") and *nuhai hen haokan* ("girl very pretty"). Examples abound of the structure "noun + qualifying adjective": In English, "the tall man" is also "The man is tall"; in Chinese *gaoger*, *gaogezi* ("tall height") is also *zhege nanren hen gao* ("this man height tall"). In both languages one finds a junction and its related nexus. However, even here we see the difference in the usage of these structures. For instance in Chinese *nuhai hen haoken* we find the emphasizer *hen* ("very"), which is almost indispensable, especially when the predicative adjective is a monosyllabic word and there is no link verb in the Chinese nexus as normally expected in English. However, the internal differences in the structures between the two languages will not prevent us from seeing the fact that both languages share the two structures. The question presents itself, Do the two structures function in the same way in the flow of information or structuring of information in the two languages? This involves issues such as How does each of the two languages make the textual choice? What structural resources are available in the two languages that facilitate the choice. This paper aims to examine the differences in the use of the two structures between English and Chinese from a discourse perspective. A functional approach is adopted, and Jespersen's terms "junction" and "nexus" are used for the two structures for want of better ones. Data for the study were taken from English novels such as *The armies of the night* (Mailer 1968), *The master of the game* (Sheldon 1982), *Rich man, poor man* (Shaw 1969) and *The joy luck club* (Tan 1989), and Chinese novels such as *A dream of red mansions* (Cao 1982), *The song of youth* (Yang 1958), and *Selected essays by Yang Shuo* (Yang 1978). A number of examples were also taken from newspapers.

Differences. The following contrastive pairs may point to the fact that where English favors a junction, Chinese shows a marked inclination for a nexus:

English	Chinese
wet paint	*you qi wei gan* "paint not dry"
wet floor	*di ban chaoshi* "floor wet"
small world	*shijie hen xiao* "world very small"

The point will become clearer when we contrast the following examples:

1E I have got a flat tire/My car got a flat tire.
1C *wo chetai bie le*
("I car tire flat")

As a message the sentence "I have got a flat tire" consists of a theme, which is what the message is concerned with or the starting point of the message (Halliday 1985) used to orient the hearer to the information he is about to process (Fries 1992)—realized in this sentence as "I"—and a rheme, which is the remainder of the message or the part in which the theme is developed (Halliday 1985)—realized in this sentence as "had a flat tire". In terms of information structure, the sentence begins with what is given information and proceeds to what is new information. There seems to be a general correlation between the rhematic status and the culmination of the new information marked by the location of tonic prominence. In 1E what the speaker wants to draw the hearer's attention to is the junction "flat tire", which is presented as new information bearing the tonic prominence. This is how English presents the message. In 1C *wo* ("I") is made the starting point of the message, that is the first theme. Then comes the second theme *chetai* ("car tire"), which serves to narrow down what is being talked about. The speaker prepares the hearer for the information that he is going to give about *chetai*. The rheme that carries the new information is realized as *bie le* ("flat"), where the end focus is placed. *Le* is an aspectual particle, but it is a well known fact that it is difficult to tell adjectives from verbs in Chinese. *Bie le* could mean "deflated" or "flat". Grammarians call this kind of adjective an "adjectival verb" (Li and Thompson 1981: 142). Whichever way we choose to treat the word *le*, we still have a nexus. This is how Chinese presents the same message.

Now let us contrast another pair of sentences:

2E Poverty in the developing countries has been ascribed to low productivity, inappropriate domestic policies and inadequate national effort.
2C *Fazhanzhong guojia de pinkun shi yinwei shengchanli di, guonei zhengce bu dang, zisheng nuli bugou.*
("Developing country PARTICLE poverty be because productivity low, national policy not appropriate, self effort not adequate")

Here the three junctions after the preposition "to" are turned into nexuses in Chinese, which are more natural and free-flowing to the Chinese ear than junctions would be.

Now let us look at two more examples. The first set (3C,3E) is a rendering from Chinese (*A dream of red mansions*) into English where we find a series of nexuses translated into junctions in English. We find the order of the two components in each of the nexuses reversed, turning them into junctions in English. The second set (4E,4C) is a sentence translated from English (*Vanity Fair*) into Chinese:

3C ... *jun ren chen liang fu ci zi xiao.*
("princes benevolent minister good father kind son filial")

3E ... benevolent princes, good ministers, kind father and filial sons.

4E She had such a kindly, smiling, tender, gentle, generous heart of her own.

4C *Ta xindi houdao xingge wenrou keteng, qiliang you da weiren you leguan.*
("She moral nature honest kind character gentle tender tolerance also great disposition also optimistic")

The English junction with five premodifiers is rendered into a series of nexuses in Chinese. It is not impossible to use a junction with a number of premodifiers, but the nexuses are definitely more in tune with the Chinese language.

The difference in the choice of the structures is in fact a difference in signaling and using the information structure and the thematic structure, a difference in structuring the clause as a message; more specifically, it is a difference in choosing what to start the message with and in telling the hearer what is important in the message.

Structural resources. The difference in the use of the two structures between English and Chinese is due to the choice each of the two languages makes of the textual function of language. Making the choice imposes the structure on the language. As a matter of fact, each of the two languages has developed a number of structural resources that make the choice possible. In English, quite a number of resources are available that facilitate the choice of a junction. To use a junction as a subject complement, it is necessary to have some devices that can initiate the clause as a message. This leads to the question, What element is usually chosen as theme in such an English clause? The following examples show the variety of choices commonly found in the data.

Impersonal "it" is most often used as the theme in English, usually followed by an inflected form of "be":

5E It's a hell of a long trip to Japan.

5C *Dao riben de lucheng chang de yao ming.*
("to Japan PARTICLE journey long PARTICLE terrible")

6E It was a cold clear day.
6C *Tian qi han leng qing lang.*
("weather cold clear")

Since there is no such pronoun as impersonal "it" in Chinese, it is necessary to begin the Chinese sentence with *lu cheng* ("journey") in 5C and *tian qi* ("weather") in 6C. This is how the English junctions are rendered into Chinese nexuses.

Personal pronouns followed by a form of "be" are also often used as the theme in such clauses:

7E You're a hopeless case.
7C *Ni bu ke jiu yao.*
("you hopeless")

In 7E the personal pronoun "you" is used. Here again the English junction is rendered into a Chinese nexus.

Personal pronouns used as the theme take "have" as the main verb:

8E She had uncommon features, bright eyes and graceful eyebrows.
8C *Ta sheng de yi rong bu su mei mu qing ming.*
("she grow PARTICLE features uncommon eyebrows eyes graceful bright")

Here the junction in English ascribes some permanent features to the theme. This use of "have" is even more common when its object is a noun derived from a verb such as "walk", "laugh", or "smile". I shall discuss this more when I discuss structural compensation. The junction in 8E is rendered into a nexus as usually done by native speakers of Chinese when they express similar ideas.

"There" as an introductory word is also used to introduce a junction in English:

9E There was an awful predicament.
9C *Qing kuang zhen zao gao.*
("situation real awful")

This introductory "there" has no counterpart in Chinese, making it necessary to use a noun as the theme in Chinese

In their nominal function, possessive pronouns such as "mine" and "ours" may also be used to introduce a junction:

10E Ours is a happy family.
10C *Women jiating hen xingfu.*
("we family very happy")

In 10E "our" is used to avoid the repetition of the word "family" from a previous sentence, and at the same time maintains the tendency to use a junction as the complement. However, a nexus is used in Chinese, which also makes it possible to avoid the repetition of *jiating* ("family").

The use of a cognate object is still another way of introducing a junction:

11E Artie smiled his sad, beautiful smile.
11C *Artie xiao de qichu dongren.*
("Artie smile PARTICLE sad beautiful")

In 11E we have a cognate object, with two adjectives premodifying it, thus forming a junction, which refers to Artie's smiling being sad and beautiful. (For a detailed analysis of such a structure see Li and Thompson 1981: 625.)

From a brief survey of the major structural means by which a junction is introduced, I now turn to the formation of junctions. For example, "one" is often used after an adjective in the predicative position:

12E You are a fine one to talk about Christian charity.
12C *Tan ji du ci shan ni zhen gou hao le.*
("talk Christian charity you real enough good PARTICLE)

Without "one" the irony would be lost in English. However, the Chinese nexus retains the irony.

In English there are a number of nouns that are frequently used to form junctions. Most of them are vague in meaning, for instance "thing", "business", "story", "affair", and "situation".

13E Love is a tiresome, childish business.
13C *Aiqing lingren yanjuan, youzhi kexiao.*
(Love tiresome childish)

F.T. Wood (1981: 269) has called "thing" an overused word. Is this not perhaps dictated by the tendency to use a junction?

On the other hand Chinese accommodates a number of structural resources that contribute to the employment of a nexus to express what is encoded as a junction in English. In English, messages usually start with something that is known to the hearer or that can be inferred from the context. This calls for an entity that is linguistically definite. However, as Chinese lacks a formal distinction between the definite and the indefinite, it is possible to make the theme be whatever the speaker is concerned with at the moment of speaking. This may account for the use of *lucheng* ("journey") and *tianqi* ("weather") as the point of departure in presenting the message in 5C and 6C. In terms of functional grammar, 5C and 6C belong to the relational process in which an attribute is ascribed to an entity. Since Chinese finds it necessary to choose words like *lucheng* and *tianqi* as the carrier, the attribute naturally will come after, thus forming nexuses.

Chinese adjectives can serve as subject complements without a copula as shown in all the Chinese sentences discussed above. In *jun ren cheng liang* (3C, "princes benevolent minister good"), the adjectives come immediately after the nouns to which they attribute a moral quality.

Alongside the nexus *diban chaoshi* ("floor wet") used in the first examples, Chinese has an alternative construction with *shi* (a copula) and *de* (a particle), *diban shi chaoshi de* ("floor be wet PARTICLE"). Although the two constructions, with *shi* and without *shi*, are somewhat different—the former gives a description, the latter a comment—the fact remains that we have a nexus in each, realizing a relational process. This contributes to the frequent use of nexuses.

Unlike English, Chinese is capable of having a nexus as the predicate of a clause. For instance, structurally in 1C *wo* ("I") is the subject and *chetai biele* ("tire flat") is the predicate. In this predicate, *chetai* is the subject, *biele* the predicate. "As the notion of subject is not structurally well defined in the grammar of Mandarin" (Li and Thompson 1981: 19), I will approach this structure from a functional perspective and use "theme" to refer to the first element in the clause, as it is relevant to discourse and reflects the syntax of Chinese. For the element like *chetai* I will use the term "second theme". Themes are ordinally numbered because there may even be a third theme in a Chinese clause, as shown later in this paper. For the rest of the clause I will use the term "rheme". Whichever way the structure is analyzed, there is a nexus within the clause. Chinese abounds with such sentences, and *zhege nanren gezi gao* ("this man height tall") and *xiangbizi chang* ("elephant nose long") are examples. The same analysis may also apply to 4C, 8C, and 10C.

Both English and Chinese have a number of structural resources that facilitate the choice of one of the two structures. But how do they function? What determines the choice in either case? The answers to both of these questions are found at the discourse level, and I shall examine the context in which the structure is chosen.

Discourse determined. Functional grammar is designed to account for how language is used. Its two important features are its orientation to meaning and its orientation to text. To understand why English and Chinese differ in the choice of the two structures it is necessary to see how each organizes its text and how each encodes meaning.

The choice of one or the other structure is textually determined. It is the discourse organization that calls for the choice in either language. Examine the following text examples:

Text 1
Q: Why did you come to school by bus?
A: I had a flat tire.

Text 2
Q: Could you lend me your car?
A: Oh, sorry. It has got a flat tire.

To achieve cohesion and coherence in Text 1, "I" is used as the theme to set up a cohesive tie with "you" in the preceding sentence. In Text 2, "it" is used to refer anaphorically to "your car", part of the rheme in the preceding sentence. The theme is chosen to ensure that the text is coherently organized. Since "I" and "it" are used as themes, it is impossible to start the sentence with "the tire". This makes it necessary to use a junction "flat tire" as the rheme showing what the speaker sees as the important information for the hearer to pay attention to. If the question in Text 1 is asked in Chinese the answer is usually:

wo chetai biele
("I car tire flat PARTICLE")
or *chetai biele*
("car tire flat particle")
or *tai biele*.
("tire flat PARTICLE")

The answer to the question in Text 2 must be:

chetai biele
("car tire flat particle")
or *tai biele*
("tire flat PARTICLE")

Wo ("I") is used to relate to *ni* ("you") in the question, but the personal pronoun is optional in everyday conversational Chinese. It is more often than not omitted and the answer will be like the second with *chetai* as the theme. An even simpler answer is possible using *tai* ("tire") instead of *chetai* ("car tire"), for *che* ("car") is understood from the context. In the answer to the second question no pronoun is used, for Chinese makes a sparing use of *ta* ("it") which, when used, sounds more or less foreign. Thus *chetai* is placed at the initial position as the theme. Here *che*, which occurs in the question, is repeated to make the answer relevant, but since it is made the theme or second theme in the Chinese translation of Text 1, the adjective *bie* can only occur in the rheme to show the state the *chetai* is in. The result is a nexus.

Thematic development correlates with the structure of a text. The following texts conform to the major patterns of theme-rheme (T-R) progression in English. (Parts I wish to emphasize appear in bold print.)

Text 3: Six months later he had a heart attack. It was a **mild one.**

The thematic development of Text 3 may be presented as T1-R1 for the first sentence and T2(=R1)-R2 for the second sentence. "It" in the second sentence refers back to "a heart attack" as part of the rheme in the preceding sentence, and yet "one" also stands for the same noun phrase and therefore has to be preceded by a modifier to present what is important in the message. This results in the use of a junction in which the attributive adjective "mild" bears the focal stress with "one" weakly stressed.

The counterpart of Text 3 in Chinese is something like *Liu ge yue hou ta xinzangbing fazuo, bijiao qing* ("six month after he heart trouble attack comparative mild"). The Chinese translation of the second English sentence is a nexus with a zero pronoun as the theme, so what is explicitly expressed is the adjective *qing* modified by *bijiao* ("comparatively") which, like emphasizer *hen*, is inserted to make the sentence flow more smoothly. As mentioned above, Chinese rarely uses *ta* ("it"). The nexus is added to the previous statement as part of the sentence. By parataxis the two nexuses are related, clarifying what the predicative adjective refers to.

To this we may add the following similar examples:

Text 4: On his desk there was a letter. **It was a short one.**

Text 5: And for the first time Jordan laughed. **He had a great laugh.** It washed away the remoteness and coldness you always felt coming off him.

Text 4 displays the same pattern of thematic progression as Text 3. In Text 5, however, the pattern is T1-R1, T2(=T1)-R2(=R1), T3(=R2)-R3. In Text 5, "laugh" in the second sentence needs a premodifier to make the rheme newsworthy.

For the junction in the parts of Text 4 and Text 5 in bold print, the Chinese translations would have a similar rendering into a nexus with a zero pronoun—*hen kailang* ("very cheerful"), *hen duan* ("very short")—as part of the sentence, just as the Chinese translation of Text 3. Thematic progression in the structure of the text calls for the choice of junction in English and of nexus in Chinese.

In English, "there is a feeling that the predicate of a clause should where possible be longer than the subject, thus a principle of structural compensation comes into force" (Quirk et al. 1985: 1401). For "He smoked", English prefers "He had a smoke." Text 5 shows that such a syntactic process is a valuable resource for textual structure. But in many cases the noun is a repetition of its corresponding verb in the preceding sentence, which makes it necessary to modify the action noun to make the rheme newsworthy. Sentences like "She has a fine laugh" is frequently used in spoken and written texts. This is in fact one of the means by which a text can be given added unity and coherence. It is also conducive to the employment of junctions in English.

Another aspect of discourse structure is local discourse organization. Text often consists of subtexts, each having its local structure that contributes to the macrostructure of the text. The kind of local organization that is relevant to this discussion contains a number of sentences or clauses, all of which maintain a unified orientation. This particular local organization is further constrained in that it forms a segment of the theme of the paragraph in which it occurs. It usually consists of three elements that are successively ordered: (1) Initiation, which is usually realized as an objective account or description, or a statement of fact; (2) continuation, which takes the form of further elaboration or description, or states the consequence; and (3) conclusion which, referring back to the previous statements, offers a subjective comment, generalization, or summary.

> Text 6: Early this morning he had put his name on the list for the telephone, and so had been able to make a call to his wife just a little while ago. **It had been a merry call.**

The first clause is a statement of fact—what happened, or what "he" did "early this morning". As the first element it serves to initiate the local organization. Then comes the second element, introduced by "and so" but with the subject ellipted, which states the consequence of the previous action. Finally comes the conclusion, which begins with "it", referring back to "a call" in the second clause. Then in the rheme the word "call" is repeated, which would convey no information unless it is modified. It is the modifier that carries the focus and gives new information. This form of local organization calls for the use of a junction. As a segment it serves to develop the central theme of showing how Norman Mailer was anxious to get out of jail.

A few more examples will show that this kind of local discourse organization is fairly systematic:

Text 7: The solution, then, was television. Here the candidate could address the electorate effectively, but at a safe remove; **it was a costly procedure, but a prudent one**.

Text 8: I wanted to be honorable because I felt more comfortable telling the truth than lying. I felt more at ease innocent that guilty. I had thought it out. **It was a pragmatic desire, not a romantic one**.

The third element in each of the two texts serves to offer a judgment. The pronoun "it" refers back to the previous statements, and the nouns "procedure" and "desire" serve to sum up what is said in the previous clauses. The focus falls on the adjectives in the junctions. "One" is used as a prop word to present a contrast in either case.

However, in many cases the second element is optional, as can be seen in the following texts:

Text 9: The orchestra leader ... signaled for "Chinatown, My Chinatown." **It was a well-intentioned but entirely superfluous gesture.**

Text 10: They had to stop twice because Billy got car-sick, but aside for that the trip was **a pleasant one**.

The subjective conclusion comes immediately after the objective statement of fact. This kind of local discourse organization is possible partly because English has a fairly large number of nouns—such as "account", "charge", "criticism", "excuse", "question", "reference", and "warning"—which can be used to refer back in a general way to what has already been said. They refer to whole sections of spoken or written text (Sinclair 1990: 389). Observe the following:

Text 11: "I must go. I've taken a leave of absence at school."
"For how long?" **It was a nervous question.**

Sometimes we find minor sentences, which are just junctions, used as the third element:

Text 12: Malomar had the rest of the day and evening scheduled for the cutting room. **His greatest pleasure**.

Text 13: "Your father's blood," his mother said. **Dreadful charge**.

As "it is" or "it was" has low information value, their deletion will not affect comprehension on the part of the hearer or reader.

This kind of English discourse segment can be transplanted into Chinese, for the elements are logically arranged. But in Chinese the third element will in most cases take the form of a nexus. A few examples will make the point clear. The final clause in Text 6 is likely to be translated as:

Dianhua shang liao de hen kaixin.
("telephone on talk PARTICLE very delightful")
Our talk on the phone was delightful.

The last clause in Text 7 finds its Chinese counterpart like this:

zheyang zuo huaqian hen duo dan bijiao jinshen.
("this way do cost very much but relatively prudent")
It costs much but is prudent to do like this.

The change in structure is necessary because a similar local discourse organization in Chinese usually ends with a nexus:

Text 14:
Ta zai yinian zhinei dapo liangci shijie jilu shifen nande.
("he in one year within break twice world record very rare")
He's broken a world record twice in one year. It's a rare feat.

The first part of the sentence states a fact and the last gives a comment, using a nexus with a zero pronoun.

So far I have shown the difference between English and Chinese in the choice of the two structures: Where English favors a junction, Chinese favors a nexus. But this does not mean that English does not employ a nexus in which an adjective is used predicatively, nor that Chinese avoids the use of a junction in which an adjective is used attributively. Alongside "She is a pretty woman," English has "She is pretty." But there is a subtle semantic difference between the two constructions. While the junction puts an entity into a specific class giving it some kind of permanent feature, the nexus usually has a temporary reference. This difference can be tested by adding an adverb of time like "today" to the two sentences. It would be acceptable to say "She is pretty today," but people are not likely to make such a remark as "She is a pretty woman today." This test brings out the distinction between the temporary and the permanent. The same is true of the semantic difference between "He is skeptical" and "He is a skeptical man." The former may imply that he is skeptical about something specific, while the latter ascribes a permanent feature to "he" to mean "He is generally skeptical about things." Similarly "a courteous man" is a man who is courteous normally, not merely at this moment. This permanent feature of an English junction may justify the use of a junction in the third element of the discourse segments discussed above. Some kind of stable quality is compatible with the function of the element of conclusion.

A subtle semantic distinction between a junction and a nexus is also found in Chinese, but it is of a different kind. While a nexus is a straightforward statement in Chinese, a junction may admit of more than one interpretation. Compare the following:

Zhe ben shu hen hao.
("this QUANTIFIER book very good)
This book is good.

Zhe shi ben hao shu.
("this is QUANITIFER good book")
This is a good book.

The first sentence simply means that the book is well written or informative. The junction *hao shu* may have the same meaning, but it may also mean a book free from filth and pornography. Compare also:

Ta hen congming.
(he very clever)
He is very clever.

Ta shi ge congming ren.
("he is QUANITIFIER clever man")
He is a clever man.

The first sentence has only one reading. But in the second sentence, *congming ren* may imply—often in a derogatory way—that *ta* is one that has common sense and knows what to do for his own good. Because of its clarity of meaning, the Chinese nexus lends itself to frequent use in discourse.

It must be noted that English also makes use of nexus with an adjective as the subject complement. The choice is made because of the temporary sense of the predicative adjective and is determined by discourse organization.

Text 15: Suddenly Cleo starts laughing and points ... Tessa is staring too, **only her eyes are big**, her mouth dropping open.

The part in bold print is a clause in which "her eyes" is used as the theme, because the word is semantically associated with "staring" in the previous clause. Thus the two clauses cohere through an association of lexical meaning. The nexus presents a temporary state: While "Tessa is staring", she keeps her eyes wide open. If "she" became the theme, there would be a junction, like "She has big eyes", suggesting a permanent feature that is somewhat out of place in this context.

Chinese sometimes uses junction with an adjective as a premodifier.

Text 16:
Na ge guniang sheng de gao biliang, da yanjing, shencai gaogao de, zhuangjian de hen.
("that girl grow PARTICLE high nose ridge big eyes height tall PARTICLE healthy PARTICLE very")
The girl has a long-bridged nose and big eyes. She is tall and healthy.

Here the subject complement consists of two junctions that run parallel, followed by two parallel nexuses. It would sound unnatural if only one junction were used. Most Chinese would consider the sentence incomplete if it ended with the second junction. One would expect the description to go on until one reaches a nexus. This has much to do with the information structure in Chinese, discussed in the next section.

Typological differences. There are typological differences between English and Chinese in how a message is presented and how information is structured. Each clause has a thematic structure, which assigns the functions theme and rheme. Thematic status is signaled in English by initial position in the clause. This is also assumed to be the case in Chinese. Information structure is not directly determined by the clause, but by the information unit. Information units are signaled in the spoken language as tone groups. Each tone group contains information which is presented as given and information which is presented as new. (For a detailed discussion see Fries 1992.) The theme is the point of departure for the clause as a message. The speaker has, within certain limits, the option of selecting any element in the clause as theme.

In the English language data presented in this paper, the theme is in most cases realized as a pronoun—most often "it", a personal pronoun, or the existential "there". This conforms to Halliday's observations, which ordered themes as follows: The item most often functioning as an unmarked theme in a declarative clause is the first person pronoun "I"; after that comes the other personal pronouns—"you", "we", "he", "she", "it", and "they"—and the impersonal pronouns—"it" and "there"; then come other nominal groups (Halliday 1985: 45). In English the theme in a clause is justifiably referred to as a peg on which the message is hung. It is not the peg that really counts; it is the message that hangs on it that really matters. Thus the theme in an English clause has low information value. Conversely in Chinese, theme is not just a peg or a starting point for the information, but rather it is the basis on which the information is built. In Chinese the theme assumes a more important role than it does in English. Two facts testify to this:

(1) Theme in Chinese is more often realized as noun phrases—as in 5C, 6C, and 9C—rather than pronominal substitutes.

(2) Even when the clause begins with a pronoun, it is often followed by a second theme to specify what is being talked about—as in 1C, 4C, 8C, and 12C.

Sometimes there is a third theme in the clause:

Text 17:
Jiali renren sheti jiankang.
("family everyone body health")
Everybody in the family is in good health.

Here *jiali* ("family") and *renren* ("everyone") stand in a part-whole relationship in which the first theme is the whole of which the second theme is a part. The second theme is possessed by the first. Similarly the third theme, *jiankang* ("health") is possessed by the second. The sense of the clause is made progressively more and more specific. It is the third theme that specifies what is really being talked about. In contrast to the English clause, in which the principle of end weight leads to a structural compensation that requires the predicate to be longer than the subject, the Chinese clause tends to be top-heavy, giving the theme more weight. Thus the rheme in English tends to be more complicated than the rheme in Chinese. This difference entails the difference in the choice of the two structures. In English information structure, given information is always realized by an element that is linguistically definite or generic. In Chinese, however, there is no overt distinction between generic and specific, definite and indefinite. It is the initial position in the clause that makes an element definite or generic. This gives Chinese more freedom in thematic choice. In the above example *jiali* is made definite by its initial position, referring to a family that the speaker expects the hearer to know. In English, the principle of end focus reserves the end position of the clause for new information. "Flat tire" in "I have got a flat tire" bears focal prominence. The same tendency obtains in Chinese in *wo chetai biele*, where *biele* bears the nucleus. End focus usually highlights new information, but in Chinese the tendency is more pronounced than in English:

> Text 18:
> *Xue yingyu de ren yuelaiyueduo.*
> ("study English PARTICLE people more and more")
> More and more people are studying English.

In the English translation of Text 18, the focus is on "more and more". But in its Chinese counterpart, *yuelaiyueduo* still comes at the end of the clause. The tendency to place end focus on the new information in Chinese may account for the use of a nexus to end a discourse segment, for the predicative adjective unmistakably has focal prominence.

The difference in the choice of the two structures also sheds light on the typological difference between English and Chinese. The thematic choice in the languages points to the fact that English is a subject prominent language while Chinese is a theme prominent language. The frequent use in English of pronominal substitutes as unmarked themes—i.e. both as theme and subject—is the result of making the clauses conform to the syntactic patten embodying the subject-predicate relation. However in Chinese, the use of noun phrases as theme/subjects, and the reinforcement of the theme by a second or even third theme, testify to the fact that Chinese is a language in which theme is prominent. This typological difference has direct bearing on the ordering of elements in the thematic structure. English orders its elements in the clause by consideration of grammatical functions, whereas in Chinese "the order is governed to a large extent by consideration of meaning" (Li and Thompson 1981: 20). As has been stated, Chinese has more freedom to choose any element for the theme in a clause. For instance it is common in Chinese to say:

> Text 18
> *Zhege xiaoxi zhidao de ren bu duo.*
> ("this news know PARTICLE people not many")
> There are few people who know this news.

In Chinese *zhege xiaoxi* ("this news") is made the theme. But in English, it is hardly possible to make "this news" the theme and say "This news there are few people who know." Text 18 shows that a Chinese speaker may place what is uppermost in his mind at the moment in the initial position without regard to the grammatical relation between the theme and the verb. This is especially true when the first element is followed by a nexus in which another noun phrase serves to set the frame for the presentation of the theme. Neither the notion of subject nor the subject-predicate relation in English totally applies to Chinese.

Subject and theme are concepts that belong to different levels of linguistic study. The subject is a syntactic element that is related to grammar, whereas the theme is a discourse element that is related to the organization of meaning. In light of this it may be sensible to regard English as a sentence-oriented language and Chinese as a discourse-oriented language. An example taken from a Chinese newspaper will make the point:

> Text 19:
> *Shi zhi shen qiu, tianqi jian han, zhouye wencha da, zheduanshijian xiaohai kesou fabinglu gao shijian chang, guanyu man.*
> ("time happen deep autumn weather gradual cold day and night temperature difference big, this period child cough incidence high time long, recover slow")
> It was late autumn. It is getting cold with a great difference in temperature between day and night. During this period children are liable to have a bad cough. It lasts long and recovery is slow.

The single Chinese sentence consists of six nexuses, each with its own theme and rheme in thematic structure, but the English translation has four sentences, of which three have "it" as the theme. The Chinese sentence is in fact a subtext. In terms of rhetorical structure, the first three nexuses combine to provide the background, the fourth is the nucleus, and the last two perform the function of elaboration. They are so related semantically that they are logically sequenced together to serve the communicative goal of the speaker. They constitute a semantic unit, which is what grammarians call "text". Halliday defines "text" as a semantic unit, realized as lexicogrammatical units (1975: 23). Furthermore, the six clauses cannot be made sentences, although there are no overt connecters between them. It is meaning that binds them together. To separate them would damage the coherent flow of the language. Text 19 thus indicates that Chinese is a text- or discourse-oriented language.

Cultural impact. How is it that English and Chinese function the way they do? The factors that shape the languages can be found in their cultures.

Halliday defines semiotics as the study of sign systems—in other words, as the study of meaning in its most general sense. Linguistics, then, is a kind of semiotics. It is an aspect of the study of meaning. Language is the most important way of conveying meaning. But there are many other modes to convey meaning, in any culture, which are outside the realm of language. These will include both art forms—such as painting, sculpture, music, dance, etc.—and other modes of cultural behavior such as modes of exchange, structures of the family, among others. All of these things bear meaning in a culture. Indeed we can define a culture as a set of semiotic systems—a set of systems of meaning, all of which interrelate (Halliday and Hasan 1989: 4). It then follows that a language, whether Chinese or English, is interrelated with other kinds of semiotic systems and shaped by the culture in which it is used.

China has a long cultural heritage. Insofar as this cultural heritage bears on the Chinese language, two features stand out prominently. One feature is its dynamism. In Chinese philosophy, "change" is the word. Traditionally, Chinese philosophy makes a distinction between "the formal" and the "formless". The two notions were interpreted in different ways by different schools of thought, but it was a consensus view among ancient Chinese philosophers that the formal and the formless represent two stages in the flow of *qi*, that is *yin* and *yang*. This means that one can change into the other. There are sayings that embody such a philosophical idea of change in Chinese:

- "Running water is never stale and a door-hinge never gets worm-eaten."
- "As there is no definite shape for water, so there is no fixed strategy for the military."

Thus things are viewed as constantly moving and changing. In Chinese painting, painters usually take a nonfocal perspective when they work on landscape. The scenery is presented as if it were viewed by the painter moving from place to place. It is a dynamic way of creating an aesthetic effect and conveying some kind of meaning. In Chinese calligraphy, the essential point is to be natural. To be natural, the calligrapher does not follow any conventional type of arrangement but aims to achieve overall harmony, as in group dancing. For instance what is called "regular script" is characterized by its abstract aesthetic value which can be appreciated without regard to the characters themselves, for each dot or stroke is usually suggestive of something in the outside world and shaped by following the dictates of the mind or will of the calligrapher. He works with facility, making sure to use the right size of characters and to vary the thickness of strokes so that he gives expression to vigor or delicacy as he sees fit. In calligraphy as in the language, what is important varies in the presentation.

We need not look into other realms to see that Chinese culture is characterized by a dynamism that manifests itself in change and variation to achieve a natural, aesthetic value. This feature of Chinese culture has its impact on the Chinese language, making it fluid, pliable, or flexible in comparison with English. Chinese orders the elements in the clause according to the needs of meaning or communication. The elements in the sentence *Tushuguan you mei you zheben shu* ("library have not have this book") can be flexibly ordered in six different ways, but in English the same idea can only be expressed in two ways, "I don't know whether the book is available at the library" or "Whether the book is available at the library, I don't know." As has been shown above in many cases, the Chinese sentence is not a sentence in the sense in which it is used in English. For one thing, Chinese sentences are not well defined. If you leave out all the punctuation marks in a Chinese passage, and ask some people to punctuate it, it is not likely that they will do it in exactly the same way. This means that the same passage may be regarded as consisting of different numbers of sentences to different people. For another, many Chinese sentences defy analysis in terms of a subject–predicate relation. Take 4C for instance:

4C *Ta xindi houdao xingge wenrou keteng, qiliang you da weiren you leguan.*
("She moral nature honest kind character gentle tender tolerance also great disposition also optimistic")

The theme/subject is followed by four nexuses, each ascribing a feature to one aspect of the theme. Having four nexuses as a predicate does not conform to Western grammar, but the use of a series of nexuses in Chinese makes the language flow naturally.

In Western philosophy, "form" means the structure, pattern, organization, or essential nature of anything. Form is thus regarded as the deciding factor. In Western painting, the usual practice is to take a focal perspective with a figure and a background in the picture. There is some kind of form underlying the work of art. In language it is the form of a sentence that determines the construction of utterances. The subject and the predicate are of fundamental importance:

> Any doubts concerning their legitimacy or even their mere usefulness therefore betray a crisis of grammatical thought, a new departure in grammatical thinking. They affect the whole system of grammar and not merely part of it. (Sandman 1954: 1)

Thus English sentences are well defined. It is true that they permit variation, but not to the extent that they deviate from the subject– predicate pattern. This explains why English is sentence-oriented and uses pronominal substitutes as the theme/subject that only perform a structural role, making utterances conform to the form of the sentence. This may also account for its preference for junction.

The other feature of Chinese culture that is related to the Chinese language is explicitness. Another important word in ancient Chinese philosophy—especially in moral philosophy—is *ren* ("benevolence"). *Ren* stands for the most important principle for social behavior and family relations. Of interest in language is *ren*'s application to people who hold different positions in social institutions and the family structure. In 3C we have four adjectives—*ren* ("benevolent"), *liang* ("good"), *ci* ("kind"), and *xiao* ("filial")—each denoting a moral code for people in different positions. Encoded in different words, *ren* is made quite explicit. In addition to the general word *ai* ("love"), Chinese has *ci* ("paternal/ maternal affection"), *xiao* ("filial piety"), and *di* ("brotherly love") to specify different kinds of love between family members. An even more revealing example is the various terms for different relatives for which English has a single word, "uncle": *bo* ("father's elder brother"), *shu* ("father's younger brother"), *jiu* ("mother's brother"), *gufu* ("husband of father's sister"), and *yifu* ("husband of mother's sister"). Here a distinction is made between the maternal side and paternal side, and an even finer distinction is made between the younger and the elder brother of one's father.

Explicitness is not limited to vocabulary, but is also reflected in clause structure. The theme, as has been noted above, may be followed by a second or even a third theme. The tendency is to move from the general to the specific, progressively narrowing down what is being talked about, thus achieving explicitness. On the other hand, the choice of a nexus with a predicative adjective probably owes to the effort to avoid the ambiguity that may arise in its corresponding junction containing a premodifier. Furthermore, in translation, Chinese tends to employ a higher-level linguistic unit for the English structure, that is use a phrase for a word, a clause for a phrase, or a sentence for a clause. For instance in "Yet, on these thoughts, he took a drink of water" the prepositional phrase "on these thoughts" must be expanded into a clause in Chinese. Such structural expansion contributes to explicitness in Chinese.

It seems that universal love, which is encouraged in Western culture, makes it unnecessary to specify different kinds of love among people and to distinguish between relatives on the maternal or the paternal side. But at the syntactic level English has its own way achieving explicitness. In complex noun phrases English usually starts with the specific and proceeds to the general. For *jiali ren renren shenti jiankang* ("family everyone body health") in Text 17, English moves the other way round, saying "everybody in the family" or even "the health of everybody in the family." While the elements are linearly sequenced in Chinese, they are hierarchically structured in English with the help of prepositions. But when it comes to the sentence structure, English tends to use hypotaxis, whereas Chinese usually uses parataxis. With the connecters, English sentences are well-knit. In contrast, parataxis renders Chinese sentences loosely structured.

How culture shapes language is a subject that calls for a separate, careful study. What I have been trying to do in this section is to examine the impact of culture on language, which may result in some general features—for instance dynamism and explicitness in Chinese, and form-dominance and compactness in English—that may shed light on language use.

Teaching implications. It is assumed that the difference in the use of the two structures may cause difficulty in foreign language teaching and learning. To find out how Chinese students of English make use of the two structures, I conducted an experiment. The subjects for the study were English majors, twenty from each of three classes: (1) a third year English class (Group A), (2) a fourth year English class (Group B), and (3) graduate students majoring in English language and literature (Group C). Half of each group was asked to do translations from Chinese into English, the other half from English into Chinese. The testing materials were designed so that the English passages contained five junctions that had to be translated into Chinese as nexuses—for instance "It was a cold, clear day"—and the Chinese passages contained eight nexuses that had to be rendered into English as junctions—for example *shenti jiankang* ("body healthy").

The findings did not turn out to be what we expected. Group B did not do much better than Group A, and Group C did slightly better, but the difference in scores was insignificant. Overall the translation from English into Chinese was better: Nearly 85% of the students rightly used nexuses for English junctions. This might be due to their intuition in the Chinese language. But when it came to translation from Chinese into English, the results were far from satisfactory. For Chinese sentences like *wo chetai biele* ("I've got a flat tire"), only 30% of Group C and 10% of Group B gave the correct translation. Noone in Group A used the desired structure. Quite a number of students used sentences like "My tire was flat": 40% in Group A, 30% in Group B, and 10% in Group C. This was not surprising, for teachers of English often come across sentences like "My family is big" in their students' essays. Grammatically there seems to be nothing wrong about the sentence, but it sounds foreign to native speakers of English. The findings indicated that while the students advance in their studies, they become only dimly aware of the differences in the use of the two structures.

The difficulty that Chinese students have in using English junctions was incidentally confirmed by a student project which aimed to find out how linguistic difficulty and content familiarity affect Chinese students' reading comprehension. As part of the testing materials, a text was simplified by a well-educated native speaker of English. Unexpectedly, the subjects—second year English majors—found the simplified version more difficult than the original. The students' rating for the degree of difficulty for the simplified version was 1.88, but for the original was 1.67. It was this anomaly that attracted my attention. On a close examination of the two texts I found there were sixteen changes made in the simplified version, out of which nine involved the substitution of a familiar word for a more difficult one—for instance "defeated" for "eliminated", "won" for "triumphed", and "reached" for "advanced to"—and in three of which the original structure was expanded, for instance an infinitive phrase "to qualify for the finals" was expanded into a clause "The Czech pair were now ready for the finals." It was quite obvious that all of these changes made the text easier. However, the other four changes involved a condensation of the structures. In two of these changes we found the use of a single verb "consulted" for "had a consultation", and a participial phrase "Having played together" for a clause "as we had played together". The other two changes were brought about by replacing nexuses with junctions: "P and H were boisterously greeted" was replaced by "boisterous greetings"; and "We lost the first game 9–21, which was quite disappointing" was replaced by "We lost the first game—a disappointing 9–21." The comparison may suggest an explanation for the anomaly: These last four changes that create compactness—a prominent feature of English—may cause difficulty to Chinese students of English. This includes changes from nexuses to junctions. We may, therefore, be justified in saying that junction, as compared to nexus, is more difficult to Chinese students in their comprehension. What difficulty American students of Chinese may have in using nexuses we cannot say for certain. But we shall not be surprised if some of them use sentences like *woyou ge bietai* ("I have a flat tire").

Conclusion. Our study suggests that while two languages may share the same structures in their language systems, they may also differ in how they use those structures. In communication the difference emerges, and discourse organization calls for the different choice. The study may also be seen as providing an insight into the relation between grammar and discourse: Grammar provides a basis for discourse analysis, and discourse perspectives may help to account for lexicogrammatical features, such as the use of "one" in the rheme in English and the use of more than one theme in Chinese. In our study, the differences in the choice of the two structures shed light on typological differences between English and Chinese, and may bc attributable to the difference between the two cultures. In foreign language teaching it is not enough to acquaint the students with the rules of the language systems. The differences in language use should be brought to their attention as well, so that they will make a conscious effort to prevent mother tongue interference and use the right structures.

REFERENCES

Cao, Xuegin. 1982. *A dream of red mansions*. Peijing: People's Literature Press.
Chomsky, Noam. 1957. *Syntactic Structures*. The Hague: Mouton.

Fries, Peter H. 1993. "Information flow in written advertising". In James E. Alatis (ed.), *Language, communication, and social meaning*. Georgetown University Round Table on Languages and Linguistics 1992. Washington, D.C.: Georgetown University Press. 336–352.

Gleason, Henry A., Jr. 1965. *Linguistics and English grammar*. New York: Holt, Rinehart and Winston.

Halliday, M.A.K. 1967. "Notes on transitivity and theme in English, (Part I)". *Journal of Linguistics* 3(1): 37–81.

Halliday, M.A.K. 1975. *Learning how to mean: Explorations in the development of language*. London: Edward Arnold.

Halliday, M.A.K. 1985. *Introduction to functional grammar*. London: Edward Arnold.

Halliday, M.A.K. and Hasan, Ruqaiya. 1989. *Language, context and text: Aspects of language in a social-semiotic perspective*. Oxford University Press.

Jespersen, Otto. 1924. *The philosophy of grammar*. London: George Allen & Unwin Ltd.

Jespersen, Otto. 1933. *Essentials of English grammar*. London: George Allen & Unwin Ltd.

Jespersen, Otto. 1937. *Analytic syntax*. Chicago: University of Chicago Press.

Li, Charles N. and Sandra A. Thompson. 1981. *Mandarin Chinese: A functional reference grammar*. Berkeley and Los Angeles: University of California Press.

Mailer, Norman. 1968. *The armies of the night: History as a novel, the novel as history*. New York: New American Library.

Quirk, Randolph, et al. 1972. *A grammar of contemporary English*. London: Longman.

Quirk, Randolph, et al. 1985. *A comprehensive grammar of the English Language*. New York: Longman.

Shaw, Irwin. 1969. *Rich man, poor man*. New York: Dell.

Sheldon, Sidney. 1982. *The master of the game*. New York: Warner.

Sinclair, John (ed.). 1990. *Collins cobuild English grammar*. London: Collins.

Tan, Amy. 1989. *The joy luck club*. New York: Ivy.

Wood, F.T. 1981. *Current English usage*. London: Macmillan.

Yang, Frederick M. 1958. *Song of youth*. Peijing: Writers' Press.

Yang, Shuo. 1978. *Selected essays by Yang Shuo*. PBeijing: People's Literature Press.

Teaching global interdependence as a subversive activity

H. Douglas Brown
San Francisco State University

Nagasaki is one of my favorite Japanese cities. All the advantages of an urban center are present, but one can very quickly escape to its surrounding mountains and look down at the beautiful fjord-like inlets characteristic of the western side of Kyushu. It was here that I had the privilege a few years ago of visiting the Nagasaki Peace Museum, commemorating the dreadful event of August 9, 1945. After a sobering walk through three of its five floors, each with vivid depictions of the catastrophic destruction, I asked my gracious hostess to escort me out. I couldn't bear to see the other two floors.

A few years earlier, my family and I visited the Arizona Memorial in Pearl Harbor, Hawaii, a somber reminder of the attack on Pearl Harbor, December 7, 1941. Among those touring the site that day were people from many different countries. At the end of the guided tour, as we exited the area, a Japanese couple—obviously shaken by the experience—turned to us and said, "We are so sorry."

These two incidents are indelibly etched into my memory. Both are dramatic reminders of the consequences of choices that human beings made some five decades ago, but more importantly, both are reminders of the collective guilt we feel as interdependent human beings inhabiting this globe. Can we harness such guilt-driven emotions, turn them around into positive, assertive action for peaceful coexistence, and guide them toward productive educational programs? I think we can. I think we must. But sometimes doing so involves a degree of "subversive activity" in our classrooms.

Teaching as a subversive activity. Twenty-five years ago, Neil Postman and Charles Weingartner (1969) shook a few educational foundations with their best-seller, *Teaching as a subversive activity.* In this stinging critique of American educational systems, they described our schools as "entropic, ... the tendency of all systems to 'run down,' reduce to chaos and uselessness" (3) and challenged schools to become anti-entropic:

> What is the necessary business of the schools? To create eager consumers? To transmit the dead ideas, values, metaphors, and information of [a

> century] ago? To create smoothly functioning bureaucrats? These aims are truly subversive since they undermine our chances of surviving as a viable, democratic society. And they do their work in the name of convention and standard practice. We would like to see the schools go into the anti-entropy business. Now, that is subversive, too. But the purpose is to subvert attitudes, beliefs, and assumptions that foster chaos and uselessness. (15)

Students, according to Postman and Weingartner, need to become "crap detectors" who can deal with (a) major *changes* in our social, economic, and political systems, (b) burgeoning *bureaucracies* (repositories of conventional assumptions and standard practices), and (c) a communications revolution in which the *mass media* is creating its own version of censorship. "There are many forms of censorship, and one of them is to deny access to 'loudspeakers' to those with dissident ideas, or even any ideas. This is easy to do (and not necessarily conspiratorial) when the loudspeakers are owned and operated by mammoth corporations with enormous investments in their proprietorship" (9).

Those words were printed in 1969. Now, a quarter of a century later, isn't it ironic

- that we are still beset with the very same problems in our educational systems?
- that we still haven't truly been effective in subverting the attitudes, beliefs, and assumptions that foster chaos and uselessness?
- that many of our schools have fallen into pedagogical disrepair as we dribble fewer and fewer dollars into public school budgets?
- that, more than ever, "subversive" teachers are few and far between?

The call for subversive teaching is a challenge all teachers can and should take up in the present day. Those of us who teach languages have a special responsibility to subvert attitudes and beliefs and assumptions

- that language teaching is neutral, sterile, and inorganic and has nothing to do with political issues
- that global conflict and other forms of international aggression are no longer serious threats in the "post-cold-war" era
- that there is no particular urgency to act assertively to stave off an imminent global environmental crisis.

It is this last topic—environmental interdependence—that I would now call to your attention as a rallying point for subversive activity in our language classrooms.

A Western view of progress. One of the major causes of what I see as an impending worldwide environmental crisis is something that may loosely be termed a "Western" view of progress. Much of current Western thought and morality is colored by Judeo-Christian and Cartesian beliefs. Genesis 1:28 depicts God commanding human beings to "subdue" the Earth and have "dominion" over "every living thing that moves on the Earth." Descartes likewise viewed the natural world as a resource to be managed. In this reductionist view that has now come to characterize not just Western thinking, but "modern" thinking in general, human beings are seen both as objective, autonomously rational observers of the world and as "masters and processors of nature." (Descartes 1637: 119) Science therefore becomes a means of controlling and *perfecting* nature for human ends. So-called advanced modern science and technology are based on a root metaphor or worldview in which human beings are *not* interdependent with natural systems. Instead, as Bowers and Flinders (1990: 229) note, "... the environment has been viewed as a resource to be exploited and, in more progressive circles, to be 'managed.' ... The modern Western mindset ... views the future in terms of an ever-widening expansion of economic development, technological possibilities, and personal freedoms."

Bowers and Flinders (1990: 249) see the need for altering basic cultural foundations in order even to begin to solve the problem:

> The conceptual foundation of industrial society (and now the society of the "information age") has been based on assumptions that, if we continue to live by them, will further accelerate the rate of environmental damage. ... In effect, the evidence of environmental disruption and system breakdown is a clear message that our most basic cultural assumptions are going to have to be reexamined and, in many instances, reconstituted in ways that take into account the interdependence of culture and natural environment.

The global environmental crisis that we now find ourselves on the verge of experiencing may well be impossible to prevent. Clearly, in a world where *economic* equilibrium is directly linked to technology, which is in turn firmly rooted in a "subdue-the-Earth" ethic, the prospect of adjusting cultural patterns around the world to achieve global *ecological* balance is even more formidable than the prospect of world peace!

Ecology and interdependence. In contrast to the Cartesian worldview is Gregory Bateson's metaphor of an ecology: a natural system that includes humans and other life forms sustained through information and energy exchanges. "The unit of survival is not the breeding organism, or the family line, or the society. ... The unit of survival is a flexible organism-in-its-environment. ... Thus, in no system ... can any part have unilateral control over the whole" (Bateson 1972: 451, 316). Perhaps if our educational institutions—and I daresay our language classrooms—were themselves more responsive and responsible, we might not place the self on such a lofty Cartesian throne. Instead, we might see the interdependence of life on this planet.

The ecology metaphor is exemplified in the ethic and religion of many Native American cultures. Jamake Highwater (1981: 18) once noted:

> From the Native American perspective the most fearsome dogma of Western reality is probably the fact that personal identity is both absolute and final at the same time that it is unavoidably public. It is inconceivable to the traditional Indian that the self is not allowed to exist in the West unless it is willing to be on perpetual public display. Indians find it incredible that a person must retain one identity, one name, one persona for his or her entire existence, no matter what immense changes may take place in that person's life. These contrasting attitudes about personal realities and the place of the self in the group make it clear that there are great differences between the way Indians and people of the West regard identity.

This contrast in culture was poignantly illustrated in 1854 when President Franklin Pierce made an offer for a large area of Indian land in the Pacific Northwest. Following are some excerpts of the eloquent reply given by Chief Sealth (Seattle):

> When the Great Chief in Washington sends word that he wishes to buy our land, he asks much of us. How can you buy or sell the sky, the warmth of the land? The idea is strange to us. If we do not own the freshness of the air and sparkle of the water, how can you buy them?
>
> Every part of the earth is sacred to my people. Every shining pine needle, every sandy shore, every mist in the dark woods, every clearing, every humming insect, the sap which courses through the trees—these carry the memories of the red man.
>
> We are part of the earth and it is part of us. The perfumed flowers are our sisters, the deer, the horse, the great eagle, these are our brothers. The rocky crests, the juices in the meadows, the body heat of the pony, and man—all belong to the same family.
>
> This shining water that moves in the streams and rivers is not just water but the blood of our ancestors. Each ghostly reflection in the clear water of the

lakes tells us of events and memories of the life of my people. The water's murmur is *the voice* of my father's father.

How can you buy or sell this sky, this land, this water? I do not know. Our ways are different from your ways. The sight of your cities pains the eyes of the red man. But perhaps it is because the red man is a savage and does not understand.

Responsive language teaching. Bowers and Flinders (1990) remind educators everywhere that *responsive* teachers will treat the classroom itself as an ecology of behavioral, mental, and cultural patterns. Responsive teachers, as I view the term, empower not only themselves but also their students by squarely facing issues of ultimate importance to the lives of students. We teachers are "transformative intellectuals," Giroux and McLaren remind us, "who connect pedagogical theory and practice to wider social issues ... and embody in our teaching a vision of a better and more humane life" (1989: xiii). Surely, then, our commission as teachers includes the goal of helping learners to become informed about the crucial issues that intrinsically affect their lives. We as Earth's stewards, rather than seeking further "dominion" over the planet's life, are more likely to "be fruitful ... and replenish the Earth" (Genesis 1:28) by helping our students to engage in an international, cross-cultural dialogue.

That dialogue is taking place across the TESOL profession in multiple contexts. A brief set of examples of how the dialogue is manifesting itself:

- NYSTESOL's *Idiom* recently (1993–1994) published an issue exclusively devoted to peace and environmental education.
- In Japan, a special interest group on "Global Issues in Language Education" is going strong with a bimonthly newsletter and many supporters.
- Recent issues of two of Japan's major language teaching periodicals, *The language teacher* and *Cross currents,* featured special issues on global educational language teaching activities.
- One of the 1993 issues of *TESOL matters* published material by Darlene Larson and Sylvia Mulling on peace/global education.
- Hockman, Lee-Fong, and Lew (1991) have compiled a large number of activities for teaching global and environmental education in the ESL classroom, called "ESL: Earth Saving Language."
- *The English teaching forum,* a periodical published by the United States Information Agency, devoted its October 1993 issue exclusively to "Environment and ESL," complete with a plethora of practical activities for EFL classrooms.

- The latest National Symposium on English Teaching in Egypt focused on teaching English in a "global age," highlighted by presentations on global/environmental education.
- A 1993 catalogue called *Global education* is replete with dozens of pages of materials for teaching environmental awareness and action in K–12 classrooms.

I hope that you are or soon will be incorporating into your classrooms the critical thinking implied in such activity. This kind of subversive teaching helps our students not just to become aware of information, but to become participants in a global partnership of involvement in solution-seeking. The little differences here and there that teachers make can add up to breaking the perilous momentum of the now worldwide mindset that gives transitory technological progress priority over basic survival. If we don't act swiftly and decisively, we or our children may witness "The Death of the Earth," as poetically and dramatically depicted by Abraham Akaka of Honolulu's Kawaihao Church:

> It began with the processions of gods departing. Pele, who would no more do her earthbuilding fiery dances. Laka, who would no more hula nature's lovely nuances of joy. Kane, who would no longer green the islands.
>
> Hawaii's gods joined the parade of departing deities, back toward the darkness and formlessness and void that was, before God said, "let there be light." And then we saw the Earth die. And we died with her. We could see no more.
>
> We smelled the Earth die in its searing acid breath. And we died with her. We could smell no more.
>
> We felt Mother Earth die, her great heart broken, the cells of her beautiful body put asunder, no more to bring forth life, and we died with her. We could feel no more.
>
> We heard the Earth die, with a great ghastly groan. And we heard God's voice saying, "I gave you freedom to choose—between death and life, between hate and love, between greed and giving, between wasting and renewing." And God wept—and he left to tend his other planets.

REFERENCES

Bateson, Gregory. 1972. *Steps to an ecology of mind.* New York: Ballantine.

Bowers, C.A. and David J. Flinders. 1990. *Responsive teaching: An ecological approach to classroom patterns of language, culture, and thought.* New York: Teachers College Press.

Descartes, Réné. 1637. "Discourse on Method, Part IV." In E.S. Haldane and G.R.T. Ross (eds.), 1955, *Philosophical works of Descartes.* New York: Dover.

Giroux, Henry A. and Peter L. McLaren. 1989. *Critical pedagogy, the state, and cultural struggle.* Albany, N.Y.: State University of New York Press.

Highwater, Jamake. 1981. *The primal mind: Vision and reality in Indian America.* New York: New American Library.

Hockman, Barbara, Kim Lee-Fong, and Eunice Lew. 1991. "ESL: Earth saving language." Workshop presented at the TESOL Convention, New York, March 1991.

Postman, Neil and Charles Weingartner. 1969. *Teaching as a subversive activity.* New York: Dell.

Educational linguistics and the knowledge base of language teaching[1]

Donald Freeman
School for International Training

Introduction. In 1989, I made a statement that has come back to haunt me. In an article titled, "Teacher training, development, and decision-making: A model of teaching and related strategies in language teacher education," which appeared in the *TESOL Quarterly,* I argued that the knowledge that teachers use in teaching languages[2] differs from the disciplinary knowledge that commonly defines the field. I wrote:

> Applied linguistics, research in second language acquisition, and methodology each contribute to the knowledge on which language teaching is based, but they are not, and must not be, confused with language teaching itself. They are ancillary to it and thus they should not be the primary subject of language teacher education. (Freeman 1989: 29)

This formulation caused a great deal of discussion. A recent electronic mail exchange gives some of the flavor of the argument:

> I am deeply concerned that more and more people believe Freeman's assertion that knowledge of applied linguistics, second language acquisition research, and various methodologies is not central to learning to be a language teacher.

Or another comment:

---

1. Preparation of this paper was supported in part by the Spencer Foundation through a Fellowship grant to the National Academy of Education. The opinions are those of the author and do not reflect positions of the Academy or the Foundation. I thank Patrick Moran and Kathleen Graves for their helpful comments on an earlier draft of this paper.

2. I use the term "languages" or "language teaching" to encompass both second- and foreign-language teaching (see Stern 1983: 15–18).

> Just before [the] TESOL [convention], the "Quote of the Week" was from Donald Freeman's 1989 *TESOL Quarterly* article. It said that applied linguistics, second language acquisition research, and methodology are ancillary to language teacher education. I found that claim rather strange. I thought those three areas represent the core knowledge of that any language teacher should have. Would anyone seriously argue that knowledge of U.S. history is ancillary to American history teacher education?

What has interested me in these responses, and in the broader debate, are the different ways the relationship between teaching knowledge and disciplinary knowledge is perceived and the seeming reluctance to untangle these competing perceptions. In "teaching knowledge" I include what teachers know in order to do what they do in their classrooms; disciplinary knowledge encompasses knowledge of subject matter, about learners and their learning processes, and about teaching as it ought to be done. While the two are not mutually exclusive, neither are they identical.

On one level, this is an argument between descriptive versus prescriptive views of what teachers know. One e-mail writer takes the prescriptive position that disciplinary knowledge is "the core knowledge that any language teacher should have." In contrast, the descriptive position, for which I argue, seeks to understand what teachers know and how that knowledge relates to their classroom practice. On another level however, the argument is about the control and definition of epistemological territory, over who and what defines what language teachers know. It is a basic debate about what constitutes the knowledge base of language teaching.

I see the knowledge base of language teaching as falling somewhere between the specificity of what Larsen-Freeman (1990) called a "theory of second language teaching," which includes knowledge of language learners, learning, and pedagogy, and the breadth of Stern's (1983) T1 type theory, which positions language teaching within the larger social and disciplinary milieu. I take the establishment of such a knowledge base to be primarily a descriptive enterprise, simultaneously grounded in classroom practice, teachers' professional lives, and the contexts in which they work. I also see it as a cognitive undertaking in the broadest sense, aimed at uncovering the understandings that animate what teachers do in their teaching.

My position is straightforward, simply that teaching knowledge and disciplinary knowledge are not isomorphic. The knowledge base of language teaching is the composite of knowledge, beliefs, and perceptions that shape what language teachers know, and therefore what they do, in their teaching.[3] Thus, I believe it needs to be approached through the professional lives and practices of classroom teachers. Others, among them some of my e-mail critics, argue the obverse position: that to determine the knowledge base of language teaching we need to specify, and agree upon, the disciplinary knowledge teachers need to know in order to teach. They propose starting with the knowledge; I propose starting with the teacher.

While disciplinary knowledge may well inform teaching knowledge, I believe that we can only understand how the two interrelate if we examine teaching per se. After all it is teachers, as classroom practitioners, who ultimately act upon whatever knowledge base others may prescribe or advocate. Thus it seems clear that we will not learn more about that knowledge base by reviewing disciplinary knowledge, we must study teachers and their understandings of what they do. To support this approach, I reach outside the domains of linguistics and psychology that usually inform discussions of knowledge in language teaching to research traditions in general education and teacher education that I believe are more suited to this debate. Because these are questions about teachers and their teaching, such research is well positioned to help us to grapple with them.

Various education researchers and theorists have established the grounds for such discussions. Schon (1983, 1987) asserted that basic differences exist between professional knowledge in action and what he called "technical rationality." His work precipitated a major shift in teacher education and research on teaching that now emphasizes teachers coming to understand their own thinking through reflective practice (Calderhead and Gates 1993). In the domain of subject matter knowledge, Shulman (1987, 1986), drawing on the work of Schwab (1978), has argued for a distinction between pedagogical content knowledge and disciplinary content knowledge (see Wilson, Shulman, and Richert 1987; also Freeman 1992a: 28-30). In a related perspective, researchers at the U.S. National Center for Research on Teacher Learning have argued that content and pedagogical activity are basically inseparable in teaching. They contend, therefore, that "subject-matter representation"—learning how to represent subject matter to learners—is the central challenge in learning to teach and therefore of teacher education (McDiarmid, Ball, and Anderson 1989; see also Kennedy 1990). Educational philosophers, drawing from the work of John Dewey, have examined the distinction between knowledge in

3. In elaborating "knowledge, beliefs, and perceptions," I intend to encompass the epistemological categories generally used in researching teacher cognition (see Clark and Peterson 1986; see also Clandinin and Connelly 1987) and theorizing about teachers' knowledge (see Carter 1990). However, given the as-yet fluid nature of this area of inquiry, it would be premature to consider these categories as exhaustive.

practice and scientific or disciplinary knowledge in teaching (see McEwan and Bull 1991; see also Freeman and Richards 1993).

In that this work falls outside the field of language teaching, it has not influenced our professional conversations as much as I believe it should have. Indeed, it seems to me that we in language education have tended to place more emphasis on language, through the study of linguistics and psychology, than we have on education, with a resulting imbalance in our discussions. There has, however, been some related work in our field (see van Lier in this volume for a fuller discussion). Strevens (1976), Spolsky (1978), Campbell (1980), and Ingram (1980) each proposed frameworks or models, some almost two decades ago, of the relationship between language teaching and the various disciplines that seem to inform it. Stern's (1983a) book presents a truly impressive summary of the then-work-to-date that bears on a general model of language teaching. And this Round Table has, from time to time, had various papers on the topic as well (Larsen-Freeman 1990; Jarvis 1983; Stern 1983b).

Clearly a substantial base of theory and research exists, both in general education and in our area of endeavor, on which to propose separating disciplinary from teaching knowledge. To revive these discussions in language teaching seems to me both necessary and timely. Discipline-derived prescriptions about what makes "good" language teaching have not demonstrably improved either teacher education or classroom practice. In fact, the hegemony of such prescriptions has oftentimes interfered with establishing a careful, disciplined examination of what language teachers do and the basis on which they do it. To examine the knowledge base of language teaching is to return to language teachers, to their purposes, contexts, and forms of activity in order to better understand both their practice and the thinking that motivates that practice.

This paper proposes a broad framework of elements in response to the question: What must a knowledge-base of language teaching account for? In so doing, I hope to clarify the position I took in the 1989 article and to advance discussions of what constitutes teachers' knowledge in language teaching. For I believe it is inadequate, as a field, to simply make prescriptive arguments about what language teachers should know or do without simultaneously examining what they do know—in other words the epistemological landscape in which they do their work. What must a knowledge base account for?

It seems to me that there are three broad groups of issues that a knowledge base must address: the nature of teacher learning, the nature of schools and schooling, and the nature of teaching. These clusters can be abbreviated as *the teacher-learner*, *the context*, and *the process*. Taken together, they outline an ecological view of the knowledge base of language teaching in framing the deceptively simply question: *Who teaches what to whom, where?* By presenting this ecological view as a question, I mean to emphasize the constant and critical interdependence of the three clusters. Further, as I discuss later on, I want to suggest that the distinction between subject matter and learners that is now taken as basic in discussions of the knowledge base can be recast. Thus I outline three clusters—the teacher-learner, the process, and the context—where some argue for breaking the cluster of process down into teaching, content, and learners, thus having a total of five clusters—the teacher-learner, teaching, the content, the language learners, and the context.

Proposals to modify or improve teaching, as well as prescriptions for what language teachers should know, must address the framework of this ecology. Within the three broad elements of the framework we can ask: What do we know about each element and its relation to the other two, and on that basis what do we need to investigate and to learn? These questions then help to shape a general research agenda that can elucidate the knowledge base of language teaching, a point to which I will return at the close of the paper.

The learner: the nature of teacher learning. In defining the knowledge base of language teaching, the learner is the teacher not the language student. This simple yet crucial fact is often disregarded. We know that classroom language learning is an extremely complex process (Larsen-Freeman and Long 1990) and that language students learn from many sources within that environment, among them the teacher (Allwright 1984). In the push to understand this complexity, however, teachers are often overlooked. They are generally portrayed as conduits to students rather than as individuals who think, and are learning, in their own right (Freeman forthcoming).

A knowledge base of language teaching must account for how individuals learn to teach and for the complex factors, influences, and processes that contribute to that learning. While we know very little that is specific to learning to teach second languages (see Freeman and Richards forthcoming), more is known about the phenomenon through research on teachers of other subject matters. I would summarize these somewhat disparate findings in five points:

- the role of prior knowledge in learning to teach
- the ways such teaching knowledge develops
- the role of context in teacher learning
- the role of teacher education as a form of intervention in these first three areas
- the role of input in changing teachers' beliefs about content and learners.

Since Lortie's 1975 study *Schoolteacher: A sociological study,* which became a seminal work in teacher socialization, it has been increasingly clear that individuals do not enter teaching tabula rasa. Rather they begin their professional careers with developed images of who teachers are and what they do, images that prove to be quite resilient and resistant to change. In summarizing research on this aspect of teacher learning, Kennedy (1991: 6–7), Director of the National Center for Research on Teacher Learning, notes:

> One important finding is that teachers develop strong conceptions of the practice of teaching while they are still children. From their experiences as students they form views about the nature of school subjects, about the teacher's role in facilitating learning, and about the pedagogical implications of diversity. These views constrain their ability to grasp alternative views.

In the field of language teaching, this finding is complicated by the fact that language is both a school subject and a phenomenon that exists and can be learned naturally in the world. There is some evidence to suggest that beginning language teachers are concerned with addressing this duality and that they are drawn to language teaching not for how they have experienced it as students but for the richness of language learning in the world (see Freeman 1991).[4] Thus a knowledge base of language teaching must account for the influence of these prior understandings on any new pedagogical information to which teacher–learners are introduced.

The next issue addresses the development of what teachers know. As a longitudinal phenomenon, however, teacher learning is yet to be closely studied to examine the development of teachers' knowledge over the course of a career.[5] Studies of teacher expertise and how it evolves focus on how time, which we normally refer to as experience, guides teachers' actions. These studies fall into two broad groups: those that focus on the development of generic teaching knowledge (e.g. Berliner 1988) and those that focus on the development of teachers' subject matter or pedagogical content knowledge (e.g. Grossman 1992; see also Shulman 1987). It is perhaps not surprising that novice teachers have been found to interpret their classroom worlds differently from their more experienced colleagues; however, the specific textures of those differences are quite interesting.

Novices, defined as teachers with no prior teaching experience, have been found to be more rigid and to rely more heavily on formulaic knowledge, such as rules, principles, and theories encountered in preservice education. When that

---

4. To date these findings only refer to language teachers who are not teaching their mother tongue. It is clearly worth investigating whether the findings apply to native-speaking language teachers as well.

5. The major TELT (Teacher Education and Learning to Teach) Studies, conducted by the U.S. National Center for Research on Teacher Education at Michigan State University, ran for five years, following cohorts of college juniors who were entering teaching through their third year of classroom teaching (see Kennedy 1992).

formulaic knowledge breaks down, as it often does, novices will fall back on their prior experience as students to resolve problems. In this way, conservative pedagogy is often seen to perpetuate itself, and changing classroom practice—through pre- or inservice teacher education—is a complex undertaking. With three years of teaching, this rigidity begins to dissipate as intermediate teachers begin to establish what works in their teaching. So-called expert teachers, with five or more years' experience, tend to interpret and respond to classroom events in a much more contextual fashion, drawing on the knowledge they have developed about students and school norms more than on educational theory or curricular design (see Genburg 1992; see also Berliner 1988).

In view of this general trajectory of development, from formulaic, rule-based to contextual, interpretative judgments in practice, it is logical to ask what causes the change. This raises the critical role of schools in shaping teachers' learning. Under the rubric of teacher socialization, research that has examined how schools influence the practices of entering teachers has found, perhaps not surprisingly, that the norms and values of the environment are a powerful factor in shaping what new teachers see as feasible in their teaching (Bullough 1989). The conserving and conservative nature of schools as normative environments cannot be underestimated in understanding how teachers learn their practice and why they do what they do.

These major findings—that teachers harbor resilient prior images of teaching from their own experience, that these images, coupled with professional training, seem to provide a rigid scaffolding that becomes more flexible over time, and that the norms and values of school environments shape the specific directions of that flexibility—together add up to rather bad news for teacher education. In fact, these broader influences suggest that teacher education may not be a major factor in shaping what teachers know and how they teach. As I have written elsewhere, teacher education, as it is currently practiced, may well be a very weak form of intervention in teaching regardless of subject matter (Freeman 1992b). Studies of development and change in teachers' beliefs suggest that external input, in the form of information or theory from teacher education courses, generally has little enduring impact on teachers' classroom practices (Kennedy 1992; Britzman 1991). It seems that the breadth and complexity of teacher learning is only slightly touched by the formal input received in teacher education. However, this does not mean that we abandon formal teacher preparation. Rather, it means we must understand the processes that are at work in teacher learning in order to be more influential and effective within them.

This insight highlights the critical importance of understanding the knowledge base of language teaching. Without a careful examination of the developmental and contextual factors that shape teachers' learning, prescriptions for teacher education will remain disconnected from the actual fabric of what teachers know. Thus, to say that the knowledge base must account for the learner is to say that we must take stock of the actual processes that occur in learning to teach and the factors that impinge on those processes. This is hardly a retreat from the importance of professional knowledge; it is an acknowledgment of the landscape in which that knowledge must operate. To begin to understand teacher learning is to begin to understand why teachers do what they do. These purposes are animated by experience, by professional education, and by the contexts in which teachers work.

The context: The nature of schools and schooling. The nature of schools and schooling is a vast topic. Hardly neutral, it is colored by debates over knowledge, power, and the role of education in sustaining or altering the social order (see Apple 1985). To address this topic, we need to determine which aspects of the nature of schools and schooling are germane to the knowledge base of language teaching.

The distinction between schools and schooling is a useful point of entry. In schools, the focus is on places in which teaching and learning happen. In schooling, the focus is on the wider social processes, of which teaching is one important part, that happen in schools. By including the nature of schools and schooling within the knowledge base, we are recognizing that we cannot understand language teaching apart from the environments in which it takes place and the other social processes in which it is embedded. These environments and processes shape in critical ways what language teachers can do. They also provide two facets of the notion of context: *context as place* and *context as process*.

This dual meaning of context operates in the knowledge base. As far as place is concerned, two points are centrally important about schools. First, schools are powerful places that create and sustain meanings and values (Lightfoot 1983). Second, it is a misreading to see them merely as settings in which educational practices are implemented. Schools and classrooms function as frameworks for interpretation in which certain actions and ways of being are valued and encouraged, while others are downplayed, ignored, and even silenced (see Fine 1986). Learning how to negotiate these powerful environments is critical to becoming an effective teacher (Sizer 1983).

Often, because they are not adequately prepared for this environment, novice teachers can be defeated by it (Bullough 1989). This may be particularly true of language teachers, who often work at the margins of administration, policy, and curriculum in schools, in part because of the students whom they teach (Benesch 1991). Language teacher education is weakened to the extent that it does not explicitly address the role of language teachers in schools and prepare novice teachers for that environment. When it does address schools, too often the knowledge base of language teaching has been defined in terms of materials, curricula, and teaching practices, with little or no attention given to how schools function as systems, how power and meaning are sustained within them, and how teachers can act on those dynamics.

To consider schools from this perspective, one must address schooling, which provides context in its second sense. As a social process, schooling integrates learners into the world. The role of language in schooling processes, in creating or denying access to curriculum, and in sustaining dominant cultural values, has been researched for both first and second language learners. Such research has also documented the central role that teachers play in these linguistic and sociocultural encounters (see Cazden 1988).

In general education, however, the role of language in schooling, as a medium of instruction as well as a vehicle of knowledge construction, is usually subsumed within the broader debates of access and power in curriculum. A knowledge base of language teaching can make a specialized contribution here. Language teachers work with language on a daily basis and are thus sensitized to its fundamental role in any learning situation.[6] Understanding how their perspective is potentially different from that of their colleagues in other subject matters, and further advocating for that perspective as fundamentally important to any teaching and learning, can create a base of power and influence for language teachers within schools.

By grasping the basic role of language in schooling, language teachers have the potential to move their work and their professional concerns from the periphery toward the core of education and what happens in schools. Until very recently, any de facto knowledge base of language teaching treated context as a sort of movable feast, emphasizing the mobility that language as a subject matter can afford language teachers. The assumption, widely supported in their professional preparation, has been that these teachers should be able to go anywhere and teach anyone (see Larsen-Freeman 1983). While this view may have been romantically attractive, I think it has contributed in part to the marginalization of language teachers within the educational hierarchy.

The changing demographics of the student population in North American as well as in many European school systems shows a sustained increase in the number of learners whose home languages are not those of the school. Further geopolitical changes have rendered English a central force in development and internationalization. The pushes toward, and the resistance to, multiculturalism in education is one current in these changes, a current that reveals how schools are communities of meaning and how schooling works to sustain those meanings. Thus, bringing new values into schools, and defining new meanings within them, is a form of social change.

---

6. While not written by a language teacher, Lemke's study (1986) of the role of language in mathematics instruction is a good example of what I mean.

In this changing global environment, the peripatetic view of context in language teaching is less useful. Instead, we need to see language teachers as central in the educational process, just as teachers of math, science, or social studies are. This entails recognizing context as a central element in what language teachers need to know in order to understand their professional world. It also means taking a more sophisticated view of context as simultaneously place and process, in which schools and schooling are closely studied and carefully analyzed. Teaching contexts should not be treated as backdrops for methods and materials; rather they need to be approached as the media through which teaching and learning operate. Other professions, like medicine for example, have seen that understanding and managing the contexts of their practice is key to any effort at defining a professional knowledge base (see Starr 1982). Education must seriously consider the same lesson. Understanding contexts of practice is a central element in the knowledge base of language teaching.

Teaching: The nature of the activity. The third broad cluster of elements in the knowledge base is the activity of teaching itself. While many who have written about the knowledge base put the specific activity of teaching at the core, I would argue otherwise. Teaching as an activity cannot be understood without understanding both the teacher as the person who is learning to do it and schools and schooling as the contexts in which it is done. Thus each domain is contingent on the other two. I arrive at teaching third in this analysis to emphasize this interrelationship and the fact that I believe the knowledge base is therefore broader than others may construe it to be.

Discussions of teaching in the knowledge base generally fall into two categories: One I would call "grounded" (see Glaser and Strauss 1967) and the other I would call a priori. In the "grounded" category I include analyses of language teaching that start with the activity as it is practiced in the classroom; thus they are grounded in the phenomenon itself. There are unfortunately very few such analyses available, which was my point in the 1989 *TESOL Quarterly* statement (see Richards in this volume as an example of the exception). In the a priori category, I include proposals and discussions of what we believe language teachers should know. These are by definition not researched or empirically documented proposals since they have not been tested against the knowledge that teachers actually draw on in their teaching. Rather, these a priori proposals are our best guesses about the knowledge we think teachers are using in their teaching.

Arguments over the relevance of discipline-derived knowledge, such as applied linguistics or second language acquisition for example, fall within the a priori category. Herein lies an important distinction. While I have said that a priori proposals are not based in empirical study of what teachers know, these proposals often derive from research and study in fields other than—although related to—language teaching. Thus, for example, information on learning styles has been developed through psychological studies, often of learners in classrooms (see Oxford in this volume). However, such research proceeds from the point of view of what the learner is doing and not from how the teacher perceives that learner. Juxtapose this view with the now well-known studies of the "Pygmalion" effect in which teachers' perceptions of learners were experimentally manipulated in order to assess the influence of those perceptions on learning (Jacobson and Rosenthal 1989). In this case, researchers took teachers' perceptions of learners, for better or worse, as the starting point of their inquiry. In the study of learning styles, the reverse has happened. Researchers have extrapolated from their understanding of what learners are doing to infer how teachers should act in order to support that learning. Thus, what makes these approaches to teaching knowledge a priori is the fact that they do not proceed from what the teacher knows and does in teaching.

I would place the proposals for frameworks of language teaching mentioned earlier in this a priori category as well. The conceptual maps proposed by Strevens (1976), Spolsky (1980), and Stern (1983) share certain important characteristics.[7] They assume as the starting point the two-step argument: First, that knowledge from other disciplines, principally linguistics and psychology, is relevant to language teaching; but second, that such knowledge alone is not adequate to account for what teachers do. There is some discussion of which elements, including which disciplines, should go into the framework. However, the central problem is not one of inclusion but of how these elements may relate to language teaching.

These frameworks are all based on the major trinity of learning and the learner, pedagogy, and content, although they define and weigh the areas somewhat differently. Context is a backdrop against which these three elements play themselves out. Further, each framework recognizes the transformation that must occur for disciplinary knowledge about one of these three elements to be brought to bear on that dimension in the classroom. Thus, for example, psychological theories or second language acquisition research must somehow be transformed—or transform themselves—into teaching knowledge about learning and learners. Stern (1983: 47) describes this process as the principle of interaction, saying that "The teacher is therefore not the recipient in the development of theory. The practice of language teaching, a teacher's or learner's intuitions and experiences can contribute ideas, information, problems, and questions, to theory development of language pedagogy and to the basic disciplines."

---

7. Stern (1983: 35–52) presents an invaluable summary analysis of this work.

Disclaimers to the contrary however, these frameworks are all constructed in a top-down fashion, with the major elements—be they social factors or disciplinary knowledge—at the top and classroom teaching at the bottom. While Stern's principle of interaction intends the mutual informing of top and bottom, there is an inescapable sense that teaching is somehow the recipient of other forms of knowledge. For this reason, some sort of mediation is necessary. Again, Stern (1983: 49–50): "We regard it as imperative to assume a mediating interdisciplinary level between the disciplines and the practice of language education. Spolsky's term 'educational linguistics' has been adopted to describe this mediating discipline." If we understand educational linguistics as this "mediating discipline," what then is its role in the knowledge base of language teaching?

The role of educational linguistics. I have argued thus far in this paper that a knowledge base of language teaching must account for the teacher-as-learner and how teaching is learned, for the contexts of place and social process in which it is learned and practiced, and for what teaching is (see Figure 1).

Figure 1. Knowledge-base of second language teaching.

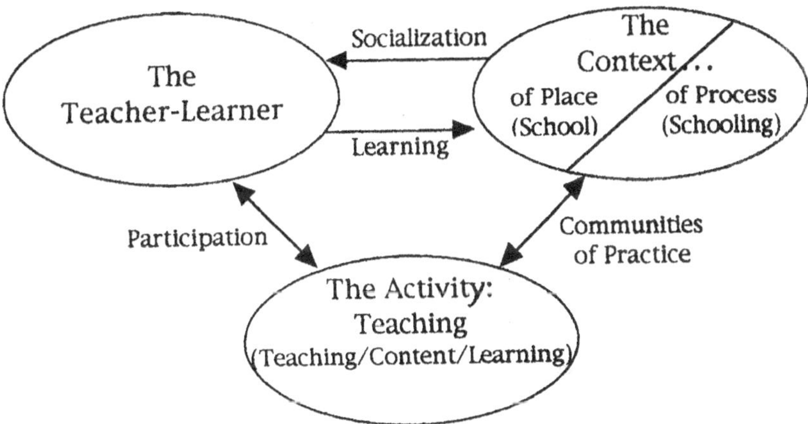

Through research, something is known of the first two areas; however, although much is said, relatively little is actually known about the third: the activity of teaching itself. Clearly, teaching relates somehow to learning, and yet as Larsen-Freeman (1990: 265) points out, "Learning is not caused by teaching. Rather opportunities for learning emerge through the interactions of teachers and students."

The relationship between classroom interactions and the content of instruction is an equally complex one (see Pica in this volume for a review). Here I find it useful to distinguish between *content*, which I define as the teachers' and the learners' particular perceptions of what is being taught in a lesson or course, and *subject matter*, which is the professional or disciplinary perception. Thus content and subject matter are differing, yet convergent, perceptions of the same phenomenon in much the same way ethnographers speak of emic and etic views of a situation, event, or phenomenon. In writing about such emic or indigenous categories, Patton (1990: 393) quotes Pelto and Pelto to describe the distinction as follows:

> Cultural behaviour should always be studied and categorized in terms of the inside (or emic) view—the actors' definition—of human events. That is, the units of conceptualization in anthropological theories should be "discovered" by analyzing the cognitive processes of the people studied, rather than "imposed" from cross-cultural (or etic) classifications of behaviour.

Research, teacher education, and classroom practice have long been served by an etic conception of subject matter as what is taught. Thus teaching becomes the transmission of that subject matter and learning becomes its reception.[8] Within this equation, content has needed to be substantively defined as subject matter, and applied linguistics has fulfilled that function. However, defining language as subject matter, and thus as the content in language classrooms, is, at least in part, a function of the transmission model of education and the accompanying views of teaching as "telling" and learning as "getting" particular information or skills.

With the advent of other views of learning, however, the teaching-content-learning equation has been shifted. Research on the social construction of knowledge has led to a different perspective in which learning is understood not as mastery of content but as increasingly proficient participation in a social community of which that content, as a social practice, is a part. In the field of language teaching, we are perhaps most familiar with this social constructivist view of learning in the teaching of writing as "process writing" or in literacy with the use of "whole language" pedagogy. In both cases, learning is seen to involve apprenticeship within a community of writers or readers, and the activity of teaching then involves fostering those apprenticeships.

In this analysis, one of the weaknesses of the classroom, in contrast to the wider world, is that the larger community is generally represented only by the teacher and, to a certain extent, by students who are more proficient in the social practice. If the teacher is not herself a fluent and recognized participant

---

8. The process-product research paradigm (Dunkin and Biddle 1964) depends on this view.

in that larger community of social practice, as may be the case in math or science teaching for example, the opportunities for successful apprenticeship are diminished (see Tharp and Gallimore 1988).

In this view of learning as social participation, content is an epiphenomenon, a by-product of that apprenticeship. Cognitive psychologists Lave and Wenger have labeled learning a process of "legitimate peripheral participation." Through that participation, learners become members of a community in which the content is part of the modus operandi of the social practice:

> Activities, tasks, functions, and understandings do not exist in isolation; they are part of broader systems of relations in which they have meaning. These systems of relations arise out of and are reproduced and developed within social communities, which are in part systems of relations among persons. The person is defined by and defines these relations. Learning thus involves becoming a different person with respect to the possibilities enabled by these systems of relations. To ignore this aspect of learning is to overlook the fact that *learning involves the construction of identities.* (Lave and Wenger 1991: 53, emphasis added)

A complete examination of social constructivist views of learning and their implications for teaching would be the subject of another paper. However, my point here is to introduce an alternative way of conceptualizing the learning–content–teaching relationship and its relationship to context. This alternative view suggests that context is central since it circumscribes the social processes operating within it. Learning is a social process of becoming recognized as a participant in a certain set of particular practices within a social context. Content is then a by-product of that learning/participation rather than its object, and teaching is the assistance and management of that social participation (see Tharp and Gallimore 1988). In this view, teaching and learning depend on social contact and participation. They are organized and constrained by factors, which we usually call contextual, that shape participation and not by the transmission of certain knowledge and information.

When applied to language teaching, the social constructivist view serves in a useful way to integrate the three clusters in the knowledge base: the teacher–learner, the social context, and the process of teaching and learning. Like everyone else, language teachers learn a great deal about teaching and their subject matter from participation in their own schooling as well as from participation with language in the world, as I have suggested earlier in this paper (see also Freeman 1991). The disciplinary knowledge that is introduced quite late in their schooling through professional education is accompanied by a different type of participation, one that bears little resemblance to the school environments in which these novice teachers will work. Thus, when they come to teach in schools, the forms of participation new teachers know and the types of knowledge about language learners, teaching, and subject matter that they are supposed to invoke through their professional training do not correspond.

This distance between differing forms of participation and different social communities, usually referred to as the gap between theory and practice, becomes a major focus of attention and concern in the knowledge base of language teaching. Instead of addressing the different forms of social participation and practice, we attempt to "fill the gap" with new information and knowledge. For educational linguistics, this alternative view implies that disciplinary knowledge per se may play a less central role in shaping language teaching. Instead, if, like any activity, language learning and teaching are done in a social context and, therefore, if we are concerned with what language teachers know in order to do what they do, we must examine how these contexts of teaching and learning operate and how teachers and students learn to participate in them.

This is a lateral, rather than a hierarchical, view of the knowledge base of language teaching. It suggests that the need for educational linguistics as "a mediating discipline," as Stern (1983) called it, has been brought about not so much by the nature of language teaching but rather by the inherently differential status in various forms of knowledge. Simply put, it may be the perceived hierarchical relationship between the academic disciplines and language teaching that has created the need for educational linguistics. Without that perception of hierarchy among forms of knowledge, there would be no need for mediation.

Closing. In language teaching, for many reasons, we seem to accord status to disciplinary knowledge and to depend on a priori prescriptions from that knowledge to define teaching. In part it may be because language teaching is fairly new as a professional field, still striving for academic and professional recognition, and because language as its subject matter has undergone periodic redefinition since World War II (see Brown 1987), and further because teaching has only recently been studied as a socio-cognitive activity (Clark and Peterson 1986). However, accounting for what language teaching is and prescribing what language teaching ought to be are two different undertakings. For a knowledge base of language teaching to be useful in a pragmatic, as opposed to a political, sense, I believe it must address teaching as it is learned and as it is practiced. Defining the knowledge base in this way has political ramifications. It means acknowledging existing practices, in all of their less-than-desirable aspects, and trying to understand why those practices happen as they do.

To do so will mean, I believe, examining the nature and experiences of language teacher-learners throughout their careers, from the time they first participate in the practices of schooling. This will entail, therefore, examining the contexts of that participation both in and over time. Synchronic examination will help us to understand more about schools as communities of meaning that shape language teaching and learning. Diachronic examination will shed light on the formative nature of schooling and how those meanings develop and are sustained. Understanding the language teacher as participant, schools as settings for participation, and schooling as a means of participation will place language teaching in the full, rich, and messy environment in which it actually happens both in and over time. Only then, I believe, can we position ourselves to examine the activity of language teaching itself.

To get to this point, however, we need to recognize that arguments over the role and contributions of disciplinary knowledge in language teaching are, in many ways, independent of the teaching itself. To articulate a knowledge base I have suggested that we must begin with the activity of language teaching, the context in which it is practiced, and the teacher as participant. However, insofar as the teaching and the taught are inseparable, we must understand what makes teaching *language* teaching. This will undoubtedly involve discipline-derived understandings from applied linguistics, second language acquisition, psychology, and curriculum development, among other areas, in a deeper examination of our subject matter. Through grounded examinations of language teaching within the broader framework of teacher–learner, context, and process will emerge a deeper understanding of how language teachers teach and how their students learn.

REFERENCES

Allwright, Dick. 1984. "Why don't learners learn what teachers teach? The interaction hypothesis." In David Singleton and David Little (eds.), *Language learning in formal and informal contexts*. Dublin: IRAAL. 3–18.

Apple, Michael. 1985. *Education and power*. New York: Routledge.

Benesch, Sarah (ed.). 1991. *ESL in American: Myths and possibilities*. Portsmouth, N.H.: Heineman.

Berliner, David. 1988. *The development of expertise in pedagogy*. Washington, D.C.: American Association of Colleges for Teacher Education.

Britzman, Deborah P. 1991. *Practice makes practice: A critical study of learning to teach*. New York: The Press of the State University of New York.

Brown, H. Douglas. 1987. *Principles of language learning and teaching, Second edition*. Englewood, N.J.: Prentice Hall.

Bullough, Robert V. 1989. *First year teacher: A case study*. New York: Teachers College Press.

Calderhead, James and Peter Gates (eds.). 1993. *Conceptualizing reflection in teacher development*. London: Falmer Press.

Campbell, Russell N. 1980. "Statement in a symposium on 'Toward a redefinition of applied linguistics'" In Robert B. Kaplan (ed.), *On the scope of applied linguistics*. Rowley, Massachusetts: Newbury House. 36–38.

Carter, Kathy. 1990. "Teachers' knowledge and learning to teach." In W.R. Houston (ed.), *Handbook of research on teacher education*. New York: Macmillan Publishing. 291–310.

Cazden, Courtney. 1988. *Classroom discourse: The language of teaching and learning*. Portsmouth, N.H.: Heineman.

Clandinin, D. Jean and Michael Connelly. 1987. "Teachers' personal knowledge: What counts as 'personal' in studies of the personal." *Journal of Curriculum Studies* 19: 487–500.

Clark, Christopher and Penelope Peterson. 1986. "Teachers' thought processes." In Merlin C. Wittrock (ed.), *Handbook of research on teaching, Third edition*. New York: Macmillan Publishing. 255–297.

Dunkin, Michael and Bruce Biddle. 1974. *The study of teaching*. New York: Holt, Rinehart, and Winston.

Fine, Michelle. 1986. "Silencing in public schools." *Language Arts* 64(2).

Freeman, Donald. (forthcoming). "Redefining the relationship between research and what teachers know." In Kathy Bailey and David Nunan (eds.), *Voices and viewpoints: Qualitative research in second language correction*. New York: Cambridge University Press.

Freeman, Donald. 1992a. "Mistaken constructs: Re-examining the nature and assumptions of language teacher education." In James E. Alatis (ed.), *Language, communication, and social meaning*. Georgetown University Round Table on Languages and Linguistics 1992. Washington, D.C.: Georgetown University. 25–39.

Freeman, Donald. 1992b. "Language teacher education, emerging discourse, and change in classroom practice." In John Flowerdew, Mark Brock, and Sophie Hsia (eds.), *Perspectives in second language teacher education*. Hong Kong: City Polytechnic of Hong Kong. 1–21.

Freeman, Donald. 1991. "'To make the tacit explicit:' Teacher education, emerging discourse, and conceptions of teaching." *Teaching and Teacher Education* 7(5/6): 439–454.

Freeman, Donald. 1989. "Teacher training, development, and decision-making: A model of teaching and related strategies in language teacher education." *TESOL Quarterly* 23(1): 27–47.

Freeman, Donald, and Jack C. Richards. (forthcoming). *Teacher learning in language teaching*. New York: Cambridge University Press.

Freeman, Donald, and Jack C. Richards. 1993. "Conceptions of teaching and the education of second language teachers." *TESOL Quarterly* 27(2): 193–216.

Genburg, Victoria. 1992. "Patterns and organizing perspectives: A view of expertise." *Teaching and Teacher Education* 8(5/6): 485–496.

Glaser, Bruce and Anselm Strauss. 1967. *The discovery of grounded theory*. Chicago: Aldine Press.

Grossman, Pamela. 1990. *The making of a teacher: Teacher knowledge and teacher education*. New York: Teachers College Press.

Ingram, David E. 1980. "Applied linguistics: A search for insight" In Robert B. Kaplan (ed.), *On the scope of applied linguistics*. Rowley, Massachusetts: Newbury House. 37–56.

Jacobson, Lenore and Robert Rosenthal. 1989. *Pygmalion in the classroom: Teacher expectations and pupils' intellectual development*. Irvington, N.Y.: Irvington Press.

Jarvis, Gilbert A. 1983. "Pedagogical knowledge for the second language teacher." In James E. Alatis, H. H. Stern, and Peter Strevens (eds), *Applied linguistics and the preparation of second language teachers: Toward a rationale*. Georgetown University Round Table on Languages and Linguistics 1983. Washington, D.C.: Georgetown University. 234–241.

Kennedy, Mary. 1992. *Findings on learning to teach*. East Lansing, Michigan: National Center for Research on Teacher Learning.

Kennedy, Mary. 1991. *An agenda for research on teacher learning*. East Lansing, Michigan: National Center for Research on Teacher Learning.

Kennedy, Mary. 1990. *A survey of recent literature on teachers' subject matter knowledge*. East Lansing, Michigan: National Center for Research on Teacher Learning.

Larsen-Freeman, Diane. 1990. "Towards a theory of second language teaching." In James E. Alatis (ed.), *Linguistics, language teaching and language acquisition: The interdependence of theory, practice and research*. Georgetown University Round Table on Languages and Linguistics 1990. Washington, D.C.: Georgetown University. 261–270.

Larsen-Freeman, Diane. 1983. "Training teachers or educating a teacher?" In James E. Alatis, H. H. Stern, and Peter Strevens (eds.), *Applied linguistics and the preparation of second language teachers: Toward a rationale.* Georgetown University Round Table on Languages and Linguistics 1983. Washington, D.C.: Georgetown University. 264–274.

Larsen-Freeman, Diane and Michael H. Long. 1990. *An introduction to second language acquisition research.* London: Longman.

Lave, Jean and Etienne Wenger. 1991. *Situated learning: Legitimate peripheral participation.* New York: Cambridge University Press.

Lemke, Jay. 1986. *Using language in classrooms.* Victoria, Australia: Deakin University Press.

Lightfoot, Sara Lawrence. 1983. *The good high school: Portraits in character and culture.* New York: Basic Books.

Lortie, Dan. 1975. *Schoolteacher: A sociological study.* Chicago: University of Chicago.

McEwan, Hunter and Bruce Bull. 1991. "The pedagogic nature of subject matter knowledge." *American Educational Research Journal* 28(2): 316–334.

McDiarmid, G. William, Deborah Ball, and Charles W. Anderson. 1989. "Why staying one chapter ahead doesn't really work: Subject specific pedagogy." In M. Reynolds (ed.), *The knowledge-base for beginning teachers.* Tarrytown, N.Y.: Pergamon. 193–206.

Patton, Michael Quinn. 1990. *Qualitative evaluation and research methods, Second edition.* Newbury Park, California: Sage.

Rosenholtz, Susan. 1989. *Teachers' workplace: The social organization of schools.* New York: Longman.

Schon, Donald A. 1987. *Educating the reflective practitioner.* San Francisco: Jossey-Bass.

Schon, Donald A. 1983. *The reflective practitioner: How professionals think in practice.* New York: Basic Books.

Schwab, J.J. 1978. "Education and the structure of the disciplines." In Ian Westbury and Nicholas J. Wilkof (eds.), *Science, curriculum, and liberal education.* Chicago: University of Chicago Press. 229–272.

Shulman, Lee S. 1987. "Knowledge-base and teaching: Foundations of the new reform." *Harvard Educational Review* 57(1): 1–22.

Shulman. Lee S. 1986. "Those who understand: Knowledge growth in teaching." *Educational Researcher* 15(2): 4–14.

Sizer, Ted. 1983. *Horace's compromise.* Boston: Houghton Mifflin.

Spolsky, Bernard. 1978. *Educational linguistics: An introduction.* Rowley, Massachusetts: Newbury House.

Starr, Paul. 1982. *The social transformation of American medicine.* New York: Basic Books.

Stern, H. H. 1983a. *Fundamental concepts of language teaching.* Oxford: Oxford University Press.

Stern, H. H. 1983b. "Language teacher education: An approach to the issues and a framework for discussion." In James E. Alatis, H.H. Stern, and Peter Strevens (eds.), *Applied linguistics and the preparation of second language teachers: Toward a rationale.* Georgetown University Round Table on Languages and Linguistics 1983. Washington, D.C.: Georgetown University. 242–261.

Strevens, Peter D. 1976. "A theoretical model of the language learning/teaching process." *Working Papers on Bilingualism.* 129–152.

Tharp, Roland G., and Ronald Gallimore. 1988. *Rousing young minds to life: Teaching, learning, and schooling in social context.* New York: Cambridge University Press.

Tucker, G. Richard. 1983. "Developing a research agenda for second language educators." In James E. Alatis, H. H. Stern, and Peter Strevens (eds.), *Applied linguistics and the preparation of second language teachers: Toward a rationale.* Georgetown University Round Table on Languages and Linguistics 1983. Washington, D.C.: Georgetown University. 386–394.

Wilson, Suzanne, Lee Shulman, and Anna Richert. 1987. "'150 different ways' of knowing: Representations of knowledge in teaching." In James Calderhead (ed.), *Exploring teachers' thinking*. London: Cassell Publications. 104–124.

Educational linguistics: Field and project

Leo van Lier
Monterey Institute of International Studies

Introduction. Linguists are fond, in a masochistic sort of way, of telling the story about being asked in a bar or airport lounge what they do and finding that their answer, "I'm a linguist," is interpreted as someone who knows or teaches foreign languages. Now imagine that someone answered: "I'm an educational linguist," or "I'm an applied linguist." It is likely that now the questioner would have even more trouble in getting a clear picture of the other's activities.

It is possible that other professionals experience a similar lack of comprehension, but in those cases it would most likely involve unusual names such as ichthyologist or histopathologist. Others, from anthropologist to archeologist, and from psychologist to pediatrician have an easier time convincing the public that they have a decent and interesting line of work. Interestingly, many professionals whose work might fit snugly under the umbrellas of educational or applied linguistics find their activities well understood: language teacher, professor of literature, speech therapist, interpreter, and so on.

There appears to be something, then, in the nature of the discipline of linguistics, or at least in the way it is typically conducted, that makes it unfamiliar and hard to grasp for the average person in the street. This difficulty, I will argue, is closely linked to both the problems and the necessity of setting up the hybrid discipline of educational linguistics. The difficulty is also related to the problems of identity that the field of applied linguistics has had in its relatively short history.

In this paper I will trace the fortunes and misfortunes of past and present links between education and language, focusing especially on problems of (1) relating theory to practice, and (2) relating language knowledge—including knowledge about language, or KAL, (see Carter 1990)—to language pedagogy. These problems are, I suggest, the two main reasons why the person in the bar does not understand what the linguist does.

Historical antecedents of educational linguistics. Any discussion of educational linguistics (EL) must begin with Bernard Spolsky's sketch of the field in 1978, particularly the first chapter entitled "The field of educational linguistics." The points that Spolsky makes there are as valid now as they were then; for example, his discussion of the tensions between theoretical and practical matters, and his analysis of applied linguistics. Spolsky defines EL as "a sub-field of linguistics ... [with] very close ties with education." I will elaborate on this definition later on.

In some ways EL has had a long history, in other ways it has had none at all. If defined as a relationship between language study and education study, it has had a very long history. If defined as an academic field, subfield, profession or discipline,[1] I would argue that it does not exist at all. I will primarily be talking about EL as a field, but it will be useful first to comment briefly about the "natural connection" between language and education.

The relationship between language study and education goes back a long way, from the Medieval structure of education, the "Trivium" (grammar, rhetoric, and logic), to the dedicated work of a long list of scholars through the ages (see Howatt 1984 for a comprehensive survey). Comenius, Humboldt, Vygotsky, Jespersen, and Dewey are merely a few of the names that stand out, and it is immaterial whether we regard them primarily as linguists, psychologists, philosophers, or educators, since in most cases they were all of these things, a concern with language and education being quite incompatible with narrow specialization.

Focusing more closely on linguistics, we also find a steady progression of scholars whose language work was closely intertwined with pedagogical affairs, for example Sweet, Firth, Bloomfield, Palmer, Fries, and Lado. These scholars, as well as many others, were in most cases influential theoretical linguists, but with a strong interest and grounding in practical activity, especially in language teaching. Bloomfield, for example, whose classic book *Language* (1933) is one of the most important publications of structural linguistics, also wrote the *Outline guide for the practical study of foreign languages* (1942), which can be seen as a manifesto for the audiolingual method.

In our current day there is no less a connection between linguistics and education. This is clear in the work of sociolinguists such as Dell Hymes, Susan Ervin-Tripp, William Labov, and Ralph Fasold. The excellent video *American tongues* (Center for New American Media 1987) is a good example of sociolinguistic expertise applied to educational materials (the *Instructional guide* for the video was prepared by Walt Wolfram). One may further mention the connections between education and language in the work of Ruqaiya Hasan,

1. For the purposes of this paper it is not necessary to distinguish between words like field, profession, or discipline, though I am not assuming that they are entirely synonymous.

Michael Halliday, Gillian Brown, Shirley Brice Heath, and many others.[2] University centers or departments that might be called educational linguistics have begun to be established in various places, including the University of Pennsylvania, Philadelphia (established by Dell Hymes), The Centre for Language in Education at the University of Southampton (headed by Christopher Brumfit and Rosamond Mitchell), the Centre for Language in Education at the University of Nottingham (Ron Carter and Mike McCarthy), the Centre for Language in Social Life at Macquarie University (Christopher Candlin), and a good number of others.

One might therefore say that the historical precedent, the infrastructure, and the key personnel of EL are firmly in place. However, in spite of this there are a number of reasons why it is still premature to speak of a discipline or field called educational linguistics. I will address some of these reasons below, but before doing that it will be useful to look at a field whose fortunes are closely intertwined with EL: applied linguistics (AL).

Applied linguistics: The rise (and fall?). Howatt (1984) traces the term AL to the journal *Language learning* which was first published in 1948 by Fries, Pike, and colleagues. Fries himself drew on the suggestions for practical uses of linguistics in education[3] in Bloomfield's 1933 book *Language*. Bloomfield's work also influenced Palmer and others in Britain. To avoid an overly Anglo-Saxon bias, we might mention the highly influential work of Vietor in Germany, and Gouin and Passy in France, particularly in the area of phonetics, which contributed to the famous Reform movement around the turn of the century.

AL itself has thus had a long history as well (for further detail of its origins and progress I recommend Howatt's indispensable guide, 1984; see also Kelly 1969). Since AL and EL are so closely related, it is important to take a look at what has happened to AL in the last few years, especially since it has had a longer and stronger identity than EL.

For our present day conception of AL, and for any future conceptualization of EL, a key work to consider is Halliday, McIntosh and Strevens (1964). The following quote from that seminal book pinpoints the tension between theory and

---

2. It is interesting to note how in our current generation women occupy a prominent position in EL. This contrasts sharply with the entire history of the field which, as Howatt (1984) shows, has been, until very recently, an all male affair.

3. Note how AL is primarily identified with language teaching. Although it is certainly true that professionals other than language teachers could be called applied linguists (speech therapists, interpreters, lexicographers, copy editors, and so on) I do not believe any of them actually call themselves applied linguists, and that is significant. It is therefore appropriate for me to take it as given that AL in practice means language teaching.

practice in AL, a tension that would later also be noted by Spolsky in EL (1978).

> Until fairly recently it was often assumed that linguistics had no applications; the subject was thought of as knowledge for its own sake. Now that it has turned out, on the contrary, to have very specific and practical applications affecting the lives of large numbers of people, it is worth remembering that its usefulness is entirely due to the hard work and insight of scholars who were simply seeking knowledge ... Theories can always be replaced by better theories, new facts elicited and new syntheses made. The applications themselves are an important source of feedback: a theory is constantly reexamined in the light of ideas suggested in the course of its application. If a theory is allowed to stand still, it soon ceases to be useful.
>
> Quite naturally, it is when a theory turns out to have applications that it becomes of general interest. Until that time, it will impinge on only a small minority. (Halliday, McIntosh and Strevens 1964: 139).

Following the rapid growth of ESP (English for Specific Purposes) which drew heavily on Halliday et al., AL was firmly established in Great Britain by works such as Pit Corder's *Introducing applied linguistics* (1973) and the four volumes of the *Edinburgh course in applied linguistics* (1973–1977). At the same time, in the United States, linguistics took an emphatically theoretical turn in Chomsky's generative grammar (1965), which resisted attempts to find practical applications for it. The language teaching profession therefore quickly turned its eyes towards the work of Dell Hymes, whose notion of communicative competence, plus the growth of sociolinguistics in general, and the work of second language researchers such as Dulay, Burt, and Krashen (see, e.g., Richards 1974; Krashen 1981; Savignon 1983) gradually led to an emphasis on communication in the process of second language learning (or acquisition, as Krashen would say).

Then, in the 1980s, it seems that a serious rift occurred in the AL ranks, due to the enormous upsurge of interest in and studies of second language acquisition (SLA) research, which had started with second language studies inspired by first language development studies such as those of Roger Brown (1973). In the years since then, many SLA researchers have consciously and overtly distanced themselves, or expressed a desire to distance themselves, from practical educational matters, leaving the field of AL seriously fractured (see, e.g., Beretta 1993).

At the same time, a new field of AL research, known as teacher research or action research, has sprung up which takes an explicitly pedagogical rather than a linguistic focus. It may be too early to take stock, but as a result of these developments it seems that the linguistics in AL has veered off in the direction of theory (in a sense, therefore, has left AL), leaving pedagogy to cope with the practical side of things. The mutually strengthening relationship between theory and practice described by Halliday et al. in 1964, and illustrated in the work of earlier scholars, seems therefore to have disappeared.

There has thus occurred a sort of "double split"—linguistics (and SLA) for theory and education for practice—and this split needs to be resolved before we can once again speak of a healthy AL, and before we can undertake the project of EL.

The field of EL. Following Bourdieu (1990), I define a "field" as a historically constituted area of activity with its specific institutions and its own laws of functioning. It should be clear that, from this perspective, linguistics (at least since de Saussure) is a field, and education is a field, but EL is not. I believe that there are two main reasons why EL is not a field:

(1) It would necessitate an integration of theory and practice; and
(2) it would require adjustments in other academic fields.

Let me elaborate a little on these points. As regards (1), theory and practice often turn into irreconcilable opposites in academic circles. But EL cannot just be linguistic theory applied to educational practice, a sort of one-way flow of advice from top to bottom, where linguistics would be "top," and educational practice "bottom." Rather, the relationship must be reciprocal and dynamic, in the sense of Halliday et al. (see the quotation above; I will elaborate on this below, under project). To forge a field which attempts a dynamic unity between theory and practice would be somewhat like an attempt to introduce a new pronoun into the language that is neutral between "she" and "he." Given recent demands to reduce gender bias in language, attempts to do just that have been made, e.g., the pronoun "hesh," which I believe a professor of English in Iowa proposed some years ago. To my knowledge no attempt to introduce a new pronoun has ever caught on in any significant way, the reason being that the pronoun system is a closed system of words, which resists change. I venture to suggest that academic institutions are much more like closed systems than like open classes, and the introduction of a new member that fundamentally reclassifies time-honored criteria of "fieldness" can therefore not be expected to be easy.

As regards (2), let us use the analogy of birds on a wire. Let us say that our fledgling EL is a bird trying to join a row of other birds on the academic wire. One can observe that birds on a wire sit at equal distances from one another. If a new bird lands in their midst, all the other birds will shift and reposition themselves until, once again, equal (but now slightly smaller) distances obtain between them. If they refuse to budge, the newcomer will have to fly off again. In a similar way, to create a new field such as EL, space must be made available for it.

To sum up the discussion of field, it should be clear that fields are socially as well as ideologically and conceptually (to say nothing of economically) constituted. To establish EL as a field, therefore, requires much more than justifying its subject matter and even its rationale and action plan. It requires political action and institutional policy (and a budget, of course).

Conceptually, EL has to break new ground and be innovative by creating a discipline in which practice and theory are not seen as separate entities. It will also have to create curricula and textbooks that are correspondingly innovative and unorthodox. Politically, EL will presumably have to engage in the usual activities of lobbying, fundraising, arm twisting, and whatever else works in politics.

EL as project. Looking at EL as project, I see two major areas that are related:

(1) The relevance of education for linguistics. This has two aspects to it:
  (a) Teaching method, and
  (b) research data.
(2) The relevance of linguistics for education.

I will discuss these points in turn. I have put the relevance of education for linguistics first, since this reverses the direction in which most people perceive the relationship, a direction implied in the terms applied linguistics and educational linguistics (linguistics—presumably linguistic theory—applied to education, presumably educational practice—the double split I referred to earlier). I think it is extremely important that this direction be taken seriously, if EL is going to work at all. Let me quote some comments by Halliday and Chafe that illustrate what I am talking about:

> I would like to reject categorically the assertion that a course of general linguistics is of no particular use to teachers. I think it's fundamental. But I don't think it should be a sort of watered down academic linguistics course. It should be something new, designed and worked out by linguists and teacher trainers together. (Halliday 1982: 13).

Halliday further argues that linguistics may not be directly and obviously applicable at all times, but that it underlies our classroom practices and our understanding of learning. Chafe comments on the traditional problems of grammar instruction:

> ... it is not outrageous to suppose that some explicit attention to the nature of language will be helpful. ...
>
> It is possible, however, that the fault is not in teaching students to look systematically at language, but in the irrelevance of the grammar instruction that entered into these studies. (Chafe 1991: 46).

What is at stake here is the way in which linguistics is taught to future and current teachers, if it is taught at all. To speak bluntly, it seems that when teaching linguistics to educators, you first have to select the most irrelevant and uninteresting aspects of language, and then you proceed to teach them in the most unpalatable way that can be imagined. This obviously has to change, and here linguistics has a lot to learn from education, since our ways of teaching linguistics and grammar to student teachers have turned generations of teachers away from these vital areas of concern. Those that for some reason have managed to avoid rejecting linguistics have then proceeded to teach it to their own students in the same unpleasant way, thus compounding the problem.

What is to be done about this? Hymes (1992) suggests elementary linguistics courses for teachers, as "... the linguistics someone needs, not to write a grammar, but to read one," and "elementary literacy" in linguistics. This is a useful starting point, but an important caveat needs to be added. We cannot afford to formulate this "elementary literacy" as a list of items similar to that proposed by Hirsch (1987) for "cultural literacy," since this would merely lead to the piecemeal transmission of linguistic trivia. Rather, we need a methodology for teaching linguistics which is not based on what Paulo Freire calls "the banking model" (1972), but which is based on the following principles:

(1) **An *experiential* approach.** Acknowledge that teachers already have a wealth of knowledge about language which must serve as a point of departure.

(2) **Language as *process*, not product.** Language does not "consist of" words, sentences, and so on, which can be scrutinized, evaluated, and analyzed, but it is a process of making sense of the world and finding a place in it.

(3) **Language as *critical* study.** Language is used to think, debate, argue, control, and so on. It is an instrument of power, sometimes used to manipulate, and it can either constrict or liberate our thinking processes. It is important to analyze the power of language.

(4) **Task-based linguistics.** Rather than amassing facts and rules for periodic regurgitation, linguistics classes need to examine language issues in context. This involves selecting relevant instances of language use, designing tasks on their basis that allow for discussions of aspects

of language, analysis of language-related problems, and critical consideration of pedagogical strategies for language teaching.

There already is an increasing amount of work in this area (Andrews 1993; James and Garrett 1991; MacAndrew 1991; Rutherford 1994; van Lier 1991), but EL must make it one of its central commitments to develop an innovative methodology for teaching linguistics to teachers and student teachers. Without it, linguistics will remain at best a fringe element in a teacher's professional life.

A second way in which education is relevant to linguistics is in the form of data for linguistic theories. Educational practice and practices, as evidenced in classroom interaction for example, can and do provide crucial data for theories of language and language development (Bourdieu and Passeron 1977; Heath 1983; Cessaris and Bollinger 1991). The history of science provides an abundance of examples of theoretical discoveries made in the pursuit of practical ends (see van Lier 1994a for detailed discussion on this point). Feyerabend puts the issue quite strongly: "The knowledge we need to advance the sciences does not come from theories, it comes from participation" (1987: 284). Similarly, Vygotsky said of psychology that it is

> erroneous ... to perceive practical psychology as an application of previously established theories. The relationship should be reversed, with practice selecting its own psychological principles and ultimately creating its own psychology. (Kozulin 1990: 101).

The second point concerns the relevance of linguistics for education, more familiar territory, about which I can therefore be relatively brief. I will list a few points where linguistics can and does contribute to educational concerns, and where a new field of EL could stake out a series of research and action plans.

- **First-language/second-language classrooms.** This relates to the constraints and resources operating in settings in which more than one language is represented in the population, for example bilingual education, dual immersion, English as a second language, foreign language instruction, sheltered instruction, and so on. In all these settings issues relating to the pros and cons of using more than one language are in constant need of research and monitoring.
- **Language across the curriculum.** Education depends on language, not only in language arts or foreign language classes, but in all subjects, including Math and Science. EL needs to investigate how consistent language policies and an interdisciplinary focus on language skills and knowledge can be fostered (see Carter 1990 for detailed discussion).

- **School–community relations.** The first issue that comes to mind on this point is the interaction between teacher and parents. However, in many places schools increasingly serve as clearing houses or information sources for a variety of community services relating to children and family concerns. There is a constant and varied flow of information from school to parents and vice versa, and the discourses in which this information is packaged are an important topic for EL research.
- **School–work relations.** When students leave school in order to enter the workplace they need to master a whole range of new ways of language use, both written and spoken. Schools are increasingly interested in making the school-to-work transition easier, as well as possibly more gradual. One area for research is the systematic comparison of work discourses and school discourses; others are the investigation of apprenticeship programs, the treatment of minorities in the workplace (Roberts et al. 1993), crosscultural training in schools and at work, and many others.
- **Critical linguistics.** This relates to issues of power and control. In massive schools of two thousand or more students, and classes of forty students or more, education can easily become focused more on control, discipline, and orderliness than on academic excellence and motivating activities. Indeed, academic evaluation (approval) and docility may become inseparable. Language use in such environments gives important clues to the establishment and maintenance of control, and a study of these matters can in turn provide ways to improve instructional discourse.
- **Classroom interaction.** This will probably continue to be the core of the educational process, and its fine-grained study therefore will be at the core of the EL research enterprise. Elsewhere I have suggested that a key element in the provision of learning opportunities is the notion of contingency in talk (van Lier 1992, 1994b).

Conclusion. Many of us have been combining insights from linguistics and education for a long time and would therefore be justified in calling ourselves educational linguists, should we so wish. However, as I have tried to show in this paper, the establishment of a new field requires more than positive interest and good reasons.

For the field of EL to become a reality, departments of EL must be established which offer programs and degrees (including Ph.D.'s) in EL, offer courses in educational theory as well as linguistic theory, use textbooks and task-based materials in EL, and offer educational insights to linguists and linguistic insights to educators. The following are some basic prerequisites for this to happen:

(1) For linguists, the establishment of EL as a field requires a redefinition of language and a reexamination of the pedagogy (or andragogy, if the reader prefers) of teaching about language. Also, a redefinition of the roles of theory and practice, and their relationships, in language study.
(2) For educators, the establishment of EL as a field requires a realization that language is central to all educational activity, that the pedagogies of first and second language education are related, and that a systematic approach to language across the curriculum is necessary. Further, an understanding of the power of language—and the language of power—in interaction between and among teachers, students, and other participants in educational endeavors.
(3) The establishment of integrated programs of professionalization in which linguistics and education play an equal role, and both have a theoretical as well as a practical dimension.
(4) One way or another, for EL to become a field with its own professional identity, room must be made for it on the wire of academic discourse. It may require a little pushing and shoving, but most of all the persistent and concerted effort of all those who are committed to education and language study.

REFERENCES

Allen, J.P.B., S. Pit Corder, Henry G. Widdowson, et al. 1973–1977. *Edinburgh course in applied linguistics, Volumes 1-4.* Oxford: Oxford University Press.

Andrews, Larry. 1993. *Language exploration and awareness.* New York: Longman.

Beretta, Alan (ed.). 1993. *Theory construction in SLA* (thematic issue), *Applied Linguistics* 14(3).

Bloomfield, Leonard. 1933. *Language.* New York: Holt.

Bloomfield, Leonard. 1942. *Outline guide for the practical study of foreign languages.* Baltimore: Linguistic Society of America.

Bourdieu, Pierre. 1990. *The logic of practice.* Stanford, California: Stanford University Press.

Bourdieu, Pierre and Jean-Claude Passeron. 1977. *Reproduction in education, society and culture.* London: Sage.

Brown, Roger. 1973. *A first language: The early years.* Cambridge, Massachusetts: Harvard University Press.

Carter, Ron (ed.). 1990. *Knowledge about language and the curriculum: The LINC reader.* Sevenoaks, Kent, U.K.: Hodder and Stoughton.

Center for New American Media. 1987. *American tongues.* (*Instructional guide* by Walt Wolfram).

Cessaris, Ann and Dwight Bollinger. 1991. "The teaching of intonation: Classroom experiences to theoretical models." In Thom Huebner and Charles A. Ferguson (eds.), *Crosscurrents in second language acquisition and linguistic theories.* Amsterdam: John Benjamins. 291–303.

Chafe, Wallace. 1991. "Grammatical subjects in speaking and writing." *Text* 11(1): 45–72.

Chomsky, Noam. 1965. *Aspects of a theory of syntax*. Cambridge, Massachusetts: M.I.T. Press.
Corder, S. Pit. 1973. *Introducing applied linguistics*. Harmondsworth, U.K.: Penguin.
Feyerabend, Paul. 1987. *Farewell to reason*. London: Verso.
Freire, Paulo. 1972. *Pedagogy of the oppressed*. New York: Herder and Herder.
Halliday, M.A.K. 1982. "Linguistics and teacher education." In Ronald Carter (ed.), *Linguistics and the teacher*. London: Routledge.
Halliday, M.A.K., Angus McIntosh, and Peter Strevens. 1964. The linguistic sciences and language teaching. London: Longman.
Heath, Shirley Brice 1983. *Ways with words*. Cambridge, U.K.: Cambridge University Press.
Hirsch, Ed. 1987. *Cultural literacy*. Boston: Houghton Mifflin.
Howatt, Anthony P.R. 1984. *A history of English language teaching*. Oxford: Oxford University Press.
Hymes, Dell. 1992. "Inequality in language: Taking for granted." *Working Papers in Educational Linguistics* 8(1): 1–30.
James, Carl and Peter Garrett (eds.). 1991. *Language awareness in the classroom*. London: Longman.
Kelly, Louis G. 1969. *Twenty five centuries of language teaching*. Rowley, Massachusetts: Newbury House.
Kozulin, Alex. 1990. *Vygotsky's psychology: A biography of ideas*. New York: Harvester Wheatsheaf.
Krashen, Stephen. 1981. *Second language acquisition and second language learning*. Oxford: Pergamon.
MacAndrew, Richard. 1991. *English Observed*. Hove, Sussex, U.K.: Language Teaching Publications.
Richards, Jack C. 1974. *Error analysis*. London: Longman.
Roberts, Celia, Tom Jupp, and Evelyn Davies. 1993. *Language and discrimination: A study of communication in multi-ethnic work places*. London: Longman.
Rutherford, William. 1994. "Teaching linguistics and the acquisition research literature." Presentation at AAAL, Baltimore, March 1994.
Savignon, Sandra. 1983. *Communicative competence: theory and classroom practice*. Reading, Massachusetts: Addison-Wesley.
Spolsky, Bernard. 1978. *Educational linguistics: An introduction*. Rowley, Massachusetts: Newbury House.
van Lier, Leo. 1991. "Language awareness." In James E. Alatis (ed.), *Linguistics and language pedagogy: The state of the art*. Georgetown University Round Table on Languages and Linguistics 1991. Washington, D.C.: Georgetown University Press. 528–546.
van Lier, Leo. 1992. "Not the nine o'clock linguistics class." *Language Awareness* 1(2): 91–108.
van Lier, Leo. 1994a. "Forks and hope: pursuing understanding in different ways." *Applied Linguistics* 15(3): 328–346.
van Lier, Leo. 1994b. "Language awareness, contingency, and interaction." *AILA Review* 11: 69–82.

Locating contingency in e-mail

Celeste Kinginger
University of Maryland

Background. This paper discusses one role of computer-mediated communication in interactive language pedagogy.[1] The electronic mail (e-mail) exchange is described using data from a study examining language learners' use of e-mail for long-distance, collaborative project work. In the analysis, I have searched for a quality identified by van Lier as "contingency," a feature of language in action for which he claims a major role in language development (1992). Interactive approaches to language teaching depend crucially upon the negotiation of meaning within contingent action; certain aspects of communication via e-mail facilitate this, while others do not.

As Cummins (1988) has pointed out, questions about the computer's role in language teaching are not questions about computers. Rather, they are questions about definitions of language and philosophies of education. A useful distinction has been described by Hermann in her study comparing modes of computer use in French language teaching (1992). For a schematic comparison of the two modes and the philosophies that underlie them, see Table 1.

Table 1. Computer use and teaching philosophy

Language is defined as	product	process
Education is viewed as	information transmission	interactive/ experiential
Computer use is	"agentive"	"instrumental"

On the one hand there is the "agentive" use of the computer as "mentor," a term that describes much of the software currently available for language teaching. In the agentive mode, language is defined as a teacher-owned commodity (Barnes 1976) that must be effectively transmitted to the mind of the

1. This research was funded by the Consortium for Language Teaching and Learning, whose support is gratefully acknowledged.

learner through systematic drill and practice. The advantage of an anthropomorphized computer "agent" is its patience and efficiency as a tutor.

In opposition to this is the "instrumental" use of the computer as a tool for the enhancement of human activity. This mode corresponds to interactive, experiential, and learner-centered pedagogies combined with a view of language as process (Savignon 1983). Instrumental computer-based teaching encompasses various uses of local-area networks (LANs) and wide-area networks (WANs) to enable communication among learners within a class, between classes, or even between learners and the second language community.

Although the literature on this type of teaching is sparse because the medium is new, a range of instrumental computer uses has already been reported. These include synchronous or "real-time" computer-mediated conversation within Portuguese and French language classes (Kelm 1992; Beauvois 1992) and asynchronous, long-distance exchanges via e-mail in a Japanese composition course (Lunde 1990) and in a content-based French course (Sanaoui and Lapkin 1992). Cononelos and Olivia (1993) have also described a content-based Italian course centered around students' participation in an Italian language "newsgroup," a type of topical electronic bulletin board.

All of these experimental pedagogies rely upon the use of the computer as a support tool for learners as they create their own learning tasks and contexts for interaction. In the reports, there is much anecdotal evidence suggesting that this kind of computer-based teaching is both well received by the learners and very productive for language development. Various explanations for this success can be proposed, including simple enthusiasm for new ways of organizing the classroom. Another possible explanation would suggest that interaction via the computer network is useful because of "the unpredictable language negotiations" invoked by communicative tasks (Hermann 1992: 4).

While it is clear that qualities of participation in classroom discourse affect learning outcome and learners' attitudes, there is little consensus among classroom researchers as to what constitutes "good" or "productive" classroom discourse. One promising avenue is represented in van Lier's theory of contingency, focusing on language development through social interaction. The overall construct of contingency relies upon a Vygotskian theory of development, wherein social activity precedes and is transformed into cognitive activity (Vygotsky 1978). Within this theory, unpredictable language negotiations are viewed as valuable to learners because participation requires learner initiative and attention to the ongoing interaction. In other words, contingency is the essence of language in action, and as van Lier claims, "the quality of contingency in talk is crucial for the transformation of social interaction into language development" (van Lier 1992: 100). The definition of contingency as "ways of displaying attentiveness towards other turns" (van Lier 1992: 98) makes it possible to follow its development across a series of turns in particular interactions.

The study

Setting. The present study examined contingency within learners' uses of electronic mail for long-distance collaborative project work. The Harvard/Stanford/Pittsburgh collaborative project began six years ago with correspondence between French language students at Harvard and at Stanford. The project has since expanded to include French language classes at the University of Pittsburgh. This work is described in detail in a recent publication by the educators who have carried it out (Barson, Frommer, and Schwartz 1993). Briefly, second-year French classes at different institutions are paired and required to realize a collaborative project. Most of the collaborations have produced newspapers or magazines with fanciful titles such as "Le Réve de Soleil et de Neige" ('Dream of Sun and Snow'), or "L'Assiette de Crevettes" ('Plate o' Shrimp'). More recently, students have begun to produce video-based projects in connection with these courses.

The results reported here form one component of a larger-scale study carried out through participant observation over the course of two ten-week academic quarters (fall and winter 1991–1992) in John Barson's second-year French classes at Stanford University. In the fall quarter the students worked with a comparable class at Harvard to produce a news magazine, "La Voix Divine" ('The Divine Voice'), and its tabloid insert , "La Vérité" ('The Truth'). In the winter the students worked on several projects, including a film produced with a class at the University of Pittsburgh. The classes took place in a room equipped with twenty-four networked Macintosh II student stations and one Macintosh II with overhead projection capability for the instructor. Space on the classroom file server was reserved for individual and class files.

The initial phase of this research was carried out by a team consisting of the author and two graduate students who assisted with the collection and initial analysis of data. Data analyzed for this part of the study are archived e-mail messages from the files of the Stanford students. These files include all of the messages that were sent by the students as well as those received from their correspondents at the other participating schools.

Results. The "virtual classroom" (Barson 1991) provides a communication environment that offers several clear advantages to language learners. On the one hand, as compared to more traditional "lockstep" classrooms (Long et al. 1976), the right to speakership is distributed in a far more equitable manner. In principle, every participant has equal access to every other participant regardless of social status or institutional hierarchy. A further significant advantage is that e-mail can be generated and read in any place and at any time of day, provided there is access to a networked computer. For learners, the freedom to time one's own contribution is important, since it reduces the potential information processing overload of classroom communication (VanPatten 1986) and thereby is likely to reduce the anxiety of participation (Horwitz, Horwitz, and Cope 1986).

On the other hand, e-mail is a relatively channel-poor medium, one that offers little beyond a typed message. E-mail users do not necessarily have any information about the social status, rank, or appearance of their interlocutor. Furthermore, the tone or spirit of a message is very difficult to convey using e-mail. In several studies it has been shown that participants view e-mail as a socially anonymous medium precisely because it offers so little information about interlocutors. For example, in a study carried out in a corporate context (Murray 1988), co-workers who had not met face-to-face strongly preferred to begin their interaction in a medium that offers richer social information, such as the telephone. In another study, Sproull and Kiesler (1991) documented the presence of a phenomenon known as "flaming," where participants engage in online emotional outbursts and obscenity. According to the authors, this abusive online behavior may be attributed at least in part to participants' relative anonymity, hence to the paucity of social cues offered by the medium.

A range of participants' experience was evident in the classroom under study. It would not be possible to account for all of the data in this brief paper; however, the examples below were typical and serve to illustrate the qualities of contingency in these interactions. At the beginning of the academic quarter, after the students had become familiar with the computer equipment and mail software, they were given a list of the names and addresses of the students in the collaborating class at the other university. They were then faced with the problem of starting a correspondence with one or more of those students. Some responded to this task by sending a brief self-description to everyone on the list, while others selected one or two names and wrote only to those addresses. What followed, for individuals, was largely a matter of whether or not they could get a response from their correspondents and build some momentum in their interaction. Laura,[2] a student who eventually established a successful correspondence, attempted several approaches and wrote numerous messages before she received a response. Her reaction in example (1) is one of manifest relief.[3]

(1) Date: Thu, 17 Oct 91 11:49:22 -0700

merci beau coup pour votre message, m! [...] votre message est mon premier message (que j'ai recu) j'existe!!! [...]

---

2. Pseudonyms have been assigned to the participants to assure their anonymity.

3. All of the examples are extracted directly from the archived files, with no attempt to correct spelling errors or nonnative forms. Approximate translations are provided.

thank you very much for your message, m! [...] your message is my first message (that I have received) I exist!!!

While several of those who were not so persistent as Laura did not ultimately find a regular correspondent, many eventually became engaged in interactions such as the ones illustrated in examples (2) through (7), in which John and Linda exchange personal information on everyday conversational topics. Example (2) is the first message in this exchange, showing how Linda introduces herself to John, who replied in Example (3).

(2) Date: Wed, 29 Jan 1992 13:05 EST
Subject: francais

Bonjour John! Ca va? Moi, tres bien! Je m'appelle Linda et je vais a Pitt, mais j'aime California aussi! Quand je ne suis pas a l'universite, j'habite a Ohio! Dis-moi de toi! Au revior.

Hello John! How are you? I am fine! My name is Linda and I go to Pitt but I like California too! When I am not at the university I live in Ohio! Tell me about yourself! Good-bye.

(3) Wed Jan 29 12:41:37 1992
Subject: reponse

Bonjour, Linda! Je suis un etudiant dans la premiere annee a Stanford. Pendant mes vacances, j'habite a Illinois. Je n'ai pas un "major," mais je pense que j'etudierai l'anglais; specifiquement les poesies. Aussi, je joue le mellophonedans l'... orchestre marchant. A Bientot,
John

Hello, Linda! I am a first-year student at Stanford. During my vacation I live in Illinois. I don't have a "major" but I think I'll study English, specifically poetry. Also, I play the mellophone in the ... marching band.
More later,
John

About a week later, Linda writes back to John to ask him about his weekend, and John provides a detailed response. Then, writing late at night, he asks her to tell him about her preferences in music and other interests in example (5). Examples (6) and (7) are messages that were written at the same time, one after the next, in response to John's request.

(4) Date: Mon, 3 Feb 1992 13:33 EST
Subject: bonjour

Bonjour John! Ca va? Moi, tres bien! ... Comment etait ce week-end? Je suis allee a Ohio. Ecris-moi!
Au revoir
Linda

Hello John! How are you? I am fine! How was this weekend? I went to Ohio. Write to me!
Until later,
Linda

(5) Mon Feb 03 23:28:36 1992
Subject: nouveau message

Bonjour, Linda! Cette week-end, je suis alle au cinema pour voir le film Easy Rider. *C'etait vendredi. Samedi soir, je suis alle au match du basketball. L'equipe de Stanford a joue l'equipe d'Arizona State. Alors, dimanche, je n'ai pas fait grand chose. Mon frere me visite cette semaine, et nous avons fait un tour du campus. Il est un etudiant de la quatrieme annee a Illinois Wesleyan, dans Illinois, ou j'habite.*

J'aime beaucoup la litterature et les poesies, et aussi l'histoire du Pays de Galles. Quels interets as-tu? Quelle sortes de musique aimes-tu? Moi, j'aime beaucoup de sortes: la musique de Mozart, Tchaikovsky, Dvorak, et Bach. Aussi, j'aime des groupes modernes, comme les Beatles, les B-52's, REM, les Rolling Stones, et U2. J'aime aussi jazz. Ecris-moi, s'il vous plait!
Au revoir,
John

Hello, Linda! This weekend, I went to the movies to see the film *Easy Rider*. That was Friday. Saturday night, I went to the basketball game. The Stanford team played the Arizona State team. Then Sunday, I didn't do much. My brother visits me this week and we went on a tour of the campus. He's a fourth year student at Illinois Wesleyan in Illinois where I live.

I really like literature and poetry and also Welsh history. What interests do you have? What kinds of music do you like? I like all kinds: the music of Mozart, Tchaikovsky, Dvorak, and Bach. Also, I like some modern groups, like the Beatles, the B-52's, REM, the Rolling Stones, and U2. I also like jazz. Write to me, please!

Until then,
John

(6) Date: Wed, 5 Feb 1992 13:25 EST
Subject: French

Bonjour John! Ca va? Moi, tres bien! Tu habites a Illinois, maintenant je comprends. Aimes-tu jouer basketball ou regarder basketball? J'aime le regarder, mais je n'aime pas le jouer.

Hello John! How are you? I am fine! You live in Illinois, now I understand. Do you like to play basketball or watch basketball? I like to watch it but I don't like to play it.

(7) Date: Wed, 5 Feb 1992 13:35 EST
Subject: French

Bonjour John. (I accidentally made an error on the last message!) J'aime REM et U2 aussi. J'aime "Love Shack" de les B52s. J'aime les Eagles, Bad Company, et Bryan Adams. J'aime "le soundtrack" de Robin Hood. *C'est un bon film! J'espere que tu a un bon jour! Au revoir!*
A bientot, Linda!

Hello John! [sentence in English] I like REM and U2 also. I like "Love Shack" by the B52s. I like the Eagles, Bad Company, and Bryan Adams. I like the *Robin Hood* soundtrack. Its a good movie! I hope you have a good day! Good-bye!
See you later! Linda!

John and Linda's interaction continues in this manner until the end of the academic quarter. Throughout, they display attentiveness to each other's contributions; in other words, contingency is present in an asynchronous form that is relatively accessible to learners. There is little in-depth discussion of these or other topics, however. Later in their interaction, John reports that he is reading Locke in one of his other classes, and he asks Linda her opinion of that philosopher. She replies that she thinks Locke is *interssant* [sic] ("interesting") then drops the topic.

In the two classes studied, most of the learners in this study became engaged in useful and apparently satisfying French language interactions over the network. Others had more difficulty, and a few did not succeed in their efforts to become involved. The learners' problems can be attributed to any combination of a range of explanations involving learning style, motivation, previous experience with computers, and the like. Another explanatory factor may be the presence of constraints on the quality of e-mail communication, hence on the extent to which the medium itself supports contingent interaction.

Two limiting factors based on these data can be identified. The first of these is timing: if a sender can generate an e-mail message anywhere at any time, the same can be said for the individual who will respond. In this study there were several interactions that simply did not survive long intervals between contributions. A second factor, perceived social anonymity, means that people must work harder than usual to forge interpersonal bonds via e-mail. Just as in any other context, interaction by e-mail requires a certain momentum that can turn out to be somewhat fragile, especially when the correspondents have never met. When the interaction is successful, most people eventually switch to another medium. Notably, at the end of the quarter John and Linda exchanged "snail mail" addresses with a promise to continue their relationship through the post.

Conclusion. This study has examined some features of electronic mail communication by learners of French, illustrating both advantages and potential difficulties associated with the classroom use of this medium. There are few constraints on the distribution, location, or timing of participation in e-mail exchanges. For learners this means that the right to speakership and access to interlocutors are much easier to obtain than has traditionally been the case in classrooms. In other words, this new technology has the potential to expand classroom discourse options (Kramsch 1985) beyond any limits previously imaginable.

This paper has also illustrated the presence of contingent interaction among learners engaged in active use of French over the electronic network. Van Lier's theory (1992) suggests that contingency may be the key to language development through social interaction, yet in many language classrooms contingent interaction between individuals is difficult to sustain. These new forms of contingency may be particularly significant for language learners because they occur without the distribution, location, and timing constraints of face-to-face conversation. It is also apparent that the liberating effects of e-mail communication can turn out to be problematic in some instances. Nonresponse or slow response to messages as well as the paucity of social cues afforded by the medium can contribute to impeding communicative exchange.

Further study is needed both to refine a definition of learners' contingent interactions via this medium and to document the effects of e-mail in language classrooms. Meanwhile it is clear that communicative language teaching can benefit by the new forms of computer-mediated communication now available.

References

Barnes, Douglas R. 1976. *From communication to curriculum*. Harmondsworth, U.K.: Penguin Press.

Barson, John. 1991. "The virtual classroom is born—What now?" In Barbara Freed (ed.), *Foreign language acquisition research and the classroom*. Lexington, Massachusetts: DC Heath. 365–383.

Barson, John, Judith Frommer, and Michael Schwartz. 1993. "Foreign language learning using e-mail in a task-oriented perspective: Inter-university experiments in communication and collaboration." *Journal of Science Education and Technology* 2(4): 565–584.

Beauvois, Margaret H. 1992. "Computer-assisted classroom discussion in the foreign language classroom: Conversation in slow motion." *Foreign Language Annals* 25(5): 455–464.

Cononelos, Terri and Maurizio Olivia. 1993. "Using computer networks to enhance foreign language/culture education." *Foreign Language Annals* 26(4): 527–534.

Cummins, J. 1988. "From the inner city to the global village: The microcomputer as a catalyst for collaborative learning and cultural interchange." *Language, Culture and Curriculum* 1(1): 1–13.

Hermann, Franloise. 1992. *Instrumental and agentive uses of the computer: Their role in learning French as a foreign language*. San Francisco: Mellen Research University Press.

Horwitz, Elaine, Michael B. Horwitz, and JoAnn Cope. 1986. "Foreign Language Classroom Anxiety." *Modern Language Journal* 70: 125–132.

Kelm, Orlando. 1992. "The use of synchronous computer networks in second language instruction: A preliminary report." *Foreign Language Annals* 25(5): 441–454.

Kramsch, Claire. 1985. "Classroom interaction and discourse options." *Studies in Second Language Acquisition* 7: 169–183.

Long, Michael, Leslie Adams, Marilyn McLean, and Fernando Castaños. 1976. "Doing things with words: Verbal interaction in lockstep and small group classroom situations." In Ruth Crymes and John Fanselow (eds.), *On TESOL 1976*. Washington, D.C.: TESOL. 137–153.

Lunde, Ken R. 1990. "Using electronic mail as a medium for foreign language study and instruction." *CALICO Journal* 7: 68–78.

Murray, Denise. 1988. "The context of oral and written language: A framework for mode and medium switching." *Language in Society* 17(3): 351–373.

Sanaoui, Rita, and Sharon Lapkin. 1992. "A case study of an FSL senior secondary course integrating computer networking." *Canadian Modern Language Review* 48: 525–553.

Savignon, Sandra. 1983. *Communicative competence: Theory and classroom practice*. Reading, Massachusetts: Addison-Wesley.

Sproull, Lee and Sara Kiesler. 1991. *Connections: New ways of working in the networked organization*. Cambridge, Massachusetts: MIT Press.

van Lier, Leo. 1992. "Not the nine o'clock linguistics class: Investigating contingency grammar." *Language Awareness* 1(2): 91–108.

VanPatten, Bill. 1986. "Second language acquisition research and the learning/teaching of Spanish: Some research findings and implications." *Hispania* 69: 202–216.

Vygotsky, Lev. S. 1978. *Mind in society: The development of higher psychological processes*. Reading, Massachusetts: Harvard University Press.

Computer-based classrooms for language teaching

Stephanie J. Stauffer
Georgetown University

Introduction. When the words "computer" and "language classroom" appear in the same phrase, a certain picture often comes to mind: That of an individual seated at a personal computer, using instructional software that might present grammar drill and practice, or, with more recent and more sophisticated software, interactive audio and video lessons for listening and reading comprehension. Until recently, in fact, many discussions of the success or failure of the computer with respect to language instruction did not even recognize that it could be used in any other way (LeBlanc and Guberman 1988; Rivers 1989). While computer-assisted language learning (CALL) software certainly has its place in a well-rounded approach to teaching, this paper will not touch on the uses of CALL.

Where the CALL approach is individualized and self-contained, the computer-based classroom aims to increase student involvement with peers, instructors, and the outside world. What this paper will offer is a description of how the computer can be used as a tool and as a medium of communication in ways that fit in very well with the need to motivate language students and to provide authentic materials and opportunities for communication.

Discussion of the computer-based classroom will be framed in terms of curriculum plans being made for an Intensive International Executive Program (IIEP) conducted for ten weeks every summer on the campus of the International University of Japan (IUJ) in Niigata Prefecture. It should be emphasized that the arguments and examples provided here could be extended, with very little modification, to other language programs with access to networked computers.

The computer-based classroom defined

Computers as tools. The computer-based language classroom makes use of the computer not as a surrogate instructor but as a tool for completing tasks that in turn motivate learning of linguistic forms and functions (Long and Crookes 1992; Nunan 1989). The most common courses of this type teach students how to operate the computer and run its various applications, such as word processors, spreadsheets, and databases. Healey (1993), for example, describes a one-semester university ESL course that introduces Microsoft Works, integrating word processors, spreadsheets, and databases, along with graphics, to produce class projects, including a newsletter.

At IUJ, instructors have chosen to present similar lessons on Macintosh computers to exploit its graphic user's interface (GUI).[1] Language teachers find that GUI software written with the business market in mind offers advantages that so-called educational software often cannot provide. The human interface is painstakingly designed and extensively tested to make the best possible use of visual, kinesthetic, and aural feedback (Apple 1992). Documentation is well-written and easy to adapt for nonnative speakers of English. Procedures for running common functions such as printing or saving documents remain consistent across applications, so that once students have invested the time to learn one application, they have a head start on learning the others. In addition, the GUI is comprehension-based: Students need only recognize the commands they need, rather than having to remember and type them correctly. Software manufacturers provide well-designed self-paced tutorials that allow students to practice basic computer operations and to gain exposure to related vocabulary at their own pace. Finally, the metaphors upon which the GUI is based are powerful aids to learning.

In this type of computer-based language classroom, tasks are selected and graded according to the difficulty of the computer procedure. The content of language lessons is determined by what features of language are relevant to the main task or by what can be worked in naturally. The approach often works especially well when students bring assignments from other courses to use as material while they learn to use the word processor or spreadsheet. In this way, they reinforce their learning of language and concepts for both classes because they are working with the same material, and they also receive evaluation from both instructors. Such coordination has been possible in the past within the IIEP's sister program at IUJ; students benefit from the process of creating a polished product.

Computer-mediated communication (CMC). Rather than emphasizing the technological aspects of computers, language instructors can highlight the communicative functions of existing networks (Maule 1993). For the large majority of users, computer-mediated communication (CMC) simply means electronic mail (e-mail). Computers may be connected within an office or university (local area networks, or LANs), or they may be part of a larger service such as Bitnet or the Internet (wide area networks, or WANs), connecting organizations world-wide. Individuals type and "send" electronic messages to their colleagues' "mailboxes," where the messages wait to be read.

E-mail, however, is only one of the many faces of CMC. In addition to e-mail, organized discussions are carried out with worldwide participation, information is made available for others to examine and use, and the network itself

1. Of course, IBM's Windows offers a good alternative.

Table 1. Models of CMC and network use

a) one →	distributor/archiver →	many	• automatic distribution = discussion list • individual initiative = usenet/BBS
b) one →		many	• automatic distribution = e-mail list
c) one →		one/few	• automatic distribution = e-mail, chat
d) many ↔	distributor/archiver →		• individual initiative = database search = file transfer (ftp) = ftp mail
e) many ↔	interface → archiver		• individual initiative = gopher, WAIS, etc.

can be searched like a huge database. Listed in Table 1 is an outline of the types of communication possible and the means by which messages are distributed.

Discussion lists and UseNet newsgroups are organized by topic. There are thousands of such public lists active at any one time, most with a global membership or readership, covering topics from where to dine in Tokyo to how to publish your first novel. Discussion lists require an intial "subscription," and messages are then sent automatically to the user's mailbox. Newsgroup messages, on the other hand, are accessed through a "newsreader" that presents a directory of group names and subdirectories of discussion topics. Users choose which messages they want to read.

E-mail lists are set up by individuals for communication within working groups: Distribution is usually more limited and more private than for discussion lists. Personal e-mail (discussed above) and "chat" allow private messages to be passed. "Chat" differs from e-mail in that messages appear on the users' screens rather than entering a mailbox, and an interactive conversation can take place.

Database search and file transfer (ftp) allow public access, copying, and keyword searches of many different types of archives, from the records of discussion lists to United States White House press releases. Gopher and other interfaces allow active, net-wide information searches guided by convenient menus.[2]

Language programs all over the world, especially those serving adult students with an interest in crosscultural interaction, are beginning to tap the resources of the Internet. Sanaoui and Lapkin (1991) studied the use of networked computers in a secondary level French as a second language course in Canada. Students enjoyed conducting online interviews, submitting personal journals, and participating in small-group conferences. Paramskas (1993/4) mentions the possibility of using of e-mail for language teaching; Bedell (1994) provides a list of discussion groups and newsgroups conducted in foreign languages; the TESL-L discussion list has been archiving files on how to use e-mail in the classroom along with addresses of students who wish to participate in exchanges; and Cononelos and Oliva (1994) outline a university-level Italian course in which students were required to read and eventually participate in the newsgroup soc.culture.italian.

Though not intended to teach language, Cotlar and Shimabukuro's (1993) experiment of inviting guests to lecture electronically could easily be adapted for the language classroom. Acker and Slaa's (1993) "international academic joint venture" involving Ohio State University and the University of Amsterdam, another project that was not part of a language course, did involve crosscultural communication between native and nonnative speakers of English. Participants on either side of the Atlantic conducted a policy-making simulation on the topic of the European Community and telecommunications. They communicated through fax, telephone, video conferences, and electronic mail, and in the end the Amsterdam team traveled to Ohio to complete the exercise. While such a travel opportunity may be extremely rare, the e-mail components of this exchange are within reach of many language programs, should they invest the time in organizing the exercise.[3]

CMC and the IIEP.

The IIEP. The ten-week Intensive International Executive Program at IUJ takes in between thirty and forty students, mainly male, mainly Japanese, with an average age of thirty and an average TOEFL score of about 460.[4] Non-Japanese students typically come from Indonesia or China. The students are

---

2. For a more complete overview of Bitnet and the Internet, see Hahn and Stout (1994).

3. An outline of a similar exercise aimed at less-sophisticated students can be found in the archived file "Project IDEALS" (Promoting an International Dimension in Education via Active Learning and Simulation), by D. Crookall and C. Schreiber-Jones, listserv@cunyvm.cuny.edu (no date given).

4. Tom Hayes, Director, personal communication, March 1994.

employees of companies or government offices, and most are to be posted abroad very shortly.

Table 2. IIEP daily schedule

Mornings
International Business English
Comunications Skills for
International Management

Afternoons
Cross-Cultural Exercises
Case Studies
Guest Speakers
Negotiations Simulation:
FINS (Moxon 1994)

The IIEP allocates class time according to the daily schedule in Table 2. Afternoon classes revolve around international business case studies, crosscultural exercises, and other activities as listed. All reading and interaction are done in English, and high levels of participation are expected. Morning classes allow students to focus primarily on features of English. The first class makes use of Jones and Alexander's (1989) text for international business English, along with Munter's *Guide to Managerial Communications* (1992); the second recycles material from the afternoon's case studies and other projects (e.g. Moxon 1994) to develop students' presentation and discussion skills. Both English classes use, to a certain extent, the adjunct content-based language instruction model discussed by Brinton, Snow, and Wesche (1989). Instructors attend afternoon classes, read the assigned materials, and prepare language lessons that facilitate comprehension and production of English for the content courses. Rather than being purely communicative, these lessons do incorporate the focus on forms (Long 1991) expected and preferred by many of these students.

Incorporating CMC. The IIEP has been providing English language, cross-cultural, and international management training very successfully for a number of years. It has included some computer-based components, but only as they serve the needs of the other parts of the curriculum. Why, at this point, should the program expand its curriculum to encompass the use of e-mail and other network services? CMC is relevant to the IIEP in three major ways.

First, business use of local networks and extended networks, including the Internet and commercial services, is increasing not only in the United States but around the globe (*The Internet Letter* 1994). For executives who are about to be sent overseas, awareness of what tools are available and what strategies are possible is extremely important.[5] This means that if the IIEP is to include a computer component, it should emphasize networked computing. The program

5. Bickson et al. (1985), Sproul and Keisler (1991), and Swanson (1993) discuss the impact of CMC in the workplace and provide good material for discussion.

will continue to teach wordprocessing skills to enable students to produce and edit their own messages and to cut and paste material they find that they would like to keep or forward to colleagues. Spreadsheets will be taught as needed to present or process the numerical data attached to case studies or other projects. Other applications will be included if and when they are requested.

Second, the language of Bitnet, the Internet, and many of the large commercial services is English. What's more, the English is not always of the textbook variety. Because the program has decided that these students should be familiar with the 'net and its services, it makes sense to tailor some language instruction to what they're going to encounter on the networks.

Finally, though it's true that the language of internetworking is English, participation in discussion lists, bulletin boards, and all form of CMC is international. In the course of one thread of discussion on a political list, for example, there may be contributions from nationals of Nigeria, India, Spain, Canada, Japan, Egypt, Germany, Korea, China, and the United States.

Such discussions are useful for IIEP students in at least two ways. To begin with, they are direct sources of information and perspectives on issues (for the Management component of the IIEP), and they are direct "comprehension checks" and "production tests" (for the English component of the IIEP). In other words, discussion lists are ready-made opportunities for students to "listen" and participate, communicating in English within domains that are directly relevant to the Management section of the IIEP and in ways that can be exploited by the Language focus of the program.

Discussion lists also provide many examples of cross-cultural misunderstanding, leading to the negotiation of meaning between people who may or may not realize that they are each attaching a different definition to the same word or a different interpretation to the same situation (cf. Bantz 1993). Again, these instances of breakdown and negotiation have relevance to both the Management and Language components of the IIEP.

Given the fact that CMC seems to be such a valuable addition to a program like the IIEP, how will it be worked into the existing curriculum? There are a number of needs that can be thought of as three overlapping phases.

Introductory phase. The first phase is an introductory phase, where the computer system and applications are the content focus of instruction. This involves introduction to the personal computer along with basic utilities like word processing and number crunching, introduction to the mainframe using local electronic mail, and introduction to the network and what it offers. For this introductory phase, instructors will use the commercially developed training materials provided by Apple for the Macintosh and also adapted versions of the help manuals and networking guides available online. These networking guides, free from newsgroups and discussion lists, have undergone years of use by an

Example 1. Usenet etiquette guidelines

```
NETIQUETTE for USENET

Newsgroups: gtu.infoage
Subject: Usenet Etiquette
Date: 6 Oct 92 15:54:42 -0400
Original-from: chuq@sun.COM (Chuq Von Rospach)
[Most recent change: 21 Jan 1991 by spaf@cs.purdue.edu (Gene Spafford)]

A Primer on How to Work With the USENET Community
Chuq Von Rospach

*** You now have access to Usenet, a network of thousands of computers.
Other documents or your system administrator will provide detailed
technical documentation. This message describes the Usenet culture and
customs that have developed over time. All new users should read this
message to find out how Usenet works. ***

*** (Old users could read it, too, to refresh their memories.) ***

[...]

This document is not intended to teach you how to use USENET. Instead,
it is a guide to using it politely, effectively and efficiently.
Communication by computer is new to almost everybody, and there are
certain aspects that can make it a frustrating experience until you get
used to them. This document should help you avoid the worst traps.

The easiest way to learn how to use USENET is to watch how others use
it. Start reading the news and try to figure out what people are doing
and why.

[...]

Because your interaction with the network is through a computer it is
easy to forget that there are people "out there." Situations arise
where emotions erupt into a verbal free-for-all that can lead to hurt
feelings.

 Please remember that people all over the world are reading your words.
Do not attack people if you cannot persuade them with your presentation
of the facts. Screaming, cursing, and abusing others only serves to
make people think less of you and less willing to help you when you
need it.

 If you are upset at something or someone, wait until you have had a
chance to calm down and think about it.

[...]
```

international audience and are easy to read and understand (see Example 1).

Implementation phase. After a staggered introduction to applications and networking comes the second phase: implementation. Now the computer network acts as a medium for students to communicate and to collect information. Here the focus should be on the content of the other modules of the IIEP.

Students and faculty will participate in an IUJ discussion list set up by the systems operator, the contents of which will be automatically archived. From time to time, discussion topics will be assigned and discussion leaders will be required to manage the talk generated on the list. The discussion list should produce both highly monitored and less monitored styles of writing. The archives will give instructors access to a "transcript" of the talk, which may serve as material for English classes if instructors notice recurring patterns of error and so forth.[6]

A second project will require students to prepare a case study involving the marketing of a given product in a given region; they will collect some of their data through file transfer ("anonymous ftp" or "ftp mail") or through personal contacts that have been set up for them in advance on the network or that they have made themselves. These case studies will be carefully prepared so that instructors will have pointers to existing data files and can point students in the right direction.[7]

As Example 2 shows, searching for information on a gopher server requires the ability to skim and scan a large quantity of text, picking out appropriate titles and following promising leads. Such practice is valuable to students who will need to sift through this type of data daily, immersed in an English-language information culture. Example 2 shows the screens for a search for construction data from Hong Kong, performed through the gopher server at UCSD. The document was just a few days old when it was retrieved.

Students will also "listen to" at least one discussion group or newsgroup and participate when they feel ready. This will afford a chance for them to follow personal interests and develop electronic friendships (if they wish): Newsgroups exist for every hobby a student has ever proclaimed.

Finally, toward the end of the summer, students will be asked to communicate via e-mail with a group of Americans, first to become acquainted, and then to develop a strategy with team members for a negotiations simulation project (Moxon 1994). This should be very much like a short term version of the project described by Acker and Slaa (1993; and above), complete with a visit by the

---

6. Concordancing software is useful in creating such materials; Sinclair (1991) is one source to consult for approaches.

7. Harvard College, Babson College, the University of California at San Diego, and the Univeristy of Missouri at Saint Louis are just a few of the many sources of relevant information. Each of these institutions has a gopher server and a World-Wide Web home page that include business sources in their directories.

Example 2. Search for construction data performed through gopher server.

(Screen 1)

```
              Internet Gopher Information Client v1.11
               Root gopher server: infopath.ucsd.edu

     1.  About InfoPath/
     2.  What's New (March 12, 1994).
     3.  The Library/
     4.  Encyclopaedia Britannica.
     5.  Campus Information/
     6.  Computing Services/
 --> 7.  News & Services/
```

(Screen 2)

```
                         News & Services
     1.  About News & Services.
     2.  Weather - Report from Scripps Pier.
     3.  Weather - San Diego Area.
     4.  Weather - California Forecasts/
     5.  Weather - North American Forecasts (via Gopher)/
     6.  Weather - National Information Service <TEL>
     7.  Weather - From U of IL (oriented for pilots and meteorolo-
         gists)/
 --> 8.  Economic Bulletin Board/
```

(Screen 3)

```
                      Economic Bulletin Board
     1.  IMPORTANT! About the EBB and UMich.
     2.  Current Business Statistics/
     3.  Defense Conversion Subcommittee (DCS) Info/
     4.  EBB and Agency Information and misc. files/
     5.  Eastern Euopean trade leads/
     6.  Economic Indicators/
     7.  Employment Statistics/
     8.  Energy Statistics/
     9.  Foreign Trade/
     10. General Information Files/
     11. Industry Statistics/
 --> 12. International Market Insight (IMI) reports/
```

(Screen 4)

```
--> 73. HONG KONG - AIRPORT PROJ - IMI940301.
    74. HONG KONG - AIRPORT PROJ - IMI040310.
    75. HONG KONG - ENVIRONMENTAL PROJ - IMI940307.
    76. HONG KONG - LIGHT RAIL PROJ - IMI940301.
    77. HONG KONG - LIGHT RAIL PROJ - IMI940307.
    78. HONG KONG - ROAD TOLL COLLECTION PROJ - IMI940310.
    79. HUNGARY - BUS CONTRACT - IMI940303.
    80. HUNGARY - EBRD TELECOM PROJ - IMI940303.
    81. HUNGARY - HIGHWAY PROJ - IMI940303.
    82. INDIA - AMATEUR RADIO OVERVIEW - IMI940301.
    83. INDIA - AVIATION INDUSTRY STATISTICS - IMI940301.
    84. INDIA - CREDIT CARD TRENDS - IMI940301.
```

(Screen 5)

```
File: AAA638404.;1    Row:          1    Col:          1    (    0%)
HONG KONG - AIRPORT PROJ - IMI940301

ace
()()(-)
SUMMARY

This article is derived from a telegraphic report dated 1 March 1994,
prepared at the American Consulate - Hong Kong. It discusses a planned
airport project in Hong KOng. The article consists of 4 pages.

()()(-)
01 MAR 94

AMCONSUL HONG KONG

SUBJECT:   IMI: HONG KONG'S NEW AIRPORT KEEPS MOVING FORWARD DESPITE
POLITICAL GRIDLOCK

1.  THE REPLACEMENT HONG KONG AIRPORT PROJECT HAS KEPT MOVING FORWARD
EVEN THOUGH THE POLITICIANS ARE STILL TRYING TO RESOLVE THE POLITICAL
REFORM DEADLOCK. THE AIRPORT PROJECT HAS SEEMINGLY REACHED THE POINT OF
NO RETURN. A TOTAL OF 41 CONSTRUCTION CONTRACTS WORTH OVER USD 6.2
BILLION HAVE BEEN AWARDED BY THE HKG, THE PROVISIONAL AIRPORT AUTHORITY
(PAA), AND THE WESTERN HARBOR TUNNEL COMPANY.
2.  THE FOLLOWING IS A SUMMARY OF THE AIRPORT PROJECT PROGRESS:
(A) SITE FORMATION AT CHEK LAP KOK - OVER 37 PERCENT OF 1,248-HECTARE
    AIRPORT PLATFORM FORMED UNDER USD 1.2 BILLION CONTRACT
(B) TUNG CHUNG NEW TOWN - ABOUT 85 PERCENT OF SITE FORMATION COMPLETE
    UNDER USD 90 MILLION CONTRACT
(C) WEST KOWLOON RECLAMATION - ABOUT 70 PERCENT COMPLETE UNDER USD 1
    BILLION CONTRACTS
(D) CENTRAL RECLAMATION - USD 0.2 BILLION CONTRACT UNDERWAY
```

American group to Japan. Here, students will need to bring to bear all of the skills they have developed during the summer in terms of crosscultural and crosslanguage communication, building group cohesion, gathering information (Bantz 1993), and handling the frustrations that can arise in electronic communication. There will be a spectacular payoff when all members of the negotiating teams are united at the end of the program.

Language emphasis phase. As an adjunct to the introductory and implementation phases, there should be an overlapping language-emphasis phase, some aspects of which have been mentioned above. A few elements will be built into the syllabus, such as the form of an e-mail message. Other topics will require some flexibility on the part of the instructors.

The language class might examine, for example, how the discourse is managed on a discussion list, what constitutes a thread of discussion, what conventions participants follow, what happens when communication breaks down, what registers and jargon participants use, what special vocabulary—both domain-related and CMC-related—is needed to understand and communicate, and so forth.

The message from soc.culture.japan shown in Example 3 is an excellent example of content that can be recycled in the language classroom. The sender is Japanese, and he quotes an American. He follows the discussion list conventions of quotation in response to an argument, and he communicates effectively while still exhibiting evidence of being a nonnative speaker of English. The language instructor might focus on what makes this an effective message, what aspects of the text provide clues that the sender is a non-native speaker, and how to "correct" the text. Students might then bring the text into their own discussion list, criticize or elaborate the points, and thereby recycle the vocabulary. The course textbook might be consulted on matters of form and style. In the end, students might prepare a response to be sent back to soc.culture.japan (assuming that the class is using an up-to-date message from the list), to start the process over again.

Readings from Cronin's (1994) *Doing Business on the Internet*, a collection of short cases, Johnstone's (1994) *Wiring Japan*, and Momtaz's (1994) *Development of Internetworking in Japan*, both analyses of the difficulties encountered in connecting to the Internet in Japan, will offer challenging topics to spark discussion and lead students to further research. Possible topics include

- how information is controlled on the Internet and who does the controlling,
- how to manage information overload,
- whether those engaged in CMC have the same rights to privacy and ownership as with other types of communication, and

Example 3. IEEP student's post to discussion group

```
Subject: Re: Cultural Differences (Was: Contamination in Thai rice)
In article xxx MF says:
[beginning of article deleted]

Thanks, Mike.
 don't realize what is it mean "law is closed" and "stocks and trading
are closed." Except "stocks and trading", other markets are all deeply
concerning with the "public", aren't they? Especially concerning with
our safety and health. As I said in the pevious post, japanese people
think the "public" is very important, so we have the strict regulations
for them. Can it be called as "closed/unfair"? If you call it unfair,
I want to ask you do you intend to change the computers of NASA to
japanese one? Do you intend to change the computers of Pentagon to
japanese one? Every nation has the right to use their own products for
their important fields, hasn't they?

I think there are 4 levels of "closed/open" markets in japan. (please
correct me if wrong)
    1) Restricted by law/regulations

        ---> like rice market

    2) Not restricted by law but usually do not use foreign products.

        ---> like computer market for public office?, construction
            market? telecomunication market?

    3) Not restricted by law but there maybe some kind of barriers
     for products.(ex. strict testings ?)

        ---> like car market, grains ?

    4) there is no regulations/barriers for foreign products.

        ---> like semiconductor market, PC & WS market,
            products for daily life, cloths, AV,
            Electronics, etc.

> Now, do YOU think the above markets are open or closed? If open, why?

I think, the most important part of the above for trade imbalance
s 3) and 4). (partly 2) I think 3) is not only effective for foreigners
but also for japanese. So I don't think it is closed. But as for 2), I
think we'd better make regulations for both japanese and foreign people
who sell products in japan. And most important part for trade imbalance
is 4) and there is no restrictions for importing to japan. Isnt it
right? I don't understand why japan is called as unfair. T.
```

- questions of authenticity that arise with electronic data transfer.

Any of these could be incorporated into the presentations or discussions required by the Communication Skills class, depending on student interests, and the topics that arise in the exercises for the Management and Cross-Cultural Communications classes.

Language instructors will prepare students for their case study exercise by practicing the skimming, scanning, and vocabulary skills that students will need to use the gopher menu hierarchies efficiently. They will also help students compose introductory statements when the negotiations teams are set up with American partners and act as advisors should communications run into difficulty.

Conclusion.

The IIEP. The aim of the IIEP is to give students strategies so that they can observe, adapt, and succeed in a foreign culture. Students should also leave the program with an increased ability to participate in an English language environment and enjoy their time abroad. CMC is a powerful ingredient in this mix—a tool for communications that can stretch far beyond the campus walls and that may last far longer than the 10 short weeks of the IIEP.

The computer-based language classroom beyond the IIEP. Definitions of literacy and the workplace are changing (Tuman 1992), and it is the responsibility of language instructors to keep pace with those changes in their classroom practices. It is hoped that language instructors will begin to look beyond CALL to the possibility of using computers as the medium for task-based instruction or as aids to content-based instruction and CMC.

This is not a motion to leave behind the methods that have served language teachers well until now. It is recognized that, often, face-to-face communication can produce better results for some activities than electronic communication, especially where the creation of group cohesion or the reliance on paralinguistic cues is desirable or necessary (Caldwell and Taha 1993). However, as one approach in a well-rounded language teaching curriculum, the computer-based classroom can motivate students and provide a rich context for practice and acquisition of language skills.

REFERENCES

Acker, Stephen R. and Paul Slaa. 1993. "International academic joint ventures: Leveraging external resources through telecommunications and travel." *IPCT-J* 1(4) [Interpersonal Computing and Technology Journal, listserv@guvm.bitnet].

Apple Computer, Inc. 1992. *Inside Macintosh: Overview*. Reading, Massachusetts: Addison-Wesley.

Bantz, Charles. 1993. "Cultural diversity and group cross-cultural team research." *Journal of Applied Communication Research* 21(1): 1-20.

Bedell, David. 1994. "Review of Bitnet/Internet lists for language learning." University of Bridgeport ELI: bedell@cse.bridgeport.edu, March 18, 1994.

Bickson, Tora, Cathleen Stasz, and Donald Mankin. 1985. *Computer-mediated work: Individual and organizational impact in one corporate headquarters*. Santa Monica, California: Rand Corporation.

Brinton, Donna, Marguerite Snow, and Marjorie Wesche. 1989. *Content-based second language instruction*. New York: Newbury House.

Caldwell, Barrett S. and Lilas H. Taha. 1993. "Starving at the banquet: Social isolation in electronic communication media." *IPCT-J* 1(1).

Cononelos, Terri and Maurizio Oliva. 1994. "Teaching languages with netnews." *IPCT-J* 2(1): 40-49.

Cotlar, Morton and James M. Shimabukuro. 1993. "Stimulating learning with electronic guest lecturing." *IPCT-J* 1(1).

Cronin, Mary J. (1994). *Doing business on the Internet*. New York: Van Nostrand Reinhold.

Hahn, Harley and Rick Stout. 1994. *The Internet complete reference*. Berkeley, California: Osborne McGraw-Hill.

Healey, Deborah. 1993. TESLCA-L: Listserv@cunyvm.bitnet, December 6, 1993.

Johnstone, Bob. 1994. "Wiring Japan." *Wired* 2(2): 38-42.

Jones, Leo and Richard Alexander. 1989. *International business English*. Cambridge, U.K.: Cambridge University Press.

LeBlanc, Raymond and Solange Guberman. 1988. "L'ordinateur dans l'enseignement des langues: Un colosse aux pieds d'argile?" [The computer in language teaching: A great image with feet of clay?]. *Canadian Modern Language Review* 45(1): 103-118.

Long, Michael. 1991. "Focus on form: A design feature in language teaching methodology." In Kees de Bot, Ralph B. Ginsberg, and Claire Kramsch (eds.), *Foreign language research in cross-cultural perspective*. Amsterdam: John Benjamins.

Long, Michael and Graham Crookes. 1992. "Three approaches to task-based syllabus design." *TESOL Quarterly* 26(1): 27-56.

Maule, R. William. 1993. "The network classroom." *IPCT-J* 1(1).

Momtaz, Cameron. 1994. "The development of internetworking in Japan." In *Proceedings of the workshop on technical requirements for accessing Japanese information: Problems and solutions*. Washington, D.C.: Library of Congress. 103-116.

Moxon, Richard. 1994. *FINS* (Foreign Investment Negotiations Simulation). Bellevue, Washington: Author.

Munter, Mary. 1992. *Guide to managerial communications*. Englewood Cliffs, N.J.: Prentice Hall.

Net Week, Inc. 1994. *The Internet Letter: On corporate Users, Internetworking, and Information Services* 1(5), February 1, 1994.

Nunan, David. 1989. *Designing tasks for the communicative classroom*. Cambridge, U.K.: Cambridge University Press.

Paramskas, Dana. 1993/4. "CALL: Increasingly integrated into an ever-more electronic world." *Canadian Modern Language Review* 50(1): 124-143.

Rivers, Wilga. 1989. "Interaction and communication in the language class in the age of technology." In James E. Alatis (ed.), *Georgetown University Round Table on Languages and Linguistics 1989*. Wasington, D.C.: Georgetown University Press.

Sanaoui, Razkia and Sharon Lapkin. 1991/2. "A case study of an FSL senior secondary course integrating computer networking." *Canadian Modern Language Review* 48(3): 525-552.

Sinclair, John. 1991. *Corpus, concordance, collocation*. Oxford: Oxford University Press.

Sproull, Lee and Sara Keisler. 1991. *Connections: New ways of working in the networked organization*. Cambridge, Massachusetts: MIT Press.

Swanson, Douglas J. 1993. "Toward a policy for managing the use of CMC in the workplace." *IPCT-J* 1(1).

Tuman, Myron C. 1992. *Word perfect: Literacy in the computer age*. Pittsburgh: University of Pittsburgh Press.

Organized Babel: English as a global lingua franca

Tom McArthur
English Today, Cambridge University Press

The Bible is not so widely read as it once was, but such phrases as *the Garden of Eden*, *Noah's Ark*, and *the Tower of Babel* still lead active lives in languages long associated with Christianity and Judaism. The original Babel story is very short: The entire account is only one brief chapter, Genesis 11, which opens with the intriguing statement that "the whole earth was of one language." It then recounts that in the land of Shinar—now southern Iraq—an unnamed leader once urged his followers to undertake an enormously ambitious project. He said:

> "Goe to, let vs build vs a city and a tower, whose top may reach vnto heauen. ... And the LORD came downe to see the city and the tower, which the children of men builded. And the LORD said; Behold, the people is one, and they haue all one language: and this they begin to doe: and now nothing will be restrained from them, which they haue imagined to doe. Goe to, let vs goe downe, and there confound their language, that they may not vnderstand one anothers speech. So the LORD scattered them abroad from thence, vpon the face of all the earth: and they left off to build the Citie. Therefore is the name of it called Babel (that is, Confusion), because the LORD did there confound the language of all the earth." (King James Bible, 1611)

We still call a confusion of tongues a *Babel*, and anxious people sometimes use the term *Babelization* for what they believe can happen when we do not take proper care of a language and of the society to which it "naturally" belongs. Terms like *Babel* and *Babelization* are particularly useful when conservatives comment uneasily on such new multiethnic, multicultural, and multilingual Babylons as London and Los Angeles, Sydney and San Francisco.

In addition, wherever we go, conservatives and liberals alike, we find that the entity once safely and sufficiently known as "the English language" has become all bound up in the bedlam of vast change across our planet. Indeed, there is a paradox at the heart of present-day English, wherever it is used in the world: that it simultaneously experiences great stability and great flux, with centripetal and centrifugal tendencies in operation at one and the same time.

The stability and the centripetal tendencies are broadly associated with the so-called standard language, while the flux and the centrifugal tendencies cover just about everything else and include all the points where everything else meets and meshes with the standard language. When people say "X speaks English," they are making a blanket statement that implies a lot more stability than flux. They imply that X can handle the phonology, syntax, and lexis of the language—that is, the standard language—adequately, and maybe also some of the rest: maybe a regional accent or even a dialect or more exotically still a creole.

If, however, people speak "only" a dialect or creole, there is often doubt about whether they really do "speak English" in any meaningful present-day sense. Doubts of this kind might be expressed as a general "Well, they speak English, but ...," or, across a continuum of comment, sometimes wry, sometimes exasperated, as with "Yes, X speaks English, but it's American English," or "Well, X does speak English if that's in fact what they do in Scotland," or "X's Yorkshire/Arkansas dialect is impenetrable," or "Well, Jamaican Creole isn't really English at all, is it?"

Millions who grew up thinking they were comfortable native speakers of the language can be pushed out into all sorts of linguistic wildernesses in such ways—often because there are real barriers, some greater, some less, of unintelligibility among varieties. The title of an article we published in *English Today* (October 1993) by the West Indian poet-academic Mervin Morris says it all, as he argues the case for his mother tongue: "Is English we speaking."

Such observations point to the vast, virtually indescribable continuum of usage within English as a world language: a state of affairs in which we are all—users of English every one—faced with points where the center does not hold and there has for long been a serious peripheral confounding of tongues, however fiercely convinced many dwellers on this enormous edge are that it is indeed "English we speaking."

At the same time, however, it is now generally agreed that a range of English-using nations have, to a greater or less degree, their own standard usage. This was long ago evident in the United Kingdom and the United States, which have had dictionaries, grammars, usage manuals, and publishing industries for centuries. It has also in recent decades become increasingly clear-cut in Australia, Canada, New Zealand, and South Africa, which also have their dictionaries, manuals of style, and the like. And despite sometimes stormy discussions, many now accept that there is a strong element of standardization within the acrolects of English in India, Nigeria, Singapore, and elsewhere. Hence we use such terms as "British English," "American English," "Australian English," "Indian English," and "Singapore English."

These terms can of course be used—and often are used, and should be used—to cover all the varieties of English in such countries, but they are also often (implicitly) limited to standardization, to what is more fully covered by the formulas *Standard Somebody's English*, as in "Standard American English" and *Somebody's Standard English*, as in "Australian Standard English" (which can then be truncated as "Standard American" and "the Australian Standard"). All such standardized or standardizing varieties around the world meet in a hard-to-define but nonetheless real global space that we can call the "international standard," which is preeminently associated with print, broadcasting, and the media at large (so that we can talk usefully about *the international print standard*, *the international broadcasting standard*, and *the international media standard*. It is also associated with science, technology, and education (so that we can talk usefully about *the international scientific and technological standard* and *the international education standard*, if we so wish). These are all, it would appear, well-defined but overlapping registers of the same worldwide linguistic artifact, and they are remarkably homogeneous—or homogenous.

All English-speaking countries, however, as far as I can tell, and whatever the condition and status of their media and their academic and educational systems, have thorough-going nonstandard varieties that are often spoken by more people than use the standard variety. Some of these are so nonstandard, so distinctive in their systems, and so autonomous in their usage that they meet many—perhaps all—of the usual criteria for independent status as languages. Try for example just these two:

> Whan the gloamin cam, aa at hed fowk at wis ailin ae gate or anither brocht them til him an he laid his haunds on ilkane o them and hailit them.

That is an example of traditional Scots, from *The New Testament in Scots*, a direct translation from Greek completed in the 1960s by William Lorimer and first published in 1983—not 1783 or 1883. (Translation: When twilight came, all those who had relatives who were sick in some way or another brought them to him, and he laid his hands on each of them and healed them.)

> Tupela kilim pik na mipela karim i kam na i hevi tru, biiiikpela tru, orait, em mipela i karim long bris.

That is an example of Tok Pisin, an official language of Papua New Guinea, as recorded by Peter Mühlhäusler in 1982 and reported in Bailey and Görlach (1982). (Translation: These two killed the pig and we [exclusive] carried it and it was very heavy, really huge, well, this one we carried toward the bridge.)

Claims regarding the autonomy of such forms are increasingly common. There are scholars, myself among them, who assert that Scots is more than a northern dialect of the English of England: that it is rather one of four Germanic languages that have been spoken in Britain: Anglo-Saxon, English, Scots, and Norn, the now extinct Scandinavian tongue of Orkney and Shetland. Various

Figure 1. Map by Peter Strevens (1980), taken from Strevens in Kachru (1992).

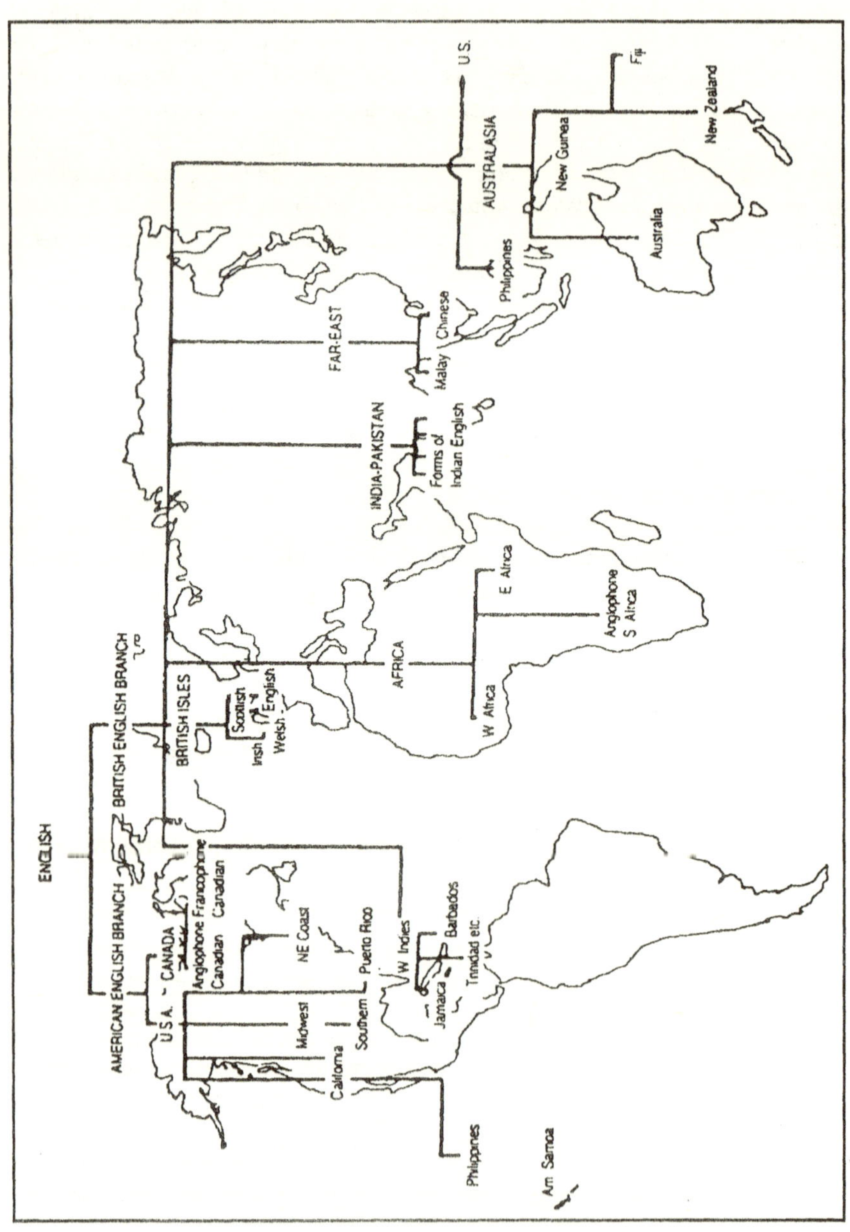

creolists also assert the distinctness not only of such a divergent form as Tok Pisin but also of Caribbean Creole and West African Pidgin. Scholars of English around the world have in recent years attempted to model this complex state of affairs, and I would like to present four of these models here.

The first consists of a map of the world on which the British applied linguist Peter Strevens (1980) has imposed a branching diagram reminiscent of the quasi-botanical models used since the nineteenth century for separating off and displaying the "mother" and "daughter" languages of, in particular, the Indo-European family. (See Figure 1, on previous page.)

The second (Figure 2) is my own "Circle of World English" (1987), which has a "world standard English" at the hub of a spoked wheel, with various standard and standardizing areas in a circle around it, then a vast ragged fringe of varieties all round the edge.

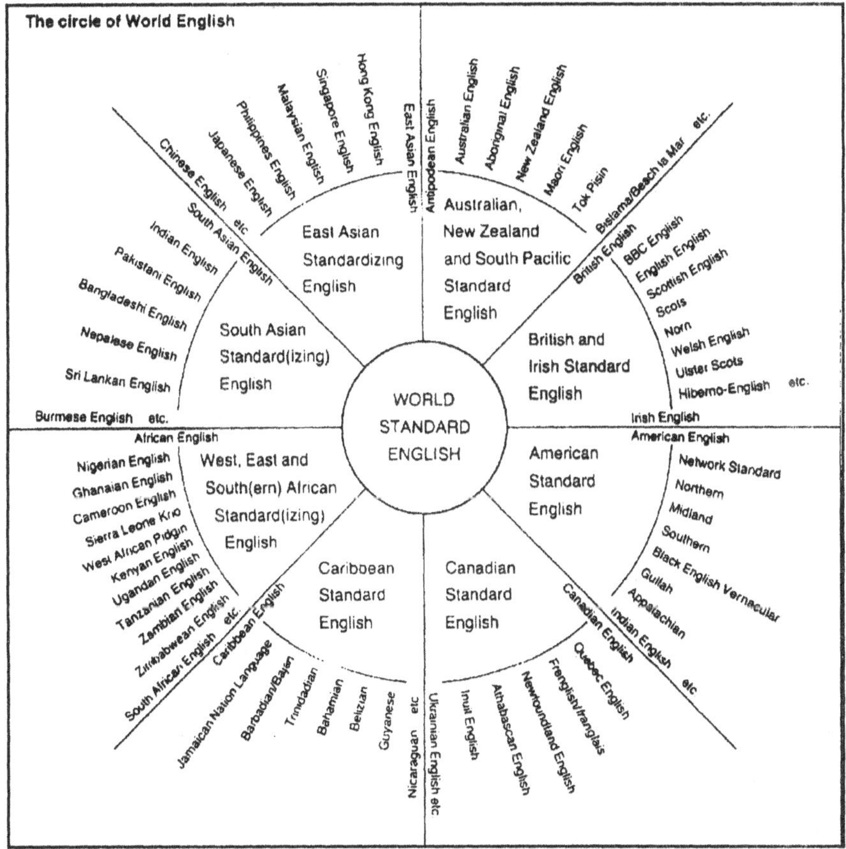

Figure 2. "Circle of World English," taken from McArthur (1987).

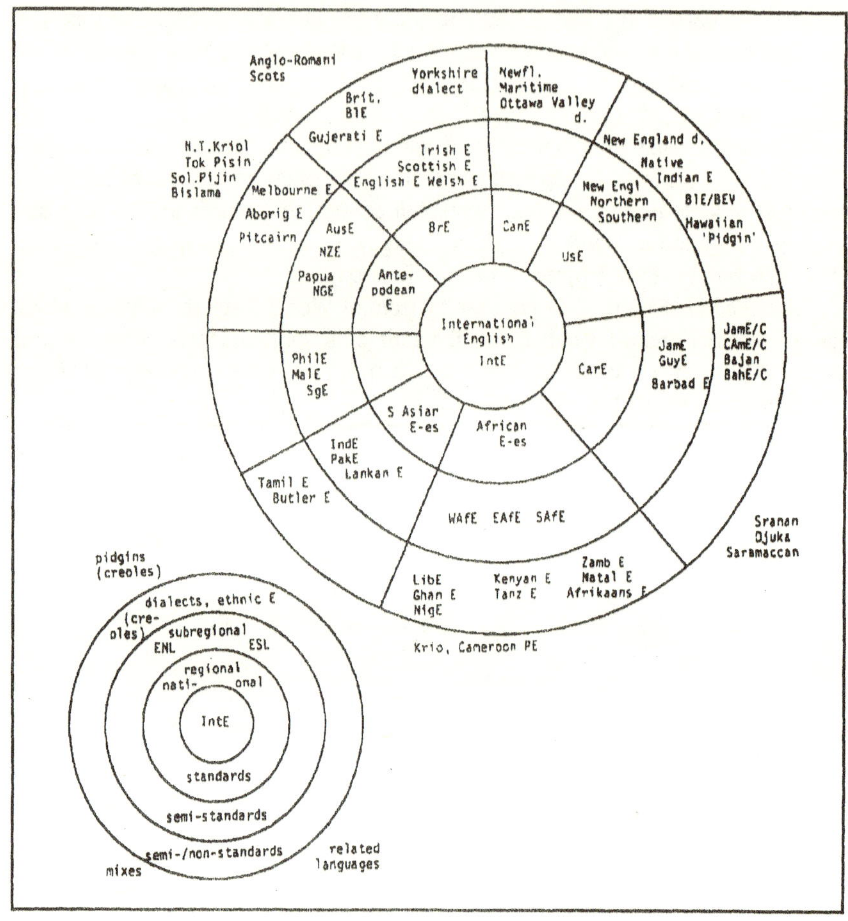

Figure 3. Manfred Görlach's circle model, taken from Görlach (1990).

The third is the German variationist Manfred Görlach's circle model (1988), which has "International English" at the hub of a similar spoked wheel, then "regional national standards" in the first outer circle, "subregional ENL and ESL semi-standards" next beyond that, then "dialects, ethnic English (creoles) semi-/non-standards" beyond, and out beyond the perimeter "related languages" such as Scots, such "pidgins" and "creoles" as Tok Pisin, and such "mixes" as Anglo-Romani in Britain (Figure 3).

The fourth is the Indian linguist Braj Kachru's model of linked ovals, in which a rising series of contiguous shapes moves from earlier unnamed states of English through an "Inner Circle" of the first English-speaking countries,

Figure 4. Braj Kachru's model of linked ovals, taken from Kachru (1992).

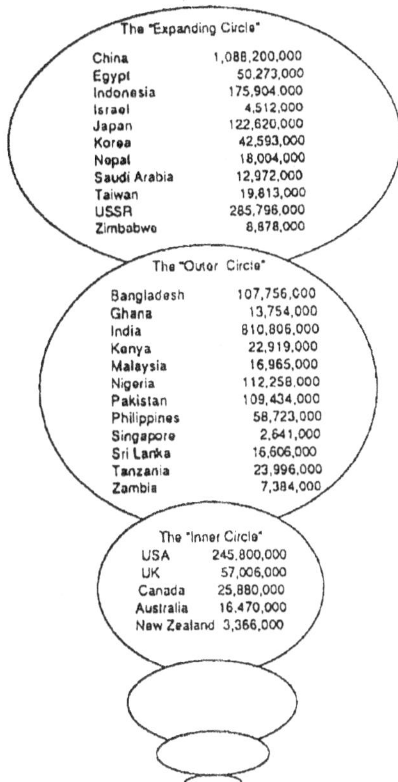

then an "Outer Circle" of post-colonial countries, to an "Expanding Circle" that takes in the rest of the world, with lists of countries and approximate populations set within the ovals (Figure 4).

These models, despite their inevitable limitations, highlight a great deal in various interesting and economical ways. Strevens implicitly expands the Indo-European language family with a whole new range of sublanguages under the heading "English," which becomes as much the name for a subfamily as ever "Germanic" or "Indo-Iranian" was; McArthur and Görlach offer core and periphery models for which standardization is the "centering" element of the English language or languages; and Kachru highlights a set of shifts from English as "mother tongue" to the furthest reaches of Enqlish as "other tongue."

All of which is fine, but none of it takes the present condition of English as far as it really stretches. What we see in the above models is explicit and well defined, but by focusing on systems that one can in some sense call "English" as traditionally perceived, all four fail to cover the whole range of phenomena affecting world English. I would argue now, in 1994, that at least one major element is missing from all of these models. What we see is a high degree of organizedness in both the description and the use of the global lingua franca and its offshoots. But for Babel in its most confounded form we must go beyond English as conventionally understood to whole new worlds of hybridization, as in the four following specimens:

- In northern India, educated, professional people commonly mix English and Hindi, as in "*mai apko batati hum,* he is a very trusting person," where the opening words are Hindi for 'I tell you' (Kachru 1992).
- In the Philippines, a comparable blend of English and Tagalog is: "*Pwede kayong magbayad* three months after arrival. *Pwede pang i*-extend up to two years *ang* payment" 'It is possible to pay three

months after arrival. It is possible to extend payment up to two years.' Filipinos have two names for this kind of blend: Taglish and Mix-Mix (Kapili 1988).

- Along the Texas-Mexican border, Latinos commonly mix Spanish and English in what is widely known as Spanglish and locally called both Tex-Mex and Border Lingo. In the following extract (Goldman 1986), a Mexican husband and wife and a sales clerk are talking in a convenience store:

Husband: "*Que necesitamos?*"
'What do we need?'

Wife: "*Hay que comprar pan, con* thin slices."
'We need to buy bread, with thin slices.'
[She turns to the sales clerk.]
"*Donde está el* thin-sliced bread?"
'Where is the thin-sliced bread?'

Clerk: "*Está en* aisle three, *sobre el* second shelf, *en el* wrapper *rojo*."
'It is in aisle three, on the second shelf, in the red wrapper.'

Wife: "*No lo encuentro*."
'I can't see it.'

Clerk: "*Tal vez* out of it."
'Maybe out of it.'

- A further illustration comes from Malaysia, in a recorded conversation (Baskaran 1994) between two women lawyers, Chandra, who is Tamil, and Lee Lian, who is Chinese:

Chandra: "Lee Lian, you were saying you wanted to go shopping, *nak perga tak*?"
'want to go, not?'

Lee Lian: "Okay, okay, at about twelve, can or not?"

Chandra: "Can lah, no problem one! My case going to be adjourned anyway."

Lee Lian: "What you looking for? Furnitures or kitchenwares?
You were saying, that day, you wanted to
beli some *barang-barang*."
'buy some things'

Chandra: "Yes lah! Might as well go window-shopping a bit at
least. No chance to *ronda* otherwise. My husband, he got
'patrol/loaf'
no patience one!"

Lee Lian: "You mean you actually think husbands got all that
patience ah? No chance man! Yes or not?"

Chandra: "*Betul Juga*. No chance at all! But if anything to do with
'true also'
their stuff—golf or snooker or whatever, then
dia pun boleh sabar one."
'he too can be patient'

Such hybridization, generally called "code-switching," is profoundly common throughout the world, linking English with an uncertainly large number of other languages. And it appears to be increasing. It is so common that many recently coined blend-names, most of them formed on the base *-lish* and used informally and often facetiously and dismissively, are nonetheless close to being technical terms in their own right. They include: *Anglikaans*; *Arablish*; *Chinglish*; *Frenglish* and *franglais*; *Gerlish* and *Deutschlish*; *Italglish* and *itangliano*; *Janglish*, *Japlish*, and *Japalish*; *Swenglish* and *Swedlish*; *Russlish*; *Spanglish*; and *Yinglish*.

In the European Union, the status and use of English (as first language among equals in a group currently of nine official languages) have been marked by five neologisms with facetious and vaguely pejorative overtones: *Euro-English, Eurolish, Eurospeak, Desperanto*, and *Minglish*. The first three also denote (and sometimes deride) the bureaucratese of the Eurocrats in Brussels, Luxembourg, and Strasbourg; the fourth, *Desperanto*, refers to a kind of anxious confusion among simultaneous translators; while the fifth, *Minglish*, the coinage of the British humorist Paul Jennings, has a serious whiff of Babel about it.

Because such labels primarily point up the amusement, anger, and so forth of their users, they do not adequately mark the significance or the scale of the hybridization itself. Such blends may be enjoyed, mocked, or denounced by teachers, linguists, the media, and others, but quite regardless of praise or blame they simply steamroller on, the daily usage of tens of millions of people. Widespread and pragmatic, they are used as much and as freely by purists—

when they relax or forget themselves—as by those who find them entirely natural.

This hybridization of English with an indefinite number of other languages is an outcome of social and linguistic necessity, and it is probably the most extensive miscegenation of languages that has ever taken place. Many people have written about "imperialist" or "killer" English supplanting and sidelining other languages; few, however, have considered whether English will under certain circumstances simply merge with these languages as, a thousand years ago, the Anglo-Saxon dialects and the French of the Normans merged to become something new in the writings of Chaucer and Malory.

The world's millions of versatile bilinguals are at least as significant for the future of the English language as the broadly unilingual communities of the U.K., the U.S., and Australia; indeed, I reckon them more significant because they vastly outnumber the unilinguals. For example, in Canada, India, Kenya, Nigeria, Pakistan, the Philippines, and Singapore, the mixers are key figures in the shaping of national usage.

Although the various Anglo-hybrids are currently unstable, the hybridity itself is stable enough. If past situations are anything to go by, those languages affected today will undergo irreversible change, as English did after the Danish invasions, the Norman Conquest, and the Renaissance. For example, Malay by government design in Malaysia and Indonesia, and Japanese by casual osmosis, are already indelibly marked by borrowings that include what English has already taken from French, Latin, and Greek. The outcome is far from clear, but it can hardly be minor, and not only the other languages but English itself will be affected in ways that we can at present barely imagine. Our future models of what has been happening in, to, and with English must somehow reflect this remarkable state of affairs.

REFERENCES

Bailey, Richard and Manfred Görlach. 1982. *English as a world language*. Ann Arbor, Michigan: University of Michigan Press.

Baskaran, Loga. 1994. "The Malaysian English Mosaic." *English Today*, January 1994

Goldman, Lorraine. 1986. "Tex-Mex." *English Today*, January 1986.

Görlach, Manfred. 1990. "The Development of Standard Englishes." In *Studies in the history of the English language*. Universitätsverlag, Heidelberg: Carl Winter. (Adapted from a 1988 paper in German.)

Kachru, Braj B. 1992. "Teaching World Englishes." In Braj B. Kachru (ed.), *The other tongue: English across cultures*. Urbana, Illinois: University of Illinois Press.

Kachru, Braj B. 1992. "Hindlish." In Tom McArthur (ed.), *The Oxford companion to the English language*. Oxford: Oxford University Press.

Kapili, Lily V. 1988. "Requiem for English." *English Today*, October 1988.

McArthur, Tom. 1987. "The English Languages?" *English Today*, July 1987.

Strevens, Peter. 1980. *Teaching English as an international language*. Oxford: Pergamon Press.

The fiction of the native speaker in L2 research

Eyamba G. Bokamba
University of Illinois

Preliminaries. On the basis of facts from native speakers of American English, this preliminary study presents a critical review of the types of data that have motivated the postulation of the theory of interlanguage (IL) and selected key concepts that underlie it. In particular, it is shown here that native speakers of American English often make errors that are analyzable as "deviant" and "fossilized" so as to be viewed as "IL," but such facts are never so characterized in the published literature. In view of these and World Englishes data, the study seriously questions the basic assumptions made in IL theory and the theoretical constructs underpinning it. It is suggested in conclusion that while concepts such as interlanguage, deviation, interference, fossilization, and transfer are useful constructs in the discussion of second language acquisition (SLA), this "usefulness" is not unique to SLA; instead, it holds across all aspects of language acquisition when sociolinguistic factors are taken into consideration. This conclusion is argued to offer a better explanation of the native and non-native speakers' data as well as a positive perspective on the notion of IL.

Objectives of language learning theory. The overarching concern of psycholinguistic research has been the discovery of the process of language acquisition by both children and adults learning one or more additional languages. In first and additional language acquisition, psycholinguistic theory aims at providing both a description and an explanation of the acquired linguistic knowledge, or what Chomsky (1986) terms internalized language. This research pursuit is guided by four fundamental questions, which, to quote Rutherford's (1982: 85) elegant statement made in reference to SLA, are as follows:

> We wish to know [1] what is acquired, [2] how it is acquired, and [3] when it is acquired. But were we to have the answers even to these questions, we would still want to know [4] why ... (cited in Ellis 1986: 249).

These questions entail three important additional subquestions: (5) what is the linguistic evidence for this internalized or acquired knowledge? (6) How can this knowledge be characterized descriptively and theoretically? And (7) what realistic inferences can be drawn from the learners' performance data or externalized language?

Interlanguage theory. SLA research has taken several different approaches in attempting to address these seven questions, among others. One of these models is the developmental or interlanguage theory articulated by, among others, Corder (1967, 1971), Nemser (1971), Richards (1971), and Selinker (1972, 1992). For the purposes of this paper I focus on the work of Selinker, who is viewed as the leading theoretician of this research paradigm.

Building on research in contrastive analysis (CA) and error analysis (EA), in 1972 Selinker published a paper that has now become a classic of SLA studies: "Interlanguage." In this lucid and internally balanced study, Selinker offers what he considers to be "...some theoretical preliminaries for researchers concerned with the linguistic aspects of the psychology of second language learning" (1972: 173). His primary interest in this regard was to provide a characterization of the learner's knowledge on the basis of actual speech data and to see what inferences could be drawn from these facts for the eventual articulation of a theory of SLA. To do this he made three crucial assumptions à la Chomskyan linguistics (Selinker 1972: 175–176):

- that there exists ideal native speakers of the target language (TL) that the learner is trying to master;
- that there is only one norm (or variety) of the language whose sentences he/she is attempting to produce;
- that from the beginning of his/her study of L2 the learner has an inherent/strong desire to develop an ideal native speaker competency in TL.

As in the classical SLA literature of the 1940s and 1950s (cf. Fries 1945; Lado 1957), Selinker assumes further that the starting point of the learner's L2 knowledge is his or her L1 and the end point is the idealized native speaker's norm.

These assumptions led Selinker to postulate the following four constructs and mechanisms, among others:

1. *Interlanguage:* The systematic knowledge of a second/foreign language that is independent of both the learner's L1 and the target language (see also Corder 1971 and Nemser 1971 for a similar characterization).
2. *Fossilization:* A subconscious mechanism which involves the retention of certain "linguistic items, rules, and subsystems" by speakers of a particular L1 in their interlanguage relative to a particular target language (IL), "no matter what the age of the learner or amount of explanation and instruction he receives in the TL" (Selinker 1972: 177).
3. *Latent psychological structure:* The ability of an adult learner to achieve native speaker competence in a second/foreign language

(Selinker 1972: 175). (cf. Lenneberg's 1967 notion of "latent language structure" for child language acquisition.)

4. *"Five central processes":* (1) language transfer; (2) transfer of training; (3) strategies of L2 learning; (4) strategies of L2 communication; and (5) overgeneralization of TL linguistic material (Selinker 1972: 179; but see also Richards 1971).

Specifically, and unlike the CA-based research and some of the earlier EA studies, Selinker considers the L2 learner's progress a developmental process that can be viewed as consisting of various stages of knowledge in which the performance data reveal systematicity or rule-governed behavior. He termed this body of knowledge "interlanguage" in the sense defined in (1). Nemser (1971) had previously termed this knowledge "the approximative systems."

According to Selinker (1972, 1992), IL is characterized by "fossilization" (2) and the mechanisms stated in (3) and (4). The involvement, consciously or subconsciously, of these mechanisms or strategies leads to a number of morpho-syntactic errors in the production of the TL—omission of function words, inconsistent use of tense-aspect markings, unnecessary pluralization, inconsistent subject-verb agreement, and the occurrence of resumptive pronouns—as illustrated in the following sentences drawn from published studies on varieties of English in the World (hereafter, World Englishes):

(1) a. He won by overwhelming majority. (cf. Kirk Greene 1971; Bokamba 1982)
b. I may continue with the interview or examine few more applications. (Sey 1973; Bokamba 1982)

(2) a. Yesterday we go for a drive and we stop near the beach ... (Richards 1971)
b. What did he intended to say? (cf. Selinker 1972)

(3) a. I lost all my furnitures and many valuable properties. (Kirk-Greene 1971; Bokamba 1982)
b. But in modern warfare ... the damages caused are great. (Sey 1973; Bokamba 1982)

(4) a. The government have broken all their promises. (van Lier 1992/1993)
b. People does whatever they have to do in order to survive.

(5) a. The boys they like to play outside even if it is cold. (Bokamba 1982)
b. The guests whom I invited them have arrived. (Bokamba 1982)

Here the first set of sentences exemplify the omission of the indefinite article: "an" (1a) and "a" (1b). The second set shows lack of tense concordance with the time adverb "yesterday" in (2a) and misapplication of the affix hopping rule (2b); the expected verbal forms should be *went* and *stopped* in (2a), and *intend* in (2b). Sentences (3a) and (3b) illustrate, respectively, the erroneous pluralization of what are generally regarded as collective nouns, and abstract nouns. Sentence (4a), which is acceptable in standard British English, exemplifies incorrect verbal and pronominal agreement in number with the head noun, *government,* which is treated as a noncollective singular element in American English. (4b) in contrast shows the opposite error: third person singular verbal agreement with a plural head noun, *people.* Finally, both sentences in (5) illustrate the unnecessary occurrence of subject, *they*, and object, *them*, resumptive pronouns. These types of facts have been claimed in the SLA literature to be characteristic of IL varieties (Corder 1967; Richards 1971; Nemser 1971; Selinker 1972, 1992; Larsen-Freeman and Long 1991).

There is considerable agreement in the SLA literature that the explicit postulation and discussion of the concepts stated in Selinker's four constructs and similar ones by Selinker (1972), and before him by Corder (1967) and Richards (1971), have immensely advanced our understanding of the process of SLA and L2 speakers' behavior in pervasively monolingual societies since the classical literature in the field. While some of the proposed concepts and mechanisms have been questioned in the recent literature (e.g. Ellis 1986; Sridhar and Sridhar 1986), most of them and the resultant IL theory have not been refuted as one of the most recent in-depth studies, Larsen-Freeman and Long (1991), indicates. Selinker (1992) returns to this topic and provides us an excellent historical overview of the relevant literature on SLA in which he not only painstakingly attempts to elucidate what he calls "founding texts" in the field but also confirms his earlier insights. The picture that emerges in the absence of any refutation is that IL theory, viz. concepts, hypotheses, and assumptions, provide us an adequate and insightful account of the ESL/EFL speaker's internalized knowledge. But is this true? This study contends that this is not the case for at least three main reasons.

First, Selinker himself recognizes a number of difficulties with his 1972 analysis. These include (1) the difficulty of unambiguously identifying which of the five processes is to be attributed to observed data (Selinker 1972: 183); (2) the considerable difficulty of systematizing fossilization so as to predict "which items in which interlingual situations will be fossilized" (Selinker 1972: 184); and (3) the problem of fitting certain types of questions to the idealized speaker and norm assumed in the study, e.g. "How does a L2 learning novice become able to produce IL utterances whose surface constituents are correct ... with respect to the TL utterances whose norm is he attempting to produce?" (Selinker 1972: 184). Selinker (1972: 185) acknowledges that the achievement of success in L2 "need not be defined absolutely," but can be defined in a communicative competence sense à la Jakobovits (1969) and Hymes (1972).

Second, the three crucial premises upon which Selinker's 1972 and 1992 studies are based may be highly useful at an abstract theoretical level of discussion, but they are empirically unwarranted otherwise. Consider in this regard, first, the cases of the existence of ideal native speakers who speak only one norm and whose sentences the L2 is attempting to produce. It has now long been recognized in both first language acquisition and sociolinguistic research that individuals learn and master the variety of language spoken in their speech community (cf. Lenneberg 1967, 1969; Ellis 1986; Labov 1972; B. Kachru 1982; Allen and Linn 1986). The study of language variation by, among others, scholars such as Labov (1972a, 1972b, 1980, 1987), Shuy, Baratz, and Wolfram (1969), and Wolfram (1969, 1974, 1983) in major cities in the United States, Trudgill (1972, 1974, 1986) and Milroy (1980, 1987) in the U.K., and B. Kachru (1982, 1983, 1986) and others on World Englishes (cf., e.g., Cheshire 1991; McArthur 1992) attest to the existence of numerous speech-community-defined norms and sociolinguistic conditions for the acquisition of additional languages. Moreover, it has been shown time and again in language variation and discourse analysis research that speakers, whether native or nonnative, actively know more than one norm. As a result, they can select an appropriate variety/dialect of that language as determined by the context of situation: interlocutor, topic, and setting.

Third, the idealized native speaker à la Chomsky (1965) and Selinker (1972, 1992) is an uncommon individual and one who is ill-defined. Now, does this mean that the native speaker is dead, as Paikeday (1985) argues? I do not believe so. He/she is alive and well as a variationist whose linguistic knowledge, both internal and external, consists of form, function, and usage. But he/she has been dead as a socially realistic linguistic construct. There is very little empirical evidence to support either the ideal speaker-hearer or the ideal linguistic norm. Consider, if you would, the data in examples (6) through (9), which were produced by native speakers of American English with various educational achievements: high school students, high school graduates, college/university graduates, journalists, and other professionals, including university professors, doctors, and lawyers.

(6) The "me and my brother" pronominal phenomenon:
- a. *Me* and my brother were driving west on Green Street when this guy suddenly leapped in front of us from nowhere. We almost hit him.
- b. *Me* and Jack are good friends. (alternate: John and me are good friends.)
- c. This is strictly between you and *I*. (van Lier, handout 1992)
- d. That day Jeff took you and *she* to the basketball game.

d. No, come on! You are not taller than *me*!

(7) The missing copular infinitivals:
a. These clothes *need washed*. (cf. van Lier, 1992, op. cit.)
b. This proposal *needs reviewed*. (Administrative Secretary, Linguistics, 1992).
c. They cool, man!

(8) Subject–verb "disagreement" (in existential constructions):
a. Here*'s* your *bags*. (receptionist, DEIL, Univ. of Illinois, March 1994)
b. There*'s* some *apples*, oranges, and spaghetti in my bag for you. [A note from a teenager to his graduate school brother, Univ. of Illinois, February 1994]
c. *There is* a lot of people in this country who do not care about foreign cars.

(9) Resumptive pronouns:
a. These journalists *they* get intoxicated every time they hear a sensational story.
b. Her sister *she* is a big Great Deadful Dead fan: she just goes anywhere with them.

As the subheadings clearly indicate, these sentences exhibit the same kind of basic morphosyntactic errors that are characteristic of IL behaviors illustrated and discussed earlier (examples 1–5). What is puzzling from attitudinal and theoretical perspectives in SLA is that data such as those in examples (6) through (9) are never discussed in the analysis of language knowledge; it is as if they never occur. In sociolinguistics, such facts are regarded as mere dialectal variation (Allen and Linn 1986): they are seldom viewed as IL or indications of inadequate proficiency in the native speaker's competence. How can SLA theory be explanatorily adequate if data such as these in L1 performance are ignored and the findings of sociolinguistics with regard to language variation are never taken into consideration? The answer to this question is obvious.

Consider, now, the long-accepted assumption rearticulated in Selinker (1972) that the L2 learner has an inherent or strong desire to achieve natural L1 proficiency in the TL. This is again an abstract assumption that is unwarranted by facts. From my own experience both as a learner of several non-L1 languages and as a teacher in and supervisor of a language program in African languages at the University of Illinois for almost twenty years, I know of perhaps one or two learners who had such a goal. The rest of my students learn a foreign language not for integrative purposes, but for instrumental ones: to meet a foreign language requirement, to be able to conduct research or to live in the TL country, and to increase their opportunities for employment nationally and internationally. In multilingual societies, for instance, where the study of a foreign language is often mandatory, the purpose is to communicate and hopefully to facilitate one's upward mobility if one is successful. As Sridhar and Sridhar (1986) correctly observe, foreign languages in multilingual societies are important additions to one's verbal repertoire: they are tools for communication. Hence, the desire to imitate ideal, even nonideal, native speakers in order to achieve native competence does not arise as a main and even perhaps a secondary concern. Further, the vast majority of the teachers of English as a second or foreign language in such societies are themselves nonnative speakers: Their varieties of English serve as the models that the students imitate and reproduce. These students' performance in English, in all structural aspects (viz. phonological, morphological, syntactic, and semantic), is further constrained by the norms of the communities in which they live and learn the language (B. Kachru 1986; Sridhar and Sridhar 1986). These learners are not free to produce native-like speech in their communities, even if they were capable of such performance, without being seen as pedantic and therefore becoming the subject of ridicule.

Implications. Several implications follow from the data and the arguments presented above. First, in view of the refutation of the premises in Selinker's assumptions (page 244 of this article) and the existence of data such as those in examples (6) through (9), it is reasonable to conclude that IL as a theoretical paradigm provides a very weak explanation to the seven fundamental questions raised in the first part of this paper. As such, it requires considerable revisions, to better account for the process of second/additional language acquisition. To be sure, IL as a concept rather than a theory is very apt because it ingeniously captures the fact that language acquisition is a continuum: L2 as well as L1 speakers develop and increase their proficiency in the target language throughout their lives (cf. Y. Kachru 1993). At any one point in this development we may depict a progression from low or zero knowledge to high knowledge, and the speaker may be placed in a particular point within the continuum. A study of his/her production (oral or written) will reveal that it is systematic and self-contained. To the extent that this is true, then, the concept of IL is applicable to L1 and L2 learners. The IL theory, therefore, cannot be maintained in its present form: It must undergo modifications to take into account research in first language acquisition (FLA) and sociolinguistics, as suggested above.

Second, the occurrence of data such as those in examples (1) through (5) and (6) through (9) indicates that the negative connotation often associated with the concept of IL must be changed to a more positive outlook: Instead of IL being viewed as a speech variety characterized by deficiencies or deviations vis-à-vis an assumed ideal norm, it should be regarded simply as a descriptor of a level of language proficiency on analogy perhaps with idiolect and dialect. It should be pointed out here that what is regarded today as "standard" American English was once viewed as a colonial substandard variety that eventually acquired prestige thanks to the work of pioneers such as Webster and Matthews (Kahane 1982).

Third, as B. Kachru (1982, 1983, 1986), Sridhar and Sridhar (1986), and Ellis (1986, in a slightly different context) argue, English as a Second Language/ English as an International Language variety data must be studied in the context of the situations in which they are produced. They cannot be analyzed in isolation as in the case of phonological and syntactic data, because while these fields can afford such abstract analysis, SLA, as an applied linguistic field with practical consequences, cannot be treated in the same fashion without hampering the ultimate objectives of this research. B. Kachru (1982) has effectively argued that studies of World Englishes that fail to take into consideration the acquisitional, sociocultural, motivational, and functional parameters under which these varieties are learned and produced cannot insightfully account for the characteristics they exhibit.

What is acquired? How is it acquired? When is it acquired? Why is it acquired? These are extremely interesting and challenging questions that have led to a proliferation of SLA theories (Ellis 1986; Spolsky 1989), but they cannot be addressed meaningfully within the scope of this preliminary study. What can be stated here is that the correct explanation for fossilization is not an inability to improve one's proficiency in a target language (L2, L3, L4, etc.), but rather an expression of one's satisfaction of having achieved the desired communicative competence. Most learners do not study an additional language so as to emulate even the most educated speakers or achieve pragmatic competence: They study it for communicative purposes. And when they have achieved that level, they stop learning unless they are linguists; this behavior is no different from that of the average native speaker (especially those without university education).

Fourth and finally, the findings of this study indicate that SLA theory needs to learn and incorporate findings from the sister disciplines of FLA and sociolinguistics, especially the ethnography of communication and language variation in the latter field (cf. Saville-Troike 1982; Allen and Linn 1986; Bryson 1990). These fields have a great deal to contribute to the study of SLA in terms of theory, description, and research methodology. Published research on World Englishes since the late 1970s constitutes an important source of both data and insights that can greatly benefit SLA theory.

Conclusion. This paper has offered a data-based analysis in which an attempt has been made to constructively criticize IL theory in the field of SLA. What the paper has attempted to show is that IL is a valid psycholinguistic concept, but as a theory it requires considerable modifications to reflect the reality of ESL/EIL. It has been suggested that SLA bridge the paradigm gaps by incorporating research findings in FLA and sociolinguistics. The paper has indicated further that language knowledge should be seen as a continuum whose starting point is either zero or low and whose end point is high. By viewing language knowledge this way, we can meaningfully and insightfully characterize different speakers, both native and nonnative, of a given language in terms of their level of proficiency relative to the standardized variety. The current view fostered by the concept of interlanguage is clearly misleading and uninsightful, and it marginalizes World Englishes without actually understanding its fundamental features.

REFERENCES

Allen, Harold B. and Michael D. Linn, eds. 1986. *Dialect and language variation*. New York: Academic Press.

Bamgboṣe, Ayọ. 1982. "Standard Nigerian English: Issues of identification." In Braj B. Kachru (ed.), *The other tongue: English across cultures*. Champaign, Illinois: University of Illinois Press. 99–111.

Bokamba, Eyamba G. 1982. "The Africanization of English." In Braj B. Kachru (ed.), *The other tongue: English across cultures*. Champaign, Illinois: University of Illinois Press. 77–98.

Broeslow, Ellen. 1988. "Second language acquisition." In Frederick J. Newmeyer (ed.) *Linguistics, the Cambridge survey, Volume III: Language: Psychological and biological aspects*. Cambridge, U.K.: Cambridge University Press.

Bryson, Bill. 1990. *The mother tongue: English and how it got that way*. New York: William Morrow.

Cheshire, Jenny (ed.) 1991. *English around the world: Sociolinguistic perspectives*. Cambridge, U.K.: Cambridge University Press.

Corder, S. Pit. 1967. "The significance of learners' errors." *International Review of Applied Linguistics* 5: 161–170.

Corder, S. Pit. 1971. "Idiosyncratic dialects and error analysis." *International Review of Applied Linguistics* 9: 149–159.

Ellis, Rod. 1986. *Understanding second language acquisition*. Oxford: Oxford University Press.

Kachru, Braj B. 1982. *The other tongue: English across cultures*. Champaign, Illinois: University of Illinois Press.

Kachru, Braj B. 1983. *The Indianization of English: The English language in India*. Delhi: Oxford University Press.

Kachru, Braj B. 1986. *The alchemy of English: The spread, functions, and models of non-native Englishes*. Oxford: Pergamon Press.

Kachru, Yamuna. 1992. Review of *Rediscovering interlanguage* by Larry Selinker 1992. Ms. To appear in *World Englishes*.

Kahane, Henry. 1982. "American English: From a colonial substandard to a prestige language." In Braj B. Kachru (ed.), *The other tongue: English across cultures*. Champaign, Illinois: University of Illinois Press. 229–236.

Larsen-Freeman, Diane and Michael H. Long 1991. *An introduction to second language acquisition research*. London: Longman.

Lenneberg, Eric H. 1964. "The capacity for language acquisition." Reprinted in Mark Lester (ed.), 1970, *Readings in applied transformational grammar*. Chicago: Holt, Rinehart and Winston. 46–80.

Lenneberg, Eric H. 1969. "On explaining language." Reprinted in Mark Lester (ed.), 1970, *Readings in applied transformational grammar*. Chicago: Holt, Rinehart and Winston. 81–105.

McArthur, Tom (ed.). 1992. *The Oxford companion to the English language*. Oxford: Oxford University Press.

Nemser, William. 1971. "Approximative systems of foreign language learners." *International Review of Applied Linguistics* 9: 115–123.

Robinett, Betty Wallace and Jacquelyn Schachter (eds.). 1983. *Second language acquisition: Contrastive analysis, error analysis, and related aspects*. Ann Arbor, Michigan: University of Michigan Press.

Saville-Troike, Muriel. 1982. *The ethnography of communication: An introduction*. Oxford: Basil Blackwell.

Selinker, Larry. 1972. "Interlanguage." *MAL* 10: 209–231.

Selinker, Larry. 1992. *Rediscovering interlanguage*. New York: Longman.

Sey, K.A. 1973. *Ghanaian English: An exploratory survey*. London: Macmillan.

Spolsky, Bernard. 1989. *Conditions for second language learning*. Oxford: Oxford University Press.

Sridhar, K.K. and S.S. Sridhar 1986. "Bridging the paradigm gap: Second language acquisition theory and indigenized varieties of English." *World Englishes* 5: 3–14.

Tanenhaus, Michael K. 1988. "Psycholinguistics: An overview." In Frederick J. Newmeyer (ed.), *Linguistics, The Cambridge Survey, Volume III: Language: Psychological and biological aspects*. Cambridge, U.K.: Cambridge University Press.

French native-speaker use of the subjunctive in speech and writing

Nadine O'Connor Di Vito
University of Chicago

1. Introduction. This paper is a preliminary report of a large, quantitative study of spoken and written French whose general purpose is the examination of a variety of grammatical structures across spoken and written French. The study examines the frequency and productivity of these grammatical forms and the diverse communicative functions these forms serve in different contexts.[1] Through such a quantitative study, my goals are (1) to provide a more accurate description of these French patterns than exists to date, (2) to further academic understanding of the relationship between spoken and written French, and of why and how the French language is evolving, and finally, (3) to offer French language teachers empirical data with which to develop accurate and appropriate contextualizations of grammar in their language classrooms.

2. The corpus. The corpus for this study consists of 53,266 independent, subordinate, and relative clauses of spoken and written French. The written corpus of 37,013 clauses includes eighteenth–twentieth century major literary prose and theater pieces as well as a variety of twentieth century popular literature, such as detective novels, folklore, travel guides, and official correspondence. The spoken corpus of 16,253 clauses was recorded and transcribed from a range of spoken discourse types, including SCOLA news broadcasts, interviews with renowned French intellectuals, academic speeches, and semiformal conversations between native speaker teachers of French. Of the linguistic patterns examined in this corpus, preliminary results of the analysis of uses of the subjunctive will be reported here.

3. Analysis of subjunctive forms and formation rules. French language teachers faced with the formidable task of teaching the subjunctive are invariably drawn into the chaotic world of lists of formation rules for a host of regular and irregular verbs and lists of abstract grammatical rules and

1. For a more complete analysis of native speaker use of the subjunctive, the reader is referred to Chapter 3 of *Patterns across spoken and written French: Empricial research, linguistic theory, and pedagogy*, B. Freed (ed.), forthcoming with D.C. Heath.

contexts, each of which contain numerous special subrules and, of course, exceptions. The nearly endless combination of forms and contexts that results typically serves then as the base for classroom exercises. But while such a procedure might help students understand the possibilities for subjunctive use, what is not at all clear is whether or not these exercises help students to understand when and why the subjunctive is used in particular discourse contexts in either the spoken or the written language. In order to appropriately understand and use the subjunctive, students should be aware of the general frequency of the subjunctive in particular discourse contexts, of the subjunctive tenses, verb types, and persons most frequently employed in these contexts, and of the various context specific functions served by the subjunctive in both the spoken and the written language. These are but a few of the issues that guided the direction of this study, and whose answers I will briefly address here.

3.1. Overall frequency of the subjunctive. With respect to the overall frequency of the subjunctive, its use is relatively limited in both the spoken and the written language, with a mere 2% overall use in the spoken language and 3% use in the written language. The highest overall frequencies found were in eighteenth century literature and twentieth century official correspondence (4% and 5% respectively). Eliminating unmarked cases of the subjunctive (i.e. cases where the subjunctive forms are the same as indicative forms), the percentages drop further to 1% in the spoken language and 2% in the written language. These low percentages should be borne in mind throughout the following discussion of subjunctive use.

3.2. Frequency of subjunctive tenses. The present subjunctive and three past subjunctive tenses (past, imperfect, and pluperfect) are represented in the data (see examples (1)–(4)).

(1) Je veux que tu *partes* tout de suite.
(Nineteenth century prose: Zola)
'I want you to leave right away.'

(2) En ce cas, dit le roi, je vais te coller au mur et tu y resteras jusqu'à ce que tu *aies changé* d'avis.
(Folklore and fairytales: Gripari)
'In that case, said the king, I am going to paste you to the wall and you will stay there until you've changed your mind.'

(3) Mais je voudrais qu'il *vînt* enfin et me *suivît*, en admirant chacun de mes mouvements.
(Twentieth century prose: Colette)
'I wanted him to come finally and follow me, admiring each of my movements.'

(4) Je n'ai pas dit que j'*eusse prêté* l'argent.
(Eighteenth century prose: Beaumarchais)
'I did not say that I had lent money.'

However, in the spoken corpus, 92% of all of the subjunctives are present subjunctive forms, with not just the imperfect and pluperfect subjunctive but also the past subjunctive frequencies negligeable. As for the written corpus, the distribution of present and past subjunctive forms is much more diverse, with official correspondence and magazines showing a very high frequency of present subjunctive forms (95% and 89% respectively) while only 56% of the subjunctive forms in nineteenth century prose are present subjunctive. Supporting previous research findings (Bryant 1985; Muller 1986), the imperfect subjunctive, while perhaps not very frequent overall in the French language, is a fairly productive tense for particular authors of literary prose.

3.3. Frequency of verbs and verb types. As for the frequency of particular verbs and verb types, 80% of all of the subjunctives in the spoken corpus and 77% of the subjunctives in the written corpus are accounted for by considering solely *être*, *avoir*, *pouvoir*, *faire*, and regular *-er* conjugation verbs (see examples (5)–(9)).

(5) Joue, belle enfant, jusqu'à ce que tu *sois* femme;
(Nineteenth century theater: Vigny)
'Play, beautiful girl, until you are a woman;'

(6) Il te faut un homme qui *ait* au moins sept ans de plus que toi...
(Twentieth century prose: Troyat)
'You need a man who is at least seven years younger than you.'

(7) On ne peut comprendre que tu *puisses* quitter tes femmes, tes parens, tes amis, ta patrie, pour aller dans des climats inconnus aux persans.
(Eighteenth century prose: Montesquieu)
'(No) one can understand that you can leave your women, your family, your friends, your country, to go into unknown Persian lands.'

(8) Si j'avais une chambre qui *fasse* le double je serais ravie.
(Conversations: Cécile[2])
'If I had a room that was twice as big I would be thrilled.'

(9) Ça ne lui a jamais plu que j'*épouse* Marthe,...
(Detective novels: Malet)
'It never pleased him that I wed Marthe,...'

Also interesting to note is that no other verb totals more than 3% of the subjunctive examples, including verbs that are generally quite common in the language, such as *aller*, *mettre*, *vouloir*, *savoir*, and *connaître*.

3.4. Verb type and person frequency of French subjunctives. Combining the results of verb type frequency and person frequency, use of the subjunctive in both spoken and written French becomes even more startling. In all spoken and written genres, the relatively high percentage of third person singular forms is noteworthy; furthermore, considering the homophony in the spoken language of the first, second, and third person singular forms and third person plural forms, approximately 80% of all spoken subjunctives, in semi-informal conversations as well as in televised interviews with such figures as Bourdieu and Ricoeur, comprise the forms: /swa/, /E/, /puis/, /fas/, and the present indicative of regular *-er* verbs. These findings, of course, have quite obvious implications for the presentation of subjunctive formation rules in French language textbooks.

4. Analysis of functions of the subjunctive in spoken and written French discourse. Moving from formation rules to contextual patterns, examination of the data indicates that use of the subjunctive is typical in certain contexts: following special conjunctions, following verbs and adjectives of subjective attitude, and following particular types of relative clauses and indefinite expressions.

4.1 Conjunctions. Certain conjunctions that typically introduce a verb in the subjunctive, such as *pour que*, *sans que*, and *bien que*, are frequent in both the spoken and written language. Conjunctions such as *le fait que* and *de sorte que* are more prevalent in the spoken language while numerous other conjunctions (*avant que*, *quoique*, *afin que*, *pourvu que*, *à moins que*, *en attendant que*, *soit que*, and *jusqu'à ce que*) are seen primarily in the written corpus. And, finally, a few conjunctions seem to be on the evolutionary

2. Unless requested by the interviewee to use his or her real name, all names of the speakers taped in the conversational and conference data are pseudonyms.

borders of the language. Whereas *malgré que* appears to be at the very least falling into certain disuse (found only three times, all in eighteenth century texts), there are a variety of conjunctions that introduce a subjunctive form in the data and with which one normally associates the indicative mood, such as *après que*, *alors que*, and *dès que* (see examples (10)–(12)). Thus, frequency distribution of subjunctive forms across discourse genres shows definite tendencies with respect to conjunction preferences in the spoken and written language and suggests particular evolutionary trends in subjunctive use.

(10) Il est distrait au volant de son auto et laisse souvent ses flèches de direction levées, même *après qu'*il *ait effectué* son tournant.
(Twentieth century prose: Camus)
'He is inattentive at the wheel of his car and often leaves his direction arrows on, even after he has made his turn.'

(11) Ou *alors que* les vieillards *soient* les seuls guerriers.
(Twentieth century theater: Giraudoux)
'Or else old people are the only warriors.'

(12) *Dès qu'*on *eût présenté* la première soupe, l'oiseau chanteur commença, sur la tête du roi, à chanter: 'Ah!...'
(Folklore and fairytales: Basque stories)
'As soon as the first soup had been presented, the singing bird began, on the head of the king, to sing: "Ah!..."'

One trend suggested by these data, of course, is that no longer is it possible to claim that the subjunctive is the mood of the unreal or unrealized; appearing now after *après que* (after) and *le fait que* (the fact that), as well as after a variety of other conjunctions that traditionally introduce verbs in the indicative mood, one is tempted to hypothesize that the subjunctive is becoming slowly grammaticalized after certain conjunctions, and now possibly signifies more a formal register in this particular grammatical context than an attitudinal disposition on the part of the speaker.

4.2. Expressions of subjective attitude. Of course, even though subjective attitude does not appear to be a significant factor in subjunctive use after conjunctions, there is certainly a considerable amount of subjunctive use after other types of expressions of subjective attitude. Winters (1989) has suggested that the primary function of the subjunctive has evolved from being an indicator of uncertainty to being an indicator of speaker subjectivity. And, in fact, expressions of subjective attitude are involved in 55% of all subjunctive examples in spoken discourse and 48% of all subjunctive examples in the written language. This subjectivity is encoded in a variety of ways: in the verb itself (*regretter*, *s'étonner*), in an adjective (*important*, *bon*) typically following the verb *être*, or in adverbs and nouns with clear subjective nuance (*bien*, *regret*). There is a very high percentage of subjunctive use in these contexts in all discourse types (39%–70%). As found with the types of verbal expressions used in the subjunctive, certain expressions of subjective attitude are much more frequent than others. Clearly *il faut que* is the overwhelming favorite context for subjunctive use, with *vouloir que*, and *croire que* also noteworthy (see examples (13)–(15)).

(13) *Il faut que* je *sois* tellement sûr de ma hauteur par rapport à lui.
(Interviews: Bourdieu)
'It is necessary that I be very sure of my level with respect to him'

(14) Qu'est-ce que tu *veux que* je *dise* d'autre?
(Magazines: *Le Point*)
'What else do you want me to say?'

(15) Et *croyez*-vous *que* ce *soit* le fils prodigue qui *ait demandé* pardon?
(Twentieth century theater: Claudel)
'And do you believe that it is the prodigal son who asked forgiveness?'

With over one hundred different verbs in expressions of subjective attitude, however, and innumerable adjectives, certainly here is one context where use of the subjunctive has real semantic value and is not a mere mechanical operation applied in a context with easily definable limits.

4.3. Negative expressions. A closer look at *croire que* expressions followed by the subjunctive suggests that negation and interrogation are factors whose presence increases the likelihood that the subjunctive will be used. In fact, not only is the subjunctive frequently used when *croire* is negated, but it is also used after many other negated verbs (approximately 20% of the time in these contexts of subjective attitude) (see examples (16)–(18)).

(16) Je *ne crois pas que* euh qu'on qu'il *suffise* de revenir à ce que vous *appeliez* la spécificité du discours philosophique de Heidegger,...
(Interviews: Derrida)

'I do not know that it is sufficient to come back to what you call the specificity of the philosophical discourse of Heidegger,...'

(17) Je *ne conçois pas qu'*un arbre *soit* fait pour autre chose,...
(Nineteenth century prose: Stendhal)
'I can not imagine that a tree is made for something else,...'

(18) On *ne peut pas dire que* le recours à saint Cornély-Corneille *soit* une simple explication d' opportunité pour le seul lieu dit Carnac,...
(Travel guides: *Les Alignements* de Carnac)
'One cannot say that resorting to Saint Cornély-Corneille is simply a timely explanation for the lone Carnac locality,...'

It is also quite interesting to note that again the notion of uncertainty does not have to be implied in order to use the subjunctive, but that negation alone may be enough to trigger the subjunctive, as suggested by the nine examples of the subjunctive after *ne pas douter que/ne pas être douteux que* found in the data (see examples (19)–(21)).

(19) *Il n'est certes pas douteux que* ce ne *soit* pas la pa– que ce ne *soit* la parole éloquente, qui pour la gloire *ait* le plus d'importance,
(Conferences: Fumier)
'There is certainly no doubt that it is not the– that it is not the eloquent word, which for glory has the greatest importance,'

(20) *Il ne douta pas que* ce ne *fût* une cigogne;
(Nineteenth century prose: Flaubert)
'He did not doubt that it was a swan;'

(21) Je *ne doutais pas que* nous ne *fussions* très pauvres.
(Twentieth century prose: Mauriac)
'I did not doubt that we were very poor.'

These data suggest once more that the subjunctive is no longer functioning primarily to indicate uncertainty but rather sometimes functions to convey subjective judgment (supporting Winters 1989) and sometimes is almost mechanically triggered by particular lexical items, such as negative particles (supporting Nathan and Epro 1984).

4.4. Croire, espérer, penser, trouver. Returning to the verb *croire* and the verbs typically grouped with *croire* when presenting the subjunctive—*penser, espérer*, and *trouver*—there is a clear preference for subjunctive use when the clause containing these verbs is either negated or interrogative, with no example of the subjunctive after these verbs in affirmative, declarative clauses (see examples (20)–(21)). Noteworthy also is the definite tendency of French native speakers to use the verb *croire* in these subjunctive contexts rather than the semantically similar options of *penser* and *trouver*.

(22) Je *ne croyais pas que* cela *fût* si monstrueux.
(Nineteenth century prose: Hugo)
'I did not believe that that was so monstrous.'

(23) Pourquoi donc *croyez-vous qu'*on les *fasse*?
(Folklore and fairytales: Gripari)
'Why therefore do you think that they make them?'

4.5. Relative and indefinite expressions. Also often associated with subjunctive use are particular types of indefinite expressions and relative clauses suggesting subjectivity or uncertainty. In fact, 11% of all subjunctives found in the spoken and written corpora are in some type of relative clause. Relative clauses preceded by superlative affirmative expressions are the most frequent type in the spoken data; in the written data subjunctives are most common in relative clauses preceded by negative (at times also superlative) expressions (see examples (24) and (25)).

(24) Et de vivre avec *la mort la plus difficile que* l'on *puisse* connaître...
(Conferences: Delart)
'And to live with the most difficult death that one can know...'

(25) De même elle *ne considérait pas* qu'un dîner chez nous *fût* pour M. de Norpois un des actes innombrables de sa vie sociale:
(Twentieth century prose: Proust)
'Even so she did not think that a dinner at our place was for Mr. de Norpois one of the innumerable acts of his social life:'

As for the frequency of general indefinite expressions followed by the subjunctive, of the eleven examples found in the spoken corpus, six were of the type *quel que* + *être* (see examples (26)–(27)):

(26) Les séropositifs qui le souhaitent pourront être pris en charge à 100% par la Sécurité Sociale *quel que soit* leur état de santé.
(SCOLA news broadcasts)

'Those HIV positive who desire it can be 100% covered by Social Security no matter what their state of health is.'

(27) *Quelle que soit* sa rancune envers Louis Martin,
(Twentieth century prose: Troyat)
'No matter what his rancor might be towards Louis Martin,'

Of course, while the writing of such expressions is typically problematic to language learners, these expressions are fairly simple to use in the spoken language, since they all sound alike and only require the learner to be familiar with the most frequently occurring subjunctive form in the spoken language (/swa/). Finally, with respect to the four examples of *quelque* + adjective/adverb/noun, all were used by Derrida (see example 28).

(28) Il se trouve que je je ne me suis pas euh intéressé en en travaillant en tout cas à de euh de grands romanciers euh *quelque quelque passion que* je *puisse* avoir pour pour n'est-ce pas pour Proust ou pour Musil ou pour ou pour des romanciers d'une— euh, antérieurs.
(Interviews: Derrida)
'It so happens that I was not interested in working in any case on great novelists no matter what passion I might have for Proust or for Musil or for the novelists of an— uh, preceding [them].'

It should be noted that these indefinite expressions are not only extremely rare in the spoken language but, together with those examples found in the written corpora, make up only 5% of the total number of subjunctive clauses which, it should be remembered, make up only a fraction of the total database.

4.6. Independent clauses and special que constructions. Finally, at times there is no preceding verbal, adjectival, or conjunctive expression provoking use of subjunctive, as in expressions such as *Vive le roi!* (May the king live!). The conjunction *que* is also used to introduce such clauses as well as hypothetical expressions presenting alternative possibilities (see examples (29)–(30)).

(29) Parce que, euh, *que ce soit* la proximité de Lacan ou non,
(Interviews: Ricoeur)
'Because, um, whether it is the proximity of Lacan or not,

(30) *Que* je *sois* à Paris ou *que* je *sois* à Chicago, cette opportunité est la même,

(Conversations: Edouard)
'Whether I am in Paris or whether I am in Chicago, this opportunity is the same,'

While subjunctives receive relatively little attention in French language textbooks until the very advanced language levels, analysis of these native speaker data suggests that subjunctives in independent clauses and in these special *que* constructions are fairly common in French. They reflect 14% of the subjunctive clauses in the written corpora and 10% of the spoken subjunctives, where they primarily function to present hypothetical alternatives especially in the form *que ce soit.* Besides their frequency in both spoken and written French, these constructions are structurally simple, have clear communicative value, and are a "cheap" way of using the subjunctive. Certainly such arguments dictate that some consideration be given to these subjunctive contexts in at least intermediate level French language textbooks.

5. Conclusion. As mentioned at the outset of this paper, these findings should be taken as preliminary. Other factors which have yet to be examined are: (1) the degree to which the indicative is also used after the many expressions of subjective attitude seen here to prompt the subjunctive (such as *(ne pas) croire que* and *ne pas douter que*), and (2) the degree to which various factors (such as negation, semantic subjectivity, and indefiniteness) may interact and result in an increased likelihood that the subjunctive will be employed. Comparison with subjunctive use in other Romance languages should also further clarify particular trends in French subjunctive use. Even when these final stages of the analysis are completed, however, clearly this study must be seen as an incomplete and somewhat biased selection of spoken and written French. Discourse samples were, as a rule, limited to approximately 10,000 words per text, and many types of popular, colloquial, and public speech were not included in the corpus at all.

Still and all, after examining 53,266 clauses from approximately fifty sources representing a variety of discourse types which are generally considered to be examples of "standard" spoken and written French, it is clear that use of the subjunctive in French is highly patterned with respect to tense, verb type, and person, and that it is linked not only to the use of other grammatical structures in the language but to particular semantic values, to the formality of the discourse context and, finally, to the subjective attitude of the speaker. Inasmuch as such patterns reflect the social life as well as the linguistic reality of spoken and written French, they merit our attention as linguists, as language teachers, and as human beings in search of crosslinguistic and crosscultural understanding.

REFERENCES

Bryant, William H. 1985. "Translating the French imperfect subjunctive." *The French Review* 58(5): 657–663.

Freed, B. (ed.). forthcoming. *Patterns across spoken and written French: Empirical research, linguistic theory, and pedagogy.* New York: D.C. Heath.

Muller, Charles. 1986. "Données quantitatives en morpho-syntaxe: L'imparfait du subjonctif dans quelque romans contemporains." *Le Français moderne* 54(3–4): 220–230.

Nathan, Geoffrey S. and Margaret Winters Epro. 1984. "Negative polarity and the Romance subjunctive." In Philip Baldi (ed.), *Amsterdam studies in the theory and history of linguistic science IV: Papers from the XII linguistic symposium on Romance linguistics.* Philadelphia: John Benjamins.

Winters, Margaret E. 1989. "Diachronic prototype theory: On the evolution of the French subjunctive." *Linguistics* 27(4): 703–730.

The language educator at work in the learner-centered classroom: Communicate, decision-make, and remember to apply the (educational) linguistics

Teresa Pica
University of Pennsylvania

Introduction. This paper will discuss ways in which classroom teachers of a second language (L2) can apply findings from educational linguistics research to their work with language learners as their traditional responsibilities of teaching grammatical and sociocultural rules are being reshaped within the context of a number of current phenomena in the field of language education—the design and implementation of a learner-centered curriculum, an emphasis on the communicative, social goals and processes of language learning, and the growth and recognition of the classroom teacher as an independent and reflective decision maker.

Of course, the reshaping of language education is not in itself a new phenomenon, as language education has been the subject of much discussion and debate over the years, indeed over centuries, as overviews on the history of the field well attest. (See for example the various perspectives of Howatt 1984; Kelly 1969; Pennycock 1989; Richards and Rodgers 1986.) Just as any other complex field, the field of language education is informed by many disciplines, influenced by a host of socioeconomic, historical, and political factors, and subject to any number of bandwagons that have been formed and re-formed over the methodologies it employs. (See Clarke 1982.) Yet even when we attempt to ignore the enormity in the scope of language education, and to reduce its ingredients to the simpler terms of a language to be learned by learners who must learn it, it is difficult to avoid questions as to the contributions of classroom teachers to this enterprise, as it is they who are expected to take on much of the responsibility for making sure that learning takes place.

What does it take to be a classroom L2 teacher? What sorts of work are required? What kinds of training are needed? What should the L2 teacher know about language? About language learners? About the range of teaching materials and strategies available to them? Such questions are all too familiar, with answers as abundant in their number as they are disparate in content. (See for example the proliferation of recent publications of relevance, including volumes by Alatis, Stern, and Strevens 1983; Fanselow 1990; Freeman 1989; Richards and Nunan 1990; Richards and Crookes 1988; and chapters in Alatis 1991.) What makes this period in language education somewhat different and cautiously optimistic is that there is now a rich and everexpanding body of research whose insights into language learning and language use can respond to these questions.

This research has come in large part from the field of educational linguistics. This a field whose research questions, theoretical structures, and contributions of service are focused on issues and concerns in education. The more obvious issues and concerns are those which in themselves pertain to language, e.g. the relationship between types of teacher questions and the syntactic complexity of learner responses in the L2 classroom. The field of educational linguistics can also include educational issues and concerns in which language plays a less direct role, but nevertheless can be addressed through language analysis. In addressing issues and concerns about student tracking, for example, the relationship between teacher questions and learner responses could also be analyzed, here to provide insight into strengths and weaknesses of the academic environments provided under different tracks.

With respect to language education, educational linguistics research has shed light on issues and concerns regarding the processes, participants, and environments of language learning and teaching and the linguistic and social goals toward which they strive. These findings have found particular focus in two current domains of interest in language education. One of these domains is the design and implementation of curricula for the communicative needs of language learners and the social processes which assist their learning; the other is the professionalization of the classroom teacher as an educator capable of conceptualizing, shaping, and accomplishing these curricular aims.

These two domains of interest hold much prominence throughout the broader field of education as well. Language education has benefited greatly from work on learner-centered instruction in the mainstream, as it has incorporated research on the first language (L1) composing process into the teaching of L2 writing and the study of L2 writing processes (Raimes 1985, 1991; Zamel 1976, 1983) and has been guided by principles of whole language curricula in its design of content based L2 and bilingual programs. (See Edelsky 1991; Rigg 1991.) And fairly obvious affiliations can be seen between learner-centered practices such as group work in the language classroom and cooperative learning in broader educational contexts (compare Pica and Doughty 1985 with Kagan 1986 and Slavin 1983), and between content-based language teaching and the integration of language arts across the broader curriculum of school subjects. (See for example Snow, Met, and Genessee 1989; Mohan 1986.) Finally, there is a mutuality of interest among language educators and other professional educators in defining an appropriate base of knowledge for the work that they do. A mutuality of goals and outcomes can be seen, for example, in Freeman and Richards (1994), who focus on language education, and Cochran-Smith and Lytle (1992) and Shulman (1987) who address broader educational themes.

Despite these ties and relationships with the broader field of education, however, the experience of language learners and teachers, taken together with research on language learning and teaching, has continued to remind us that language education carries its own special challenges and needs. As both a body of knowledge to be learned and evaluated and an instrument for communicating and evaluating that knowledge, language, after all, holds considerable distinction with respect to other subject areas of educational pursuit.

Further, languages are so rigorously complex that many of their linguistic and social rules can be difficult to discover, to understand, and to articulate, even for native speakers. Learners progress in much of their L2 study if and when they are ready to do so. In this process, they must integrate the rules and features of the language they are learning with those of the (one or many) languages already known to them, including those of their own developing interlanguage. Thus there is not a one-to-one relationship between what learners produce as output and what they are given as input. These and countless other considerations must surely be taken into account in any program of language education. And, indeed, they form the basis for the kinds of decisions that educators must make as they attempt to design and implement a successful curriculum that is both learner-centered and communicative in its aims and activities.

How then can L2 teachers turn to, and be assisted by, educational linguistics research in their decision-making responsibilities as they attempt to guide students within a learner-centered, communicative curriculum? How can educational linguistics research assist their immediate and longer range classroom concerns? How can it contribute to their current store of professional knowledge? How can it lead them toward a distinctive, professional status, shared with colleagues across the educational community? To address these questions, we will first review a number of characteristics of such curricula that both provoke reflection of and often require decision-making on teachers' roles

The learner-centered, communicative curriculum: Contributions and perspectives from educational linguistics research. The movement toward a learner-centered, communicative curriculum has been widespread across the field of language education. Much of the impetus has come from the changing face of learners' needs, more specifically from their need to learn languages quickly and efficiently for communicative purposes. Among adults, for example, the ability to communicate through the medium of another language has become a social and professional tool, not just mark of educated individuals, but a basic skill they cannot afford to be without in the interdependent economic and social conditions of the contemporary world. For younger learners, too, language learning through and for communication has come to be viewed in many countries as preparation for the adult world as well as for their own immediate academic environment.

Theoretical and empirical work from the field of educational linguistics has already contributed enormously to this effort. Educational linguists have drawn on methodologies in sociolinguistics, pragmatics, and discourse analysis to identify and record the language that is used in the professional, vocational, and academic contexts of life toward which learners aim (see for example the range of work represented in this area from Breen 1987 and Wilkins 1976 to Cohen and Olshtain 1978, 1993 and Wolfson 1981, 1983, 1984). Educational linguists have also built on and expanded theories of language competence, specifically notions of communicative competence expressed in Hymes (1972) and Savignon (1972), to provide a detailed picture of the social and strategic goals of language learners and the expectations placed upon them. (See Canale and Swain 1980.)

Throughout the learner-centered, communicative curriculum, communication is regarded as not only the purpose and outcome of learners' language study, but also the process through which such a purpose and outcome are accomplished. It is believed that by using a language to communicate meaningful information, learners can internalize the language as a system of structural and sociolinguistic rules and features. The prevailing view is that students will acquire an L2 by focusing attention not on its forms, but on the meaningful content that such forms encode. Teachers are expected to structure their classroom environment along these lines. There is an extensive, everthriving literature on this topic, but see, among others, some fundamental works by Brumfit and Johnson (1979), Krashen and Terrell (1983), Savignon (1972), and Widdowson (1978).

Along with these conceptual underpinnings have come a number of distinctive classroom practices. Thus in many communicative classrooms, L2 rules and features are not explicitly emphasized through direct instruction, but rather are drawn from subject matter content in literature, the social sciences, and/or the learner's own domain of social or professional interest. Activities are often centered on academic, occupational, or high interest materials, and are based on decisions that need to be made, problems to be solved, and opinions to be shared. Cooperative and collaborative organizational frameworks are used to emphasize learner spontaneity and initiative over teacher-directed drill and practice. These are often designed to replicate the settings and situations to which the learners aspire.

When described in the ways above, activities in the communicative classroom have obvious, distinctive, and defining aspects which contrast sharply with classroom practices that focus on isolated rules and features of language divorced from their situated use. Beyond these few distinguishing features, however, the learner-centered, communicative curriculum has taken on a host of realizations that are wide ranging and varied. From the theoretical side for example, modes for identification and organization of communicative curriculum units are numerous and are often as competing as they are complementary. (See descriptions and discussions in Breen 1984 and Long and Crookes 1992.)

And with respect to implementation, communicative curricula, when put into classroom practice, have often been shown to be less communicative than hoped for, and, in some cases, not very communicative at all. As revealed for example in work of Long and Sato (1983), Pica and Doughty (1985a, 1985b), and Pica and Long (1986), even classrooms that claim to be communicative often focus on L2 structure, with little attention to meaning. Interaction might take the form of teacher transmission of communication rules and evaluation of students on them. Such classrooms, as Prabhu (1987) has pointed out, would emphasize communication as the only goal of L2 learning. This might keep the students from engaging in any meaningful exchange with the teacher and each other and thereby deprive them of opportunities for communication as the process through which L2 learning occurs. (Again, see Prabhu 1987.)

Thus the learner-centered, communicative curriculum, conceived as most suited to the needs of language learners in today's world, has numerous actual and potential incarnations when put into a classroom context. Some curricula may meet those needs; others may overlook them or possibly work against them. A singular, "correct" curriculum is inadvisable, as it would be unable to address the great diversity of learners and their needs. Yet teachers who want to work with L2 learners within a communicative framework expect to do so in a way that is credible, respectable, and sound. They want to make sensible choices from the many options that confront them, and to work with "a sense of plausibility," informed by a multiplicity of sources, to cite Prabhu again (1993: 172).

And this is where L2 teachers can turn to educational linguistics research as one of these sources. They might see direct application of some of its findings to their own teaching circumstances. Or they might raise questions about the applicability of other findings to their work. This could lead them to design and carry out their own research. Even here, prior studies in the field could be of service, their theoretical frames provocative, and their methodologies useful. Whatever direction teachers might pursue, they can draw on many facets of educational linguistics research to guide their decisions as they implement a learner-centered, communicative curriculum in their classrooms. And by incorporating educational linguistics research into their knowledge base for program implementation and classroom decision making, they can exercise their professional role as teachers of language, an area which is distinct from other content areas. They can also expand their role as researchers and research consumers, able to address the relevance and generalizability of research findings to their specific classroom contexts, to inform current theories on language learning and use, and to contribute to, as well as implement, a research agenda in these areas.

But teachers cannot, and should not, do this on their own. The most fruitful work in this regard will be as systemic and collaborative as possible, involving all those who share comembership in the educational community. Those whose primary work is in different aspects of language education—whether that be classroom teaching, research, publication, or policy—must listen to each other's questions and concerns, as they make decisions that can truly make a difference in the lives of language learners. Such collaboration is not what these different participants may be used to doing. Not only is it unusual, it is not easy either. But it is important to the success of the learner-centered, communicative curriculum and the challenges it poses.

A good basis for launching this effort is discussion and dialogue around the body of information on L2 teaching and learning that has already come from educational linguistics research. The careful control under which much of this work was undertaken means that its findings are not directly applicable to the classroom. However, many of the questions that inspired the work are clearly classroom-oriented and a good number are classroom-based. It is in light of the relevance of educational linguistics research that the following aspects of teacher decision-making are discussed. They have to do with the planning choices and on-the-spot decisions teachers must make to select and organize course content and activities around communication and learning, to structure classroom communication to assist the learning process, and to provide other kinds of learning experiences when classroom communication is insufficient in this regard. Here they are posed as questions, followed by responses from research. These responses are not intended as answers, but rather the basis for further discussion and collaboration between and among professionals in language education.

How should a learner-centered, communicative curriculum be organized with respect to classroom content and activities?

Tasks and L2 learning processes. The multiplicity of choices in content, most of which are very attractive choices, in widespread use all over the world, offers considerable challenge to the teacher who wants to design and/or implement a learner-centered, communicative curriculum. There are structures and lexemes, notions and functions, topics and situations, and multiple combinations of same. Each has its strengths and weaknesses as a single or integrated unit of communication content, and a number of excellent reviews have been published on them. (See for example Breen 1987, Long and Crookes 1992, and Nunan 1988, 1989.) Among these authors (and others), communication "tasks" have emerged as a suitable choice for the basis of a learner-centered, communicative curriculum. Although defined in various ways, the key features of "task" are "work" or "activity" and "goal." (See Pica,

Kanagy, and Falodun 1993.) In carrying out a task, learners and interlocutors must work together, using language to achieve a goal or outcome. For example, they might have to share instructions in order to replicate a picture or assemble an object, to exchange ideas to reach a decision or solve a problem, or to pool clues to solve a mystery or complete a puzzle.

Tasks have come under the scrutiny of research more than notions and functions or any of the other units of curriculum content noted above, the basis of these latter being largely theoretical. Yet tasks have held up exceedingly well under such scrutiny, and have demonstrated a capacity to provide conditions which can nurture the kinds of communication considered essential to L2 learning. Thus there is growing amount of evidence to support learners' participation in communicative tasks with respect to both L2 learning outcomes and the processes that underlie them. With respect to outcomes, both grammatical rules and communication skills appear to be assisted, this revealed most clearly in an evaluation of the task-based program of Prabhu. (See Beretta and Davies 1986.)

Research has also revealed that learners' participation in tasks enhances their experience in L2 learning at the process level as well. This is accomplished as learners negotiate with their interlocutors over the comprehensibility of the messages they provide and those they receive in order to carry out the task and bring it to a successful outcome. Their work sets up several distinct, but interrelated conditions considered critical to successful L2 learning.

Among the conditions provided as learners negotiate for message meaning is the opportunity to be given L2 input that is modified so that they can comprehend it. Such modification often involves repetitions and rephrasings of the original L2 input, which helps to draw learners' attention to relationships of form and meaning within the L2. Their participation in negotiation also offers learners feedback on the comprehensibility of their own production. Such feedback can then be used to modify their production in ways that are important to the restructuring work they might need to do to advance their interlanguage development and eventually internalize a more target-like system of L2 rules. Such relationships are illustrated in the examples below:

Native Speaker (NS)	Learner
there's a chimney on the left *(NS original input)*	
	what? *(Learner feedback to NS)*
a chimney is on the left *(NS modified input)*	
	the windows are crozed

The windows have what? crossed? I'm not sure what you're saying there.
(NS feedback to Learner)

(Learner original input)

windows are closed
(Learner modified output)

oh, the windows are closed. oh, okay, sorry
(NS feedback to Learner)

(Data are from Pica, Holliday, Lewis, Berducci, and Newman 1991.)

Among the relevant studies on tasks, nearly all have touched on this broad range of conditions for L2 learning, but each might be singled out for its particular emphasis on one or two, for example: Long (1980, 1981, 1985) focused primarily on input modification; Pica, Young, and Doughty (1987) on input comprehension; and Crookes and Rulon (1985, 1988), Gass and Varonis (1985), Pica, Holliday, Lewis, and Morgenthaler (1989), and Pica et al. (1991), on feedback and production of modified input. The tasks used in these studies were reviewed, together with others in Pica, Kanagy, and Falodun (1993), and included in a task typology in which types of tasks were classified and compared according to their potential contributions to L2 learning. Among the most potentially effective types of tasks identified, two features were apparent. First, such tasks required, rather than simply invited, the exchange of information among task participants. Further, they were targeted toward only one possible solution rather than several acceptable outcomes. Specific examples included tasks which required participants to pool unique pieces of information known only to them in order to complete a picture (as in Pica et al. 1991; Pica et al. 1989), assemble an object or display (as in Doughty and Pica 1986; Pica and Doughty 1985a, 1985b; and Pica, Young, and Doughty 1987), unravel a mystery story (Gass and Varonis 1985), or solve a mathematics problem (Long 1980; Crookes and Rulon 1985, 1988).

Communication tasks and L2 grammar learning. Tasks are holistic in their orientation toward L2 structural forms and rules. As such, their emphasis has not been on the targeting of specific linguistic features, but rather the communication of message meaning. Recently, however, such targeting has become of great interest to researchers in the design of tasks. (See for example Bley-Vroman and Loschky 1993; Fotos and Ellis 1991.) Often referred to as grammar-based or grammar-focused, these tasks require the attainment of goals conditioned by communication and the exchange of information, as well as receptive and/or productive access to a particular linguistic feature to be used in reaching these goals. For example, a task of this kind might require the learner to assemble an item such as a car, based on interviewing an interlocutor who could provide information in that regard. The information might focus on individual and multiple parts of the car, thus setting up the need for the learner to hear and produce plural *-s* contrasts.

Similarly, a task might be organized around a particular L2 function or notion. For example, the function of request might be highlighted in a task that required learners to obtain a meal in a restaurant. The notion of space might be the focus of a task that engaged them in reading and relating measurements needed for object assembly. Although there are, no doubt, numerous other possibilities for this type of task, this is an aspect of task design which has posed considerable challenge to us. We have found it difficult to coordinate the goal-oriented criteria for task design, the need to focus on grammar, and the desire to provide learners with a context for L2 learning.

Thus we have identified difficulties with tasks of this kind, as our work has required us to choose tasks for purposes of data collection (Pica, Lincoln-Porter, Paninos, and Linnell in progress), and in so doing to analyze grammar-based or grammar-focused communication tasks and task structures, both those already available as well as our own designs. One common problem is found with activities often labeled as tasks that engage learners in deciding which structure to choose in order to complete a sentence or describe a picture. While research has shown that these tasks can be effective for engaging learners in discussions about grammar and in metalinguistic questioning and exchange—some of which even include negotiation for message meaning (see Fotos and Ellis 1991)—they differ considerably, however, from the tasks described above, which engage learners in work whose goal is not the identification or expression of language in itself, but rather the replication of a picture, the assembly of an object, the ordering of a meal, etc.

There is a danger that if these two kinds of activities are both to be considered as grammar-based tasks, other, far less communicative assignments such as fill-in-the-blank worksheets might be labeled grammar-based "tasks" as well, if only because they, too, are work-driven, goal-oriented and form-focused. This is unfortunate because grammar-based activities that are not tasks leave little possibility for the meaningful exchange characteristic of message communication and, with that, negotiation of message meaning.

Another problem we have found with grammar-based communication tasks is that they live up to the second rather than the first of their descriptive premodifiers. In other words, their emphasis is on "communication," not grammar, and within that "communication," far more attention is given to the exchange of information than to the negotiation of meaning. In Pica et al. (in progress), we have been working to develop communicative tasks that engage learners in negotiation over verb form–meaning relationships. The task we are currently using requires learners and their interlocutors to replicate the picture sequence of a picture story hidden from their view and to compose a jointly-written narrative by pooling and exchanging information on the story pictures, subsets of which they hold uniquely.

What we have found is that throughout their communication about the story sequence, learners and their interlocutors (NSs as well as other learners) provide many contexts for grammatical features, in this case the different tense and aspectual functions that coordinate the story. They also negotiate for message meaning with considerable frequency. What they do not do, however, is bring these two components together for us. Thus they seldom negotiate over the activities of the story characters in ways that focus on verb grammar. Although our task participants occasionally negotiate over the activities of the story characters in their pictures, e.g. whether one of them "telephones" or "is telephoning" the other, such exchanges are by no means common to their communication. What we have typically found across these and other tasks is that learners and NSs prefer to describe what their pictures look like rather than exchange information about what they are doing. This activity gets them into a great deal of negotiation, but their negotiation tends to be about colors, sizes, and names rather than verb tense and aspect.

We are still working on developing grammar-focused communication tasks in order to examine their actual impact on the learner, i.e. to test whether they are as worthwhile in practice as they seem to be at a theoretical level. At another theoretical level, however, we feel that this may not be worth the effort, in light of what we have come to see as important conditions for L2 learning and the differential contributions of the different task types in bringing them about. If successful L2 learning depends on learners' access to comprehensible and modified input that helps to draw their attention to relationships of L2 form and meaning, and offers them feedback to modify their production and advance their interlanguage, then tasks designed to highlight specific grammatical features need not be viewed as the basis for curricular organization. They are perhaps better viewed not as fundamental organizing units of a learner-centered, communicative curriculum, but as interventions within such a curriculum, employed to help learners when they are struggling to attain productive knowledge and use of specific grammatical features. As such, they play an important role which will be addressed below in discussion of ways to encourage learners' L2 awareness and sensitivity.

Before coming to that discussion, however, a further aspect of task implementation must be addressed, this having to do with the social organization in the classroom that can foster the sense of collaboration and cooperation that are at the heart of successful tasks in terms of setting up conditions for L2 learning. Teachers' choices of social organization are many, but at issue for most is whether to let students work together or with their teacher. Each has its strengths and shortcomings, as will be discussed next in the next section.

Which types of classroom organization are effective in providing a social and linguistic environment for L2 learning?

The cautions in L2 learner peer interaction. One of the dominant practices in the communicative, learner-centered classroom has involved letting students work together in small group and pair work. This practice is not at all unique to the L2 classroom as it has been widely espoused throughout the educational literature under other labels, e.g. cooperative, collaborative, and peer learning. Studies inside and outside language education have reported a number of positive results. (See for example Deen 1987 for the former, and Kagan 1986 and Slavin 1983) for the latter.)

Is L2 learners' interaction with peers sufficient for meeting their social and linguistic needs? The results are actually mixed. For one thing, peer interaction carries with it the potential problem of learners hearing much more of each other's nontarget-like, interlanguage input than the NS varieties toward which they strive. Thus studies of Canadian French immersion classrooms in Canada, as well as Spanish and Chinese bilingual programs in the United States, have found that students who engaged in extensive interaction with their L2 speaking classroom peers, with little opportunity to interact with standard L2 speakers in the wider environment outside the classroom, received in effect a large proportion of interlanguage input, which in turn limited their access to target-like L2 input. Such input appeared to reinforce their own production errors. (See Lightbown and Spada 1990; White 1990; Wong Fillmore 1992.) Opportunities for interaction with a teacher would seem critical, therefore, as was the finding of Chesterfield, Chesterfield, Hayes-Latimer, and Chavez (1983), who found that in bilingual classrooms in which most students were English speaking, greater proficiency in English L2 was related to peer interaction than to teacher interaction. However, where the majority of students shared the same L1 (which in this case was Spanish), interaction with the teacher was key to students' proficiency in English L2.

These findings seem particularly appropriate to classrooms where students are homogeneous in the L1, or share a common language other than the one they are studying. It is commonly reported in classroom observation that, unless their teacher carefully monitors their language choice, students working together often communicate in their common language rather than attempt to produce the L2. However, a recent study by Futaba (1994) provides needed detail on this widely reported phenomenon. What Futaba found was that when working together in dyads on communication tasks, Japanese L1 learners of English L2 seldom used their L1 to negotiate the key requirements of the task. Lapses into L1 were usually done subvocally, as learners work individually to organize information before presenting it to their partners in English L2.

The benefits of L2 learner peer interaction. Despite the concerns raised by research that learner interaction might have a negative impact on L2 production accuracy as well as invite inappropriate L1 use, another set of studies has shown that it can also assist learners' production, albeit in a fairly restricted way. In the "story task" research related above (see again Pica et al. in progress), in which learners and their interlocutors share information from pictures to compose a story, we have found distinct and potentially beneficial interactions among our learners. The most salient is an exchange in which one learner supplies an appropriate lexical item to finish the other's utterance when the other is struggling to retrieve it. We call such interactions "completions," because in such instances, one learner will pause during an utterance, providing a context for the other to offer the needed word. Such words could very well function as the "satellite units" identified by Bygate (1988) to contribute toward the building of interlanguage grammar. A typical exchange of completion is shown below:

NNS (Non-Native Speaker)	NNS
She made like a	fire?
yes, fire	okay

We have also found that here, and elsewhere, the learners' incorporation of other learners' errors into their own production has been very rare. Other researchers, too, have found similar phenomena (see Porter 1986), and ample evidence of learners' self-generated adjustments toward more correct production (Bruton and Samuda 1980) and their incorporation of each others' correct productions into their own (Gass and Varonis 1989).

Although the completions phenomenon brings a potentially beneficial contribution to peer interaction, another pattern identified when learners work together is not as reassuring, this having to do with the brevity of learner responses to each other during negotiation work. While their input to each other as they negotiate is often quite accurate with respect to L2 grammar, their utterances are commonly in the form of isolated words and short phrases. This limits learner access to L2 sentence grammar during the very time—negotiation—in which their attention is claimed to be most focused. We have also found that there is little negotiation over inflectional morphology, which in the case of our story task, would include verb endings and expressions of tense and aspect. This, as noted above, is an unfortunate, all too common finding about negotiation during communication tasks that applies to learners and NS interlocutors alike. It raises questions as to when a learner-centered, communicative curriculum might require a more deliberate focus on L2 form and grammar. It is to these questions that we next turn.

How can a learner-centered, communicative curriculum be adjusted and enhanced when exchange of message meaning is not sufficient for L2 mastery? Many concerns have been raised that L2 learners in communicative programs seldom reach NS norms. (See for example Higgs and Clifford 1982; Swain 1985.) Even highly proficient learners tend to show considerable unevenness in their L2 development. In English L2, for example, learners often acquire a high degree of accuracy in constituent order syntax, which is considered a "resilient" feature, while they manifest incomplete and variable accuracy in the "fragile" features of English such as its inflectional morphology (Bardovi-Harlig and Bofman 1989). This is not unlike the pattern reported for German L2 (Meisel, Clahsen, and Pienemann 1981). Among the more vulnerable features are those that are difficult to perceive in communicative input, are not salient when attention is focused on the comprehension and expression of the L2 message meaning, and/or bear a resemblance that is close, but not identical, to their counterparts in the learners' L1. (See Lightbown and Spada 1993; Sharwood Smith 1991; White 1987, 1991; White, Spada, Lightbown, and Ranta 1992, among others, for further exposition of this argument.)

In keeping within a learner-centered perspective, incomplete L2 outcomes may be sufficient with respect to the individual needs and goals of many learners. However, this is not the case for children who need to attain complete bilingualism or adults who aspire toward academic and professional goals that require standard language use. For such learners, it has been argued that communicative activities may not be sufficient, especially if the context for L2 learning is primarily a classroom situation. (See for example Swain 1985.) What appears to be needed are ways to enhance the communicative curriculum through activities that help learners access, internalize, and control L2 features, both structural and sociolinguistic, when they cannot do so solely on the basis of their exchange of message meaning.

How to do this appears to range from task enhancement, e.g. by engaging learners in tasks that call their attention to those structures and forms they do not appear to induce through communication alone (Doughty 1992; Bley-Vroman and Loschky 1993; Mackey 1994; and Mackey, Pienemann, and Thronton 1991), to explicit grammar instruction and feature correction (Lightbown and Spada 1993; White 1987; White et al. 1992; as well as Day and Shapson 1991 on the French conditional; and Harley 1989 and Spada and Lightbown 1993 for work on questions), to calling learners' attention to differences between target L2 structures and those they produce on their own. (See again Lightbown and Spada 1990 for English *have* and *be* distinctions and progressive *-ing*; Tomasello and Heron 1988, 1989 for a variety of French structures prone to learner misgeneralization.) Such activities get learners to engage in one or both of two processes known more popularly as "focus on form" (Long 1991) and "notice the gap" (Schmidt and Frota 1986). They have their roots in earlier constructs of "consciousness raising" (Rutherford and Sharwood Smith 1985; Sharwood Smith 1991) and language awareness (Hawkins 1984), and more recently language sensitivity (James and Garrett 1991).

"Focus on form" in the learner-centered, communicative classroom. With its findings with regard to "focus on form," research is not suggesting an all-encompassing return to grammar instruction, but rather a sensitivity to language. Meaningful tasks that focus learner's attention to form might be an ideal toward which the L2 teacher can aspire, and have already been implemented successfully in experimental settings (see Doughty 1991; Loschky 1989). However, as noted above, it cannot be taken for granted that communicative tasks that involve decisionmaking, discussion, following directions, etc. can require messages where linguistic features such as verb endings, adverb placement, phoneme clusters and phoneme voicing, for example, are so crucial to communication that learners will focus attention on these features specifically or will anticipate their inclusion in the input they receive. All too often, the language needed to encode a message is sufficiently redundant that an omitted or imprecise feature will not make a difference in successful conveyance of the message. Or the context of the message may be sufficiently shared and understood by speaker and interlocutors that, again, there is little need to attend to form to express or understand the intention underlying the message.

Another area in which "focus on form" may be needed is with respect to L2 sociolinguistic rules. As Wolfson (1981, 1983, 1984) and others have pointed out, many of these are almost impossible to discern in communication, and in a classroom context, a large number of these rules are not required at all. Learners are therefore kept from accessing them. And as Auerbach and Burgess (1986) have demonstrated, in an effort to put a communicative curriculum into practice, materials are often introduced which look authentic with respect to the sociolinguistic categories they present to learners, but the linguistic devices presented for encoding these categories are more often than not based on their author's intuition than on empirical data. As a result there is often a huge difference between the social rules that learners are taught and those that are actually used by NSs and NNSs alike.

Recent research in the area of pragmatics has uncovered a good deal of information on the appropriate encoding and applications of sociolinguistic rules in the areas of requests and apologies (Blum-Kulka, House-Edmondson, and Kasper 1989; Faerch and Kasper 1986; House and Kasper 1987), compliments (Billmyer 1990, 1992; Holmes and Brown 1987; Wolfson 1981, 1983, 1984), complaints (Cohen and Olshtain 1985, 1993; Olshtain and Weinbach 1987), expressions of gratitude (Eisenstein and Bodman 1986), disapproval (D'Amico-Reisner 1983), and refusals (Beebe, Takahashi and Uliss-Weltz 1990). Of additional interest have been specific sociolinguistic contexts in which pragmatic skills are required. Those in which a fair amount of research has already accrued are in university settings. These include academic advising sessions (see for example Bardovi-Harlig and Hatford 1990) and teaching assistant classroom interaction (see Bailey 1983; Pica, Barnes, and Finger 1989; Tyler 1992; Williams 1992).

A small but promising number of studies (e.g. Billmyer 1990, 1992; Holmes and Brown 1987) have shown that learners can be assisted in their access to such rules and their contexts of use through a combination of conversational events and explicit articulation thereof. This is certainly encouraging. To the general perspective that teachers must exercise caution about materials that claim to provide authentic discourse and sociolinguistic rules is added that evidence that there are a number of such rules that might be taught with confidence, perhaps others given more research. This instructional dimension of certain sociolinguistic rules appears to have particular import in foreign language learning contexts. In countries in which sociolinguistic competence in an L2 is becoming increasingly important, it has been shown that direct instruction in sociolinguistic skills may be an effective strategy toward meeting these ends. (See Burnaby and Sun 1989.)

Helping learners to "notice the gap" in the communicative classroom. One of the more recently held assumptions about L2 learning that has had implications for the communicative classroom is that learners make hypotheses about the L2 they are learning and that therefore their initial L2 productions should not be expected to correspond to those in their target L2. This, in turn, suggests that correction of learner error may be inconsequential to the natural path of L2 acquisition. It is believed that errors are evidence that learners are experimenting with L2 rules and patterns as they perceive them and that they will work out these rules appropriately in good time. As been pointed out, however, with respect to both L2 theory and pedagogy, there is a danger in letting this go on without the intervention of correction. Lack of correction, it is argued, may imply to the learner that what was actually an incorrect production was in fact acceptable (Bley-Vroman 1986; Higgs and Clifford 1982; Schachter 1983, 1984, 1991; White 1991).

How do these theoretical claims and examples help teachers make informed decisions about correction in the classroom? This is a difficult question to answer since, so far, research on the actual practice of classroom correction has shown it to be a highly diversified classroom phenomenon, sometimes focused on function, other times on form. Correction can be provided differentially and unsystematically to and across students, yielding confusing and, at times, contradictory results. Thus research has shown that teachers find it difficult to provide systematic correction, correcting students more often for errors in meaning than for errors in grammar, and when providing correction, they do so inconsistently to both individual students and the class as a whole (Fanselow 1977).

Still, research has shown that a number of strategies seem to work quite well. For example in Chaudron (1977), teachers' reduced repetitions of students' errors, with emphasis on the error itself, were found to be effective in learners' subsequently correct responses, much more so than for expansions or elaborations of the learners' utterances or isolated suppliance of a correct form. In another study, L2 learners who were first led "down the garden path" to produce typical errors of overgeneralization for exceptional L2 structures, performed well on these structures if they were given feedback and instruction immediately after they made the errors. Learners who were first taught the rules and exceptions for these structures had less success in using them correctly. (Tomasello and Herron 1988, 1989). These are two ways of calling students' attention to differences between their errors and the correct versions thereof that seem critical to the success of correction as an intervention in L2 learning. Further, the timing of correction seems to be of great importance. Schmidt and Frota (1986) found that in order to benefit from correction, Schmidt had to be given a corrected version of his utterance immediately following what he had just said.

One important finding from research is that correction is especially effective when coordinated into or combined with communicative activities. Thus Lightbown (1992) found that students whose teacher provided immediate corrective feedback on their substitution of *have* for *be* during communicative activities were able to overcome this error and sustain correct production well beyond their period of instruction. Students who were corrected during audiolingual drill and practice activities were also able to self-correct, but could not sustain such correction beyond the classroom (Lightbown 1992). And in Brock, Crookes, Day and Long (1986), correction had no significant effect on learners' production during half hour research sessions. However, when learners were corrected during communication games, they quickly incorporated these corrections into their responses. Two essential features of correction are evident from results of this research. First correction must bring students' attention to their own errors, and secondly it must do so in meaningful, communicative contexts.

Educational linguistics and the L2 teaching profession. The field of education is going through a burgeoning movement toward teacher professionalization and empowerment for making decisions about what to teach, how to teach, and when to do so. Much of this is taking place in ways that embrace the broader context of educational reform and school restructuring around teacher control. The classroom L2 teacher, too, is faced with new and important challenges. It was not so long ago that applied linguistics meant that structuralist linguistics was first applied to the design of classroom materials, then applied to activities grounded in behaviorist psychology. Such earlier restrictions on their knowledge and skills left classroom teachers with little to decide on beyond choosing a sound or structure for classroom drill and practice. Fortunately, they are no longer dependent on this narrow view of linguistics for their identity. Educational linguistics research on language and learning has provided a substantial knowledge base that offers teachers both strategies for assisting their students and opportunities for attaining distinctive, professional status within the wider educational community.

The research base provided by educational linguistics offers no prescriptions, but rather a source of information that teachers can apply to choices they must make about classroom strategies and materials. Teachers need not become linguists to do this, but when they incorporate findings in educational linguistics that pertain to their work, I believe that this can enrich their teaching and enhance the learning of their students. At the risk of appearing to be a top down researcher, I should note that the movement here is somewhat circular, as many educational linguists were classroom teachers to begin with. In fact, it was the questions about language learning and teaching they experienced as classroom teachers that influenced their decisions, my own included, to engage in research.

Some of you reading this paper may be linguists who teach, others may have been educated as teachers, though not as language teachers, and not in linguistics. Some of you may have even been trained as language teachers, but the orientation of your training has provided little background in linguistics. All of you, I hope, find much gratification in your work. You may feel that you have been applyinq educational linguistics throughout your career, but have just not been calling your work by that name. Perhaps I have given you a new label for this component of your work. In any case, I do hope you will turn to educational linguistics research, and be able to apply it to the work that you do and to the questions you may have. I also hope that you will raise questions about educational linguistics research when it does not apply to the teaching and learning that goes on in your classroom. Such questions will open up new areas for research that will benefit teachers and learners alike, and bring teachers and researchers together as professionals in ways that will enhance the field of language education.

REFERENCES

Alatis, James E., H. Stern, and Peter Strevens (eds.). 1983. *Applied linguistics and the preparation of second language teachers: Toward a rationale.* Georgetown University Round Table on Languages and Linguistics 1983. Washington, D.C.: Georgetown University Press.

Auerbach, Elsa Roberts and Denise Burgess. 1985. "The hidden curriculum of survival ESL." *TESOL Quarterly* 19(3): 475–496.

Bailey, Kathleen M. 1983. "Competitiveness and anxiety in second language learning: Looking at and through the diary studies." In Herbert W. Seliger and Michael H. Long (eds.), *Classroom oriented research in second language acquisition.* Rowley, Massachusetts: Newbury House. 67–102.

Bardov-Harlig, Kathleen and Beverley S. Hartford. 1990. "Congruence in native and nonnative conversations: Status balance in the academic advising session." *Language Learning* 40(4): 467–501.

Bardovi-Harlig, Kathleen and Theodora Bofman. 1989. "Attainment of syntactic and morphological accuracy by advanced second language learners." *Studies in Second Language Acquisition* 11(1): 17–34.

Beebe, Leslie M., T. Takahashi, and Robin Uliss-Weltz. 1990. "Pragmatic transfer in ESL refusals." In Robin Scarcella, Elaine Andersen, and Stephen Krashen (eds.), *On the development of communicative competence in a second language.* Cambridge, Massachusetts: Newbury House. 55–74.

Beretta, Alan and Alan Davies. 1986. "Evaluation of the Bangalore project." *ELT Journal* 39(1): 121–127.

Billmyer, Kristine. 1990. "The effects of formal instruction on the development of sociolinguistic competence: The performance of compliments." Unpublished Ph.D. Dissertation. University of Pennsylvania.

Billmyer, Kristine. 1992. "'I really like your lifestyle': ESL learners learning how to compliment." *Working Papers in Educational Linguistics* 6(2): 31–47.

Bley-Vroman, Robert. 1986. "Hypothesis testing in second language acquisition theory." *Language Learning* 36(3): 353–376.

Blum-Kulka, Shoshana. 1982. "Learning how to say what you mean in a second language: A study of speech act performance of learners of Hebrew as a second language." *Applied Linguistics* 3(1): 29–59.

Blum-Kulka, Shoshana, Juliene House-Edmondson, and Gabriele Kasper Eds. 1989. *Cross-cultural pragmatics: Requests and apologies.* Norwood, N.J.: Ablex.

Breen, Michael. 1987. "Contemporary paradigms in syllabus design: Part II." *Language Teaching* 20(2): 157–174.

Brock, Cynthia, G. Crookes, Richard Day, and M. Long. 1986. "The differential effects of corrective feedback in native speaker-nonnative speaker conversation." In Richard Day (ed.), *Talking to Learn.* Rowley, Massachusetts: Newbury House. 229–236,

Brown, H. Douglas. 1991. "TESOL at twenty-five: What are the issues?" *TESOL Quarterly* 25(2): 245–260.

Brumfit, C. J. and K. Johnson (eds.). 1979. *The communicative approach to language teaching.* Oxford: Oxford University Press.

Bruton, Anthony and Virginia Samuda. 1980. "Learner and teacher roles in the treatment of error in group work." *RELC Journal* 11(1): 49–63.

Burnaby, Barbara and Yilin Sun. 1989. "Chinese teachers' views of Western language teaching: context informs paradigms." *TESOL Quarterly* 23(2): 219–239.

Bygate, Martin. 1988. "Units of oral expression and language learning in small group interaction." *Applied Linguistics* 9(1): 59–82.

Canale, Michael and Merrill Swain. 1980. "Theoretical bases of communicative approaches to second language teaching and testing." *Applied Linguistics* 1(1): 1–47.

Candlin, Christopher N., Clive Bruton, Jonathan Leather, and Edward Woods. 1981. "Designing modular materials for communicative language learning; an example: Doctor-patient communication skills." In Larry Selinker, Elaine Tarone, and Victor Hanzelli (eds.). *English for academic and technical purposes.* Rowley, Massachusetts: Newbury House. 105–133.

Carroll, Susanne and Merrill Swain. 1992. "Explicit and implicit negative feedback: An empirical study of the learning of linguistic generalizations." *Studies in Second Language Acquisition* 15(3): 357–386.

Chaudron, Craig. 1977. "A descriptive model of discourse in the corrective treatment of learners errors." *Language Learning* 27(1): 29–46.

Chaudron, Craig. 1986. "Teachers' priorities in correcting learners' errors in French immersion classes." In Richard Day (ed.), *Talking to learn: Conversation in second language acquisition*. Rowley, Massachusetts: Newbury House. 64–84.

Chaudron, Craig. 1988. *Second language classrooms: Research on teaching and learning*. New York: Cambridge University Press.

Chesterfield, Ray, Kathleen Barrows Chesterfield, Katherine Hayes-Latimer, and Regino Chavez. 1983. "The influence of teachers and peers on second language acquisition in bilingual preschool programs." *TESOL Quarterly* 17(3): 401–419.

Clarke, Mark A. 1982. "On bandwagons, tyranny, and common sense." *TESOL Quarterly* 16(4): 437–448.

Cochran-Smith, Marilyn and Susan Lytle. 1990. "Research on teaching and teacher research: The issues that divide." *Educational Researcher* 19(2): 2–11.

Cohen, Andrew D. and Elite Olshtain. 1985. "Comparing apologies across languages." In Kurt R. Jankowsky (ed.), *Scientific and humanistic dimensions of language*. Amsterdam: John Benjamins. 175–184.

Cohen, Andrew D. and Elite Olshtain. 1993. "The production of speech acts by EFL learners." *TESOL Quarterly* 27(1): 33–56.

Crookes, G. 1986. "Task classification: A cross-disciplinary review." Technical Report No. 4. Center for Second Language Classroom Research/Social Science Research Institute. Manoa, Hawaii: University of Hawaii.

Crookes, Graham & Katherine Rulon. 1985. "Incorporation of corrective feedback in native speaker/non-native speaker conversation." Technical Report No. 3. The Center for Second Language Classroom Research/Social Science Research Institute. Manoa, Hawaii: University of Hawaii.

Crookes, Graham and Katherine Rulon. 1988. "Topic and feedback in native speaker/non-native speaker conversation." *TESOL Quarterly* 22(4): 675–681.

Crookes, Graham & Susan Gass (eds). 1993. *Tasks and language learning: Integrating theory and practice*. Clevedon, U.K.: Multilingual Matters.

D'Amico-Reisner, Lynne. 1983. "An analysis of the surface structure of disapproval exchanges." In Nessa Wolfson and Eliot Judd (eds.), *Sociolinguistics and Language Acquisition*. Rowley, Massachusetts: Newbury House. 103–115.

Day, Elaine M. and Stan M. Shapson. 1991. "Integrating formal and functional approaches to language teaching in French immersion: An experimental study." *Language Learning* 41(1): 25–58.

Deen, Jeanine. 1987. "An analysis of classroom interaction in a cooperative learning and teacher-centered setting." M.A. in TESOL thesis, University of California, Los Angeles.

Doughty, Catherine 1991. "Second language instruction does make a difference: Evidence from an empirical study of second language relativization." *Studies in Second Language Acquisition* 13(4): 431–469.

Doughty, Catherine and Teresa Pica. 1986. "'Information gap tasks': An aid to second language acquisition?" *TESOL Quarterly* 20(2): 305–325.

Duff, Patsy. 1986. "Another look at interlanguage talk: Taking task to task." In Richard Day (ed.), *Talking to learn: Conversation in second language acquisition*. Rowley, Massachu-setts: Newbury House. 147–181.

Edelsky, Carole. 1991. *With literacy and justice for all: Rethinking the social in language and education*. London: Falmer.

Eisenstein, Miriam and Jean Bodman. 1986. "'I very appreciate': Expressions of gratitude by native and non-native speakers of American English." *Applied Linguistics* 7(1): 167–185.

Ellis, Rod. 1992. "Learning to communicate in the classroom: A study of two language learners requests." *Studies in Second Language Acquisition* 14(1): 1–23.

Ellis, Rod. 1989. "Are classroom and naturalistic acquisition the same? A study of the classroom acquisition of German word order rules." *Studies in Second Language Acquisition* 11(3): 305–328.

Faerch, Claus and Gabriele Kasper. 1989. "Internal and external modification in interlanguage request realization." In Shoshana Blum-Kulka, Julienne House, and Gabriele Kaspter (eds.), *Cross-cultural pragmatics*. Norwood, N.J.: Ablex. 221–247.

Faerch, Claus and Gabriele Kasper. 1986. "The role of comprehension in second language acquisition." *Applied Linguistics* 7(3): 256–274.

Fanselow, John F. 1977. "The treatment of error in oral work." *Foreign Language Annals* 10(4): 583–593.

Fanselow, John F. 1990. *Breaking rules: Generating and exploring alternatives in language teaching*. New York: Longman.

Fotos, Sandra and Rod Ellis. 1991. "Communicating about grammar: A task-based approach." *TESOL Quarterly* 25(4): 605–628.

Freeman, Donald. 1989. "Teacher training, development, and decision making: A model of teaching and related strategies for language teacher education." *TESOL Quarterly* 23(1): 27–45.

Freeman, Donald and Jack C. Richards. 1992. "Conceptions of teaching and education second language teachers." *TESOL Quarterly* 27(2): 193–216.

Futaba, Terefumi. 1994. "Second language acquisition through negotiation: A case of non-native speakers who share the same first language." Unpublished Ph.D. dissertation, University of Pennsylvania.

Gass, Susan and Evangeline Varonis. 1989. "Incorporated repairs in NNS discourse." In Miriam Eisenstein (ed.), *The dynamic interlanguage*. New York: Plenum. 71–86.

Gass, Susan and Evangeline Varonis. 1986. "Sex differences in NNS/NNS interactions." In Richard Day (ed.), *Talking to learn: Conversation in second language acquisition*, Rowley, Massachusetts: Newbury House. 327–451.

Gass, Susan and Evangeline Varonis. 1985. "Variation in native speaker speech modification to non-native speakers." *Studies in Second Language Acquisition* 7(1): 37–58.

Gass, Susan and Evangeline Varonis. 1985 "Task variation and NNS/NNS negotiation of meaning." In Susan Gass and Carolyn Madden (eds.), *Input in second language acquisition*. Rowley, Massachusetts: Newbury House. 149–161.

Gass, Susan and Evangeline Varonis. 1984. "The effect of familiarity on the comprehensibility of non-native speech." *Language Learning* 34(1): 65–89.

Harley, Birgit. 1989. "Functional grammar in French immersion: A classroom experiment." *Applied Linguistics* 10(3): 331–359.

Hatch, Evelyn. 1978a. "Acquisition of syntax in a second language." In Jack C. Richards (ed.), *Understanding second and foreign language learning*. Rowley, Massachusetts: Newbury House. 34–70.

Hatch, Evelyn 1978b. "Discourse analysis and second language acquisition." In Evelyn Hatch (ed.), *Second language acquisition: A book of readings*. Rowley, Massachusetts: Newbury House. 401–435.

Hawkins, Edward. 1984. *Awareness of language: An introduction*. Cambridge, U.K.: Cambridge University Press.

Higgs, Theodore and Ray Clifford. 1982. "The push toward communication." In T. Higgs (ed.), *Curriculum, competence and the foreign language teacher*. Skokie, Illinois: National Textbook Co. 57–79.

Holmes, Janet and Dorothy F. Brown. 1987. "Teachers and students learning about compliments." *TESOL Quarterly* 21(3): 523–546.

House, Julieane and Gabriele Kasper. 1987. "Interlanguage pragmatics: Requesting in a foreign language." In Wolfgang Lorscher and Renate Schulze (eds.), *Perspectives on language in performance: Festschrift for Werner Hullen.*The Hague: Mouton. 157–185.

Howatt, Anthony. 1984. *A History of English Language Teaching.* Oxford: Oxford University Press.

Hyltenstam, Kenneth and Manfred Pienemann (eds.). 1984. *Modeling and assessing second language acquisition.* Clevedon, U.K.: Multilingual Matters.

Hymes, Dell. 1972. *Towards communicative competence.* Philadelphia: University of Pennsylvania Press.

James, Carl and Peter Garrett (eds.). 1991. *Language awareness in the classroom.* London: Longman.

Johns, Ann M. 1990. "L1 composition theories: implications for developing theories of L2 composition." In Barbara Kroll (ed.), *Second language writing:: Research insights for the classroom.* New York: Cambridge University Press. 24–36.

Kagan, Spencer. 1986. "Cooperative learning and sociocultural factors in schooling." In California State Department of Education, *Beyond Language: Social and cultural factors in schooling language minority students.* Los Angeles: California State University Evaluation, Dissemination, and Assessment Center. 231–298,

Kelly, I. 1969. *Twenty-five centuries of language teaching.* Rowley, Massachusetts: Newbury House.

Krashen, Stephen. 1980. *Second language acquisition and second language learning.* Oxford: Pergamon Press.

Krashen, Stephen. 1983. "Newmark's ignorance hypothesis and current second language acquisition theory." In Susan Gass and Larry Selinker (eds.), *Language transfer in language learning.* Rowley, Massachusetts: Newbury House. 135–156.

Krashen, Stephen. 1985. *The input hypothesis: Issues and implications.* London: Longman.

Krashen, Stephen and Tracey Terrell. 1983. *The natural approach.* Oxford: Pergamon Press.

Lightbown, Patsy. 1983. "Exploring relationships between developmental and instructional sequences in L2 acquisition." In Herbert Seliger and Michael Long (eds.), *Classroom-oriented research in second language acquisition.* Rowley, Massachusetts: Newbury House. 217–243.

Lightbown, Patsy. 1984. "Can language acquisition be altered by instruction?" In Kenneth Hyltenstam and Manfred Pienemann (eds.), *Modelling and assessing second language acquisition.* Clevedon, U.K.: Multilingual Matters. 101–112.

Lightbown, Patsy. 1992. "Getting quality input in the second/foreign language classroom." In Claire Kramsch and Sally McConnell-Ginet (eds.), *Text and context: Cross-disciplinary perspectives on language study.* New York: Heath. 187–197.

Lightbown, Patsy and Nina Spada. 1990. "Focus-on-form and corrective feedback in communicative language teaching: Effects on second language learning." *Studies in Second Language Acquisition* 12(4): 429–448.

Lightbown, Patsy and Nina Spada. 1993. *How Languages are Learned.* Oxford: Oxford University Press.

Long, Michael. 1980. "Input, interaction, and second language acquisition." Unpublished Ph.D. dissertation. University of California, Los Angeles.

Long, Michael. 1983. "Does second language instruction make a difference? A review of research." *TESOL Quarterly* 17(3): 359–382.

Long, Michael. 1984. "A role for instruction in second language acquisition: Task-based language teaching." In Manfred Pienemann and Kenneth Hyltenstam (eds.), *Modelling and assessing second language acquisition.* Clevedon, U.K.: Multilingual Matters. 77–99,

Long, Michael. 1985. "Input and second language acquisition theory." In Susan Gass and Carolyn Madden (eds.), *Input in second language acquisition*. Rowley, Massachusetts: Newbury House. 377–393.

Long, Michael. 1991a. "The least a theory of second language acquisition needs to explain." *TESOL Quarterly* 24(4): 649–666.

Long, Michael. 1991b. "Focus on form: A design feature in language teaching methodology." In Kees de Bot, D. Coste, Ralph Ginsberg, and Claire Kramsch (eds.), *Foreign language research in cross-cultural perspective*. Amsterdam: John Benjamins. 39–52.

Long, Michael H. (in press). *Task-based language teaching*. Oxford: Basil Blackwell.

Long, Michael, Leslie Adams, Marilyn McLean, and Fernando Castanos. 1976. "Doing things with words—verbal interaction in lockstep and small group classroom situations." In John Fanselow and Ruth Crymes (eds.), *On TESOL '76*. Washington, D.C.: TESOL. 137–153.

Long, Michael and Graham Crookes. 1992. "Three approaches to task-based syllabus design." *TESOL Quarterly* 26(1): 27–56.

Loschky, Lester 1989. "The effects of negotiated interaction and premodified input on second language comprehension and retention." *Occasional Paper No. 16*. Manoa, Hawaii: Department of E.S.L., University of Hawaii.

Loschky, Lester and Robert Bley-Vroman. 1993. "Grammar and Task based methodology." In Graham Crookes and Susan Gass (eds.), *Tasks and language learning: Integrating theory and practice*. Clevedon, U.K.: Multilingual Matters. 123–167.

Mackey, Alison. 1994. "Targeting morphosyntax in children's ESL— An empirical study of the use of communicative tasks." *Working Papers in Educational Linguistics* 10(1): 67–91.

Mackey, Alison, Manfred Pienemann, and Ian Thornton. 1991. "Rapid profile: A second language screening procedure." *Language and Language Education* 1(1): 61–82.

Mohan, Bernard A. 1986. *Language and content*. Reading, Massachusetts: Addison-Wesley.

Meisel, Jurgen, Harald Clahsen, and Manfred Pienemann. 1981. "On determining develop-mental stages in natural second language acquisition." *Studies in Second Language Acquisition* 3(2): 109–135.

Nunan, David. 1988. *The learner-centered curriculum*. Cambridge, U.K.: Cambridge University Press

Nunan, David. 1989. *Designing tasks for the communicative classroom*. Cambridge, U.K.: Cambridge University Press.

Olshtain, Elite and L. Weinbach. 1987. "Complaints: a study of speech act behavior among native and nonnative speakers of Hebrew." In J. Verschueren and M. Bertucelli-Papi (eds.), *The pragmatic perspective*. Norwood, N.J. Ablex. 195–208.

Penfield, Joyce, 1987. "ESL: The regular classroom teacher's perspective." *TESOL Quarterly* 21(1): 21–40.

Pennycock, Alastair. 1989. "The concept of method, interested knowledge, and the politics of language teaching." *TESOL Quarterly* 23(4): 589–618.

Pica, Teresa. 1985. "The selective impact of classroom instruction on second language acquisition." *Applied Linguistics* 6(3): 214–222.

Pica, Teresa. 1987. "Interlanguage adjustments as an outcome of NS-NNS negotiated interaction." *Language Learning* 37(4): 563–593.

Pica, Teresa, Gregory Barnes, and Alexis Finger. 1990. *Teaching matters: Skills and strategies for international teaching assistants*. New York: Newbury House.

Pica, Teresa and Catherine Doughty. 1985a. "Input and interaction in the communicative classroom: A comparison of teacher-fronted and group activities." In Susan Gass and Carolyn Madden (eds.), *Input in second language acquisition*. Rowley, Massachusetts: Newbury House. 115–132.

Pica, Teresa and Catherine Doughty. 1985b. "The role of group work in classroom second language acquisition." *Studies in Second Language Acquisition* 7(2): 233–248.

Pica, Teresa, Lloyd Holliday, Nora Lewis, and Lynelle Morgenthaler. 1989. "Comprehensible output as an outcome of linguistic demands on the learner." *Studies in Second Language Acquisition* 11(1): 63–90.

Pica, Teresa, Lloyd Holliday, Nora Lewis, Dom Berducci, and Jeanne Newman. 1991. "Language learning through interaction: What role does gender play?" *Studies in Second Language Acquisition* 13(3): 343–376.

Pica, Teresa, Ruth Kanagy, and Joseph Falodun. 1993. "Choosing and using communication tasks for second language research and instruction." In Susan Gass and Graham Crookes (eds.), *Tasks and language learning: Integrating theory and practice*. London: Multilingual Matters. 9–34.

Pica, Teresa, Felicia Lincoln-Porter, Diana Paninos, and Julian Linnell. (in progress). "What can second language learners learn from each other? Only their researcher knows for sure." University of Pennsylvania.

Pica, Teresa and Michael Long. 1986. "The linguistic and conversational performance of experienced and inexperienced teachers." In Richard Day (ed.), *Talking to learn: Conversation in second language acquisition*. Rowley, Massachusetts: Newbury House. 85–98.

Pica, Teresa, Richard Young and Catherine Doughty. 1987. "The impact of interaction on comprehension." *TESOL Quarterly* 21(4): 737–758.

Pienemann, Manfred. 1984a. "Learnability and syllabus construction." In Kenneth Hyltenstam and Manfred Pienemann (eds.), *Modelling and assessing second language acquisition*. Clevedon, U.K.: Multilingual Matters. 23–76.

Pienemann, Manfred. 1984b. "Psychological constraints on the teachability of languages." *Studies in Second Language Acquisition* 6(2): 186–214.

Porter, Patricia. 1986. "How learners talk to each other: input and interaction in task-centered discussions." In Richard Day (ed.), *Talking to learn: Conversation in second language acquisition*. Rowley, Massachusetts: Newbury House. 200–224.

Prabhu, N.S. 1987. *Second language pedagogy: A perspective*. Oxford: Oxford University Press.

Prabhu, N.S. 1990. "There is no best method—Why?" *TESOL Quarterly* 24(2): 161–176.

Richards, Jack C. and Theodore Rodgers. 1986. *Approaches and methods in language teaching*. Cambridge, U.K.: Cambridge University Press.

Raimes, Ann. 1985. "What unskilled ESL students do as they write: A classroom study of composing." *TESOL Quarterly* 19(2): 229–258.

Richards, Jack C. and Graham Crookes. 1988. "The practicum in TESOL." *TESOL Quarterly* 22(1): 9–27.

Rigg, Pat. 1991. "Whole language." *TESOL Quarterly* 25(3): 521–542.

Rutherford, William & Michael Sharwood Smith 1985. "Consciousness-raising and universal grammar." In William Rutherford and Michael Sharwood Smith (eds.), *Grammar and second language learning*. Rowley, Massachusetts: Newbury House. 107–116.

Rulon, Katherine and Jan McCreary. 1986. "Negotiation of content: teacher-fronted and small group interaction." In Richard Day (ed.), *Talking to learn: Conversation in second language acquisition*. Rowley, Massachusetts: Newbury House. 182–199.

Sato, Charlene. 1984. "Phonological processes in second language acquisition: Another look at interlanguage syllable structure." *Language Learning* 34(4): 43–57.

Sato, Charlene 1986. "Conversation and interlanguage development: Rethinking the connection." In Richard Day (ed.), *Talking to learn: Conversation in second language acquisition*. Rowley, Massachusetts: Newbury House. 23–48.

Savignon, Sandra. 1972. *Communicative competence: An experiment in foreign-language teaching*. Philadelphia: Center for Curriculum Development.

Scarcella, Robin & Corrine Higa. 1981. "Input, negotiation, and age differences in second language acquisition." *Language Learning* 31(2): 409–438.

Schachter, Jacqueline. 1983. "Nutritional needs of language learners." In Mark A. Clarke and Jean Handscombe (eds.), *On TESOL '82: Pacific Perspectives on Language Learning and Teaching*. Washington, D.C.: TESOL. 175–189.

Schachter, Jacqueline. 1984. "A universal input condition." In William Rutherford (ed.), *Universals and second language acquisition*. Amsterdam: John Benjamins. 167–183.

Schachter, Jacqueline. 1991. "Corrective feedback in historical perspective." *Second Language Research* 7(2): 89–102.

Schmidt, Richard and Sylvia Frota. 1986. "Developing basic conversational ability in a second language: A case study of an adult learner of Portuguese." In Richard Day (ed.), *Talking to learn: Conversation in second language acquisition*. Rowley, Massachusetts: Newbury House. 237–326.

Sharwood Smith, Michael 1991. "Speaking to many minds: On the relevance of different types of language information for the L2 learner." *Second Language Research* 7(2): 118–132.

Shulman, Lee. 1987. "Knowledge and teaching: Foundations of the new reform." *Harvard Educational Review* 57(1): 1–22.

Slavin, Robert. 1983. *Cooperative learning*. New York: Longman.

Snow, Marguerite, Myriam Met, and Fred Genesee. 1989. "A conceptual framework for the integration of language and content in second/foreign language instruction," *TESOL Quarterly* 23(2): 201–217.

Spada, Nina. 1987. "Relationships between instructional differences and learning outcomes: A process-product study of communicative language teaching." *Applied Linguistics* 8(1): 137–161.

Swain, Merrill. 1985. "Communicative competence: Some roles of comprehensible input and comprehensible output in its development." In Susan Gass and Carolyn Madden (eds.), *Input in second language acquisition*. Rowley, Massachusetts: Newbury House. 235–256.

Swain, Merrill and Sharon Lapkin. 1989. "Aspects of the sociolinguistic performance of early and late French immersion students." In Robin Scarcella, Elaine Anderson, and Stephen Krashen (eds.), *On the development of communicative competence in a second language*. Cambridge, Massachusetts: Newbury House. 41–54.

Tomasello, Michael and Carol Herron 1988. "Down the garden path: Inducing and correcting overgeneralization errors in the foreign language classroom." *Applied Psycholinguistics* 9(3): 237–246.

Tomasello, Michael and Carol Herron. 1989. "Feedback for language transfer errors." *Studies in Second Language Acquisition* 11(4): 385–395.

Tyler, Andrea. 1993. "Discourse structure and the perception of incoherence in international teaching assistants' spoken discourse." *TESOL Quarterly* 26(4): 713–729.

Varonis, Evangeline and Susan Gass. 1982. "The comprehensibility of non-native speech." *Studies in Second Language Acquisition* 4(1): 41–52.

Varonis, Evangeline and Susan Gass. 1985a. "Miscommunication in native/non-native conversation." *Language in Society* 14(3): 327–343.

Varonis, Evangeline and Susan Gass 1985b. "Non-native/non-native conversations: A model for the negotiation of meaning." *Applied Linguistics* 6(1): 71–90.

Wesche, Marjorie Bingham. 1994. "Input and interaction in second language acquisition." In Claire Gallaway and Brian J. Richards (eds.), *Input and interaction in language acquisition*. Cambridge, U.K.: Cambridge University Press.

White, Lydia. 1988. "Against comprehensible input: The input hypothesis and the development of second language competence." *Applied Linguistics* 9(1): 89–110.

White, Lydia. 1991. "Adverb placement in second language acquisition: Some effects of positive and negative evidence in the classroom." *Second Language Research* 7(2): 133–161.

White, Lydia, Nina Spada, Patsy Lightbown, and Leila Ranta. 1992. "Input enhancement and L2 question formation." *Applied Linguistics* 12(4): 416–432.

Widdowson, Henry. 1978. *Teaching language as communication.* Oxford: Oxford University Press.

Williams, Jessica. 1993. "Planning, discourse marking, and the comprehensibility of international teaching assistants." *TESOL Quarterly* 26(4): 693–711.

Wong-Fillmore, Lily. 1992. "Learning a language from learners." In Claire Kramsch and Sally McConnell-Ginet (eds.), *Text and context: Cross-disciplinary perspectives on language study.* New York: Heath. 46–66.

Wolfson, Nessa. 1981. "Compliments in cross-cultural perspective." *TESOL Quarterly* 15(1): 117–124.

Wolfson, Nessa. 1983. "An empirically based analysis of complimenting in American English." In Nessa Wolfson and Eliot Judd (eds.), *Sociolinguistics and language acquisition.* Rowley, Massachusetts: Newbury House. 82–95.

Wolfson, Nessa 1984. "Rules of speaking." In Jack C. Richards and Richard Schmidt (eds.), *Language and communication.* London: Longman. 61–87.

Yalden, Janice. 1983. *The communicative syllabus: Evolution, design, and implementation.* Oxford: Pergamon.

Zamel, Vivian. 1976. "Teaching composition in the ESL classroom: What can we learn from research in the teaching of English?" *TESOL Quarterly* 10(1): 67–76.

Zamel, Vivian. 1983. "Writing: The process of discovering meaning." *TESOL Quarterly* 16(2): 195–210.

Crosscultural communication and comparative terminology

Faina Citkina
Kent State University, Ohio
and Uzhgorod State University, Ukraine

Crosscultural communication and crosscultural approach to foreign language teaching in Ukraine. Today, the newly independent Ukraine as an emergent nation faces a severe crisis—a result of many years' economic stagnation and political instability. It is necessary now to catch up with Western technology and to become integrated with the European and world economy; therefore, the drive toward establishing many levels of international links and crosscultural communication is coming to the foreground. While in former years, Ukrainian economic, sociological, and educational contexts were unfavorable for the development of culture studies in foreign-language teaching, the reaction to the present-day economic crisis is one of increasing urgency in regard to the necessity of learning foreign languages—especially those of Western Europe. So nowadays, steps are being taken for foreign-language teaching to be naturally integrated into the broader context of international education and development of transcultural competence; transcultural competence implies a type of language teaching that includes not only the new language discovery—a traditional procedure—but also a deeper learning, which would include, for example, culture shock.

The concept of "interculturality," so popular now, is consistent enough with foreign-language teaching methodology: Indeed, if we believe a language to be a realization of a culture (and so part of a culture), we can assume that foreign-language teaching is also an "intercultural communication" activity. It is our growing belief that a foreign language should be taught along with a foreign culture and that contrastive-comparative studies of both language and culture should precede this teaching in order to create for it an adequate systematic factual basis.

This paper presents the conclusions derived from our English-language teaching experience—about the absolute necessity to integrate teaching the language with teaching about the language. Lack of knowledge about language and culture is an impediment to language learning in general, but being taught both of and about the language, the student will tend to build correspondence rules between L1 and L2 as well as C1 and C2 (i.e. between first and second languages and between first and second cultures). This leads to the well-documented language and culture bias in the student's approach to learning L2. Such an approach was first put into practice in the recently opened Kievo-Mohyljans'ka Academy in Kiev. However, for the vast majority of higher-education institutions in Ukraine, the significant reorientation of foreign-language teaching is practically impossible at present due to lack of proper funding.

Foreign-language teaching and contrastive studies in Ukraine. Speaking about the state of the art in this field, one should first and foremost say that there exists a bridgeable gap between what we have and what we need. It is easy to explain. Foreign language teaching and learning were traditionally a subject of low interest in the former Soviet Union. With the seventy years of isolation of my country from the outside world, with the fear we had for years of communicating with foreigners, with the enormous difficulties we had in publishing our works abroad, even university students and scientists demonstrated no enthusiasm for foreign-language learning, to say nothing of the rest of the population.

It is only with the beginning of *perestroika* that things began to slowly change for the better: Tourism and international contacts at large are now available to many "humbler" people, not to the select few, and this has influenced the growth of interest in foreign languages (especially English and ESP) and laid down the social basis for the real explosion of new information processing. Numerous foreign-language courses are opening up every day; specialists with a knowledge of foreign languages are increasingly in great demand. And this is to be expected, because these processes are characteristic of all the countries of the former East European bloc. However, the process in Ukraine has peculiarities of its own.

Thus after the coup of August 1991 came freedom and independence for Ukraine, with outcomes that were both expected and unexpected. So we found ourselves living in a newly independent Ukraine, with Russia being just another foreign country—instead of in the "senior brother" position it had for centuries—and with the Russian language being, or rather turning into, just another foreign language, due to the consistent straightforward language policy adopted by the Ukrainian government. Since Ukraine is a large country, this language policy is treated differently in its different parts. In Western Ukraine and Transcarpathia we have always used Ukrainian (or mostly Ukrainian) as a language of communication and instruction, whereas in the vast regions of Eastern and Southern Ukraine the population speaks mainly Russian and now, very slowly, it is switching into Ukrainian, beginning with officialese, academic and other publications (including textbooks), mass media, etc. Thus, the language situation is far from simple, and it affects foreign-language teaching in several ways.

First, new developments significantly enhance interest and raise motivation for foreign-language learning. Second, it makes the teachers almost spontaneously change the language of instruction from Russian into Ukrainian, and they face the lack of terminology in many subject fields. Third, with mixed Russian- and Ukrainian-speaking audiences, and with many students being practically bilingual, foreign-language teachers should expect interference from both Russian and Ukrainian; consistent contrastive studies can forecast the "weak points" that are susceptible to interference.

The little time we have had trying to use only Ukrainian in all spheres of communication has already shown how unpredictable language interference can be. It is quite clear now that without a well-grounded, contrastive linguistic analysis of different kinds of communication activities on different language levels, we will get nowhere. What we need is an adequate linguistic foundation for human- and machine-assisted translation, for foreign-language teaching, for terminography, for modern information processing—in other words, for practical purposes first and foremost. Meanwhile, the state of the art in English–Ukrainian contrastive studies is, briefly, as follows.

Contrastive English–Ukrainian analysis was pioneered by the late Prof. Jury Zhluktenko in early 1960s (Zhluktenko 1960, 1964) and then proceeded at slower pace in the 1970s (Zhluktenko 1979, 1981). Even the small textbook we have, *Introduction to Comparative Typology of English, Russian, Ukrainian* (Shvachko et al. 1977) is based on the pilot study on the subject.

Let me exemplify what sorts of problems the English teacher faces in the Russian–Ukrainian community and what kinds of mistakes can be avoided by paying attention to the contrastive English–Russian–Ukrainian data.

Divergences of three main types can be clearly seen here:

- *Constitutive divergences:* presence in every language of some constitutive specific features
- *Productivity/usage divergences:* different degree of productivity of various means of expression, or different usage
- *Correlation divergences:* different correlation between the constitutive language means or between the frequencies of their usage

From a pragmatic, foreign-language-teacher point of view, it is the constitutive divergences that are most important. Four random examples on different language levels follow, two of them illustrating constitutive divergences and two illustrating usage.

A typical example of word-building constitutive divergences is nonparallelism in word building. The layout of the examples in Table 1 shows a *decrease*

Table 1. Regularity in word building.

Ukrainian	Пан	Пані	Панночка
dialect	Паніка	Панянка	
English	Mr.	Mrs.	Miss (mistress*)
Russian	Господин	Госпожа	Барышня
German	Herr	Frau	Fräulein

in systemic character and/or regularity. In this example German looks the least systematic, but this is not really significant, as it is a random example and it would take volumes to prove which language shows more regularity in its word-building and word production. Therefore, what can be recommended to the language learner, translator, or interpreter is to simply commit to memory many things and be careful with word-building. In fact, phenomena like word-building lie on the surface of language potential. If we imagine the language potential as an iceberg, then, they say, the visible part of the iceberg, the part on the surface, constitutes one-eighth of the whole. So seven-eighths of the iceberg is under water, but it is just the underwater part, which is not accessible to immediate, direct observation, that gives power and stability to the whole of the iceberg and that is of paramount importance.

Therefore we come to quite a different level of comparison when we contrast the phenomena referring to the language norm, especially when we investigate the complex relationship between communicative function and natural language forms. The typical example here will be contrasting the different theme-and-rheme divisions of sentences in different languages. The function of expressing something old and something new (topic and comment) is expressed differently:

(1) English:
A candle was lit.

Russian:
Зажгли свечу.
was lit candle

Ukrainian:
Запалили свічку.
was lit candle

So in Ukrainian and Russian, the focus on the new is *normally* placed at the end of the sentence, as contrasted with English. In other words, we have the end-weight/end-focus in Russian and Ukrainian, which must be taken into account in translation. The complementing example is the one with the focus on the "old":

(2) English:
They lit the candle

Russian:
Свечу зажгли
candle they lit

Ukrainian:
Свічку запалили
candle they lit

The change of the place of "theme–rheme" in translation is taking place within a sentence, and it is important for establishing proper communication that a budding translator should acquire the differing language norms and the differing theme and rheme placement.

As we now turn to discourse level, it is necessary to mention Wolfgang Dressler, who rightly pointed out that the predictive power of contrastive parameters is *more limited* on the textual/discourse level, although they may be involved in the explanation of linguistic phenomena and their cross-linguistic and crosscultural distributions (Dressler 1992). It should also be noted that this area of contrastive analysis is practically a complete blank in English–Russian–Ukrainian studies. Our pilot study into the subject has shown that the divergences here are those of degree and not of kind; here we deal with a spectrum that admits blends and overlappings. Both examples I am going to give demonstrate interaction of cultural and language norms. They consider one of the most general features ascribed to the English language, namely that of understatement. The Russian mode of speech, however, is that of straightforwardness, while the Ukrainian one tends to both straightforwardness and overstatement.

Thus, the Russian and Ukrainian phrases that often correspond to the typical English phrase:

(3) English:
He didn't exactly come early.

Russian:
Он себе мнóго позволяет, постоянно опаздывая.

Ukrainian:
Він собі занадто позволяє, постійно спізнюючись.
He allows himself too much being late so often.

Moreover, in Ukrainian, overstatement may be realized in ironic/satirical remarks:

(4) Ukrainian:
О, пан знову затримався.
Oh, the respected person is late again!

In Modern Ukrainian the word пан *merely* corresponded to "mister" in pre-Soviet times, but nowadays, after years of using "comrade" for addressing a person, пан has acquired a somewhat high-flown shade of meaning. Besides, in Russian and Ukrainian culture, it is typical to issue different sorts of remarks depending on who is late, a boss or a rank-and-file colleague. And when we speak of a boss, straightforwardness is completely out of place, there is even a saying: "Bosses are not late, they are delayed."

(5) Russian:
Начальство не опаздывает, а задерживается.

Ukrainian:
Начальство не запізнюється, а затримується.

Another example concerns rendering the typically English pair of phrases with different meanings: "an 'animal lover'" and "an animal 'lover'," where the first phrase normally corresponds to

(6) Russian:
любитель животных

and Ukrainian:
любитель тварин

while the second one has no exact correspondences either in Russian or in Ukrainian, and can be rendered only descriptively, by a sentence. There is just no such notion formed in the Russian or Ukrainian mentality which for many years has been preserved intact, and is rather puritan; even such words as *sex, sexy, sexuality* present difficulty in translation (see, for instance, Azhnjuk 1989: 109–110) due to cultural and psychological differences; they are not as frequently used as in English, and the connotations are not very positive. It is interesting that language puritanism has been maintained in nations and cultures that were practically devoid of religion for seventy years.

Objectives and perspectives of comparative terminology and foreign-language teaching. As mentioned above, the results of the English-Ukrainian contrastive studies are only preliminary, the full-scope analysis of all language levels in the contexts of the respective cultures being the task of the future. Taking into account the immediate needs of crosscultural special communication in different subject fields, we suggest a strategy of parallel work in several directions: first, building up a contrastive study of general languages enveloped in their cultural contexts; second, building up a practice-oriented contrastive LSP project; third, drawing the contrastive outlines of different terminological subsystems. Thus, it is a systematic, "building-from-within" approach that we are after, with the expansion from the nucleus—comparative terminology investigation—to comparative LSPs investigation to comparative-contrastive general languages and cultures investigation.

The sequence of the research procedures suggested here is especially necessary in Ukraine, where, as in the case of all emerging nations, the situation with terminology is really dramatic, demanding great efforts for improvement. During the many years of Soviet hegemony, the influx of new terminology into Ukrainian was almost exclusively through Russian, and most standardization materials were not created but were translated from Russian, with all the attending circumstances, such as, borrowed synonymy: "forcing":

(7) Russian:
вынуждение, форсинг

Ukrainian:
вимушення, форсінг

But the most important thing was that Russian terminologies (and LSPs) for years dominated specialist usage in Ukraine, and at present Ukrainian scientists face a problem of improving—or in some cases creating anew—a national Ukrainian terminology for computer and military sciences and for certain branches of medicine, economics, law, etc. The national renaissance of terminology can be very chaotic—with no ill effect—provided comparative terminology research helps to create a sound scientific basis for the process in question, to orient terminologists and specialists in different subject fields to not a blind borrowing on the one hand or purism on the other, but to adhere to the best, time-tested traditions of various national terminographies and, especially, to English terminology accepted worldwide.

Now, to what extent can comparative terminology science (CTS) be of help here, and what is the state of the art itself? Analysis of specialized literature shows us clearly that comparative terminology science can be considered to be a relatively autonomous trend bordering on comparative linguistics, general terminology science, and translation studies. CTS's separate status as a trend in its own right is supported by the fact that it has its own subject and object of study, its own specific system of methods and procedures of investigation, and its own specific theoretical and applied products (Citkina 1988, 1990).

From a theoretical point of view, CTS aims to create a general theory for comparing terminological systems on the basis of interlingual and inter-terminological regularities established after investigating different language pairs and terminologies of different types. These regularities represent a higher level of abstraction than those established in the investigation of individual terminological systems in bilingual and/or multilingual situations. Therefore, at present we cannot claim to have reached the point where we can make any universal conclusions based on CTS. Our strategic purpose today must be to consolidate theoretical and applied works in CTS, while our tactical purpose consists in working out an adequate system of unified methods and procedures and applying them to a wide range of terminological systems in different languages. Consequently, we think that a general theory of CTS can be achieved only after we have accumulated sufficient comparative empirical data and worked out consistent universal methods for analysis.

These methods are essential in CTS for obtaining comparable results in a wide range of terminological systems and national languages (Citkina 1993). As a matter of fact, a great deal of serious research has been conducted in CTS worldwide, including research in the multilingual former Soviet Union, where it was prompted by general ignorance of foreign languages and a need to have all scientific-technical literature translated. At the same time, the data obtained have been compared with a considerable degree of approximation because of the great discrepancies in methods employed. Work aimed at unifying the methods of investigation is in full swing now, but it is a time-consuming process.

From the applications point of view, CTS is translation-oriented; it involves establishment of interlingual correspondences and correlations between terms and terminological systems on different language levels. This provides adequate terminological maintenance for computer-assisted translation and multilingual terminological databases, bilingual terminography, international unification and harmonization of terminologies, etc.

One of the major tasks, as I see it, is to disseminate the results of research, to make future specialists and budding LSP translators terminology-wise. Performance of this task is embedded in the existing curriculum in university departments. At this point, mention should be made of the systemic differences between higher education in Europe or America and in the former Soviet Union, where practically all the subjects in the curriculum are compulsory. The latter system may be open to criticism in many ways, but its positive value undoubtedly consists in the opportunity to arrange all the theoretical courses in such a way that they form a logically linked complex with a well-balanced distribution of the knowledge to be acquired all through the years of study. Thus, in Uzhgorod State University, Ukraine, students study foreign literature, history, geography and culture of Britain and the United States, lexicology, theoretical grammar, phonetics, and functional stylistics in their first, second, and third years, theory and practice of translation in their fourth year, scientific-technical translation in spring semester of their fourth year, and general and comparative terminology and business English in their fifth year. All the basic courses are followed by some special ones, which are optional (students must choose one course of those suggested for the given semester). Thus, students come to the translation courses well-prepared linguistically.

The main objectives of terminology and translation courses are (a) to make students realize the structural typological differences between English and Ukrainian/Russian; (b) to make them aware of the differing lexical laws, i.e. semantic structure of the word/word-combination, lexical valency, context-dependent words and other language universals that are a must of a compulsory education of any translator; (c) to give the students some practical experience in translation, resulting in a set of patterns, formulae, cliches—the educational basis necessary for further professional perfection. The curriculum in other universities is very similar. As mentioned above, what we really are after is to extend and deepen the crosscultural component of all our courses. Needless to say, the crosscultural and crosslinguistic education of students in non-linguistics departments is just beginning, and it proceeds at an extremely slow pace due to the lack of funds and specialists. A breakthrough in this area is a task for the future.

REFERENCES

Aznjuk, Bohdan. 1989. *English phraseology from the cultural-ethnic point of view* (in Ukrainian). Kiev: Naukova Dumka.

Citkina, Faina. 1988. *Terminology and translation* (in Russian). Lviv: Vischa Shkola.

Citkina, Faina. 1990. "Comparative terminology theory: Problems, goals, methods, applications." In Klaus-Dirk Schmitz (ed.), *TKE '90: Terminology and knowledge engineering, Volume one*. Proceedings of the Second International Congress. Frankfurt: Indeks.

Citkina, Faina. 1993. "Methods and procedures in comparative terminology science." In Klaus-Dirk Schmitz (ed.), *TKE '93: Terminology and knowledge engineering*. Frankfurt: Indeks.

Dressler, Wolfgang. 1992. "Between grammar and discourse." In Martin Putz (ed.), *Thirty years of linguistic evolution*. Amsterdam and Philadelphia: John Benjamins.

Shvachko, Karp, Peter Terentjev, Tatjana Janukjan, and Svetlana Shvachko. 1977. *Introduction to comparative typology of English, Russian, and Ukrainian* (in Russian). Kiev: Vischa Shkola.

Zhluktenko, Jury. 1960. *Contrastive English-Ukrainian grammar* (in Ukrainian). Kiev: Vischa Shkola.

Zhluktenko, Jury 1964. *Ukrainian-English interlanguage relations: Ukrainian in the U.S.A. and Canada* (in Ukrainian). Kiev: Vischa Shkola.

Zhluktenko, Jury (ed.). 1979. *Essays in contrastive linguistics* (in Ukrainian). Kiev: Naukova Dumka.

Zhluktenko, Jury (ed.). 1981. *Contrastive studies in English, Ukrainian, and Russian Grammar* (in Ukrainian). Kiev: Naukova Dumka.

The pleasure hypothesis

Stephen Krashen
University of Southern California

The hypothesis explored in this paper is that those activities that are good for language acquisition are usually perceived by acquirers as pleasant, while those activities that are not good for language acquisition are not consistently perceived as pleasant, and are, in fact, often perceived to be painful.

Before detailing how language acquirers react to different activities, we first need to discuss which activities are good for language acquisition.

Comprehensible input is good for language acquisition. In previous publications (e.g. Krashen 1985), I have argued that we acquire language in only one way: when we understand messages or get "comprehensible input." Comprehensible input results in subconscious linguistic competence, which underlies most of our ability to use language for communication.

The evidence for this "input hypothesis" can be summarized as follows: Assuming affective barriers are not present, more comprehensible input leads to more language acquisition and more literacy development. This relationship holds for both the informal (outside the classroom) and formal (classroom) environment and for both beginning and intermediate levels of instruction in the formal environment. In this section. I briefly review the evidence.

Second language acquisition.

The informal environment. Consistent with the input hypothesis, studies of second language acquisition in the informal environment show that longer length of residence in the country where the target language is spoken results in more proficiency as long as the acquirer is competent enough in the language to understand some of the input and has a chance to get input, e.g. to interact with speakers of the language (Krashen 1982, 1985).[1]

1. Very advanced acquirers may cease profiting from the informal environment after a while because the input no longer contains new language (i+1). I have suggested (1991a) that language acquisition in the informal environment follows an S-shaped curve, with little progress at the beginning and a flattening out of growth at advanced levels.

The formal environment—beginning level. Method comparison studies show that comprehensible-input-based methods are clearly and consistently superior to traditional methods when communicative measures are used. When form-based measures are used, students in comprehensible-input-based classes are at least as good as traditional students and sometimes better (Krashen 1982, 1985, 1991a).[2]

The formal environment—intermediate level. Intermediate language teaching, in my view, is sheltered subject matter teaching, classes in which intermediate students are taught subject matter through the second language in a comprehensible way. In sheltered subject matter teaching, students are not tested on language but are completely focused on subject matter. From my review of sheltered subject matter teaching and related approaches (Krashen 1991b), I have concluded that students in these classes acquire as much or more of the second language as students in traditional intermediate level language classes, and they learn impressive amounts of subject matter at the same time.

Literacy development.

The informal environment. Research consistently shows that those who live in a more print-rich environment show superior literacy development. and research also confirms that those who say they read more typically read better

---

2. There is the perception that students in comprehensible input-based classes are not as grammatically accurate as traditional students, that methods such as Natural Approach trade fluency for accuracy. Tracy Terrell (personal communication) explained to me the reasons for this perception: Natural Approach students sound less accurate because they can actually speak with some fluency; students in traditional classes can hardly speak at all. If traditional students could produce language with any fluency, they would be less accurate than Natural Approach students. Terrell's explanation is consistent with findings showing that students in comprehensible-input-based class do as well as or better than traditional students on grammar tests.

A similar complaint has been made by some foreign-language teachers who note that students who enroll in higher-level classes after comprehensible input methodology are not up to the standard of previous years' students. Steven Sternfeld (personal communication) investigated these charges informally at one university and found that they were, in fact, true. There was, however, a very good reason for these "declining standards": Many more students were continuing on to higher levels. In previous years, most of the students who took higher-level foreign-language courses were those who had had considerable exposure to the language outside the classroom, a conclusion consistent with Graman's results (Graman 1987). (See page 15 for empirical data supporting Sternfeld's observations.)

and write better (research reviewed in Krashen 1993a). The latter result holds for both first and second language development (Krashen 1993a).[3]

Of course, these conclusions can be challenged: Perhaps those who read more do other things as well. Perhaps they write more, study harder, or are even hooked on phonics. Case studies of individual readers (see e.g. Krashen 1993a: 16–18), as well as studies of free reading in school (see below), make these possibilities unlikely.

As an example of the former, Cho and Krashen (1994) asked a small group of female adult acquirers of English as a second language to do light reading at their own convenience. Several subjects were hesitant English speakers and had never read a book in English. After it was determined that novels from the Sweet Valley High and Sweet Valley Twins series were too difficult, subjects began reading novels from the Sweet Valley Kids series (second grade reading level). They became fanatic Sweet Valley Kids readers, made impressive gains in vocabulary, and reported that their overall English competence improved greatly.

The formal environment—beginning level. A comprehensible-input-based approach to beginning literacy is reading stories outloud to students. Research confirms that this activity is highly effective; students who are read to regularly easily outperform comparison students on a variety of measures of literacy development. This result has been confirmed both in first language acquisition (Cohen 1968; Feitelson, Kita, and Goldstein 1986) and second language acquisition (Romney, Romney, and Braun 1989).

The formal environment—intermediate level. Perhaps the most effective means of promoting literacy at the intermediate level in school are programs in which a specific amount of time is set aside for free voluntary reading. From my review of this research, I have concluded that students in these programs typically outperform comparison students on tests of literacy development if the programs are given sufficient time to run (Krashen 1993a)

In a recent study, Pilgreen and Krashen (1993) managed to get impressive results in a short term sustained silent reading program (four months). High school ESL students gained nearly one month for every week they participated in the program, moving, as a group, from a mean of 3.7 to 5.3 on the Stanford Diagnostic Reading Comprehension Test (grade equivalent scores). In addition, students reported doing more reading after the program, and most felt they had

3. As was the case for second language acquisition (see note 1), an S-shaped curve appears to fit the data for the development of literacy over time in the informal environment, with acquirers making somewhat less progress at more advanced levels as less i+1 is present in what they read (Greaney 1980; Anderson, Wilson, and Fielding 1988).

improved a great deal. The success of this program may be due to the fact that students had an excellent supply of interesting reading material easily available, were encouraged to read at home, were allowed to take books home, and were informed about the advantages of free reading.

Activities that do not help language acquisition. The above survey makes it clear that comprehensible input, in the form of aural or written input, helps language acquisition. I focus here on three activities that do not help: forced speech, correction, and grammar study.

Forced speech. Forced speech is output that the acquirer is forced to produce but that is beyond his or her current level of acquisition, that is, it is at "i+1" or beyond. The input hypothesis predicts that forced speech will not be helpful; according to the input hypothesis, the ability to speak is a result, not a cause, of language acquisition. A competing hypothesis, the comprehensible output hypothesis, claims that forced speech is one of the ways we acquire language (Swain 1985).

I have argued (Krashen 1991a) that the evidence does not support the comprehensible output hypothesis. First, studies show that people simply do not produce enough language for output to make a significant contribution to language development (Krashen 1991a). Such evidence damages all output hypotheses. Second, studies typically show no relationship between written output quantity and writing quality (Krashen 1991a).

In addition, studies of the frequency of comprehensible output itself are not encouraging. The comprehensible output hypothesis claims that we acquire when, in the face of communicative problems, we adjust our output and improve it. This improvement appears to happen only some of the time that conversational adjustments are made (31% of the time for beginners (Pica 1988) and 51% in intermediates [Pica et al. 1989]), and rarely in writing (30% of the time for second language writers, with many decisions being lexical [Cumming 1990]).

Nobuyoshi and Ellis (1993) claim to have provided data supporting the comprehensible output hypothesis. In their study, six adult EFL students in Japan of "fairly low-level proficiency" but who were "capable of using at least some past tense verb forms correctly" (1993: 206) were asked to participate in a jigsaw task with their teacher in which they described actions in pictures that, they were told, occurred the previous weekend or previous day. During the first session of the study, the three experimental subjects received requests for clarification if the verb was not in the past tense or if the past tense was incorrectly formed. During the second session, one week later, they only received general requests for clarification (when the teacher did not understand).

The three comparison subjects only received general requests for clarification each time.

Nobuyoshi and Ellis report that comparison subjects did not improve their past tense accuracy. Two experimental subjects (E1 and E2) were able to improve their performance, but the third experimental subject (E3) did not. Nobuyoshi and Ellis claim that E1 and E2 sustained their gains to time 2, with E1 increasing accuracy from an original level of 31% to 89% and E2 increasing from an original 45% to 89%. Nobuyoshi and Ellis conclude that their study "provides some support for the claim that pushing learners to improve the accuracy of their production results not only in immediate improved performance but also in gains in accuracy over time" (1993: 208).

As Nobuyoshi and Ellis point out, however, their conclusions are based on a very small sample size. In addition, it is based on a very low number of obligatory occasions. E1, who showed the clearest gains, went from 4 correct out of 13 at time 1 to 8 correct out of 9 at time 2. E2 went from 9 correct out of 20 at time 1 to 16 correct out of 26 at time 2. In addition, according to my calculations, gains for neither E1 nor E2 were statistically significant (for E1, chi square = 2.061 (just short of the .10 level); for E2, chi square = 1.246, df = 1 in both cases). Data supporting a central hypothesis should be made of sterner stuff.

Thus, for one subject there was no evidence of the value of comprehensible output (E3), and for the other two, gains were not statistically significant. In addition, the number of obligatory occasions was very small. Note also that all three subjects had studied the past tense rule and had been clearly focused on it in session 1. It is reasonable to expect that when you focus a subject on form, then put the subject back in the same environment, the subject will be focused on form again, especially if the conversational partner is their teacher. The near-significant effect on subject E1, in other words, may simply have been a performance effect—he or she was simply more inclined to try to use a consciously learned rule for the past tense and was a more successful Monitor user than E2 and E3.

Correction. In previous publications, I have argued that correction is consistently ineffective. I have hypothesized that correction affects only conscious learning, not acquisition. Studies show either no effect for correction or a very small effect, and this small effect occurs just where theory predicts it should: on form-based measures when performers have time and knowledge of the rule (Krashen 1991a). Current research, in my view, is fully consistent with this position.

Jafarpur and Yamini (1993), in a study of 39 English majors at the university level in Iran, concluded that practice with dictation did not improve English language competence. Their data, however, also bear on the issue of correction.

All subjects took a conversation class in English that met for four one-hour sessions per week and that focused on direct instruction in English pronunciation. The experimental group took a total of 60 dictations, about one per class period, during the class. Dictations consisted of 55 to 156 words and took about five minutes each. Dictations were read three times, once at normal speed (students only listened), once with pauses at "natural boundaries" (1993: 363) with punctuation marks dictated, and finally again at normal speed.

Crucial to the correction issue is the fact that the experimental students' efforts were corrected and returned to them at the next session and were reviewed with them. This took about three minutes per session. To compensate for time spent on the dictation, three extra sessions were scheduled for comparison students.

Jafarpur and Yamini reported no significant differences between groups on pre- or post-test measures. In addition, there was no difference found on a listening comprehension test administered to a subset of experimental and comparison students one semester later.

In both Carroll, Swain, and Roberge (1992) and Carroll and Swain (1993), correction, in my interpretation, was shown to be of more value the more the conditions for Monitor use were met, as predicted by theory. Because the designs were complex, detailed description and my analyses are presented in the appendix on p. 19.

DeKeyser (1993) studied two classes of high school students in the Netherlands studying French as a foreign language. One class (n=19) was corrected for one year, while another (n=16) was not. Students had had an average of seven years of previous study of French.

DeKeyser found no overall difference between the classes on tests of grammar and oral communication at the end of year. Interestingly, inspection of the pre- and post-tests revealed little progress by either class; the corrected class gained from 77% to 80% on grammar, while the comparison class gained from 71% to 72%.

DeKeyser also reported three significant interactions: First, students with high pre-test grammar scores who were corrected did better on the grammar post-test. According to theory, this is not unexpected. Better "learners" should increase their accuracy more from correction, and the effect was seen on a grammar test. Second, students with low anxiety did better on the grammar test after correction. Again, as predicted, the impact of correction was on a grammar test.

Finally, DeKeyser reported that students with low extrinsic motivation were better on oral accuracy and fluency after correction. This result is not consistent with theory, but the effect was due entirely to the performance of a few students. Six students from the corrected group had high motivation ratings and low oral fluency scores, and five students had high motivation and low oral accuracy scores. Only two students in the corrected group had low motivation ratings and high scores on both oral tests.

Grammar study. The effect of grammar study has been widely researched in recent years. I have concluded (Krashen 1992, 1993b) that studies claiming to show the effectiveness of grammar instruction have succeeded only in showing a short-term effect.

Scott and Randell (1992) present results very consistent with those of other studies. First-year French students studied three rules of French. "The grammar lessons included two pre-reading questions, an introductory dialogue illustrating the meaning of the targeted grammar structure and a one-sentence rule followed by examples in context with translations" (1992: 358). Students were tested on the rules immediately and again four weeks later. The test contained multiple choice and completion exercises, as well as "communicative tasks requiring students to write personalized sentences using the structures" (1992: 359). Scott and Randell's results are shown in Table 1.

Table 1. Percent correct on three rules of French (from Scott and Randell 1992)

	negation		comparative		relative pronouns	
test	1	2	1	2	1	2
% correct	91	91	82	68	57	48
% of subjects who improved on test 2	36		18		0	
% of subjects who did worse on test 2	9		36		43	

As in previous studies, subjects showed clear drops in accuracy on the second test. In this study, in fact, the decline occurred more rapidly than the decline seen in other studies; this may be due to the fact that the study period for the grammar rules was very brief (four minutes).

Working much harder, however, only delays the inevitable: While Day and Shapson's subjects had six weeks of instruction on the French conditional and held their gains for eleven weeks (Day and Shapson 1991), Harley's subjects spent eight weeks (about twelve class hours total) on the passé composé and imparfait, but they lost their advantage over a comparison group on tests administered three months later (Harley 1987). Subjects studied in White (1991) had five weeks of instruction on adverb placement and held their gains for five weeks, but had lost them when tested one year later. An exception is Spada and Lightbown (1993), whose subjects had nine hours of instruction on English question formation over two weeks and actually showed some improvement on a post-test administered six months after the instruction. The comparison group also improved at a comparable rate on the target structure during this time, however.[4]

In a recent study, Fotos (1993) investigated the role of grammar study in "consciousness raising." Her subjects, 160 EFL students in Japan, were divided into three groups: One group did grammar tasks in which there was a focus on grammatical form, a second group had traditional grammar lessons, and a third group participated in communicative tasks with no focus on grammatical form. After each treatment, one for each target rule in groups 1 and 2, all subjects were asked to do a "noticing task" in which they read a story and were asked to underline any "special use" of English. One week later, they did a similar noticing task with a dictation. The story and dictation contained exemplars of the target structures included in the grammar task and grammar lesson. After three weeks of treatment, subjects in groups 1 and 2 took a grammaticality judgement test and production tests that focused on the target structures (unscramble sentences, sentence-combining).

Fotos reported that subjects in the first two groups were better able to notice examples of the target structures in the noticing task. She reported, however, no relationship between the ability to notice and combined scores on the proficiency measures (with the exception of the grammar lesson group, and only for one structure of out three, indirect object placement. the correlation was modest, r = .354). In addition, there was clearly less noticing on the second administration of the noticing task, one week after instruction on the target structure. Moreover, noticing frequency was not high, with subjects from the grammar groups noticing about two to three items out of five. Fotos's results, in my view, provide good evidence that consciousness raising does not play a role in language acquisition. (For the record, there was no difference between the grammar task and grammar lesson groups on the grammar test; the communicative task group did not take the grammar test.)

In addition to the arguments presented above, one can also argue that forced speech, correction, and grammar study are not essential because many acquirers have attained high levels of competence without them. No acquirer, however,

4. The comparison group teacher promoted a focus on form, frequently correcting students' use of question forms. While students in the experimental classes produced more questions and had more total feedback, Spada and Lightbown point out that the comparison teacher might have emphasized form more in the months preceding the treatment, which in their view explains why this group also did well on the delayed post-test. Comparison students, however, also heard far more questions (Spada and Lightbown, table 3, p. 214). Clearly, this one study does not help us decide among competing hypotheses.

has been shown to develop high levels of competence without comprehensible input (Krashen 1991a).

Comprehensible input is pleasant. If the pleasure hypothesis is correct, we should easily be able to find evidence that activities that promote comprehensible input are pleasant. In addition, it would be strong evidence for the pleasure hypothesis if we could find evidence that these activities are perceived as more pleasant than activities that attempt to promote language development in other ways.

Reading outloud. Research confirms what nearly every parent knows; children like to be read to. Walker and Kuerbitz (1979) interviewed 36 children and reported that 35 of them said they enjoyed being read to. Mason and Blanton (1971) interviewed 180 children, ages three to five, and 171 of them said they liked to have stories read to them. Wells (1985) asked the mothers of small children how much their children enjoyed doing different activities, and found that being read to was among the most popular: 89% of the children enjoyed being read to "very much" or "quite a lot." Trelease's *Read aloud handbook* (Trelease 1985) contains a great deal of anecdotal evidence confirming that hearing stories is pleasant. Here is an example:

> Assigned at mid-year to teach a sixth-grade class of remedial students, Mrs. (Ann) Hallahan shocked her new students by reading to them on her first day of class. The book was *Where the red fern grows*.
>
> A hardened, street-wise, proud group (mostly boys), they were insulted when she began reading to them. "How come you're reading to us? You think we're babies or something?" they wanted to know. After explaining that she didn't think anything of the kind but only wanted to share a favorite story with them, she continued reading *Where the red fern grows*. Each day she opened the class with the next portion of the story and each day she was greeted with groans. "Not again today! How come nobody else ever made us listen like this?"
>
> Mrs. Hallahan admitted to me later, "I almost lost heart." But she persevered, and after a few weeks (the book contained 212 pages), the tone of the class's morning remarks began to change. "You're going to read to us today, aren't you?" Or "Don't forget the book, Mrs. Hallahan."
>
> "I knew we had a winner," she confessed, "when on Friday, just when we were nearing the end of the book, one of the slowest boys in the class went home after school, got a library card, took out *Where the red fern grows*, finished it himself, and came to school on Monday and told everyone how it ended." (Trelease 1983: 9).

There is also suggestive evidence that children prefer being read to to traditional language arts activities. Earlier, I cited Feitelson et al. (1986) as showing that more reading outloud to children resulted in more literacy development. Feitelson et al. also described how their subjects, first graders in Israel, reacted to the story books. The set used was a series called Kofiko, which dealt with the adventures of a monkey. The following is a quote from a teacher's observational record two months after the reading program began:

> 11:20: The class is busy copying home assignment questions from the blackboard. At 11:25 the teacher reminds the children that "we need to hurry because we want to read Kofiko." There are immediate shouts of approval and children hurry to finish the task. A few faster children go to the desks of slower ones and assist them. Cries of "hurry up" and "let's get it done so we don't lose time" are heard from various directions. (1986: 348).

In addition to the enthusiasm for hearing stories in the classroom, Feitelson et al. reported that children asked their parents to buy them Kofiko books: "By the end of the study 13 of the 31 children in the experimental class personally owned one or more Kofiko books; all together the children owned 45 Kofiko books. Four additional children were borrowing Kofiko books from relatives, neighbors, or the public library. In comparison, there were single Kofiko volumes in each of three homes in one control class, and one Kofiko book each in four homes and two in a fifth home in the second control class. In every case these belonged to older siblings and the interviewed first grader had not read them" (p. 350).

Clearly, these children enjoyed the stories more than the usual school activities. It is hard to imagine a similar response to spelling and reading comprehension exercises.

Free reading.

Evidence that reading is pleasant—outside of school. There is abundant evidence that free reading outside of school is pleasant. I have documented (Krashen 1993a) several cases of extremely high motivation resulting from reading light literature. Haugaard (1973) describes the case of her son, a reluctant reader until he discovered comic books:

> "He devoured what seemed to be tons of the things ... The motivation these comics provided was absolutely phenomenal and a little bit frightening. My son would snatch up a new one and, with feverish and ravenous eyes, start gobbling it wherever he was—in the car on the way home from the market, in the middle of the yard, walking down the street, at the dinner table. All his senses seemed to shut down and he became a simple visual pipeline" (1993: 85).

Teen romances seem to have similar effects. Parrish (1983) quotes one 14 year old girl: "I am the kind of person who hates to read, but when my mother brought home a Silhouette book for me to read, I just couldn't put it down" (1983: 615).

Recent evidence showing that free reading is pleasant comes from work by Csikszentmihalyi (1990), who introduced the concept of "flow." Flow is the state one reaches when one is deeply but effortlessly involved in an activity. In flow, the concerns of everyday life and even the self disappear—one's sense of time is altered and nothing but the activity itself seems to matter.

Cross-cultural studies indicate that flow is easily recognized by members of widely different cultures and groups. For example, members of Japanese motorcycle gangs experience flow when riding (Sato 1992), and rock climbers experience flow (Massimini, Csikszentmihalyi, and Fave 1992) when climbing.

Of special interest is the finding that reading "is currently perhaps the most often mentioned flow activity in the world" (Csikszentmihalyi 1990: 117). This finding is consistent with the reports of individual pleasure readers. A resident of Walse in Northern Italy noted that when he reads "I immediately immerse myself in the reading, and the problems I usually worry about disappear" (Massimi et al. 1992: 68). One of Nell's subjects (Nell 1988) reported that "reading removes me ... from the .... irritations of living ... for the few hours a day I read 'trash' I escape the cares of those around me, as well as escaping my own cares and dissatisfactions" (240). W. Somerset Maugham, quoted in Nell (1988), had similar comments: "Conversation after a time bores me, games tire me, and my own thoughts, which we are told are the unfailing resource of a sensible man, have a tendency to run dry. Then [I] fly to my book as the opium-smoker to his pipe ... "(Nell 1988: 232).

Nell (1988) provides interesting evidence showing why bedtime reading is so pleasant. Pleasure readers were asked to read a book of their own choice, while their heart rate, muscle activity, skin potential and respiration rate were measured; level of arousal while reading was compared to arousal during other activities, such as relaxing with eyes shut, listening to white noise, doing mental arithmetic, and doing visualization exercises. Nell found that during reading, arousal was increased, as compared to relaxation with eyes shut, but a clear *decline* in arousal was recorded in the period just after reading, which for some measures reached a level below the baseline (eyes shut) condition. In other words, pleasure reading is arousing, but then it relaxes you.

Consistent with these findings are Nell's results showing that bedtime reading is popular. Of 26 pleasure readers he interviewed, 13 read in bed every night, and 11 "almost every night" or "most nights" (1988: 250). In view of these results and the positive effect reading has on literacy development, Trelease's suggestion that children be given a reading lamp for their beds at an early age is a good one (cited in Krashen 1993a).

EVIDENCE THAT READING IS PLEASANT—IN SCHOOL. Children find free reading in school very pleasant, and there is evidence that strongly suggests that they like free reading better than traditional activities.

When children are allowed to include light reading during in-school free reading sessions, "the period [is] eagerly looked forward to" (Sperzl 1948). Sperzl noted in her study of comic book reading during sustained silent reading that comic book reading resulted in intense absorption: "as far as the rest of the world was concerned, it simply did not exist for these boys and girls" (1948: 111).

The research on in-school reading is filled with such informal reports. Here are several examples of the effect of free reading on behavior. Johnson (1961) reported that when her sixth graders were allowed to do recreational reading "there were no discipline problems" (1961: 655) and children would occasionally ask for more reading time when the free reading period was over. Do they ever ask for more drill and exercise?

Petre (1971) reported on the effect of 35-minute "reading breaks" in public schools in Maryland:

> The most unusual happening when the reading break begins is total quietness ... One middle school principal reports a 50 percent drop in discipline cases after the school began such a reading environment. (1971: 192)

Similarly, Thompson (1956) found that "most of the teachers using self-selection evaluate it by saying 'I like it because my children like it. All my discipline problems are solved ...' One teacher asked 'How do you *stop* them from reading? Mine take out a book as soon as they come in from recess, and start reading again as soon as spelling and arithmetic assignments are completed'" (1956: 487). In addition, Oliver (1976) noted that SSR had "a quieting effect" on fourth, fifth, and sixth graders and that it "exerts an inhibiting pressure on potentially disruptive behavior of individuals" (1976: 227). Farrell (1982) noted that junior high school students doing sustained silent reading showed "a reluctance to put [their books] aside when the bell rang" (51).

The following reactions suggest that children like free reading better than traditional language arts. McVey (1960), in another study of sixth graders doing recreational reading, reported that "In my slower readers, I found the most wonderful change of attitudes. In the beginning most were not reading up to their ability level and at the mention of reading sneered. Their other work suffered also. After one semester of 'self-selectors,' they were reading many books and enjoying themselves. In the words of one, 'Reading sure is fun now'" (1960: 308). Schwartzberg (1962) reported that the fifth graders he interviewed "uniformly expressed a preference for the individualized program over the reading groups they had done previously" (1962: 86).

Davis and Lucas (1971) studied seventh and eighth graders who did free reading for one year, and noted:

> From personal interviews, teacher anecdotal records, and from an experimenter designed survey, it was quite apparent that changes in attitude toward reading and in some cases toward school were overwhelmingly favorable on the part of individualized reading center subjects. Almost without exception the students endorsed the concept and asked for similar classes in ensuing years. It may be significant to note that the center counselors received many complaints that the fifty-minute periods were not long enough. The students wanted at least one hour daily in the center (1971: 743).

Bailey (1969) asked parents of 22 children in in-school free reading programs how their children reacted:

Does your child ever complain of reading in the classroom?

yes: O	no: 22

Does your child seem more or less interested in reading this year?

more: 21	neither more nor less: 1

Gray (1969) asked 27 children how they felt about in-school free reading:

Do you like the individualized reading program?

yes: 27	no: O

If you were to choose your reading program for another year, which would you choose?

individualized reading: 27	grouping: O

Pilgreen's high school ESL students (Pilgreen and Krashen 1993) were very positive about SSR. Of Pilgren's subjects, 56% reported that they enjoyed the SSR sessions "very much," while 38% said they enjoyed them "some" and only 7% reported that they only enjoyed them "a little."

Similarly, Sadowski (1980) asked high school students how they liked a seven-week SSR program: "Of those responding (49%), 58% gave the program strong praise and asked for its continuation, while only.09% gave the program strong negative criticism and called for its elimination" (1980: 724).

Greaney (1970) compared two groups of sixth graders in Dublin and found evidence that students prefer free reading to traditional language arts activities.

Table 2. Free reading vs. traditional language arts

Rating	Exper.	Control
very interesting	28	8
reasonably interesting	9	13
neutral–boring	3	17

While both groups had 40 minutes per day of reading class, the experimental group was allowed to choose their own reading material that they could read at their own rate. After the eight-month program, experimental subjects rated their reading class as significantly more interesting than the comparison groups rated their traditional class.

There has been no research I know of that sheds light on reading enjoyment in a foreign language, which is undoubtedly because so few foreign-language programs use free reading. A hint that free reading might be pleasant for foreign-language students comes from Young (1990). Her foreign-language students rated silent reading in class as the least anxiety-producing of twenty-one different activities. In addition, Jeanne Egasse (personal communication) has told me that she has a classroom library for her second-semester college Spanish students that includes light reading, such as comics and magazines. About a third of the students regularly take selections from the collection home to read on their own. This reading is completely voluntary. I know of no case where foreign-language students have voluntarily done extra traditional homework, unless they were preparing for an exam.

Before ending this cheerful section, I must note that in at least one in-school free-reading study, free reading was not perceived to be pleasant. Minton (1980) studied the impact of SSR in a high school over one semester. Both students and faculty were negative about the program (only 19% of the students thought it was an "excellent idea") and were less likely to be reading after the SSR program; 28% said they were currently reading a book after the SSR program, compared to 55% before the program began. Minton discusses several possible reasons SSR flopped. The most compelling to me was the fact that SSR was implemented at the same time every day, which was very awkward and disruptive. Some students were in PE, some in industrial arts, etc.

Second-language teaching. Are comprehensible input-based classes more pleasant? Koch and Terrell (1991) asked first-semester Natural Approach students to compare Natural Approach to other methodologies they had experienced. While 40% of the sample said that Natural Approach was less anxiety-provoking than other methods, 34% said it was more anxiety-provoking. As I will argue below, these students may feel anxiety over the lack of traditional techniques because they have incorrect personal theories of language acquisition.

Indirect evidence for the hypothesis that CI-based methods are more pleasant are findings showing that more foreign-language students in beginning level CI-based classes continue on to advanced levels. Swaffer and Woodruff (1978) reported that enrollment in second-semester German classes increased after students experienced a comprehension-based first-semester course. The attrition rate between the first and second semesters under traditional instruction was 45% and 47% in the two years studied. After comprehension-based instruction, attrition dropped to 28% and 22% in two consecutive years.

Cononelos (1988; cited in Sternfeld 1992) compared students who had completed five quarters of traditional skill-based foreign-language instruction with students at the same university who had completed five quarters of an "immersion/multiliteracy" program, which was sheltered subject-matter teaching focusing on culture and civilization. Of 109 traditional students, only four went on to take more advanced courses in the foreign language, a finding very consistent with Graman (1987). In contrast, nine out of twenty-two former sheltered students went to higher levels. (According to my calculations, this difference is highly significant, using the Fisher test, $p < .0001$.) While "immersion/multiliteracy" students made up only 17% of all fifth-quarter students surveyed, "they accounted for fully 69% of the students enrolled in upper-division classes" (Sternfeld 1992: 425).

Similarly, in Lafayette and Buscaglia (1985), more students from a sheltered subject-matter fourth-semester French class said they intended to enroll for advanced French (50%, compared to 36% of comparison students). In addition, 94% of the sheltered class said the course was more interesting than other French courses they had taken at the same university.

Are activities that do not help language acquisition unpleasant? We now discuss those activities that theory predicts will not help language acquisition, that ask the brain to acquire language in unnatural ways. In each case, we will see evidence that these means are not universally perceived to be pleasant, but that a substantial percentage of students want them. When they are provided, however, students are less enthusiastic.

Forced speech. Price (1991) interviewed a group of ten subjects who considered themselves to be anxious about foreign-language study. When asked what bothered them the most about foreign-language classes, "they all responded that the greatest source of anxiety was having to speak the target language in front of their peers. They all spoke of their fears of being laughed at by the others, of making a fool of themselves in public" (1995: 105). In other words, their fear was speaking and having their output evaluated.

In addition, another source of stress for Price's subjects "was the frustration of not being able to communicate effectively" (1991: 105). Methods based on comprehensible output put students in this kind of situation repeatedly.

Loughrin-Sacco (1992), in his report of a beginning French class at the university level, reported that "for nearly every student, true beginner or false beginner, speaking was the highest anxiety-causing activity" (1992: 93). As was the case with Price's subjects, a major part of this anxiety was the fear of making mistakes. As one subject stated: "Every time I go to say something, I want to say it right. I don't want to make mistakes." (94)

Four of the five activities (out of twenty-one) rated as the most anxiety-provoking by Young's subjects (Young 1990), foreign-language students, entailed speaking (present a prepared dialogue, make an oral presentation or skit, speak in front of the class, role-play a situation spontaneously in front of the class). Students apparently think that the way to overcome this anxiety is more speaking.

In Young (1990), most foreign-language students agreed with the statement "I would feel more confident about speaking in class if we practiced speaking more" (1990: 543).

Grammar study. It is possible to find evidence that some people like the study of grammar, and I must admit that I am one of these people. We are, however, in the minority.

There are anecdotal reports in the literature about students' dislike of grammar study. Warner (1993) for example, commenting on grammar instruction in language arts, notes that "students generally dislike grammar exercises, which they see as boring and irrelevant" (1993: 78).

The research, however, indicates that opinions about grammar study are divided. Lalonde (1990) asked 216 high school students of German as a foreign language "What does 'grammar' in foreign language instruction mean to you?," with these responses:

dry, boring work: 18%
fun: 24%
interesting exercises: 37%

When Horwitz, Horwitz, and Cope (1991) asked college foreign-language students whether they were "overwhelmed by the number of rules you have to learn," only 34% agreed, while 33% disagreed and 32% responded "neither."

A de-emphasis on grammar in Natural Approach Spanish was "comforting" to 35% of Koch and Terrell's subjects, but it made 26% of them "anxious" (Koch and Terrell 1991). Students, however, apparently adjust to the new methodology, with only 11% of third-quarter students reporting anxiety from reduced grammar study (of course, it is possible that grammar-loving students drop out before the third quarter).

Students may say they want grammar, but do they act on this stated preference? Jeanne Egasse (personal communication) has informed me that in her first-year Natural Approach Spanish class at a community college, she invites questions on grammar at the beginning of every class period. Typically, during an entire semester, only one or two students ask such questions.

Error correction. A large percentage of language students, victims, in my view, of incorrect personal theories of language development, feel uncomfortable when they aren't corrected in class. There is reason to suspect, however, that when correction is provided, it is not welcome.

Chenoweth, Day, Chun, and Luppescu (1983) confirmed that students desire correction. Their subjects, adult ESL students, showed a positive attitude toward correction and indicated that they would like their native-speaker friends to correct them more. Similarly, Nemni, Huovelin, Rondeau, and Vadnais (1993) reported that most adult students (79%) of French as a second language in Quebec approved of correction of errors of both grammar and pronunciation, and the overwhelming majority (94%) preferred that the correction be accompanied by a statement of the rule. In addition, most (86%) felt that correction did not have a negative effect on their ability to express themselves.

Cathcart and Olsen (1976) also asked their adult ESL students whether they wanted their teacher to correct their mistakes: All (n=188) responded in the affirmative, and 91% of the sample said they wanted to be corrected "all or most of the time." Cathcart and Olsen then provided them with total correction and obtained results that conflict with the opinions of subjects in Nemni et al.'s study:

> An interesting informal experiment was conducted by one of the teachers following the questionnaire. She told her students she would correct all their errors in a discussion and proceeded to do so. Afterwards, the students agreed that it was impossible to think coherently or produce more than fragmented sentences when they were interrupted constantly. (1976: 50)

Other studies confirm this ambivalence. Young (1990) reported that high school and university foreign-language students appeared to desire correction. When asked if they would enjoy class "if we weren't corrected at all," most subjects disagreed. In addition, most students said they would be uncomfortable if the instructor never corrected their errors. But most agreed with the statement "I would be more willing to volunteer answers in class if I weren't so afraid of saying the wrong thing" (p. 543), which suggests some discomfort with correction.

Taylor and Hoedt (1966) present evidence strongly suggesting that correction can have devastating affective effects. In their study, fourth graders received either positive comments (praise) or negative comments (criticism) on ten essays, whether earned or not, written over a period of ten weeks. Typical positive comments were "Excellent work!" "What an expressive phrase," "I really like this." Typical negative comments included "I'm sure you can do much better!" "Are you really trying?" "Your word choice could be better."

While there was no difference in writing quality between the groups (both groups improved), the praised group wrote significantly more and had much better attitudes toward writing. The criticized group was clearly discouraged from writing. Taylor and Hoedt noted that "When papers where returned to the children ... children from (the praised group) seemed pleased and shared their papers with others. Children in [the criticized group], however, usually folded or hid their papers from sight. From [the criticized group], 53 papers were excessively wrinkled or torn, but only one from [the praised group] was in such a condition (1966: 83).

Taylor and Hoedt noted that six cases of plagiarism occurred among the criticized children, but no cases were detected among the praised children. Also, "while children in [the criticized group] sat idly waiting for the end of the class period when they had completed their required theme for the day, on 15 occasions a child from [the praised group] asked for more paper so he might write more than one theme in the allotted time" (1966: 83). Taylor and Hoedt conclude that "quality of children's work will not deteriorate if criticism and correction are withheld in favour of praise" (1966: 83).

Actual experience with comprehensible input methodology may be part of the cure for the unnatural desire for correction. Koch and Terrell (1991) found that 40% of first-quarter students in a Natural Approach Spanish class said they were uncomfortable with the lack of correction, but this percentage dropped to 26% among third-quarter students. While a selection bias may be operating (perhaps those uncomfortable with Natural Approach do not continue to the third semester), it may be the case that these students, with experience, are beginning to understand that correction is not the way language is acquired.

Conclusions. Language acquisition is, in Frank Smith's terms, one of the processes "that the brain does well." Language learning, on the other hand, is one of the processes that the brain does not do well. Trying to develop linguistic competence via conscious learning, via output plus correction, studying rules, and trying them out in performance, is, in a real sense, an unnatural process, an attempt to acquire language using parts of the brain that are not designed for language acquisition. Conscious language learning is one of those tasks "for which humans have no special abilities" (Chomsky 1975: 26).

It is thus no surprise that what the brain does well, for tasks that we have a "special design" for (Chomsky, 1975: 27), it does without effort and even with pleasure. For most people, using the brain for tasks it doesn't do well is not especially pleasant.

I should make it clear that I do not consider the study of grammar (linguistics) an unnatural act. The study of language and solving problems in grammatical theory gives a lot of people, including me, real pleasure. Attempting to use this knowledge for language production, however, is another matter. Those who manage to do it sometimes derive some satisfaction from it, from managing to carry off a difficult, and in my opinion, an unnatural task. Normal people, however, get their pleasures elsewhere.

REFERENCES

Anderson, Richard, Paul Wilson, and Linda Fielding. 1988. "Growth in reading and how children spend their time outside of school." *Reading Research Quarterly* 23: 285-303.

Bailey, Auline. 1969. "How parents feel about individualized reading." In Sam Duker (ed.), *Individualized reading: Reading*. Metuchen, N.J.: The Scarecrow Press. 325-326.

Carroll, Susanne, Yves Roberge, and Merrill Swain. 1992. "The role of feedback in adult second language acquisition: Error correction and morphological generalizations." *Applied Psycholinguistics* 13(2): 173-198.

Carroll, Susanne and Merrill Swain. 1993. "Explicit and implicit negative evidence: An empirical study of the learning of linguistic generalizations." *Studies in Second Language Acquisition* 15(3): 357-376.

Cathcart, Ruth and Judy Olsen. 1976. "Teachers' and students' preferences for correction of classroom conversation errors." In John Fanselow and Ruth Crymes (eds.), *On TESOL '76*. Washington, D.C.: TESOL. 41-53.

Chenoweth, N. Ann, Richard Day, Ann Chun, and Stuart Luppescu. 1983. "Attitudes and preferences of ESL students to error correction." *Studies in Second Language Acquisition* 6: 79-87.

Cho, Kyung Sook and Stephen Krashen. 1994. "Acquisition of vocabulary from the Sweet Valley Kids series: Adult ESL acquisition. *Journal of Reading* 37: 662-667.

Chomsky. Noam. 1975. *Reflections on language*. New York: Pantheon Books.

Cohen, Dorothy. 1968. "The effect of literature on vocabulary and reading achievement." *Elementary English* 45: 209-217.

Csikszentmihalyi, Mihaly. 1990. *Flow: The psychology of optimal experience*. New York: Harper Perennial.

Cumming, Alister. 1990. "Metalinguistic and ideational thinking in second language composing." *Written Communication* 7: 482-511.

Davis, Floyd and James Lucas. 1971. An experiment in individualized reading. *The Reading Teacher* 24: 737-747.

Day, Elaine M. and Stan M. Shapson. 1991. "Integrating formal and functional approaches to language teaching in French immersion: An experimental study." *Language Learning* 41(1): 25-58.

DeKeyser, Robert. 1993. "The effect of error correction on L2 grammar knowledge and oral proficiency." *Modern Language Journal* 77(4): 501-514.

Farrell, Ellen. 1982. "SSR as the core of a junior high school reading Program." *The Reading Teacher* 36: 48–51.

Feitelson, Dina, Bracha Kita, and Zahava Goldstein. 1986. "Effects of listening to series stories on first graders' comprehension and use of language." *Research in the Teaching of English* 20: 339–355.

Fotos, Sandra. 1993. "Consciousness raising and noticing through focus on form: Grammar task performance versus formal instruction." *Applied Linguistics* 14(4): 385–407.

Graman, Tomas. 1987. "The gap between lower- and upper-division Spanish courses: A barrier to coming up through the ranks." *Hispania* 70(4): 929–935.

Gray, Glenda. 1969. "A survey of children's attitudes toward individualized reading." In San Ducker (ed.), *Individualized reading: Readings*. Metuchen, N.J.: The Scarecrow Press. 330–332.

Greaney, Vincent. 1970. "A comparison of individualized and basal reader approaches to reading." *The Irish Journal of Education* 19: 19–29.

Greaney, Vincent. 1980. "Factors related to amount and type of leisure reading." *Reading Research Quarterly* 15(3): 337-357.

Harley, Brigit. 1989. "Functional grammar in French immersion: A classroom experiment." *Applied Linguistics* 10: 331–359.

Haugaard, Kay. 1973. "Comic books: A conduit to culture?" *The Reading Teacher* 27: 54–55.

Horwitz, Elaine, Michael Horwitz, and Jo Ann Cope. 1991. "Foreign language classroom anxiety." In Elaine Horwitz and Dolly Young (eds.), *Language anxiety*. Englewood Cliffs, N.J.: Prentice Hall. 27-36.

Jafarpur, Abdoljavad and Mortaza Yamini. 1993. "Does practice with dictation improve language skills?" *System* 21(3): 359–369.

Johnson, Blair. 1989. *DSTAT: Software for the meta-analytic review of research literature*. Hillsdale, N.J.: Erlbaum.

Johnson, Mabel. 1951. "Individualizing reading experience." *New York State Education* 38: 654–655, 673.

Koch, April and Tracy Terrell. 1991. "Affective reactions of foreign language students to Natural Approach activities and teaching techniques." In Elaine Horwitz and Dolly Young (eds.), *Language Anxiety*. Englewood Cliffs, N.J.: Prentice Hall. 109–126.

Krashen, Stephen. 1985. *The input hypothesis*. Torrance, California: Laredo Publishing Co.

Krashen, Stephen. 1991a. The Input Hypothesis: An update. In James E. Alatis (ed.), *Linguistics and language pedagogy: The state of the art*. Georgetown University Round Table on Languages and Linguistics 1991. Washington, D.C.: Georgetown University Press. 409–431.

Krashen, Stephen. 1991b. "Sheltered subject matter teaching." *Cross Currents* 18: 183–189.

Krashen, Stephen. 1992. "Under what circumstances, if any, should formal grammar instruction take place?" *TESOL Quarterly* 26(2): 409–411.

Krashen, Stephen. 1993a. *The power of reading*. Englewood, Colorado: Libraries Unlimited.

Krashen, Stephen. 1993b. "The effect of formal grammar teaching: Still peripheral." *TESOL Quarterly* 27(4): 722–725.

Lafayette, Robert and Michael Buscaglia. 1985. "Students learn language via a civilization course—A comparison of second language classroom environments." *Studies in Second Language Acquisition* 7: 323–342.

Lalonde, John. 1990. "Inquiries into the teaching of German grammar." *Die Unterrichtspraxis* 23: 30–41.

Loughrin-Sacco, Steven. 1992. "More than meets the eye: An ethnography of an elementary French class." *Canadian Modern Language Review* 49(1): 80–101.

Mason, G. and W. Blanton. 1971. "Story content for beginning reading instruction." *Elementary English* 48: 793–796.

Massaimi, Fausto, Mihalyi Csikszentmihalyi, and Antonella Delle Fave. 1992. "Flow and biocultural evolution." In Mihalyi Csikszentmihalyi and Isabella Selega Csikszentmihalyi (eds.), *Optimal experience: Psychological studies of flow in consciousness*. Cambridge, U.K.: Cambridge University Press. 60–81.

McVey, Marcia. 1960. "Reading sure is fun now." *Elementary English* 37: 307–309.

Minton, Marilyn. 1980. "The effect of sustained silent reading upon comprehension and attitudes among ninth graders." *Journal of Reading* 23: 498–502.

Nell, Victor. 1988. *Lost in a book*. New Haven, Connecticut: Yale University Press.

Nemni, Monique, Mirja Houvelin, Daniel Rondeau, and Marguerite Vadnis. 1993. "L'erreur: les intéressés prennent la parole." *Journal of the Canadian Association of Applied Linguistics* 15(2): 119–135.

Nobuyoshi, Junko and Rod Ellis. 1993. "Focused communication tasks and second language acquisition." *ELT Journal* 47: 203–210.

Oliver, Marvin. 1976. "The effect of high intensity practice on reading achievement." *Reading Improvement* 13: 226–228.

Parrish, Berta. 1983. "Put a little romantic fiction into your reading program." *Journal of Reading* 26: 610–615.

Petre, Richard. 1971. "Reading breaks make it in Maryland." *The Reading Teacher* 15: 191–194.

Pica, Teresa 1988. "Interlanguage adjustments as an outcome of NS-NNS negotiated interaction." *Language Learning* 38(1): 45–73.

Pica, Teresa, Lloyd Halliday, Nora Lewis, and Lynelle Morganthaler. 1989. "Comprehensible output as an outcome of linguistic demands on the learner." *Studies in Second Language Acquisition* 11(1): 63–90.

Pilgreen, Janice and Stephen Krashen. 1993. "Sustained silent reading with ESL high school students: Impact on reading comprehension, reading frequency, and reading enjoyment." *School Library Media Quarterly* 22: 21–23.

Romney, J. Claude, David Romney, and Carl Braun. 1989. "The effects of reading aloud in French to immersion children on second language acquisition." *The Canadian Modern Language Review* 45(3): 530–538.

Sadowski, Mark. 1980. "An attitude survey for sustained silent reading Programs." *Journal of Reading* 23: 721–726.

Sato, Ikuya. 1992. "Bosozuku: Flow in Japanese motorcycle gangs." In Mihaly Csikszentmilhalyi and Isabella Selega Csikzentmihalyi (eds.), *Optimal experience: Psychological studies of flow in consciousness*. Cambridge, U.K.: Cambridge University Press. 92–117.

Schwartzberg, Herbert. 1962. "What children think of individualized reading." *The Reading Teacher* 16: 86–89.

Scott, Virginia and Sarah Randell. 1992. "Can students apply grammar rules for reading textbook explanations?" *Foreign Language Annals* 25(4): 357–367.

Spada, Nina and Patsy Lightbown. 1993. "Instruction and development of questions in L2 classrooms." *Studies in Second Language Acquisition* 15(2): 205–224.

Sperzl, Edith. 1948. "The effect of comic books on vocabulary growth and reading comprehension." *Elementary English* 25: 109–113.

Sternfeld, Steven. 1992. "An experiment in foreign language education: The University of Utah's immersion/multiliteracy program." In Robert J. Courchene et al. (eds.), *Comprehension-based second language teaching*. Ottawa: University of Ottawa Press. 407–432.

Swaffer, Janet King and Margaret Woodruff. 1978. "Language for comprehension: Focus on reading." *Modern Language Journal* 62(1–2): 27–32.

Swain, Merrill. 1985. "Communicative competence: Some roles of comprehensible input and comprehensible output in its development." In Susan Gass and Carolyn Madden (eds.), *Input in second language acquisition*. New York: Newbury House. 235–256.

Taylor, Winnifred F. and Kenneth C. Hoedt. 1966. "The effect of praise upon the quality and quantity of creative writing." *Journal of Educational Research* 60(2): 80–83.

Thompson, Mildred. 1956. "Why not try self-selection?" *Elementary English* 33: 486–490.

Trelease, Jim. 1985. *The read-aloud handbook.* New York: Penguin Books.

Walker, G. and I. Kuerbitz. 1979. "Reading to preschoolers as an aid to successful beginning reading." *Reading Improvement* 16: 149–154.

Warner, Ann. 1993. "If the shoe no longer fits, wear it anyway?" *English Journal* 82: 76–80.

Wells, Gordon. 1985. *Language development in the pre-school years.* Cambridge, U.K.: Cambridge University Press.

Young, Dolly. 1990. "An investigation of students' perspectives on anxiety and speaking." *Foreign Language Annals* 23: 539–553.

APPENDIX

In Carroll, Swain and Roberge (1992), 79 students of French as a foreign language were given exposure and correction on the use of two suffixes, *-age* and *-ment.* All subjects first participated in a training session, in which they were presented with cards with French sentences and translations, such as:

Marie a bien attelé les chevaux.
Marie harnessed the horses well.

Marie a fait un bon attelage des chevaux.
Marie did a good harnessing of the horses.

It was explained to subjects, in English, that both sentences were possible and that their meanings were similar. Subjects saw and heard two examples that were explained, and then they were presented with two more sentences and were asked to fill in a blank in the second sentence, supplying an *-age* noun corresponding the verb in the first sentence, which was highlighted. Subjects in the experimental group were given the correct response if they made an error, but subjects in the control group were "never corrected" (1992: 180). Following this, subjects saw and heard two more model sentences and three more sentences with blanks. When this session was complete, the procedure was repeated with *-ment* formation.

After the training session, subjects participated in three "experimental sessions." In the first part of the experimental session, the "feedback session," subjects received fifteen cards with two sentences similar to those they received in the training session. Experimental subjects received correction in this session, but control subjects did not. In the second part of the experimental session, the "guessing session," neither group received feedback. In this session, subjects received fifteen cards similar to what they had seen and heard during the training session and fifteen cards containing sentences with new verbs; subjects "were asked to read the French sentence aloud and to come up with the appropriate word corresponding to the verb" (1992: 180). The third part of the session was similar in format but contained "completely exceptional" items.

All together, experimental subjects were corrected on 45 stimuli and received 45 guessing items with no correction, while controls received 90 items with no correction. For 39 of the 90 items, the correct answer was an -age word, for 38 it was an -ment word, in 13 cases, neither was correct.

The Monitor hypothesis claims that successful Monitor use is dependent on three conditions:

1. Know the rule.

2. Focus on form.
3. Have enough time.

In terms of the Monitor hypothesis, it can be argued that the focus-on-form condition was met in all cases; subjects clearly knew they were not in a real communication situation. Also, it can be argued that there was sufficient time. Even though responses were oral, there was no time pressure. Only the experimental group was given help in figuring out the rule, that is, correction/feedback that provided confirmation or disconfirmation for their conscious hypotheses, so this group came closer to meeting the "know the rule" condition. We would thus predict higher performance from the experimental group.

This is exactly what was found. On recall tests using the guessing format administered after the treatment, the experimental group was significantly better than the comparison group. On recall tests taken one week later, the experimental group was still superior but the effect was smaller (see Table 3 for my calculation of effect sizes from Carroll et al.'s data. Data from Carroll et al.'s measure of accuracy based on subjects' performance as compared to native-speaker norms ["attested words," Table 1, p. 182]. In all cases, effect sizes were corrected for sample size bias [Johnson 1989: 19] and calculated using pooled standard deviations.) Thus, the results are entirely consistent with the Monitor hypothesis and the claim that the impact of conscious grammatical knowledge is peripheral and fragile (Krashen 1993b).

Table 3. Effect sizes on recall tests

Level	recall 1	recall 2
Intermediate	.605	.280
Advanced	1.016	.818

Results from Carroll and Swain (1993), in my view, are also consistent with the Monitor hypothesis. Five groups of adult ESL students were provided exposure to the English dative alternation rule under different conditions. This rule is complex. It describes which verbs can be used in both of the following contexts: John sent a letter to Mary./John sent Mary a letter. As Carroll and Swain note, there are semantic constraints on this rule ("verbs that alternate express transfer of possession in addition to the movement of the theme toward a goal," p. 363), phonological constraints ("this category of stems corresponds to a metrical foot," p. 363, and, in addition, "verbs that can occur in the alternation tend to belong to the [+native] class of stems" (p. 363).

All five groups went through a training session in which they simultaneously heard and saw eight pairs of sentences such as the following:

Peter wrote a letter to Theresa. / Peter wrote Theresa a letter.

They were told that the two sentences had the same meaning. Members of these pairs were alternated in a guessing activity in which subjects were shown one sentence and asked to guess the alternating form. Subjects were told that "some but not all of the items they would see alternated and that they would have to decide which ones did and which ones did not" (365). If subjects gave any incorrect answers during the training session, the entire session was repeated.

This training session was followed by the experimental session. which consisted of four parts: two feedback sessions and two guessing sessions, each containing twelve items. A recall test of forty-eight items was administered immediately after the sessions and again one week later.

The five groups were as follows:

1. An "explicit hypothesis rejection" group: This group was told when they made a mistake during the feedback session, and were given an explicit rule, either a semantic or phonological explanation.

2. An "explicit utterance rejection" group: This group was "simply told they were wrong whenever they made a mistake" (365).
3. A "modeling/implicit negative feedback group": They were given "a reformulated correct response whenever they made a mistake" (365),
4. An "indirect metalinguistic feedback group": Subjects in this group "were asked if they were sure that their response was correct whenever they made a mistake" (365) and were not given a model of the correct form.
5. No feedback of any kind.

These five conditions can be analyzed in terms of the Monitor hypothesis. Group 1 was given explicit information about the target rule, but the other four groups were not. It can easily be argued that groups 1, 2, 3, and 4 were all focused on form more than group 5 was. Even though subjects responded orally, members of all groups had enough time to access consciously learned rules because they were not under time pressure.

Thus, the "know the rule" condition was satisfied most completely by group 1, the "focus on form" condition was satisfied more by the four experimental groups than by the control (no feedback) group, and the "time" condition was satisfied by all five groups. This analysis predicts that group 1 should do the best, as all three conditions are met the most completely by this group, followed by groups 2,3, and 4, in turn followed by the control group. This is precisely what Carroll and Swain reported.

All four treatment groups outperformed the control group on recall tests 1 and 2, and group 1 performed the best of all. Carroll and Swain did a separate analysis of the guessing items only, that is, words that were not presented on feedback trials, to see if the rules acquired had generalized. Once again, all the treatment groups were better than the controls, and group 1 was significantly better than groups 2 and 4.

The greater effect of correction with increased satisfaction of the conditions for Monitor use can be confirmed by the use of effect sizes. Computing effect sizes from Carroll and Swain's Table 1 (p. 367) for the first recall test, the advantage of group 1 over group 5 ($d = 2.32$) is clearly larger than the advantage of the other experimental groups over group 5 ($d = 1.79$, d computed using the average mean of groups 2, 3, 4). As was the case in Carroll, Roberge, and Swain (1992), the advantage of the corrected groups over the noncorrected group was smaller one week later (for group 1 compared to group 5, $d = 1.66$; for groups 2, 3, and 4 compared to group 5, $d = .786$).

A model for learning strategies instruction in the foreign language classroom

Anna Uhl Chamot
Georgetown University

Georgetown University's Language Research Projects has been conducting a research program on the application of learning strategies instruction to foreign language classrooms since 1990.* Two studies were completed in late 1993, and three additional related studies in progress will be completed in 1996. This paper describes the methodology and accomplishments of the completed learning strategies studies and suggests areas of future research in language learning strategies instruction.

The first study investigated the feasibility of teaching learning strategies to beginning level high school and college students of Japanese; the second study sought to develop effective learning strategies instruction in high school beginning and intermediate level Russian and Spanish classrooms. Both studies had similar designs and objectives, and are therefore discussed together. The major purposes of the studies were to identify appropriate learning strategies for the languages and levels studied, to develop and refine instructional materials to teach the strategies, and to describe the impact of the instruction on students and teachers. In addressing these major purposes, additional objectives included issues in the professional development of teachers, materials design, student affect and motivation, and teacher attitudes.

Theoretical Background. These studies have built on an emerging interest in a cognitive perspective in second and foreign language acquisition research. While cognitive learning theory has become a well-established model for instruction in general education, the theory's contributions to the area of second language acquisition are relatively recent.

---

* This research is conducted by the Georgetown University/Center for Applied Linguistics National Foreign Language Resource Center and through additional grants from the International Research and Studies Program of the U.S. Department of Education. The views, opinions, and findings reported in this paper are those of the author and should not be construed as an official Department of Education position, policy, or decision unless so designated by other official documentation.

A theoretical model in second language acquisition is important as a basis for explaining how a language is learned and how second and foreign languages can best be taught. Moreover, for purposes of research on language learning processes, a theoretical model should describe the role of strategic processes in learning. A cognitive theoretical model of learning (e.g. Anderson 1983, 1985; Gagné 1985; Gagné, Yekovich, and Yekovich 1993; Shuell 1986) accomplishes these objectives because the theory is comprehensive in explaining how learning takes place for a variety of tasks, including both linguistic and content-oriented tasks, and because cognitive theory provides valuable insights into second language acquisition (Chamot and O'Malley 1993; McLaughlin 1987; O'Malley and Chamot 1990).

In cognitive theory, learning is seen as an active, constructivist process in which learners select and organize informational input, relate it to prior knowledge, retain what is considered important, use the information appropriately, and reflect on the outcomes of their learning efforts (Gagné 1985; Gagné et al. 1993; Shuell 1986). In this dynamic view of learning, second language acquisition should be most successful when learners are actively involved in directing their own learning in both classroom and non-classroom settings. Second language learners would select from target language input, analyze language functions and forms perceived as important, think about their own learning efforts, anticipate the kinds of language tasks they may encounter, and activate prior knowledge and skills to apply to new language learning tasks. It is because of this intricate set of mental processes, which includes learning strategies, that second language acquisition has been described as a complex cognitive skill (McLaughlin 1987; O'Malley and Chamot 1990).

Learning strategies are the steps, plans, insights, and reflections that learners employ to learn more effectively. Learning strategies are intentional on the part of the learner, and are used for the purpose of facilitating learning (Weinstein and Mayer 1986). A learning strategy may cause an observable behavior such as note-taking, but frequently learning strategies are unobservable mental processes such as associating new information with prior knowledge or visualizing a story one is listening to.

Extensive research in first language contexts has verified the beneficial effect of learning strategy use with a variety of learning tasks including reading, composing, and problem-solving (see, for example, Palincsar and Klenk 1992; Pressley and associates 1990; Silver and Marshall 1990), but not listening or speaking skills. Research conducted with ESL and foreign language students, while less extensive, has included all language skills, vocabulary, and problem-solving. The research indicates as well that better learners use more appropriate strategies, and that learning strategy instruction may help students achieve success with both language and content learning (Chamot, Dale, O'Malley, and Spanos 1993; Padron and Waxman 1988; O'Malley and Chamot 1990; Oxford 1990; Rubin, Quinn, and Enos 1988).

Learning Strategies Studies on Japanese, Russian, and Spanish. This section describes the objectives, subjects, instructional context, instruments, methodology, and results of the two language learning strategies studies recently completed by Georgetown University's Language Research Projects.

Objectives. The main objective of the Japanese learning strategies study was to find out whether learning strategies instruction could be applied to beginning level Japanese study. Previous research on teaching language learning strategies, focused on English as a foreign or second language (Brown and Perry 1991; Chamot et al. 1993; O'Malley, Chamot, Stewner-Manzanares, Russo, and Küpper 1985; Rost and Ross 1991), French (Hosenfeld, Arnold, Kirchofer, Laciura, and Wilson 1981), Spanish (Rubin et al. 1988), and learning in first language contexts (e.g. Harris and Graham 1992; Pressley and associates 1990). The Japanese learning strategies study, however, was the first to investigate learning strategies in Japanese as a foreign language.

The main objective of the study on teaching learning strategies in high school Russian and Spanish classrooms was to develop effective learning strategies instruction for beginning and intermediate level high school Russian and Spanish classrooms. The questions addressed in the Japanese, Russian, and Spanish studies included which strategies would be most appropriate for high school and/or college classes, how the strategies could be implemented within the curriculum, and what effects strategies instruction has on students.

Subjects and Instructional Context. Both studies were conducted in a mid-Atlantic metropolitan area with high school Japanese, Russian, and Spanish teachers and their students and with college Japanese instructors and their students. Three public school districts and one private school participated in the studies. High school teachers participating in the studies included two Japanese teachers, four Russian teachers, and seven Spanish teachers. Four Japanese instructors participated at the college level. Over the three years, high school students participating included a total of 93 students of Japanese, 239 students of Russian (of which 26 participated for two consecutive years), and 390 students of Spanish. In addition, 50 intensive beginning level college students of Japanese took part in the Japanese study.

During the pilot-testing year and the first year of instructional intervention, differences existed in curriculum and instructional approaches between participating high school teachers. The curriculum was textbook-based in some of the classes, whereas the other high school classes followed a proficiency-based curriculum developed by the school district and individual teachers. In the third year of the project, all participating classrooms were in the same school district and followed a similar theme-based curriculum which used a variety of both teacher-developed and commercially produced instructional materials.

Differences in instructional approach were also evident between high school and college Japanese classes. For example, high school students were introduced to written Japanese from the beginning of the first year course, whereas college students began with oral skills and were introduced to writing later.

Instructional Design and Implementation. Instructional materials designed to explicitly teach learning strategies were developed and implemented for the Japanese, Russian, and Spanish classrooms participating in the learning strategies studies. These lessons were integrated with the specific curriculum each teacher was using. Thus, for the proficiency-based curriculum in the Japanese and Russian high school classrooms, and in the Year 3 Spanish classrooms, the learning strategies lessons provided activities related to each unit theme. Learning strategies lessons for Year 2 Spanish high school and for the college Japanese classrooms were linked to the textbook unit being studied. The lessons provided an introduction to students about the value of learning strategies, definitions and explanations of how to use the strategies, and both individual and cooperative activities for practicing and evaluating the strategies. The guidelines for teachers included additional explanations, suggestions for modeling the strategies, and directions for conducting and evaluating the strategies activities. Strategies instruction was developed for learning vocabulary, listening comprehension, reading comprehension, speaking, and self-regulated learning (see Table 1). Not all strategies were taught every year or in all three languages.

In the third year of the study a problem-solving process model for comprehension was developed and implemented in participating classrooms. This model provided a metacognitive framework for explaining and practicing the strategies.

Instruments. Instruments were developed to collect data from both students and teachers. Parallel forms of the student instruments reflected the language being studied and the types of language activities encountered in the class. Questionnaires administered to students in the learning strategies study included: a background questionnaire to gain information about students' age, gender, native language, and previous language study; a learning strategy questionnaire (LSQ) designed to elicit the frequency with which students used strategies for the types of language tasks they encountered in their class; a self-efficacy questionnaire (SEQ) which asked students to rate their degree of self-confidence for accomplishing different learning tasks in the target language; and open-ended questionnaires administered to students at the mid-year point and end of year (for Spanish in Year 3) to explore the degree to which they found the strategies instruction useful. Information about students' language proficiency and achievement was collected through criterion-referenced language tests (LTs), and a teacher ranking scale in which teachers used criteria developed jointly by

Table 1. Learning Strategies and Definitions

Metacognitive Strategies	**Classroom Definition**
Directed Attention	Decide in advance to pay close attention to the task and to ignore irrelevant distractions.
Self-evaluation	Test yourself to see how well you've learned the material.
Selective Attention	Decide in advance to focus on specific information.
Metacognitive Planning	Make a list of personal objectives for each theme and select strategies to reach your objectives.
Cognitive Strategies	
Transfer	Recognize words which are similar to your native language or any other language you know.
Imagery or Visualization	Picture or visualize the meaning of the word or sentence.
Personalization	Relate information to yourself and your own experiences; use your background knowledge.
Contextualization	Imagine yourself using the material in an appropriate life situation.
Grouping	Put words into personally meaningful groups.
Inferencing	Make guesses based on the context or what you already know.
Prediction	Predict information based on background knowledge before you read or listen.
Social Strategies	
Questioning for Clarification	Ask for confirmation that you have understood correctly.
Cooperation	Work with classmates to help each other solve problems.

teachers and researchers to rank their students' proficiency levels.

Classroom observations were recorded on an observation summary form, and teachers' attitudes and recommendations about the learning strategies instruction were elicited through structured interviews guided by a teacher interview guide. Spanish teachers in Year 3 also completed a teacher questionnaire about the effectiveness of the strategies instruction using the scripted strategies lessons developed by the project staff.

Procedures. The design of the learning strategies studies called for development activities during the first year, followed by implementation of strategies instruction in Japanese, Russian, and Spanish classrooms in the second and third years.

Activities in the first year focused on securing teacher and school district collaboration, observing classrooms to gain an understanding of the instructional approaches being implemented, and interviewing students to discover the strategies they used for different language tasks. Information gathered from classroom observations and student interviews was used to develop a form of the LSQ for each language, and these were piloted with students who would not be participating in the studies. Responses from the pilot LSQs were compared to responses on the student interviews, and LSQ items were revised as necessary to reflect the language that students used to describe particular strategies. Draft versions of the other instruments were also developed. A major activity was the selection of learning strategies to teach beginning level Japanese, Russian, and Spanish students, and the development of preliminary learning strategies lessons in the form of resource guides for teachers to use in subsequent years of the study. The lessons were designed to be integrated with the regular class work that each participating teacher was planning for the following year, and were correlated with the textbook or other instructional materials used by each teacher.

In the second year of the studies, the strategies lessons in the resource guides were used by participating teachers to implement strategies instruction in a quasi-experimental design in some of the participating classrooms. Three Russian and two Spanish high school classrooms implemented language learning strategies instruction, while one classroom for each language served as a control in which no strategies instruction took place. Two college beginning intensive Japanese classes team-taught by the same instructors also took part in the quasi-experimental design, with one class receiving strategies instruction and the other class serving as the control class. All participating students were pre- and posttested with the LSQ, SEQ, and LT, and the background questionnaire was administered at the time of the pretest. At the time of the posttest, teachers ranked their students as high, medium, or low in language abilities and achievement. Students also completed a mid-year questionnaire on which they recorded their independent use of strategies and gave reasons why they used or did not use the strategies that had been taught. Correlations were conducted between the instruments and comparisons were made between the classes receiving learning strategies instruction and the control classes.

In the third year of the study, strategies instruction was developed and implemented for intermediate level Russian and Spanish, and revised resource guides were implemented in both high school and college Japanese classrooms. The instruments were revised to reflect changes in the instructional focus, and administered as pretests and posttests. A quasi-experimental design was used to compare a high school strategies instruction class with a non-strategies class in Russian, and a similar design was used to compare two college level Japanese classes. Six intermediate level Spanish classrooms were randomly assigned as either control classrooms or experimental classrooms receiving strategies instruction, and two other Spanish classes also received strategies instruction. A teacher interview guide and observation summary form were used to gather information on teachers' perceptions of the strategies instruction and on classroom observations.

Results. In this section the results of the two learning strategies instructional studies are discussed in terms of language learning strategies identification, implementation of strategies instruction, and strategies use by students.

IDENTIFICATION OF LANGUAGE LEARNING STRATEGIES. Researchers worked with participating teachers to identify the learning strategies that would be most beneficial to students for each teacher's curriculum. Through consultations with teachers and classroom trials, a number of appropriate strategies were identified for beginning level Japanese, Russian, and Spanish classes (see Table 1).

In the third year of the study, strategies were organized within a problem-solving process model which emphasized metacognitive knowledge and strategies for planning, monitoring, problem-solving, and evaluating.

IMPLEMENTATION OF LANGUAGE LEARNING STRATEGIES INSTRUCTION. A primary task in these studies was developing a system for the effective implementation of strategies instruction in the foreign language classroom. Since teachers were to be the ones implementing the instruction, an important achievement was the identification and development of a framework for teaching learning strategies. The framework described the technique of scaffolding strategies instruction so that in the early stages teachers had responsibility for explaining and modeling the strategies, but then students gradually increased their responsibility until they could independently use the strategies (Chamot and O'Malley 1993).

In addition, a significant improvement in the delivery of strategies instruction was the development of a problem-solving process model which not only organized the strategies by task (i.e. planning, monitoring, problem-solving, evaluating), but also provided structure for developing metacognitive knowledge in both teachers and students. The model used an analogy of a mountain climber to illustrate the sequential stages of a task and the types of strategies that could be selected for each stage (Chamot and O'Malley 1993). Teachers found the strategies model successful in communicating a rationale and concrete examples for a strategic approach to language learning.

Professional development activities also included workshops in which the framework and model were introduced to teachers, and sample strategies lessons with guidelines were provided to teachers for developing their own lessons. As teachers developed their own strategies lessons and integrated them into regular class activities, it became apparent that teachers preferred developing lessons themselves and that students' reactions to the teacher's strategies lessons were positive. Observations also indicated that the teachers' lessons were explicit and spontaneous.

Interviews with teachers and classroom observations revealed some patterns in the implementation of strategies instruction. The strategies teachers and students identified as most effective sometimes varied across levels of language study. As beginning level tasks were different from those at the intermediate level, the selection of appropriate strategies was influenced by the type of language learning task involved. For example, beginning level teachers emphasized vocabulary development, which was enhanced by memory and recall strategies. Similarly, a main focus at the intermediate level was reading and listening, so appropriate strategies were taught to assist in these comprehension processes. The close relationship between task and strategy was further supported through evidence provided by students' reactions, which became negative when a strategy was inappropriately chosen (e.g., trying to use visualization for a reading passage that was not visually-oriented).

STRATEGIES USE BY STUDENTS. Teachers believed that the instruction had more of an impact on students with average learning abilities than students who were above or below average. However, they also indicated that all students could benefit from the instruction because it helped students to become more aware of their own and others' learning processes, and provided opportunities for teachers to show concern for *how* students were learning as well as *what* they were learning. Teachers also pointed out that the strategies instruction provided students with a structured approach to language tasks, thus maintaining student attention throughout language activities.

The majority of students found the strategies instruction helpful. Many students said that the strategies helped them understand better and see new ways for learning. Some students who did not find the instruction helpful responded that they already used the strategies or had other preferred strategies. In either case, it was clear at the conclusion of each year's strategies instruction that students were familiar with the instructed strategies and knew how to apply them. Students could also report preferences for strategies that they personally found effective, rejecting strategies that did not work for them. These expressions of strategy preferences seemed to indicate that students had become aware of their own language learning processes.

High school students of Japanese reported significant gains in self-confidence each year, and in the last year also significantly increased their overall frequency in using learning strategies. In particular, high school Japanese students' level of confidence in using Japanese communicatively was positively correlated with increased use of learning strategies. In contrast, college Japanese students did not gain overall in level of self-confidence, and gained in frequency of strategies use for only some individual strategies. For these students, greater self-confidence was positively correlated with increased strategy use only for integrative language tasks, such as listening comprehension.

Russian and Spanish students' self-confidence in their ability as language learners was, in general, strongly correlated to their use of language learning strategies. Beginning level Russian and Spanish students and intermediate Spanish students who reported an increase of learning strategies use for specific tasks also reported higher levels of confidence in their ability to complete similar tasks successfully. A moderately significant correlation was also found between self-efficacy and language performance for beginning level Russian classes and intermediate level Spanish classes. Although causal relationships cannot be determined from these data for the interaction of strategies use, self-efficacy, and language performance, the results do indicate the possibility that students' performance in a language is related to their level of self-confidence for particular language tasks, which is in turn related to their use of appropriate strategies for the same tasks.

Summary of Findings. This section summarizes the findings of the two studies, "Learning Strategies in Japanese Foreign Language Instruction" and "Methods for Teaching Learning Strategies in the Foreign Language Classroom". While some findings were similar for both studies, others differed. In addition, differences were found between high school and college students in the Japanese study.

A number of language learning strategies were identified and tested in foreign language classrooms, resulting in the identification of appropriate learning strategies for beginning level Japanese in high school and college classrooms, and for beginning and intermediate level Russian and Spanish in high school classrooms. Professional development activities for teachers were effective in assisting teachers to implement the strategies instruction.

Resource guides providing strategies lessons and teaching guidelines were developed and field tested for all three languages in high school classrooms, and separate resource guides were developed and tested in college beginning level Japanese classes. A problem-solving process model for strategies instruction was developed and proved helpful in organizing strategies instruction within a metacognitive framework. Students in Russian and Spanish classrooms using the model increased their use of learning strategies over the school year. Participating teachers implemented the learning strategies instruction in their classes as part of their regular curriculum, and provided information on the ease and effectiveness of the instruction. Teachers viewed strategies instruction positively and provided valuable information on methods of teaching language learning strategies. Most students thought the strategies were helpful, selected preferred strategies, and used many of the instructed strategies on their own.

The data collected through the SEQ indicated that high school students' levels of self-efficacy increased over an academic year for all three languages studied, but this did not hold true for college students of Japanese. As high school students increased their knowledge of the target language they apparently became more confident in their language learning abilities. Furthermore, in some cases, the degree of confidence was correlated to the students' language performance, suggesting that more effective learners are also more confident about their abilities. Positive correlations were also found for some groups between the students' levels of self-efficacy and the frequency with which they used the learning strategies, as students who reported using strategies more often also reported greater confidence for language learning. The information obtained in these studies indicates that further investigation into the causal affects between learning strategies use, self-efficacy, and performance seems promising.

Emerging Issues in Strategies Instruction. In these studies, a number of issues emerged that may be of interest to other language learning strategies researchers and practitioners. Although these issues became prominent in this study, which focused on beginning level high school and college Japanese instruction and beginning and intermediate levels Russian and Spanish instruction, they represent concerns that apply to strategies instruction for any language. Two major issues in strategies instruction that have yet to be resolved are discussed in this section.

Language of Strategies Instruction. When strategies instruction is presented in beginning level classes, the language of strategies instruction is necessarily the native language or a language that students understand well. This is because students are not yet proficient enough in the target language to comprehend explanations about strategy value and applications. However, in proficiency-based foreign language classrooms, teachers attempt to conduct almost all of the class in the target language. Therefore, any recourse to native language explanations (for example, for learning strategies instruction) may be perceived as detrimental to target language acquisition. On the other hand, if students are still thinking in their native language at the beginning stage of foreign language acquisition, then abstract concepts such as learning strategies are probably most accessible through their native language.

These studies sought to mitigate this difficulty by providing Japanese, Russian, or Spanish names for the instructed strategies. It was hoped that this approach would help teachers provide at least some of the strategies instruction in the target (rather than the native) language. This approach was successful mainly with the Spanish classes, probably because cognates could be found for most of the strategy terms. Cognates could not always be found in Russian and students perceived the Russian terms which were not cognates as additional vocabulary items, so a combination of Russian and English was used for the strategy names. Japanese students also found that Japanese strategy names were an additional vocabulary load, and preferred English names.

The issue of language of strategies instruction becomes less of a problem at higher levels of language study, when students have developed sufficient proficiency in the target language to understand the instruction without recourse to English. The third year high school students of Spanish were able to understand and even discuss learning strategies in the target language. When questioned about the difficulty of thinking aloud in Spanish, a little over half of the intermediate level students indicated that they felt it was easy to think aloud in Spanish.

A teacher's experience in implementing strategies instruction also affected the amount of target language used for the instruction. As teachers became more familiar and comfortable with the strategies, they were better able to provide instruction in the target language. Strategies lessons developed by intermediate level Spanish teachers were almost exclusively in the target language, whereas the sample lessons used early in the school year consisted of a mixture of native and target language explanations. All teachers indicated that in future strategies instruction they would be able to provide more explanation in the target language.

Amount of Strategies Instruction. Another issue in strategies instruction has to do with the number of strategies to be taught in a course and the amount of time needed for explicit instruction. Students, and even teachers, may find a large number of strategies difficult to distinguish and remember. On the other hand, students need to be exposed to a variety of strategies if they are to develop a strategic repertoire from which they can select strategies appropriate to a specific language task.

In the Russian and Spanish study, teachers who used the problem-solving model for comprehension indicated that the focus on comprehension strategies may have had an adverse effect on the development of students' productive skills in the target language. These teachers would have liked to have included production strategies in the model so that speaking and writing skills could also be enhanced. The number of strategies most effective for a class probably depends upon the individual curriculum and the types of tasks assigned in the class.

The amount of time devoted to explicit strategies instruction was difficult to ascertain in advance. Some high school and college students, for example, seemed to need only an introduction to and overview of the learning strategies, while other students indicated that they were already using the strategies. Still other students appeared to need a considerable amount of explicit instruction and activities for practicing the strategies. Gauging the right amount of explicit strategies instruction and knowing when students are ready to use the strategies independently is an issue which may have to be decided on a case by case basis, depending on the composition of individual classes.

Future Research Directions on Language Learning Strategies Instruction. An important need for future research is intervention studies involving larger numbers of students and teachers. Larger numbers increase statistical power, thus facilitating investigation of causal effects among strategies use, self-efficacy, and performance. In addition, the type of research conducted in this study needs to be extended to other languages and levels of language study. Longitudinal research on the development and continuation of strategies applications as students increase their language proficiency would help to further determine an appropriate sequence for strategies instruction at beginning, intermediate, and advanced levels of language study.

Considerable research remains to be done on teaching methods for strategies instruction. The amount and timing of explicit instruction needs to be further explored, perhaps through simple experiments with strategies for specific language tasks. Similarly, the amount and type of professional development for teachers interested in integrating strategies instruction in their foreign language classroom needs additional study.

An instructional approach which helps students gain confidence in their language learning ability would be beneficial in motivating a greater number of students to continue their foreign language study beyond the elementary level. Increasing and refining their use of learning strategies seems to help many students gain confidence in their ability to successfully complete language tasks. Continuing research on learning strategies instruction as one way of promoting successful foreign language learning is essential to the development of effective language teaching and learning.

APPENDIX

(1) This paper is based on the final reports on the two learning strategies studies:

Chamot, Anna Uhl, Jill Robbins, and Pamela Beard El-Dinary. 1993. "Learning Strategies in Japanese Foreign Language Instruction."

Chamot, Anna Uhl, Sarah Barnhardt, Pamela Beard El-Dinary, Gilda Carbonaro, and Jill Robbins. 1993. "Methods for Teaching Learning Strategies in the Foreign Language Classroom and Assessment of Language Skills for Instruction."

Both final reports are available from ERIC.

2. I would like to acknowledge the contributions to this paper of my co-researchers, Sarah Barnhardt, Gilda Carbonaro, Pamela Beard El-Dinary, and Jill Robbins. Their insights, dedication, and continuing efforts have made this research possible.

REFERENCES

Anderson, John R. 1983. *The architecture of cognition.* Cambridge, Massachusetts: Harvard University Press.

Anderson, John R. 1985. *Cognitive psychology and its implications, second edition.* New York: Freeman.

Brown, Thomas S. and Fred L. Perry, Jr. 1991. "A comparison of three learning strategies for ESL vocabulary acquisition." *TESOL Quarterly* 25(4): 655–670.

Chamot, Anna Uhl and J. Michael O'Malley. 1994. "Teaching for strategic learning: Theory and practice." In James E. Alatis (ed.), *Georgetown University Round Table on Languages and Linguistics 1993.* Washington, DC: Georgetown University Press.

Chamot, Anna Uhl, Marsha Dale, J. Michael O'Malley, and George Anthony Spanos. 1993. "Learning and problem solving strategies of ESL students." *Bilingual Research Journal* 16(3/4): 1–38.

Gagné, Ellen D. 1985. *The cognitive psychology of school learning.* Boston, Massachusetts: Little, Brown.

Gagné, Ellen D., Carol Walker Yekovich, and Frank R. Yekovich. 1993. *The cognitive psychology of school learning, second edition.* New York: HarperCollins.

Harris, Karen and Steve Graham. 1992. "Self-regulated strategy development: A part of the writing process." In Michael Pressley, Karen R. Harris, and John T. Guthrie (eds.), *Promoting academic competence and literacy in schools.* New York: Academic Press. 277–309.

Hosenfeld, Carol, Vicki Arnold, Jeanne Kirchofer, Judith Laciura, and Lucia Wilson. 1981. "Second language reading: A curricular sequence for teaching reading strategies." *Foreign Language Annals* 14(5): 415–422.

McLaughlin, Barry. 1987. *Theories of second language learning.* London: Edward Arnold.

O'Malley, J. Michael and Anna Uhl Chamot. 1990. *Learning strategies in second language acquisition*. Cambridge, U.K.: Cambridge University Press.

O'Malley, J. Michael, Anna Uhl Chamot, Gloria Stewner-Manzanares, Rocco P. Russo, and Lisa Küpper. 1985. "Learning strategy applications with students of English as a second language." *TESOL Quarterly* 19(3): 285–296.

Oxford, Rebecca L. 1990. *Language learning strategies: What every teacher should know*. New York: Newbury House.

Padron, Yolanda N. and Hershon C. Waxman. 1988. "The effects of ESL students' perceptions of their cognitive strategies on reading achievement." *TESOL Quarterly* 22(1): 146–150.

Palincsar, Annemarie S. and Laura Klenk. 1992. "Examining and influencing contexts for intentional literacy learning." In Cathy Collins and John N. Mangieri (eds.), *Teaching thinking: An agenda for the twenty-first century*. Hillsdale, N.J.: Erlbaum. 297–315.

Pressley, Michael and associates. 1990. *Cognitive strategy instruction that really improves children's academic performance*. Cambridge, Massachusetts: Brookline Books.

Rost, Michael and Steven Ross. 1991. "Learner use of strategies in interaction: Typology and teachability." *Language Learning* 41(2): 235–273.

Rubin, Joan, Joanna Quinn, and John Enos. 1988. *Improving foreign language listening comprehension*. Report to International Research and Studies Program, U.S. Department of Education, Washington, DC.

Shuell, Thomas J. 1986. "Cognitive conceptions of learning." *Review of Educational Research* 56: 411–436.

Silver, Edward A. and S.P. Marshall. 1990. "Mathematical and scientific problem solving: Findings, issues, and instructional implications." In Beau Fly Jones and Lorna Idol (eds.), *Dimensions of thinking and cognitive instruction*. Hillsdale, N.J.: Lawrence Erlbaum. 265–290.

Weinstein, Claire E. and Richard E. Mayer. 1986. "The teaching of learning strategies." In Merlin R. Wittrock (ed.), *Handbook of research on teaching, third edition*. New York: Macmillan. 315–327.

Teacher education and coherent curriculum development: The crucial link

Ronald P. Leow
Georgetown University

The role of teacher development in institutions with large language departments has recently come into prominence (e.g. Barnett and Cook 1992; Di Donato 1983; Fox 1992; Herschensohn 1992; Lee 1989). At the same time, efforts are being made to address the issue of coherence in language curriculum development (e.g. Johnson 1989).

This paper describes a Model of Coherent Language Curriculum Development in a language program that seeks to underscore the crucial link between teacher education and coherent language curriculum development. This model also clearly distinguishes teacher education from teacher development. Teacher education provides the teaching staff with educational information on areas of language learning and teaching, while teacher development takes place in the classroom setting where the teaching staff develops both personally and professionally. Instructors exposed to teacher education are referred to in this paper as being "educated."[1]

Developing a model of coherent language curriculum. Johnson (1989: xiii) describes language curriculum development largely as a decision-making process and gives the following description for a coherent curriculum:

> A coherent curriculum is one in which decision outcomes from the various stages of development are mutually consistent and complementary, and the learning outcomes reflect curricular aims. The achievement of coherence is said to depend crucially in most educational contexts upon the formalisation of decision-making processes and products. This formalisation facilitates consensus amongst those involved and is a prerequisite for effect evaluation and subsequent renewal. Decision making is therefore a continuing and cyclical process of development, revision, maintenance and renewal which needs to continue throughout the life of the curriculum.

---

1. See also Azevedo 1990; Lange 1983; Pennington 1990; Richards 1987; and Savignon 1990 for preference of terminology.

The development of a coherent language curriculum must address at least the following important components that serve as its foundation, namely student characteristics, objectives, classroom activities, assessment tasks, the teaching staff, and evaluation (Nunan 1988; Richards 1987). These components are presented in Figure 1 in a language program that includes the language program director/coordinator (LDP) and the classroom.

As Figure 1 shows, unlike conventional views of curriculum development models as solely prescriptive, rule-driven, and linear in nature (Dick and Carey 1985; Taba 1962), the curriculum (comprising students' characteristics, objectives, classroom activities, and the teaching staff) can be viewed as both a process and a product (Johnson 1989). In other words, this model does not view language curriculum only as a static entity etched in stone for eternity (product) but as a process that undergoes constant modifications during its existence in an effort to reflect a more realistic description of the formal classroom setting. The process is represented by both dark and light arrows. The dark arrows indicate a dynamic interaction between all the major components while the light arrow from the classroom (emanating especially from students' evaluations and performance on the assessment tasks) via the teaching staff to the LPD refers to the crucial feedback the LPD receives. This feedback is used to evaluate, modify, and improve the curriculum, resulting in a curriculum that is viewed as dynamic and cyclical in nature. The product is represented by the actual outcomes expressed for each component, for example the learning outcomes for students at Intermediate 2, the assessment tasks to be used at Introductory 2, etc. The product is subject to change based on the feedback received and overall evaluation of the curriculum.

In this model, the teaching staff component is symbolically placed in the center or heart of the curriculum. As can be seen, the teaching staff is one that is "educated," that is, they are aware of several of the variables that contribute to language learning, teaching, and classroom dynamics and they use this education for their personal and professional development in the classroom setting. The positions of the other components are presented rather arbitrarily.

The model also provides flexibility in its open-endedness to the choice of product different departments may want to include in their curriculum. For example linguistic knowledge, culture, literature, or community service learning may be included in the objectives component. All shaded components are subject to evaluation.

When ready to express the product of the curriculum, it is feasible to use any of the components, objectives for example, as one's starting point, but it must be kept in mind that "the coherence of the curriculum is more important than the 'perfection' of any or all of its separate parts" (Johnson 1989: xiii). A brief description of each component in the model will now be provided.

Figure 1. A Model of Coherent Language Curriculum Development

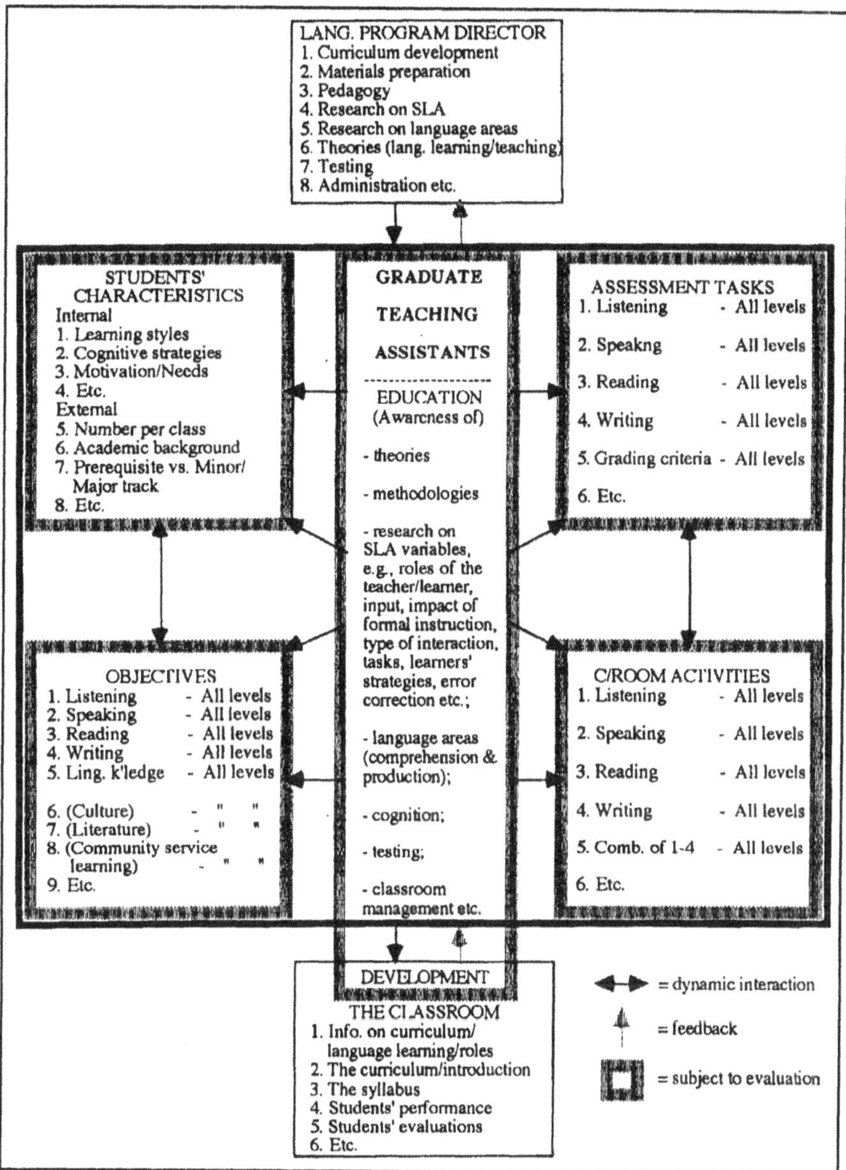

The Language Program Director. Language Program Directors possess a multidisciplinary background preparation that permits them to make informed decisions on the various components of the curriculum. Components include curriculum development, materials preparation, methodology or language

teaching pedagogy, and theoretical frameworks for language learning, teaching, and testing in addition to keeping up to date on recent research on the two language areas of comprehension (aural and written) and production (oral and written), and studies on second/foreign language acquisition (SLA), testing, and administration. The LPDs' responsibilities include the development and evaluation of the curriculum and the syllabus, the education of the teaching staff, the allocation of teaching assignments, the selection of textbooks, and the preparation of materials and exams in addition to several other administrative duties (Lee 1989). As Lee writes, the LPD is "the creative force behind basic language instruction and the administrator who keeps the bureaucratic mechanisms of the language program moving." (Lee 1989: 12)

Students' characteristics. Inherent in the decision-making on the components of objectives, classroom activities, and assessment tasks is consideration of the role of students' internal and external characteristics. For example, the selection of objectives, classroom activities, and assessment tasks can benefit tremendously from studies that have addressed cognitive processes in SLA (e.g. Leow 1993; McLaughlin 1987; Schmidt 1993; VanPatten 1990), cognitive learning strategies (e.g. O'Malley and Chamot 1990; Oxford 1992; Oxford and Ehrmann 1992), and interaction (e.g. Pica, Young, and Doughty 1987). External characteristics that need to be considered include students' academic background, the average number of students in each section, the requirements of their respective colleges or the track they are pursuing, and so forth.

Objectives. The literature abounds with proposals for objectives for different skills/functions and different levels of language experience (Freed 1984; Johnson 1989; Medley 1985; Omaggio 1993). Based on one's departmental constraints (e.g. number of hours per week/semester, students' profiles, etc.), this literature can be used to establish the objectives (desired outcomes) or functions students are required to achieve or do at each level or semester in all four skills. Some institutions may also want to include the linguistic knowledge required for each level, usually based on the current textbook. Care is taken to ensure that there is coherence between the objectives for each skill at each level of language study. In other words, the selected objectives do not only subsume but also provide a logical progression from those objectives identified below.

Some questions that need to be addressed while selecting the objectives include the following: Are students taking the program as a requirement or are they pursuing a minor or major degree in the language? Should students be provided with different tracks with different curricula, or should the tracks be the same for all students? Is there any hierarchy of skills/functions/grammatical structures, that is, are there some skills/functions/grammatical structures to which students should be exposed before others? How realistic are the selected objectives when the multiple constraints of the typical foreign language classroom are considered?

Classroom activities. The objectives can then be used to guide the selection of classroom activities for all four skills (and their combinations) and all four levels. These activities are designed to address at least the following components: academic level of the students, objectives, skills/functions to be practiced, duration of time, materials (if any), group size, a description of each step or stage in the activity, and finally a section for an evaluation of the activity. It is ensured that these activities are congruent with students' learning outcomes for each semester. In addition, a hierarchy of the activities may be established into different stages depending upon the perceived level of difficulty of each task, defined here as what students are expected to do in the activity. For example, debates may be reserved for intermediate and/or advanced levels while more guided oral presentations may be more suitable for beginners.

Questions that need to be addressed include the following: Are the selected activities ecologically valid, that is, do they include functions and skills that students will need for communicating inside and outside the classroom setting? Are they of intrinsic interest to the students? Do they consider students as mature adults with an advanced cognitive development and acknowledge their background knowledge in their native language? Do they address different learning styles? Should activities be teacher-fronted for the most part, should they be more student-centered (pair- or groupwork for example), or a combination of both? Do these choices depend on levels? Do these activities promote students' maximum participation? How much freedom or power do we want to give students in their participation? Is there an integration of skills?

Assessment tasks. Assessment tasks (e.g. quizzes, midterm and final exams, etc.) administered to students during and at the end of the semester[2] provide one major source of feedback on the success of objectives achieved. As a consequence, careful attention is given to the actual assessment tasks that are carefully designed and ideally evaluated for both their reliability and validity (Brown 1987; Henning 1987; Hughes 1989; Underhill 1987) in eliciting specific information on students' abilities. Medley (1985) proposes that assessment tasks include both achievement and proficiency tests, while Nuessel (1991: 6) suggests that assessment tasks "reflect the types of language acquisition activities carried out in the classroom prior to testing." This extension of classroom activities to

2. For different types of tests or assessment tasks, see Henning 1987; Hughes 1989; Nuessel 1991; Nunan 1988; Teschner 1991; Underhill 1987.

assessment tasks is also supported by Shohamy, Reves, and Bejarano (1986), who advocate different speech acts practiced in the classroom to be used also as tests in order to arrive at an assessment of global oral proficiency. A hierarchy of these tasks may be established for all four skills and levels based on the perceived level of difficulty. In addition, because one major concern of evaluation is interrater reliability between the teaching staff (Henning 1987; Terry 1992), grading criteria are also designed for the oral and written skills for all levels to address this concern.

Questions that need to be addressed include the following: Do the tasks reflect the appropriate knowledge to which students have been exposed in the classroom? Are the tasks of interest and challenging to the students, and do they encourage interaction between the input/task and the students? Are these tasks educational? Do they consider students' cognitive processes and strategies at each level?

Evaluation in coherent curriculum development. Once the product of the curriculum is completed, it is then evaluated continually to ensure that it continues to be informed by findings of relevant current research on the classroom setting, and that what takes place in the classroom truly reflects, for the most part, students' objectives as measured by the tasks across all levels of language study.

Coherent language curriculum development provides for both formative and summative evaluation from its inception in order to provide the essential feedback necessary for a continual improvement of the curriculum (Hargreaves 1989) and the product of its components. Formative evaluation is periodic in nature. It can be used to monitor the progress of the curriculum and its components, including the teaching staff, and students' performance (as measured on the assessment tasks) in order to make recommendations and/or adjustments if necessary. Summative evaluation, on the other hand, is used at the end of a specified period of time in an effort to address the effects of the curriculum.

With respect to the teaching staff, formative evaluation is used with a dual purpose: promoting professional growth, continuing education, and morale of both full and part-time staff while, at the same time, assessing the latter's performance with respect to a renewal of their teaching contracts. Job-related aspects of performance may include the teacher's preparation, adherence to departmental policies and procedures, curricular objectives, and syllabus, participation in mutual assignments (e.g. preparation of quizzes, exams, etc.), and his or her level of professionalism.

In light of the integrative nature of the components of a coherent curriculum, it is advisable that curriculum evaluation be divided into the following: a yearly formative evaluation with respect to each component, and a three-year summative evaluation of the entire curriculum. The yearly evaluation involves at least the teaching staff while the three-year evaluation also includes outside professionals in curriculum development if available.

Teaching staff and teacher education. To ensure the success and ongoing development of the curriculum, it is essential that the teaching staff be provided with teacher education that aims to promote their awareness of at least the following: (1) theories of language learning, (2) different methodologies in or out of vogue, (3) current research on the variables that contribute to SLA, such as the staff's role as teachers, the role of input, the impact of formal instruction, the type of interaction, learners' strategies, tasks, evaluation, and error correction, (4) representative studies or reports of current research on comprehension (aural and written), production (oral and written), and cognitive processes involved in SLA, (5) cognition, (6) the principles of testing, and (7) classroom management.

Teachers can be educated via a methodology course (especially in the case of graduate teaching assistants) or workshops before the beginning of classes, they can be educated on the job (during the semester), or at the very least they are provided with literature that can promote their awareness of the variables that contribute to language learning and teaching.

Members of the teaching staff are the heart of any language curriculum and their role in the curriculum is symbolically exemplified by their central position in the model. As can be seen in the model, this position highlights (1) the teachers' educated background preparation and (2) their interactive and dynamic contribution to the development of the curriculum with respect to the perennial evaluation and progress of the program and the improvement of the product of the curriculum. Teacher development will be discussed in the setting of the classroom.

Teacher development in the classroom. This model proposes that it is in the classroom setting where the teaching staff's personal and professional development as educated teachers blossoms. Here they put into practice their education and awareness of the variables that contribute to language learning and teaching. The teaching staff serves as the monitor of what takes place in the classroom and the provider of vital information or feedback necessary for an ongoing modification and development of the curriculum. This increased participation in the continuous monitoring of the curriculum promotes a better self-awareness of themselves not as cogs in the machinery but as essential and integral parts of the whole.

It is also in this setting that the teaching staff serves as the medium through which the different aspects of the curriculum are disseminated to the students. These aspects may include information on the curriculum, the principles of language learning that drive the curriculum, their consequences for the roles of the instructors and the students, departmental policies and procedures, and the syllabus. It is part of the teaching staff's responsibilities to be able to explain and/or defend the various aspects of the curriculum. The kind and amount of information disseminated to students in this setting will depend on the desires of individual departments.

Conclusion. This paper has attempted to present a possible approach to the development of a model of a coherent language curriculum that seeks to underscore the crucial role teacher education plays. The success of this model clearly depends on the crucial link between teacher education and coherent language curriculum development. Once installed, this proposed model can offer several benefits to language departments. These benefits include the following:

(1) It provides a language department with an up-to-date curriculum that closely resembles students' actual interaction with the foreign language in the classroom. Because the model is simple yet comprehensive, its use as a working model can also benefit smaller language departments that are interested in reviewing their present language curriculum for coherence and articulation. Furthermore, it can also provide guidance to individual language teachers who may be in charge of developing their own curriculum;

(2) Due to its flexibility, its product can be modified according to one's own departmental preferences;

(3) It provides curricular continuity between all levels of the language program and facilitates articulation between levels and coordination between several sections of one level; and

(4) It exposes an increasing number of undergraduate foreign language students to educated instructors who are capable of maximizing their interaction with and exposure to the foreign language in the formal classroom setting.

REFERENCES

Azevedo, Milton M. 1990. "Professional development of teaching assistants: training vs. education." *ADFL Bulletin* 22(1): 24–28.

Barnett, Marva A. and Robert Francis Cook. 1992. "The seamless web: Developing teaching assistants as professionals." In Joel C. Walz (ed.), *Development and supervision of teaching assistants in foreign languages*. Boston: Heinle and Heinle Publishers. 85–111.

Brown, H. Douglas. 1987. *Principles of language learning and teaching, Second edition*. Englewood, N.J.: Prentice-Hall.

Dick, W. and L. Carey. 1985. *The systematic design of instruction, Second edition*. Glenview, Illinois: Scott Foresman.

Di Donato, Robert. 1983. "TA training and supervision: A checklist for an effective program." *ADFL Bulletin* 15(1): 34–36.

Fox, Cynthia A. 1992. "Toward a revised model of TA training." In Joel C. Walz (ed.), *Development and supervision of teaching assistant in foreign languages*. Boston: Heinle and Heinle Publishers. 191–207.

Hargreaves, Peter. 1989 "DES-IMPL-EVALU-IGN: An educator's checklist." In Robert Keith Johnson (ed.), *The second language curriculum*. New York: Cambridge University Press. 35–47.

Henning, Grant. 1987. *A guide to language testing*. Cambridge, Massachusetts: Newbury House Publishers.

Herschensohn, Julia. 1992. "Teaching assistant development: A case study." In Joel C. Walz (ed.), *Development and supervision of teaching assistants in foreign languages*. Boston: Heinle and Heinle Publishers. 25–45.

Hughes, Arthur. 1989. *Testing for language teachers*. Cambridge, U.K.: Cambridge University Press.

Johnson, Robert Keith (ed.). 1989. *The second language curriculum*. New York: Cambridge University Press.

Lange, Dale L. 1983. "Teacher development and certification in foreign languages: Where is the future?" *Modern Language Journal* 67(4): 374–381.

Lee, James F. 1989. *A manual and practical guide to directing foreign language programs and training graduate teaching assistants*. New York: Random House.

Leow, Ronald P. 1993 "To simplify or not to simplify: A look at intake." *Studies in Second Language Acquisition* 15(3): 333–355.

McLaughlin, Barry. 1987. *Theories of second language learning*. London: Edward Arnold.

Medley, Frank W. 1985. "Designing the proficiency-based curriculum." In Alice C. Omaggio (ed.), *Proficiency, curriculum, articulation: The ties that bind*. Middlebury, Vermont: Northeast Conference on the Teaching of Foreign Languages. 13–40.

Nuessel, Frank. 1991. "Foreign language testing today: Issues in language program direction." In Richard V. Teschner (ed.), *Assessing foreign language proficiency of undergraduates*. Boston: Heinle and Heinle Publishers. 1–20.

Nunan, David. 1988. *The learner-centred curriculum*. New York: Cambridge University Press.

Omaggio, Alice C. 1993. *Teaching language in context, Second edition*. Boston: Heinle and Heinle Publishers.

O'Malley, J. Michael and Anna Uhl Chamot. 1990. *Learning strategies in second language acquisition*. Cambridge, U.K.: Cambridge University Press.

Oxford, Rebecca L. 1992. "Research on second language learning strategies." *Annual Review of Applied Linguistics* 13: 175–187.

Oxford, Rebecca L. and Madeleine Ehrmann. 1992. "Second language research on individual differences." *Annual Review of Applied Linguistics* 13: 188–205.

Pennington, Martha C. 1990. "A professional development for the language teaching practicum." In Jack C. Richards and David Nunan (eds.), *Second language teaching education*. New York: Cambridge University Press. 132–153.

Pica, Teresa, Richard Young, and Catherine Doughty. 1987. "The impact of interaction on comprehension." *TESOL Quarterly* 21(4): 737–758.

Richards, Jack C. 1987. "The dilemma of teacher education in TESOL." *TESOL Quarterly* 21(2): 209–226.

Savignon, Sandra. 1990. "In second language acquisition/foreign language learning, nothing is more practical than a good theory." In Bill VanPatten and James F. Lee (eds.), *Second language acquisition/foreign language learning*. Philadelphia: Multilingual Matters. 185–197.

Schmidt, Richard. 1993 "Awareness and second language acquisition." *Annual Review of Applied Linguistics* 13: 206–226.

Shohamy, Elana, Thea Reves, and Yael Bejarano. 1986. "Introducing a new comprehensive test of oral proficiency." *ELT Journal* 40(3): 212–220.

Taba, H. 1962. *Curriculum development: Theory and practice*. New York: Harcourt, Brace and World.

Terry, Robert M. 1992. "Improving interrater reliability scoring tests in multisection courses." In Joel C. Walz (ed.), *Development and supervision of teaching assistants in foreign languages*. Boston: Heinle and Heinle Publishers. 229–262.

Teschner, Richard V. 1991. *Assessing foreign language proficiency of undergraduates*. AAUSC Issues in Language Program Direction. Boston: Heinle and Heinle Publishers.

Underhill, Nic. 1987. *Testing spoken language: A handbook of oral testing techniques*. Cambridge, U.K.: Cambridge University Press.

VanPatten, Bill. 1990. "Attending to form and content in the input: An experiment in consciousness." *Studies in Second Language Acquisition* 12(3): 287–301.

An alternative to mainstream U.S. educational discourse: Implications for minority identity development

Rebecca Freeman
University of Pennsylvania

How can American public schools provide equal educational opportunities to an increasingly linguistically and culturally diverse student population? This paper presents findings from a two year ethnographic/discourse analytic study of the Oyster Bilingual School, a successful two-way Spanish–English bilingual public elementary (pre-K–6) school in which language minority students are achieving[1]. Oyster describes its bilingual program as follows:

> Oyster's Bilingual Program has been in operation since 1971. It is considered unique in the city and the country. The teaming of English dominant and Spanish dominant teachers provides language models for students in both their first and second languages.
>
> Students hear and respond to both languages throughout the day. A final average of instruction is approximately half and half for each language each day. Students read in both languages every day. Mathematics and content area groups are developed by the teaching teams. Often key vocabulary may be introduced in both languages.
>
> The end result of instruction at Oyster is the development of students who are biliterate and bicultural and who have learned all subject areas in both languages (*1988 Teachers' Handbook*: 1).

Triangulating analyses of Oyster policy statements, curriculum content, and classroom interaction with interviews of their policymakers, administrators, and teachers reveals that the Oyster Bilingual School has organized itself to provide an alternative to mainstream U.S. educational discourse with respect to minority language use and identity development. As opposed to expecting language mi-

1. By "successful" I mean as determined by students' performance on standardized tests, teachers' ongoing performance-based assessments, and the Office of Bilingual Education and Minority Language Affairs (OBEMLA)'s description of the Oyster program as a model bilingual program. By "language minority" I mean students defined as "Limited English Proficient" as well as students whose primary language or language variety is other than standard English, and by "language majority," I mean speakers of standard English.

nority students to assimilate to standard English and to white middle class norms of interaction and interpretation as prerequisite to their equal participation opportunities, Oyster expects all students to become bilingual and biliterate in Spanish and English and encourages cultural pluralism. I argue that such an educational discourse makes possible the emergence of positively evaluated minority identities whose differences are ideally expected, tolerated, and respected by language minority and language majority students alike.

This paper begins with a brief discussion of identity development and display that provides the basis for analyzing how language minority students are defined relative to language majority students in schools. I then contrast Oyster's bilingual program, curriculum content, and organization of classroom interaction with mainstream U.S. educational programs and practices to illustrate how differently language minority students are positioned and defined in the two discourse communities. The paper concludes with a discussion of systematic discrepancies between Oyster's ideal plan and actual implementation, which can be explained by the interaction of Oyster students, parents, teachers, and administrators with mainstream U.S. society and its competing assumptions and expectations about bilingualism and cultural pluralism on a regular basis.

Co-construction of identity. My work is based on the assumption that identity is co-constructed through interaction (Harré 1984; Davies and Harré 1990; Ochs 1993). Davies and Harré (1990) emphasize the constitutive force of language in identity development. If an individual is repeatedly positioned as a particular kind of social being in the micro-level interaction, over time the individual may assume that role with its associated rights and obligations in the social order. Relating this to minority students in schools, we can understand how minority and majority identities are developed relative to each other and to the school by analyzing minority and majority identity display in the classroom discourse over time.

Carbaugh's (1990) "tentative heuristic for modeling cultural communication systems" (Figure 1) provides a useful framework for analyzing minority identity display in the classroom. Carbaugh stresses that cultural identity is encoded everywhere in communication, but is not coded exactly the same way in all contexts. His review of cultural identity display though cultural communication patterns in distinct cultural contexts (see Carbaugh 1990 for examples and discussion) illustrates considerable crosscultural variation in the notion of cultural identity. He suggests that one way to unravel the variation is to ask, What cultural model(s) for the person is being coded in a situation? and How is this coding accomplished interactionally? According to Carbaugh, the cultural model for being a person consists of its targeted goals, loci of motives, and bases for social relations; analysis of cultural model(s) as displayed through interaction yields an understanding of the concepts and premises that consitute

Figure 1. The circularity of the system. *Source*: Carbaugh (1990: 166)

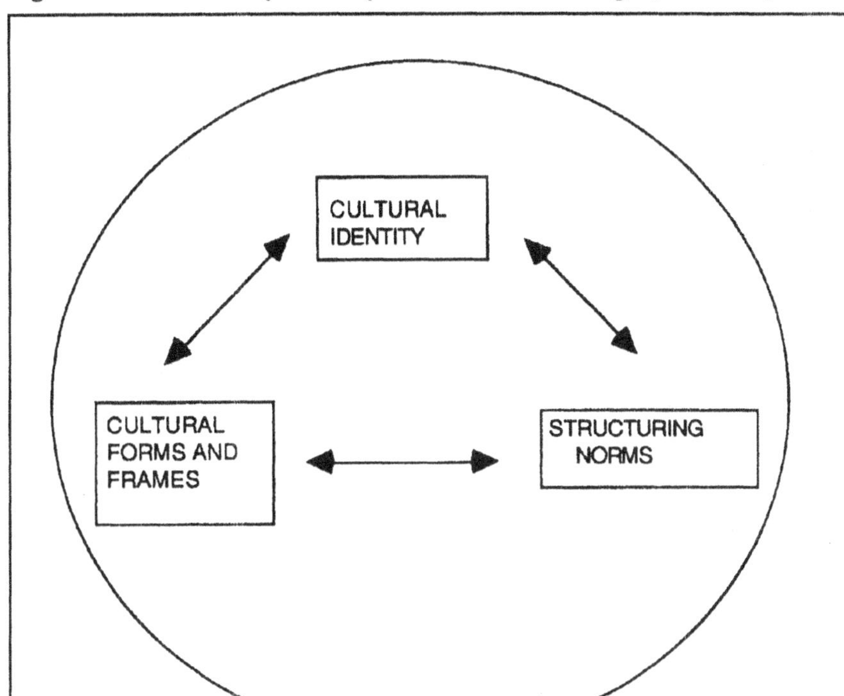

personhood within a particular cultural communication system. My concern in this study is to understand what constitutes language minority identities relative to language majority identities within Oyster's alternative educational discourse as compared to mainstream U.S. educational discourse.

With respect to "cultural frames and forms for performance," Carbaugh claims that every group can and does identify some sequences for communicating. To understand such culturally coded sequences of communication, Carbaugh suggests asking the following questions: What means of expression does the frame make available? What goals are being targeted? What is the relationship between this kind of talk and the cultural identity under study? Is this talk aligned with it? Valued? Why or why not? Relevant to this study are the mainstream U.S. educational and Oyster alternative educational frames and forms for bilingual education, teaching, and learning. My comparative analysis illustrates how differently language minority students are positioned relative to language majority students through mainstream U.S. educational definitions of bilingual education, teaching, and learning on the one hand, and through Oyster's definitions of bilingual education, teaching, and learning on the other.

The third component of Carbaugh's heuristic is "structuring norms." In order to understand how cultural identities are negotiated and displayed through cultural frames and forms for performance, Carbaugh stresses the need for a detailed analysis. He suggests that we consider structuring norms as made up of three parts: (1) the structuring of interaction, (2) the structuring of information, and (3) the structuring of content. Questions such as the following guide the analysis of this component of the cultural system: Who should talk? How much should one say? How are turns exchanged? What constitutes appropriate participation? What topics are discussed? and How are those topics organized and developed? To investigate structuring norms within the mainstream and Oyster educational systems, I investigate the curriculum content and the patterns of interaction within the classroom and throughout the school.

It is important to emphasize the nature of the relationship among the parts of Carbaugh's heuristic:

> The model is *circular* because each element contributes to the others while itself being influenced by the others. Put another way, each element is both a medium, and outcome, of the communication process. It is this dynamic that makes cultural communication systems more or less stable, and more or less resistant to change, because any element (or subpart) is being continually reinforced by others within the system (cf. Scollon and Scollon 1981: 192). (Carbaugh 1990: 166–167, emphasis in original)

In sum, by studying the norms of interaction and interpretation within the curriculum content and within the classroom interaction that structure the local definitions of bilingual education, teaching, and learning within mainstream U.S. educational discourse on the one hand and within the Oyster cultural system on the other, it is possible to compare how minority and majority identities relative to each other and to the school are negotiated and displayed in very different ways.

Language minority students in Oyster's alternative educational discourse: A comparative analysis. Recognizing the powerful role that our language use plays in identity development allows for the possibility of refusing a discourse in which the individual/group is positioned negatively and constructing an alternative in which the individual/group is positioned more favorably (Davies and Harré 1990). As my analysis of Oyster's alternative educational discourse illustrates, Oyster has refused mainstream U.S. educational programs and practices that negatively position language minority students relative to language majority students. Instead, the Oyster educators attempt to position language minority students as equal to language majority students so these students can participate and achieve in school.

My discussion of Oyster's alternative educational discourse begins with their inclusive notion of "community." I then describe their bilingual education language plan, curriculum content, and organization of classroom interaction to illustrate how language minority students are defined relative to language majority students. Because the Oyster educators describe their program as an alternative to mainstream U.S. educational discourse for language minority students, I introduce each of these sections with a brief discussion of negative implications for language minority students in mainstream U.S. schools. The comparative analysis is intended to highlight implications for language minority students in Oyster Bilingual School.

The Oyster "Community." Oyster's description of itself as a linguistically and culturally diverse "community" is central to understanding how its program functions within its particular sociopolitical context. Evidence for Oyster's inclusive notion of "community" can easily be found. According to administrators and policymakers, the program originally began as a grassroots community effort involving local politicians and parents. The parent organization is referred to as the Community Council, and is very active in all aspects of school management from raising funds to hire resource teachers to participating in the hiring of the principal. Parents, whether members of the Community Council or not, are expected to and do volunteer their services throughout the school on a regular basis. The students wear t-shirts that say "Oyster Community Bilingual School." One parent told me, "You know, the great thing about this school is it's like a community that crosses language, cultural, and class lines."

This constructed notion of comembership in the Oyster community is important to emphasize. As Erickson and Shultz point out in their discussion of comembership in counselor/student interactions, "attributes of status such as ethnicity or social class do not fully predict the potential comembership resources" (1982: 17), in this case to the Oyster school. The common goal of educating the children is the attribute that ties these individuals from diverse backgrounds into one Oyster community that they recognize and explicitly refer to. In other words, the Oyster community has *chosen* to define itself as one, rather than as several communities that are often in conflict with each other in mainstream society.

Programs for "Limited English Proficient" Students. In order to provide equal educational opportunities to students defined as "Limited English Proficient" (LEP), the Bilingual Education Act supports programs that enable these students to achieve "full competence in English" so they can participate in the all-English content area instruction. Transitional bilingual and pull-out English as a Second Language (ESL) programs are those most commonly funded through the Bilingual Education Act (Ramirez, Yuen, and Ramey 1991). Transitional bilingual education is advocated by the Bilingual Education Act for schools that have a sufficient number of students from the same language background and trained bilingual educators in that language. In the transitional model, LEP students are taken out of what is usually referred to as the "regular" program while they receive ESL instruction and content-area instruction in the native language. When the students have passed the criteria that the school uses to determine their proficiency in English, the students are "exited" from the transitional program and admitted to the "regular" all-English program. In schools where there is not a sufficient number of students from the same language background or trained bilingual educators in that language, LEP students are pulled out of the "regular" classes for ESL instruction.

Transitional bilingual and pull-out ESL programs can be understood in Ruiz's (1984) terms as following a "Language-as-Problem" orientation. That is, given that the students are defined in terms of what language proficiency they do not have ("Limited English Proficiency"), that the students are segregated from the "regular" program while they receive ESL and/or content-area instruction in their native language, that the majority of the programs do not emphasize maintenance of the students' native language, and that the goal of instruction is transition to English, these programs implicitly define languages other than English as problems to be overcome. Because language is so closely tied to group identity, by extension the LEP students themselves are positioned in these programs as problems to be overcome. In Harré's (1984) terms, such ongoing negative positioning of LEP students can contribute to the LEP students' assuming a negative role relative to the school. This kind of interactional experience in school can teach language minority and language majority students alike that languages other than English are problematic within the school context.

What can the LEP student do in these circumstances? The transitional bilingual and pull-out programs encourage assimilation to standard English as the means to improve the LEP students' negative role. In keeping with this orientation, LEP students tend to abandon the minority language and identity as quickly as possible and attempt to assimilate to monolingualism in standard English and to the majority (white middle class) identity in their effort to succeed in the mainstream school. This orientation in mainstream schools toward languages other than standard English as problems, and toward assimilation to monolingualism in standard English as the solution to these problems, reflects and helps perpetuate the stigmatization of minority languages and speakers of minority languages within mainstream U.S. society. From the Oyster perspective, such transitional bilingual programs are discriminatory. According to a paper describing Oyster's historical and political background presented by some of the Oyster parents at a National Association for Bilingual Education (NABE) conference in 1980,

> The Director of EDC (Educational Development Center) pushed hard for integrated two way bilingual education involving English and Spanish speakers. She felt that transitional bilingual education had isolated Hispanic students. In D.C. the philosophy placed emphasis on maintaining language and culture.

In order to provide native Spanish speaking students with the opportunity to acquire English without being "isolated," as well as the opportunity to maintain their native language and culture, Oyster has planned and implemented a Spanish-English acquisition plan through which all students (including native Spanish-speaking, native English-speaking, and any others who may be enrolled in the school) become bilingual and biliterate in Spanish and English in one integrated program. To fulfill this goal, there are two teachers in each class: one Spanish-dominant who ideally speaks and is spoken to only in Spanish, and one English-dominant who ideally speaks and is spoken to only in English. They are responsible for dividing up the content-area instruction so that all of the subject areas are to be taught 50% of the time in Spanish and 50% of the time in English. The practical implications of this dual language acquisition plan are that native Spanish-speaking children and native English-speaking children all need to use Spanish and English in school, and therefore acquire both languages. And since everyone is learning through their first and second language at the same time, all of the students can participate fully in the educational discourse from the first day.

In addition to the practical implications of this program, it is important to consider the symbolic ramifications of this language policy for all of the Oyster students. As opposed to the "Language-as-Problem" orientations that characterize transitional bilingual education or pull-out ESL programs, Oyster's bilingual program provides an example of what Ruiz (1984) calls a "Language-as-Resource" orientation. Oyster's language plan explicitly defines both Spanish and English as resources to be maintained and developed by defining them as equal to fulfill the educational function. Given the lower status associated with the Spanish language and speakers of Spanish in mainstream U.S. society (see Fasold 1984 for discussion of social stratification of languages and speakers of those languages), Oyster's language plan provides an example of Spanish language status planning. In this sense, the Oyster language plan, with equal distribution of content-area instruction in Spanish and English, and equal representation of Spanish-dominant and English-dominant teachers in each class, must be understood as an attempt to elevate the status of native Spanish speakers as equal to that of native English speakers. And given that Oyster is an elementary school (Pre-K–6) and therefore most of the students' first school experience, socialization through this bilingual program ideally provides the children with an understanding of bilingualism in Spanish and English as the norm.

Curriculum Content. While an understanding of the language acquisition and status planning is necessary to understanding how Oyster attempts to provide equal participation opportunities to its language minority and language majority students alike, it is certainly not sufficient. As one teacher told me, "You know, it's much *more* than language" (her emphasis). The notion of minority participation is also central to understanding Oyster's curriculum content and organization of classroom interaction.

The question to be addressed at this point is, How are minority groups represented and evaluated within the curriculum content the students are learning at school? According to Nieto (1992: 74):

> if we define curriculum as the organized environment for learning in a classroom and school, we see that it is never neutral but represents what is thought to be important and necessary knowledge by those who are dominant in a society. Given the vast knowledge available, only a tiny fraction of it finds its way into textbooks and teachers' guides.

In other words, what is included and what is omitted in the curriculum is evaluative.

With respect to the curriculum content in mainstream U.S. schools, Sleeter and Grant's (1991) extensive study of the treatment of various groups across the major subject areas currently used in grades 1 through 8 found the following:

- Whites still consistently dominate textbooks, although their margin of dominance varies;
- Whites receive the most attention and dominate the story line and lists of accomplishments in most textbooks;
- Women and people of color are shown in a much more limited range of roles than are White males;
- Textbooks contain very little about contemporary race relations or the issues that concern most people of color and women; and
- Textbooks continue to convey an image of harmony among different groups and contentment with the status quo. (cited by Nieto 1992: 75)

The exclusion or marginalization of minority students' histories, literatures, arts, etc. within the mainstream U.S. curriculum content suggests that these contributions are not important subject matter for school study. And not talking about tensions between groups but conveying an image of contentment with the status quo can be understood as denying that such tensions exist, or at least denying these topics' legitimacy within the mainstream classroom. Although the Sleeter and Grant (1991) study finds more representation of women and people of color in school textbooks than earlier studies did, they found that minority groups are often portrayed in stereotypical ways, which can perpetuate those stereotypes. Taken together, the exclusion, marginalization, and stereotyping of minority populations within the mainstream U.S. curriculum content also contributes to the negative definition of minority students relative to majority students within the school.

Evaluation can further aggravate the situation for minority students in mainstream U.S. schools. Standardized tests are the most common measure of student's achievement, and they have been found to contain a cultural bias against other than white middle class populations. Therefore, minority students may have restricted ability to demonstrate academic achievement (Mohan 1989).

The Oyster educators, in contrast, describe their curriculum as "multicultural", which in the Oyster context means that the cultures the students and teachers represent are reflected in and help determine the curriculum's content. The student population is approximately 60% native Spanish speaking, primarily from Central America, and about 40% native English speaking. The teacher population is approximately 50% native Spanish speaking, with representatives from Puerto Rico, Argentina, Peru, Cuba, Guatemala, and El Paso, Texas, and approximately 50% native English speaking. Across the native English speaking and native Spanish speaking student and teacher population, there is considerable African American representation. Therefore, as opposed to excluding, marginalizing, or stereotyping minority contributions as is the case within mainstream U.S. educational discourse, the Oyster educators bring Latino and African American contributions to the center of the curriculum.

The following discussion is intended to provide an idea of how this is accomplished. Since the Spanish dominant teachers represent many different countries, cultures and perspectives, the students are regularly exposed to Latin American geography, literature, history, politics, arts, etc. Since there is no standardized District of Columbia Public Schools (D.C.P.S.) Spanish language curriculum and 50% of the content area instruction is to be in Spanish, these Spanish-dominant teachers bring materials, teaching styles, dialects, and perspectives from their particular Spanish-speaking culture, all of which contributes to the students' understanding of diversity within the notion of "Hispanic." Similarly, the English-dominant teachers bring materials, teaching styles, dialects, and perspectives from their particular English speaking culture, which contributes to the students' acceptance of diversity within the notion of "native English speaking American." For example, as opposed to providing a Eurocentric curriculum content, Africa was the topic of the entire spring semester sixth grade social studies unit taught by Mrs. Washington, an African American and the English dominant teacher. Following a discussion about her philosophy of teaching, Mrs. Washington showed me a paper entitled, "An African View of the World," in which she wrote, "The story of Africa has not been accurately recorded. Much that is accepted today as truth will have to be changed." This stance reflects her African American pride and her passionate interest in teaching her students to think critically about many mainstream representations of African history and African peoples. In addition to what the varied teaching staff bring to the curriculum content, the students also represent a variety of countries, cultures, and perspectives. The teachers regularly incorporate the students' personal and cultural backgrounds into the curriculum, and use that background as a topic through which the students develop academic skills in both Spanish and English. And the students regularly share what they are learning with each other in small groups, with the whole class, and/or with the larger Oyster community.

A description of the 1991 Black History Sharing Assembly illustrates their approach. Like Hispanic Heritage Month in September, Black History is also celebrated for a month, in this case in February, and the celebration ends with a "culminating sharing assembly." All of the classes participated in the day-long event. There were many guest presenters and many parents attended. The Black History Celebration brochure listed the following activities which were included in the event: tie dye; listen to a story teller; make an African drum; taste African and Caribbean cooking; sing songs of Africa; wrap yourself in African cloth; taste George Washington Carver's peanut recipes; watch African dancers; watch videos about Africa; learn about the contributions of Blacks to science; look at masks, jewelry, and art from Africa; watch artists model clay into Senufo designs; watch artists paint Senufo style paintings; look at Adinkra printing and prints; make a day Mousgoum village ("A Day in Black History" schedule, Friday, March 1, 1991). As the list of activities suggests, the auditorium was transformed into a festival-like atmosphere, divided into booths and demonstration areas, and was highly interactive. Each sense was appealed to: the sound of African music; the smell and taste of Caribbean and African cooking; videos to watch; and hands-on activities to participate in. Many of these activities had been organized by the students as part of their content classes. For example, the sixth grade Science class in Spanish researched the contributions of Blacks to science, and presented an interactive demonstra-tion of their findings in which they modeled and explained the particular scientific contributions to the Black History Celebration participants. Another class had made a Mousgoum village in their art class, and were teaching participants how to do the same as their contribution to the celebration. In this Black History Month Celebration, as in the Hispanic Heritage Celebration, the focus is on including Latino, African, Caribbean, and African American contributions in the regular content classes in both Spanish and English, and then having students share their work with the rest of the school in a fun, celebratory way.

This description of the 1991 Black History Month Sharing Assembly provides an extreme example of what "multicultural" means at Oyster. What is important to emphasize is the Oyster focus on the inclusion of minority perspectives that have traditionally been excluded, but which are central to the student and teacher populations. In addition, students are regularly encouraged to relate the curriculum to their own lives. For example, in choosing to write biographies about famous African Americans, students would be asked why they had chosen to investigate their stories, that is, what the significance was of their lives for the students' own lives. Or, when reading a Mexican short story, the students would be asked which characters they identified with and why, what they would have done differently, how they would have felt if they had been treated the way one character treated another, etc.

Drawing the students' attention to diverse people's experiences, emphasizing their struggles and their accomplishments, and then helping students relate those experiences to their own lives can fulfill several functions. By including minority contributions, minority populations are represented as legitimate participants in the offical educational discourse. Such a curriculum can offer students role models of people who were discriminated against, but who continued to struggle and made great accomplishments despite the obstacles put in front of them. These role models and their strategies would then be available for the students to draw on in their own attempts to refuse negative positioning and reposition themselves so that they can achieve. Teachers can also use the multicultural curriculum content to draw students' attention to the similarity in people's experiences so that the students will learn to look for what people have in common and to work together, rather than to concentrate on what divides people. Perhaps most importantly, this type of multicultural curriculum content can be used to teach students to be aware of many different perspectives on any one topic, to think critically about what they see and hear, and to decide what to think and how to act for themselves.

Organization of Classroom Interaction. In order to understand how differently language minority students are positioned relative to language majority students on a daily basis at Oyster, I begin with a discussion of language minority students' participation in mainstream U.S. schools. Mainstream U.S. classrooms are generally characterized by the transmission model of teaching and learning (Cummins, 1989) and the Initiation Response-Evaluation (IRE) participation structure (Holmes 1978). In these teacher-centered classes, the teacher talks for the majority of the time as he/she transmits the curriculum content to the student population in a relatively competitive atmosphere, and initiates the students' participation. The students are encouraged to bid for the opportunity to respond to what Cazden (1988) describes as the "known-answer" question, and the teacher then evaluates the students' responses as right or wrong. Findings from ethnography of communication research that focus on minority students in U.S. public schools suggest the need to look critically at what "full competence in English" (the goal of the Bilingual Education Act) means in these classrooms. In order to participate and achieve in the classroom discourse, students must know (1) when to respond, and (2) how to respond as part of their academic competence in English. Research suggests crosscultural differences in appropriateness for both of these areas (see Scarcella 1992 for a discussion of many potential areas of language minority student–teacher miscommunication and culturally sensitive teacher response strategies).

For example, Philips's (1983) investigation of Warm Springs Indian students and Mohatt and Erickson's study of Odawa Indians (1981, cited by Scarcella 1992) illustrate that native American students tend to pause longer than standard English speaking, white middle class students before responding. However, the teacher may interpret the longer pause as not knowing or as uncooperative. Michaels (1981) and Heath (1983) both illustrate crosscultural differences in the appropriate way to tell a story, a typical response to a question in the mainstream U.S. elementary school classroom. If the teacher expects the story told according to white middle class norms of interaction, he/she may not be able to interpret the language minority student's way of telling a story. The mainstream preference for demonstrating active involvement in the classroom through bidding and speaking publicly can also present problems for language minority students who prefer a different way of participating, for example, silently, or in a one-to-one or small group participation framework (see Philips 1983 for discussion). As these brief examples from the ethnography of communication in schools literature demonstrate, if the language minority student does not know and use English according to white middle class standard English speaking norms, he/she can be denied equal participation opportunities and be defined negatively relative to the majority students.

Two years of observing, taping, transcribing, and analyzing micro-level classroom processes at Oyster reveals a very different organization of classroom interaction than described above. Since Oyster's goals are to provide opportunities for all students to acquire English and Spanish, and for language minority students in particular to see themselves as legitimate members of the class and school, the classroom interaction is organized to maximize student opportunities to talk with each other about the content they are learning through both their first and second languages. Because of space limitations, I do not provide examples of my actual discourse analysis here (see Freeman 1993 for extensive analysis). Rather, I list the norms of interaction and interpretation that guide behavior within the classroom interaction as they emerged from my analyses. I want to emphasize that these norms are best understood not as hard and fast rules dictating how people must and do act, but rather as preference relations or strategies that guide what is and is not appropriate behavior within the classroom. There is always deviation from the norm, the reaction to which helps make that norm explicit. My observation of systematic deviations from the norm, or systematic discrepancies between ideal plan and actual implementation, is taken up at the end of the paper.

Students.

- **50% Spanish/50% English.** Students speak only Spanish to the Spanish-dominant teacher. In the Spanish content class, students speak Spanish to each other unless they have a problem understanding, in which case whatever language aids in comprehending the content is fine. There is a reciprocal policy for English.
- **Demonstrate agency.** Students make their own choices and take responsibility for their thoughts and actions.
- **Learn from one another.** Students are taught that every individual has something unique and valuable to contribute. Students are encouraged to ask each other questions, tell each other what they think, and both agree and disagree with one another. Students think of themselves as a community with common interests and common problems that require communal effort to solve.
- **Think critically and solve problems.** Students are asked not to just passively accept what people say and do, but to challenge what they see and hear. Students are encouraged to develop creative alternatives to the problems they identify.
- **Expect, tolerate, respect, and celebrate diversity.** Everybody has the right to participate more or less equally. Students are reminded that just because groups have been excluded historically, and/or are currently discriminated against, does not make such exclusion or discrimination justifiable.

Teachers.

Spanish dominant teachers.

- Spanis

h dominant teacher speak only Spanish to their students and encourage students to speak only Spanish to them.

- They present themselves as a role models of nativc Spanish speakers who have maintained Spanish and who see bilingualism as an asset.
- They bring in materials, strategies, and perspectives from their native countries and cultures to share with the students.

English dominant teachers.

- English dominant teachers speak only English to their students and encourage students to speak only English to them.
- They present themselves as a role models of native English speakers who see bilingualism as an asset.

Both Teachers.

- Both teachers maintain high expectations for all of the students.
- They provide comprehensible input for students to acquire the second language.

- They do not assume students know anything a priori but find out what the students' strengths are and build from there.
- They organize students into heterogeneous groups.
- They provide a great variety of activities that accomodate diverse learning style preferences and that allow students to use language for different functions, in different registers, and in increasingly more complex ways so that students develop the necessary communicative competencies.
- They assess students' performance through these varied activities to see what they students *can* do.
- They try to be supportive, caring, sensitive, open, understanding, accessible, etc. and try to expect, tolerate, respect, and celebrate diversity.
- They intervene when students are having problems, in either language acquisition, academic skills development, content comprehension, or social relations.
- Each teacher works with his/her team teacher to accomplish these things.

It is important to emphasize that the team teachers have considerable autonomy in how they allocate Spanish and English content area instruction in their particular classes as long as they adhere to the general guidelines of providing instruction in Language Arts in Spanish and English to all of the students everyday, and approximately 50% of instruction in Spanish and English per week. In some cases, the Spanish dominant teacher would teach a subject area one week and the English dominant teacher would teach that same subject area the next week; in other cases the teachers switched subjects by the month or by the semester. Some teams worked very closely together, and others worked much more independently. Regardless of this surface variation, all of the teachers organized their classes so that students worked together in many different ways to acquire Spanish and English through content, develop academic skills in both languages, and learn to see each other as resources in their learning.

I will briefly describe several activities that I observed in more detail to illustrate these principles in action. The goal of a Kindergarten class in Spanish one day was for the students to make a poster which would have pictures of things that began with the letter "p" in Spanish. The teacher divided the students into groups, and gave each group magazines through which they were to look and find pictures for the class poster. In each group, there was at least one native Spanish speaking child whose role was very important to the completion of the task. The native Spanish speaking students helped the native English speaking students determine which pictures represented words that began with the letter "p", for example by encouraging them to sound out the words in Spanish. Each small group negotiated among themselves in their selection of pictures. The class later came back together as a large group to check the work that the small groups had done, which additionally served to reinforce the skills they were learning. Each small group of students then contributed their pictures to the making of a group poster, which was facilitated by the Spanish dominant teacher. When the group poster was completed, it was put up on the wall with the other alphabet posters the students had made. Through this activity, students learned to use resources (magazines), work together in groups and help each other, and share their work with the class. In addition, they were contributing to the materials development of their class, which made the job more meaningful to them, and easier on the teacher who then does not have to take responsibility for all of the materials design. The students were simultaneously acquiring literacy skills, social skills, and either acquiring Spanish as a second language or maintaining Spanish as the first language.

The following description is of an activity cycle that I repeatedly observed throughout the school. It also illustrates how the classroom organization encourages students to take responsibility for their own and the other students' learning as they simultaneously develop their academic, second language, and intergroup communication skills. The teachers often divided the students into groups who would cooperate to solve a problem or complete a task, and then the groups would compete with each other. For example, one day I observed the fifth grade science class in English working on the "Jason Project." "Jason" is an actual robot, and the National Geographic Society provides this curriculum to interested schools. The students were divided into groups of four to write a computer program together instructing Jason, the robot, to walk from a position in the class to a table, pick up a particular article off of the table, and place it in another position in the room. The next day, the teacher performed the part of the robot "Jason," and followed the directions that each small group gave her in front of the entire class. When Group 1, for example, was giving directions to "Jason" (the teacher), and the other students recognized an error, they would shout "ERROR," and Group 1 would have to collaborate to correct the error. Each group was allowed two errors before having to go back and rewrite the program. There was a competition among the groups, and the group that got the fewest errors in their computer program won. Another day, I observed a sixth grade social studies class in English in which the small groups of students competed in a women's history trivia game. In a first grade Spanish language arts class, the small groups of students competed in identifying the greatest quantity of words beginning with the letter "b" in the text they were reading.

What was common in the classes that I observed, both in Spanish and in English, throughout grade levels was, (1) the emphasis on skills development and problem solving abilities, (2) the variety of activities in which the children worked together as groups, (3) competition across groups in many cases, and (4) the use of Spanish and English to perform many different functions. Since Oyster is a D.C. public school, the students' achievement is assessed through obligatory standardized tests. It is important to mention that all the Oyster students, language minority and language majority alike, consistently score above the national norm on these tests (see Freeman 1993 for discussion). However, in order for the teachers to determine what the students can do so they know how to build upon it, the students' performance is regularly assessed through their participation in all of these activities as well as through their finished products.

Summary. This description of the Oyster bilingual program and its practices illustrates how the school has organized itself as an alternative to mainstream U.S. educational discourse for language minority students. In mainstream U.S. educational discourse, language minority students are negatively positioned as LEP and as students whose histories, arts, literatures, etc. are marginalized, stereotyped, or not included in the curriculum content. They are also negatively positioned as students whose performance is not validly assessed and who do not behave and interpret behavior according to white middle class norms. Together, these factors can contribute to a subordinate minority social role, first in the school and then in mainstream U.S. society. From the perspective of mainstream U.S. educational discourse, the language minority student has two options: Assimilate to the positively evaluated majority (white middle class standard English speaking) identity and succeed; or maintain the negatively evaluated minority identity and fail.

In contrast, Oyster has organized itself to socialize its language minority and language majority students into seeing themselves and each other as equal. Language minority students are repeatedly positioned as members of a linguistically and culturally diverse Oyster community who are encouraged to maintain and develop their native language, culture, and identity in an integrated, two way Spanish–English bilingual education program. They are also repeatedly positioned as students whose histories, arts, literatures, experiences, etc. are a focal point in the multicultural curriculum content, whose performance is assessed through a variety of measures aimed to see what these students *can* do, and who are not expected to behave and interpret behavior exclusively according to white middle class norms. Together, these factors contribute to an elevated minority role in school.

As opposed to expecting language minority students to *either* assimilate to monolingualism in the positively evaluated majority language (standard English) and to the positively evaluated minority identity (white middle class) in order to achieve in school, *or* maintain the negatively evaluated minority language, culture, and identity and fail in school, Oyster attempts to provide a third option to its language minority students: Maintain the native language and culture, acquire standard English and the associated norms of interaction and interpretation, and achieve in school. It is important to emphasize that although the school only provides instruction in Spanish and English, the "Language-as-Resource" orientation should be understood as including the maintenance and development of other languages/varieties of languages as resources. This third option provides language minority students the opportunity to develop positively evaluated minority identities in school, an opportunity not readily available in mainstream U.S. discourse. In addition, this socializing discourse provides language majority students the opportunity to see this minority identity as a legitimate participant in school and in society.

In conclusion to this section, it is important to consider implications of Oyster's alternative educational discourse for mainstream societal discourse. My discussion of mainstream educational programs and practices illustrated how the language minority students' negative positioning in the micro-level classroom interaction reflected and helped perpetuate the subordinate minority role in macrolevel mainstream societal discourse. My discussion of Oyster's program and practices illustrates how the school has organized itself to provide an alternative to mainstream educational discourse by positioning the language minority students as equal to the language majority students. As the children learn to see themselves and each other as equal relative to the school, and as they develop strategies to recognize and refuse the negative positioning of minority inividuals/groups outside of school, they have the potential to challenge and transform the minority role in mainstream society from the bottom up.

Discrepancies between ideal plan and actual implementation/outcomes: A sociopolitical explanation. Oyster's goals are to develop students who are bilingual and biliterate in Spanish and English through the equal distribution and evaluation of Spanish and English in the school, and to create a culturally pluralistic discourse community in which language minority and language majority students can participate equally and achieve. However, given that all of the individuals who make up the Oyster community interact with mainstream U.S. society and its conflicting assumptions and expectations about bilingualism and cultural pluralism on a regular basis, there are systematic discrepancies between the ideal plan, the actual implementation, and the immediate outcomes. When I returned to Oyster in 1994 to talk to the new principal about my work, she mentioned her awareness of many of these discrepancies and described measures the school is taking to address them. My inclusion of her comments is intended to emphasize the dynamic, ongoing nature of language planning at the Oyster Bilingual School, as well as to suggest future areas for research.

Since the teachers are considered integral to the successful implementation of the Oyster language plan, I begin my discussion with the teachers. There is considerable symbolic importance attached to who the teachers are, where they are from, and what languages they speak. At Oyster, representation seems to be equated with legitimacy and omission with illegitimacy. It is important to mention that at the time of my study, all of the Spanish dominant teachers could speak English but not all of the English dominant teachers could speak Spanish. The implicit message was that Spanish speakers must speak English but that English speakers do not necessarily have to speak Spanish. While bilingualism is clearly the norm and considered an asset for the English dominant teachers, it is not a necessity. In this respect, both languages are not distributed and evaluated equally within Oyster. In addition, at the time of my study there were no Salvadoran teachers, and the largest Latino student population in Oyster, as well as the largest Latino population in Washington, D.C. is from El Salvador.

In response to these discrepancies, the new principal said that all new Spanish dominant and English dominant teachers must be bilingual, preferably in Spanish and English. She said that at this point only three of the English dominant teachers are not bilingual. In addition, she said that the school currently has a full-time Salvadoran aide and a Salvadoran student teacher as part of their effort to better represent and serve the large Salvadoran population.

The ideal plan is for the English dominant teacher to speak and be spoken to only in English and for the Spanish dominant teacher to speak and be spoken to only in Spanish. Consistent with the ideal, I observed that there is little to no codeswitching from English to Spanish by the English dominant teachers, but considerable codeswitching by the Spanish dominant teachers to English. Part of this discrepancy can be explained by the fact that in both the kindergarten class and the sixth grade class that I observed for the longest periods of time, neither of the English dominant teachers were able to speak Spanish, making teacher codeswitching impossible. However, there is more to the explanation than individual teachers' language proficiencies. Given that the language of wider communication outside of Oyster Bilingual School is English, which naturally has a very strong influence on students' language choice, leakage is to be expected within the school.

To counter this leakage, one teacher explained that there tends to be less codeswitching in the lower grades:

> Pre-K and Kindergarten are where uh the system is most regimented because it's at those lower levels that the students need to really learn what they'll be expected to do for the next few years ... it's important there for the student to speak Spanish to the Spanish dominant teacher and vice versa ... later it can become more flexible

My observations of the codeswitching patterns support this teacher's explanation.

I turn now to the question of evaluation. Although the students received grades for their classes in Spanish and English, the grades were not really equal. If, for example, a student failed the third grade reading class in Spanish, that student could be promoted to fourth grade. If the same student, however, failed the reading class in English, that student could not be promoted. This is because the District only evaluates English. I repeatedly heard concern by the English dominant teachers that the different evaluation standards made the English dominant teachers more accountable for skills development than the Spanish dominant teachers. One English dominant teacher suggested that the two way bilingual model could be improved by "making Spanish instruction count as much as English."

Although I also observed an unequal emphasis on skills in Spanish and English content classes, I think this teacher's solution of "making Spanish instruction count as much as English" is practically impossible given Oyster's sociopolitical situation. Oyster cannot control mainstream society's evaluation of Spanish and English relative to one another. As long as Oyster is a United States public school, and English is the language of instruction in public schools in the United States, nothing Oyster can do can "make Spanish count as much." It can, however, make Spanish count more than it does now within Oyster through such internal measures as, for example, equal evaluation and equal promotion criteria. Addressing this discrepancy, however, assumes that equal skills development really is a goal within Oyster. When I mentioned this discrepancy to the new principal, she informed me that all students, native Spanish speaking and native English speaking alike, are currently required to take a basic skills test in Spanish (Aprenda). How the results of this test are to be incorporated into the educational program is an area for further research.

The ideal plan is for all students to become bilingual and biliterate in Spanish and English. Given that Oyster is considered a successful school by a variety of sources using distinct measures, including the District's standardized tests in English, we can assume that native Spanish speaking students become academically competent in English. This demonstrates that the explicit goals of the Bilingual Education Act are being met by the Oyster program, because it "enable(s) students to achieve full competence in English and to meet school grade promotion and graduation requirements" (Bilingual Education Act 1988). It is important to mention that most transitional bilingual and pullout ESL programs do not enable "Limited English Proficient" students to develop full competence in academic English (Adamson 1993).

However, Oyster's goals go beyond the goals of the Bilingual Education Act, and include the goal of additive bilingualism for all students. Although I do not have specific measures to support the following claims, my impressionistic observations were that while native Spanish speaking students did maintain their Spanish — at least until the sixth grade — English tended to be their stronger language at that point in their lives. Similarly, while the native English speaking students understood and expressed their ideas well in spoken and written Spanish, their fluency and grammatical accuracy, generally speaking, was not at the same level as their native Spanish speaking counterparts' fluency and grammatical accuracy in spoken and written English.

This outcome can also be explained by the sociopolitical context of the Oyster School. First of all, it is important to be aware of the difference in the second language base that the native Spanish speakers and the native English speakers bring with them to Oyster, and the opportunities and expectations for using the second language that exist outside of the official classroom discourse. At the time of this study, it was generally assumed that the majority of the Spanish dominant students had some English language base and that the majority of the English dominant students had no Spanish base. The reason that the native Spanish speakers have a stronger English base than their native English speaking counterparts have in Spanish base when they begin school, and the reason that the native Spanish speakers are more fluent in English than their native English speaking counterparts are in Spanish when they graduate, is the same. Because there are many more opportunities for the native Spanish speakers to use English outside of the official classroom than there are for the native English speakers to use Spanish, their levels of bilingualism could not be expected to be the same.

It is also important to emphasize that, in addition to the difference in the language base that the students bring with them to school, standard English and the variety of Black English spoken in Washington, D.C. seem to be attributed more status than standard Spanish and the varieties of Spanish spoken in the District. English (standard and non-standard varieties) is what the Oyster students hear most often on television and in the popular music that they listen to. Although the school goes to great lengths to create an environment in which English and Spanish are valued equally, the same conditions do not exist outside of the school's discourse.

With respect to Oyster's goal of cultural pluralism, the students seem to negotiate very well in their small groups, and they seem to expect and be able to accommodate diversity as they jointly construct meaning with each other through Spanish and English within the classroom interaction. That is, their intercultural communication skills seem very good. Based on their class discussions and samples of their work, it seems that the students recognize discriminatory practices in the school as well as outside. Some examples of this are when the teacher treats individual students or groups more or less fairly, when women's contributions and/or Asian contributions are not represented in the curriculum, or how the local police and media treated groups in the racial riots that occured in their neighborhood in 1991. The students also articulate creative solutions to the problems they identify. They may do this, for example, to the teacher in class, through petitions and protest letters they write and send, or through stories in which they describe an alternative construction of reality with women as heroes.

However, the sixth grade lunch table was particularly telling with respect to the students' choice of social groupings. Since there were only a few boys in the class and they all tended to hang around together, ethnic, racial, and class division was not apparent. With the girls on the other hand, there was a tendency for the black English speaking girls to form one group, and for the white English speaking girls to form another. Within the Spanish speaking female population, the white Spanish speaking girls generally stayed together while the darker Hispanic girls (who happened to come from the lowest income bracket) tended to socialize together. While there were exceptions, and the students all seemed to get along together in class, these patterns prevailed in their social interaction at school.

In discussing these groupings with the Spanish dominant Kindergarten teacher, Señora Rodriguez, who has been teaching in Oyster since the bilingual program began, responded:

> In Kinder eh ... they come with their home experiences but they don't uh ... they don't realize their backgrounds are different ... by third grade they tend to be equalized ... by sixth grade they are separate again ... but eh ... that's the teachers' job to make the students aware of when they're separating ... they should start tracking that here ... these stereotypes should be broken here ... it's the fault of the teacher for not watching.

Señora Rodriguez reveals her assumption that the school has the obligation and the potential for breaking such stereotypes, and that the emergence of separation by social groups is "*the fault of the teacher for not watching.*" While I do not know whether it would be possible to do what Señora Rodriguez has argued is possible, I think the discrepancies between the school's ideal policy and the actual outcomes with respect to the students' social interaction can be explained by the interaction of the Oyster alternative discourse with society's mainstream discourse. The students are all exposed to the norms of interaction within Washington, D.C. and as represented on television, movies, etc. where the opportunity to see integrated social groupings is relatively rare, and often negatively evaluated. The students are socialized into acquiring the norms of interaction of both the larger society and the Oyster institutional discourse. Since the norms about social interaction are distinct in two discourse worlds, we can expect leakage between ideal plan and actual outcomes. As part of their ongoing efforts to address these discrepancies, the new principal told me that they had contracted the Peace Education Foundation to conduct a three day program for Oyster teachers, staff, parents, and a student representative from each of the fourth, fifth, and sixth grades. The program was designed to "combat aggression and violence, and to promote peace, conflict resolution and peer mediation." Further research is required to see the outcomes of these efforts.

In sum, analysis of the implementation and immediate outcomes of Oyster's program as compared to their goals of bilingualism, biliteracy, and cultural pluralism illustrate the interaction of the Oyster educational discourse and mainstream societal discourse. With respect to bilingualism and biliteracy, the explicit goal is for all of the students to master skills in both Spanish and English through equal representation and evaluation of Spanish and English. However, close analysis of the implementation of the language plan on the classroom level reveals that there is more of an emphasis on skills in English, because only English is evaluated by the District on standardized tests and because not all of the teachers can speak Spanish. The result seems to be that all of the native Spanish speakers become competent in English, including academic English, and maintain their Spanish. The native English speakers also develop academic skills in English, but their Spanish competency, while quite good, is less fluent and less grammatically accurate than their native Spanish speaking counterparts' English competence. With respect to cultural pluralism, the students seem to develop good intercultural communication skills and work well in diverse groupings in their classes. They also talk about discrimination and about solutions to problems they identify both in school and outside. However, there are divisions in the students' social interaction at school that seem to correspond to racial, ethnic, or class lines. The teachers and administrators are aware of these discrepancies, and as my conversations with the principal in 1994 illustrate, many of these discrepancies are being addressed. There remains the need for further study to see how the policy changes impact on the actual implementation and outcomes.

Conclusion. This comparative analysis of the implications of mainstream U.S. educational discourse and the Oyster alternative educational discourse for language minority students was intended to illustrate that we have choices in how we define languages, and by extension, how we define speakers of these languages. Although mainstream U.S. educational and societal discourse has been dominated by the "Language-as-Problem" orientation (Ruiz 1984), and has encouraged assimilation to white middle class standard English speaking norms of interaction and interpretation as the solution to that problem, this is not the only choice. My analysis of the Oyster Bilingual School's successful program, in which language minority and language majority students are achieving, makes clear that other orientations, e.g. "Language-as-Resource" (Ruiz 1984), are possible.

In sum, demographics and the associated sociolinguistic realities are rapidly changing in the United States. According to Craig (1993), mainstream attitudes toward languages other than English are also changing, with native English speaking parents increasingly valuing foreign language study as a means of teaching their children to expect and tolerate diversity, and with native Spanish speaking parents increasingly valuing maintenance of the native language and culture. These demographic and attitudinal changes suggest that schools organize themselves differently to meet the needs of their increasingly linguistically and culturally diverse student populations. This paper has provided one example of a school that organized itself to meet the challenge of providing equal educational opportunities to students who do not come from identical backgrounds, which suggests the possibility for other creative solutions in other sociopolitical contexts.

REFERENCES

Adamson, H.D. 1993. *Academic competence*. New York: Longman.

Carbaugh, Donal (ed.). 1990. *Cultural communication and intercultural contact*. Hillsdale, N.J.: Lawrence Erlbaum.

Cazden, Courtney B. 1988. *Classroom discourse: The language of teaching and learning*. Portsmouth, N.H.: Heinemann.

Craig, Barbara A. 1993. "The public as language planner: Promoting grassroots bilingualism." Unpublished doctoral disseration. Georgetown University, Washington, D.C.

Cummins, Jim. 1989. "The sanitized curriculum." In Donna Johnson and Duane Roen (eds.), *Richness in writing: Empowering ESL students*. New York: Longman. 19–38.

Davies, Bronwyn, and Rom Harré. (In press). "Positioning: Conversation and the production of selves." *Journal for the Theory of Social Behavior* 20(1): 43-63.

Erickson, Frederick, and Jeffrey Shultz. 1982. *The counselor as gatekeeper*. New York: Academic Press.

Fairclough, Norman. 1989. *Language and power*. New York: Longman.

Fasold, Ralph. 1984. *The sociolinguistics of society*. Oxford, U.K.: Basil Blackwell Ltd.

Freeman, Rebecca. 1993. "Language planning and identity planning for social change." Georgetown University. Washington, D.C.

Harré, Rom. 1984. *Personal being*. Cambridge, Massachusetts: Harvard University Press.

Heath, Shirley Brice. 1983. *Ways with words*. Cambridge: Cambridge University Press.

Kessler, Carolyn (ed.). 1992. *Cooperative language learning*. Englewood Cliffs, N.J.: Prentice Hall Regents.

Michaels, Sara. 1986. "Narrative presentations: An oral preparation for literacy with first graders." In Jenny Cook Gumperz (ed.), *The social construction of literacy*. New York: Cambridge University Press. 94–116.

Mohan, Bernard A. 1992. "What are we really testing?" In Patricia A. Richard-Amato and Catherine Snow (eds.), *The multicultural classroom*. New York: Longman. 258-270.

Nieto, Sonia. 1992. *Affirming diversity: The sociopolitical context of multicultural education*. New York: Longman.

Ochs, Elinor. 1993. "Constructing social identity: A language socialization perspective." *Research on Langauge and Social Interaction* 26(3): 287–306.

Oyster Bilingual School. 1988. *Oyster Bilingual School Teachers Handbook*. (Unpublished)

Philips, Susan U. 1983. *The invisible culture*. New York: Longman.

Ramirez, J. David, Sandra D. Yuen, and Dena R. Ramey. 1991. *Executive summary final report: Longitudinal study of structures English immersion strategy, early-exit and late-exit transitional Bilingual Education programs for language-minority children*. San Mateo, California: Aguirre International.

Ruiz, Richard. 1984. "Orientations in language planning." *Journal of the National Association for Bilingual Education* 2(VIII): 15–34.

Scarcella, Robin. 1992. "Providing culturally sensitive feedback." In Patricia A. Richard-Amato and Catherine Snow (eds.), *The multicultural classroom*. New York: Longman. 126–142.

Educational linguistics: Looking to the East

Anne Pakir
National University of Singapore

Introduction. My title, "Educational linguistics: Looking to the East," is rather presumptuous. Perhaps it is better served with a change in the preposition, to read "Looking from the East" rather than "to the East." The change is possibly necessary in order to deny making any claim that the East has all the answers to issues in educational linguistics, especially those that pertain to bilingualism and bilingual education. Furthermore, the experience of a single country in the East may not be representative of the others in the region. All that I can propose here is a case study of a Southeast Asian nation, viz. Singapore, where bilingualism and bilingual education have succeeded both in terms of policy and outcome.

More than a decade ago, Fishman, in a foreword to a book called *Language and society in Singapore* (1980), had correctly assessed that from "tiny Singapore comes a wealth of data, integrative theory, considered practice, and above all informed research and training efforts" (1980: 1). Indeed, a steady stream of language research activities in the 1980s and early 1990s has resulted in the publication of a state-of-the-art volume, *Language, society and education in Singapore: Issues and trends* (Gopinathan et al. 1993).

In Singapore, where language management is a crucial factor for success, it is to be expected, and justly so, that much effort, time, and money will go into quality education that also ensures the continued use of the country's official languages, namely English, Mandarin, Malay, and Tamil.

The thesis in my paper is that although questions based on educational and psychological perspectives are important in largely monolingual countries in the West,[1] other questions are more important for smaller countries in the East that are already multilingual (for example Malaysia, Brunei, Singapore). They are questions dealing with the ultimate motivation for a country to become bilingual. Inevitably, social, cultural, political, and economic perspectives take priority.

---

1. Questions such as: (1) Will children suffer if they become bilingual? (2) Will children suffer from education that uses two languages? and (3) Isn't the "right" attitude and motivation, and not compulsion and conformity, vital in becoming bilingual and in bilingual education? take up almost all the space devoted to key issues in bilingualism and bilingual education in Baker's book (1988:ix).

Microlevel operations dovetail into macrolevel perspectives in Singapore, which can be seen as a prime example of the theme expressed in this year's Georgetown University Round Table: educational linguistics, crosscultural communication, and global interdependence. In other words, for a small country like Singapore, there is no alternative but to engage in discourse with the outside world, and education is made available for all to serve this national goal.

The concerns of educational linguistics in Singapore are closely related to those of crosscultural communication, within and outside of the nation. These concerns are usually attended to with an anxious eye on global interdependence. I would go further to say that it is because of the latter—the need to forge links in an ever-growing global village—that educational linguists need to worry less about educational and psychological perspectives and look for the larger goal of achieving success in bilingual education for the community for the purposes of global interaction and crosscultural interdependence. At the macro level, there must be a willingness to pay a high premium for increasing the human capital of the country.

The aims of a bilingual education program, the operation of bilingual classrooms, and the effects of bilingual education (cf. Spolsky 1978) are important for a bilingual education evaluation model at the microlevel, but these are made to serve the operations at the macrolevel, i.e. successful language management based on sound principles, policies, and programs, and planned in phases.

Bilingualism and bilingual education in Singapore. Singapore's rich language environment, language policies, and implementation strategies are determinants of its economic growth and success. A city-state of three million people, inhabiting 226-square miles of expensive real estate, Singapore has no natural resources except its people, a multiracial composite of mainly Chinese (77%), Malays (14%), and Indians (7%). The three labels of Chinese, Malay, and Indian cover a diversity of origins: among the 77% of Chinese origin are the Hokkien, Teochew, Cantonese, Hakka, Hainanese, Hockchia, Foochow, Henghua, and Shanghainese. The 14% Malays include persons of Malay or Indonesian origin such as Javanese, Boyanese, and Bugis. The 7% Indians include those of Indian, Pakistani, Bangladeshi, and Sri Lankan origin, such as the Tamil, Malayali, Punjabi, Bengali, and Singhalese. This multilingual community has a vast range of complex linguistic and cultural traditions.

English is taught in all schools that also offer second languages—Mandarin, Malay, and/or Tamil. All of these languages come from different language families (Indo-European, Sino-Tibetan, Austronesian, and Dravidian), and have quite distinct writing systems. English has an alphabetic writing system based on the Roman alphabet. Chinese has a "morpheme-syllable writing" system (Chao 1968, cited in Coulmas 1989: 107), traditionally using Chinese characters, although students are made familiar with hanyu pinyin, "the standard system of writing the Chinese language with Roman letters" (Coulmas 1989: 246). Malay is a language to which the Arabic alphabet was applied, and Tamil has an alphabet derived from the Grantha script, a southern Indian script.

The multilingual heritage of Singapore was made to serve two purposes in the model of a multilingual nation: First, a nation-to-nation interaction and second, the integration of a nation that is to be forged out of diverse linguistic elements (PuruShotam 1989: 508). English, the legacy of the British, was chosen for both purposes, i.e. for general international interaction as well as for the expression of a Singapore identity, of Asianness expressed in a "neutral" language belonging to none of the three major ethnic groups.

The choice of English as a working language for Singapore was opportune, for in the last 40 years the ascendancy of English as a world language has made it possible for tiny Singapore to successfully plug into the international grid of business and finance, since almost all of its populace know and use English today. English, the working language of Singapore, has become a language of international as well as interethnic communication.

Malay, the language of Singapore's immediate neighbors, is the language of interaction among nations in the region, and Singapore's policy of maintaining it as a national language as well as an official language reduces Singapore's profile as a sore thumb sticking out in a Malay-speaking region.

Mandarin, the language of the Chinese mainland and a large portion of Taiwan, was chosen to replace the other dialects spoken by the majority Chinese population in Singapore. China is now poised to become an important economic force in the coming century and the knowledge of Mandarin bodes well for the increasing numbers of Mandarin speakers in the country.

Tamil, the language of the migrant Indians, who came from South India, was chosen as the official language for the Indian community, although Punjabi, Hindi, Gujarati, and Bengali speakers do not readily identify with the language or the community practices of the South Indians in Singapore.

With its policy of multiracialism and four official languages (English, Mandarin, Malay, and Tamil) to represent the four strands of linguistic affiliation of the major ethnic groups, Singapore has managed to embark on a policy of bilingualism (and biliteracy) that in thirty years has transformed the speech and the reading and writing behavior of its people, both the young and the old, and has contributed a great deal to the small city-state's gross national product.

Hidden under this grand canvas of language management is the fact that the population of Singapore has undergone a tremendous language shift, producing a generation of Singaporeans who are English-knowing bilinguals, schooled in English and in their respective ethnic mother tongues, be they Malay, Chinese, or Indian. The other part of the dual linguistic transformation was a massive shift from the other Chinese dialects (Hokkien, Teochew, Cantonese, Hainanese, and Shanghainese) to the official Chinese language, Mandarin. As it turns out, these two important school languages, English and Mandarin, are already lan-

Table 1. Resident private households by ethnic group of head of household and predominant household language spoken, 1980 and 1990.

Predominant Household Language or Dialect Spoken	In 1980 (percent)	In 1990 (percent)
All Households		
English	11.6	20.8
Mandarin	10.2	23.7
Chinese dialects	59.5	38.2
Malay	13.9	13.6
Tamil	3.1	3.0
Others	1.7	0.7
Chinese Households		
English	10.2	21.4
Mandarin	13.1	30.0
Chinese dialects	76.2	48.2
Others	0.5	0.4
Malay Houscholds		
English	2.3	5.7
Malay	96.7	94.1
Others	1.0	0.2
Indian Households		
English	24.3	34.3
Malay	8.6	14.1
Tamil	52.2	43.7
Others	14.9	8.1

Source: Department of Statistics, Singapore, Singapore Census of Population 1990 (1993: 6).

guages of international dialogue for Singapore in its strategy of look-West and look-East for economic opportunities.

The success of Singapore's bilingual education policy is seen in Table 1, which shows the shift in language use over ten years.[2] These statistics reveal the shift to English and Mandarin in Singapore from 1980 to 1990 and the slight decrease in Malay and Tamil as predominant household languages. Many of these households are bilingual households, i.e. the residents speak more than one language.

If we compare these statistics to the ones displayed in Table 2, we see that the language shift has already established itself among primary school children. The figures here are based on the 1990 Primary 1 (grade 1) cohort and are valid for six-year-olds. The result, rather than the process of bilingualism, is presented in this table, which clearly shows the significant language shift experienced mainly by Chinese school children who are giving up the way their parents or grandparents speak to read and write in the important languages of trade and finance.

Educational and psychological questions, important as they are, are really nonquestions in countries such as Singapore where bilingualism is a way of life and where the whole educational enterprise is geared towards producing efficient and effective bilinguals, especially those with proficiency in the working language, English. Along with the perception of language as a tool is the equally important one of language as a tie. Sociocultural concerns such as understanding and respect for other cultures, while being schooled in the values and traditions of one's own, also play a part in the bilingual education program.

The bilingual education policy and the ascendancy of English. The bilingual education policy in the Republic of Singapore began in 1966, one year after its independence. The policy is based on the premise that English is crucial to Singapore's survival and that bilingualism would take a specific direction. In line with the official language policy of Singapore, bilingualism was defined "not as proficiency in any two languages, but as proficiency in English and one other official language" (Tay 1985: 5), which is usually taken to mean the ethnic mother tongue of the student. The following quotations taken from various issues of *The Straits Times*, the leading national newspaper, indicates that frequent articulation of the language policy would drive home the point of the importance of English:

---

2. Most of the statistics presented in this paper come from official surveys made by the Department of Statistics and the Ministry of Education of Singapore. Even though there might be the possible problem of underreporting or overreporting, statistics gathered by other independent bodies, such as the Survey Research of Singapore, have shown that these official figures are highly reliable.

I think that Singapore is the only [nonnative speaker] country which has adopted English as its working language. (Former Minister for Culture S. Rajaratnam, July 12, 1986)

The Prime Minister said that small countries like Singapore and Brunei must make use of the English language to plug into the international network. At the same time, he said, bilingualism should be promoted to prevent a gap

Table 2. Languages children speak at home

	Race				
	Chinese	Malay	Indian	Others	Overall
Total number	28,074	6,920	2,925	340	38,259
Most frequently spoken home language					
English	26.2%	10.6%	46.6%	70.3%	25.4%
Mandarin	67.9%	0.1%	0.4%	1.2%	49.9%
Malay	0.2%	89.3%	19.4%	27.4%	18.0%
Tamil	—	—	30.0%	—	2.3%
Chinese dialects	5.6%	—	—	—	41.1%
Other languages	—	—	3.5%	1.2%	0.1%
Second most frequently spoken home language					
English	33.8%	83.1%	48.7%	27.4%	43.8%
Mandarin	26.0%	0.3%	2.9%	20.3%	19.6%
Malay	0.4%	10.2%	8.8%	23.8%	3.0%
Tamil	—	—	24.3%	—	1.9%
Chinese dialects	28.4%	0.3%	3.2%	20.9%	
Other languages	0.1%	—	8.9%	4.7%	0.7%
Not available	11.3%	6.2%	6.1%	20.6%	10.1%

Source: Ministry of Education, Singapore

> forming between an English-educated elite and the rest of the population. (Cheng Shoong Tat, reporting on the visit of Prime Minister Lee Kuan Yew to Brunei, August 2, 1989)

> While there are other countries in the world which teach their children in more than one language, there is no other country that "tries to educate an entire population so that everyone is literate in English, and at the same time, has a reasonable knowledge of his mother tongue." (Minister for Education Tony Tan, March 17, 1990)

Such articulations came long after parents themselves had chosen to enroll their children in English-medium schools when they had the opportunity in the 1970s and early 1980s to enroll them in Chinese-medium, Malay-medium, or Tamil-medium schools. As early as 1972, the trend toward English was clearly seen by the prime minister:

> This fundamental change in our policy, of industrialization geared to a world export market ... also meant more widespread use of English, for this is the language of the investing industrialists ... This has posed a problem for the Malay, Chinese and Tamil streams. More and more parents have registered their children for the English-stream schools. This has led to sporadic and spasmodic reactions from the Chinese and Malay language newspapers, unions of school teachers, and literary and cultural groups. But despite successive campaigns, parents have continued to place the future careers of their children first, before any cultural or linguistic patriotism. (Lee Kuan Yew, *The Mirror* 8(16))

The ascendancy of English is seen also in the increasing literacy levels in English for the entire population. Along with the language shift in the spoken domain, we see a dramatic increase in literacy rates in the official languages as seen in Table 3. In the Census of Population 1990, literacy was defined as "the ability to read a newspaper with understanding" (Lau 1993: 2). The overall literacy rate rose from 84% in 1980 to 90% in 1990. According to the report on literacy, languages spoken, and education:

> The improved literacy rate was the result of the availability of universal education which was enjoyed by the young, the government's policy on bilingual education and the active promotion of continuing education and training programs for working adults (Lau 1993: 2).

When we examine literacy rates by age group, we see that the rate in the younger age groups is higher than that in the older age groups. In 1990, the

Table 3. Resident population aged 10 years and over by age group and literacy, 1980 and 1990.

Age Group (in years)	Total (%)	Literate (%)	Illiterate (%)
	1990		
10-19	100.0	99.4	0.6
20-29	100.0	98.3	1.7
30-39	100.0	96.6	3.4
40-49	100.0	90.2	9.8
Total	100.0	90.0	10.0
	1980		
10-19	100.0	94.5	5.5
20-29	100.0	95.4	4.6
30-39	100.0	88.1	11.9
40-49	100.0	72.7	27.3
50 & above	100.0	51.7	48.3
Total	100.0	83.5	16.5

Source: Department of Statistics, Singapore, Singapore Census of Population 1990 (1993: 3).

literacy rate for persons in the age group 10–19 was 99%, sliding down progressively to 64% for those in the age group of 50 years and over (Lau 1993: 3). However, what is of interest is that the corresponding rates for various age groups in 1990 is higher than for the same groups in 1980. The figures show a noticeable improvement in the literacy rates for those in the older age groups of 40–49 years and 50 years and over.

Bilingualism and biliteracy. In Table 4 below, we see that among the literate population aged 10 years and over, the rate of those who are literate in at least two official languages increased significantly from 39% in 1980 to 47% in 1990. The percentage of young persons who are literate in more than one

Table 4. Proportion of resident population aged 10 years and over who were literate by type of official language and ethnic group, 1980 and 1990.

Speakers (percent)		Official Language			
		English	Chinese	Malay	Tamil
Total	1980	56	60	17	3.3
	1990	66	63	16	3.6
Chinese	1980	53	77	1.2	—
	1990	62	80	1.5	—
Indians	1980	66	0.3	96	0.1
	1990	74	0.5	96	0.1
Malays	1980	67	0.5	18	48
	1990	82	1.1	27	50
Others	1980	95	3.3	32	0.3
	1990	93	6.5	31	0.2

Source: Department of Statistics, Singapore, Singapore Census of Population 1990 (1993: 5)

official language has increased. The proportion who are literate in two or more official languages and who are in the age group 10–19 rose from 53% in 1980 to 76% in 1990, while that of the age group 20–29 increased from 43% to 61%. This seems to have been "the result of the bilingual education policy which emphasizes English and the mother tongue" (Lau 1993: 3).

Literacy in the four official languages also shows an increase. Literacy in English (English only or English and another language) increased from 56% in 1980 to 66% in 1990, a direct outcome of the wider use of the language for both commercial and social interaction, and of the adoption of English as the main medium of instruction in schools and educational institutions. According to the report:

> Literacy in the mother tongue had also improved as a result of the bilingualism policy in which students were taught the mother tongue as the second language. The literacy rate in the Tamil language among the Indian

> community had also improved to 50 per cent from 48 per cent in 1980. Literacy in the Chinese language among the Chinese rose to 79 per cent from 77 per cent in 1980. The literacy rate in the Malay language among the Malays, however, remained unchanged at 96 per cent (Lau 1993: 5).

These results have come about after a heavy investment in educational linguistics, that is, providing an acquisition environment based on findings in current research on first- and second-language learning/acquisition in the classroom, applying methodologically and theoretically sound practices, and providing innovative and coherent curricula. Better teachers, better support from the home, better resources, improved training, and innovative curriculum planning have been provided to ensure that the children had a good chance to learn two of the official languages.

Language, education, and society in Singapore: Toward a theory of massive language shift. The questions of why language shift occurs and how it occurs are of great interest. In Singapore, we have seen that on the macrolevel, language management principles, policies, programs, and phases have helped set the ground in motion. On the microlevel, language acquisition and learning theories feed into the practices, beliefs, attitudes, values, and behaviors of the children's teachers and of the parents who want only the best for their children.

The social setting. On the microlevel, the theory of one parent, one language, or the belief in total immersion in one language or in the critical period of ages two through eight have become part of the consciousness of many parents and educators in Singapore. In addition, values attached to the languages (such as whether they serve as a tool or as a tie to cultural behavior) are examples of concerns of the community.

Parents would willingly pay for seminars such as a recent one on the topic of how to motivate children to learn the Chinese language. On July 30, 1993, 80 parents of girls in Raffles Girls' Primary School, a good primary school in Singapore, paid $5.00 each to attend such a seminar geared to help the parents of Primary 1 and Primary 2 students, particularly parents who encounter problems when their children do not show any interest in learning the Chinese language. In addition, each family had willingly enrolled their seven- and eight-year-olds in a speech and drama course given by the same consultant, Prof. Hou Jing-Hui. Prof. Hou teaches at the Central Academy of Drama in Beijing, and she has over 30 years of experience in this field and has developed her own unique teaching materials and methodology based on child psychology. Furthermore, she has trained numerous Singaporean teachers and instructors who were well sought after by schools in Singapore. The two consecutive modules cost each parent $300 for 24 weeks (1.5 hours per week). The classes were overwhelmingly oversubscribed. This enthusiastic response of parents to improving their children's learning in the second school language is just one example of community support and interest in the whole bilingual enterprise and the parents' understanding of the need to move to important languages of the future.

Toward a theory of massive language shift. For language shift to occur, there has to be an openness to change, a forward-looking vision, and cultural nonconservatism (cf. Fishman 1991: 386). Such a language shift has occurred in Singapore, especially in Chinese households (with the Malay and Indian households similarly affected though to a smaller extent), as school languages have become home languages.

In the case of Singapore, we could begin with the broad canvas of a very multilingual population, the majority of whom do not have high literacy levels in the languages that they speak. Then we move on from multilingualism to bilingualism, a step that effectively reduces the use of many available community languages to just two stipulated school languages. The multilingual but not too literate individual gives way to the bilingual individual, who is eventually also a biliterate person. The next stage is to define, in a precise way, the kind of bilingualism needed, i.e. proficiency in the first and second school languages. In Singapore, these languages are English and Mandarin, English and Malay, English and Tamil, and recently, English and some other Indian language (viz. Punjabi, Gujarati, Bengali, and Urdu). Table 5 shows the stages, in descending importance, that are needed to prepare the ground for massive language shift (cf. Fishman 1991: 395).

To ensure significant language shift, the population undergoing the shift must initially have low literacy levels and rates. Later, a higher rate of literacy, particularly defined as reading and writing in the school languages, will ensure the successful final stages of the language shift. There is an implicational scaling here from understanding to speaking, to reading, and to writing, which will feed back into the system of biliteracy. Bilingual proficiency and biliterate proficiency have come about because of the context of second language acquisition in Singapore.

It does seem that massive language shift can take place and will take place if specific conditions exist, e.g. a tacit understanding in the population that language is an important resource. However, as demonstrated in the Singapore case study, there must also be a shallowness in initial literacy levels that will allow openness to change, forward-looking vision, and cultural nonconservativism.

For most of Singapore, language is tool as well as tie. The rise of English and Mandarin in Singapore at the expense of the other languages (especially other Chinese dialects and some of the Indian languages) is linked to global events such as the increasing importance of languages of wider communication for purposes of trade, industry, and technology. English is recognized as the language of the new world order and as necessary for Singapore in order for it to plug into the international grid of business and finance. Mandarin is recognized as a potential cocandidate for that position. Malay is an import trading language for the region, Tamil for southern India.

Moreover, in Singapore, the school languages (primarily English and secondarily the other official languages) are imparted on a strong readership and writership basis, ensuring higher literacy levels. Higher literacy levels in these school languages are a necessary condition for gaining strength and becoming new dominant languages, and for remaining on the scene long after speakers of the other languages have passed on.

In brief, the Singapore experience has emphasized the importance of literacy transmission rather than intergenerational transmission in bilingualism. Parents are pragmatic and will give up their own language in order to ensure that their children will survive with the languages of the new world order. These languages are more often than not tied to education, trade, and technology, and high literacy in the languages will ensure high returns.

Table 5. Stages necessary for massive language shift

Stage 1—Nonneighborhood worksphere: Education, worksphere, mass media, government operations at the highest, nationwide level.

Stage 2—Family: Intergenerational codeswitching, exposing the weakness in the links between language use in the family.

Stage 3—Neighborhood worksphere: Reinforcing the language use in the core complex of family/ neighborhood/community (the weakness in the links among language use in family, neighborhood, and community in the other languages is compensated for with the new strength in the links in the desired languages).

Stage 4—Literacy acquisition: For the old and for the young, with an emphasis on the young in the desired languages.

Harking back to Fishman (1980), tiny Singapore does offer a wealth of data, considered practice, informed research, and training efforts in regard to education, language, and multilingualism. However, an integrated theory is yet a reality, as it may well be for all other multilingual societies, since the nature and the type of bilingualism that exist in different settings offer unique evolving contexts, necessitating unique treatments, whether in practice or in precept. Many aspects of multilingualism in Singapore remain relatively unexamined, and this search for a theory to account for multilingualism in Singapore is a step into unknown and uncharted territory.

Conclusion. Major areas in bilingualism, such as cognitive functioning, bilingual education, and attitudes/motivation, have not been expounded on here—but that was not my purpose. My purpose is, in fact, to show the operation of coherent language management, informed by the need to survive in the global marketplace. The intention here was to raise new questions (such as, How does one make an entire population give up its entrenched linguistic habits to adopt new ones?) and to ponder the language developments in Singapore that follow the linguistic marketplace principle.

Language policies and situations differ from place to place. Looking from the East to the countries in America or Europe that have developed sound language education principles and practices, one can say that the big questions raised there about speech communities and schools and related problems are not the same as the ones here.

In the 1950s, Singapore was a poor, developing nation; today, it is a model of efficiency, excellence, and progress and is considered one of the fastest-growing economies in the world. Much of this progress can be attributed to linguistic pragmatism and enlightened planning to accommodate such a pragmatic attitude to language issues.

The situation in Singapore may perhaps be unique in the entire world, East and West, and Singapore, with its mainly Asian population, heavily dependent on English for its survival, offers a distinctive example of educational linguistics for global interdependence and crosscultural communication, apt themes for a modern universe.

REFERENCES

Afendras, Evangelos A. and Eddie C.Y. Kuo. 1980. *Language and society in Singapore*. Singapore: Singapore University Press.

Baker, Colin. 1988. *Key issues in bilingualism and bilingual education*. Clevedon, U.K. and Philadelphia: Multilingual Matters.

Coulmas, Florian. 1989. *The writing systems of the world*. Oxford: Basil Blackwell.

Fishman, Joshua. 1991. *Reversing language shift: Theoretical and empirical foundations of assistance to threatened languages*. Clevedon, U.K. and Philadelphia: Multilingual Matters.

Gopinathan, Saravan, Anne Pakir, Ho Wah-Kam, and Vanithamani Saravanan (eds). 1993. *Language, society and education in Singapore: Issues and trends*. Singapore: Times Academic Press.

The Mirror, 1972. Volume 8, Number 16. Singapore: Ministry of Culture.

Spolsky, Bernard. 1978. "A model for the evaluation of bilingual education." *International Review of Education* 24(3): 347.

Lau, Kak-en. 1993. *Singapore census of population 1990: Literacy, languages spoken, and education*. Statistical Release Number 3. Singapore: Department of Statistics.

PuruShotam, Nirmala. 1989. "Language and linguistic policies." In Kernial Singh Sandhu and Paul Wheatley (eds.), *The management of success*. Singapore: Institute of Southeast Asian Studies.

The Straits Times, 1986–1990. Various issues. Singapore: Singapore Press Holdings.

Tay, Mary J.W. 1985. *Trends in language, literacy and education in Singapore*. Census Monograph Number 2. Singapore: Department of Statistics.

The sources of language teachers' instructional decisions

Jack C. Richards
City University of Hong Kong

In the field of second language teacher education (SLTE), the conceptualizations we have of the nature of teaching have a significant impact on both the content and process of our work as teacher educators. For example, if teaching is viewed as a science, scientific investigation and empirical research are seen as the source of valid principles of teaching. Good teaching involves the application of the findings of research, and the teacher's role is to put research-based principles into practice. Alternatively, teaching may be viewed as accumulated craft knowledge, and the study of the practices of expert practitioners of their craft may be seen as the primary data for a theory of teaching (Freeman and Richards 1993). In recent years, an alternative metaphor has emerged within the field of teacher education and is now making its way into SLTE. This is the notion of teaching as a thinking activity. This has been characterized as "a common concern with the ways knowledge is actively acquired and used by teachers and the circumstances that affect its acquisition and employment" (Calderhead 1987: 5). Calderhead points out that interest in teachers' thinking was a response to dissatisfaction with behaviorist approaches to the study of teaching in the 1970s.

> Ideologically, viewing teachers as active agents in the development of their own practice, as decision-makers using their specialist knowledge to guide their actions in particular situations, underlined the autonomous, responsible aspects of teachers' work, and provided an appealing rationale for considering teaching as a worthy, complex, demanding profession, especially when contrasted with the previously dominant view of teaching as the mastering of a series of effective teaching behaviours. (Calderhead 1987: 5)

The teacher-as-thinker metaphor captures the focus on how teachers conceptualize their work and the kinds of thinking and decision-making that underlie their practice. Rather than viewing the development of teaching skill as the mastery of general principles and theories that have been determined by others, the acquisition of teaching expertise is seen to be a process that involves the teacher in actively constructing a personal and workable theory of teaching.

This is the orientation to teaching I want to explore in this paper, which seeks to clarify the concept of teaching as thinking, to describe research on second language teachers that has been carried out from this perspective, and to examine implications for the field of SLTE.

The content of teachers' thinking. It might appear to be presumptious to try to characterize the thinking processes that underlie a process as complex and multifaceted as teaching. Fortunately, several scholars have tried to tease apart some of the issues that are involved (e.g. Clark and Peterson 1986; Calderhead 1987) and to reveal something of what Clark and Peterson refer to as the "cognitive psychology" of teaching. In their survey of teachers' thought processes, Clark and Peterson (1986) focus on three major categories of teachers' thought processes: teachers theories' and beliefs, teachers' planning or preactive decisionmaking, and teachers' interactive thoughts and decisions. While research on teachers' theories and beliefs tries to identify the psychological contexts that underlie teacher thinking and decisionmaking, research on teachers' preactive and interactive thinking seeks to identify the thinking and decisionmaking employed by teachers before and during teaching. In studying the knowledge and cognitive skills used by teachers, a variety of different research approaches has been employed, including:

- Thinking aloud (teachers verbalize their thoughts while engaged in tasks such as lesson planning),
- Stimulated recall (teachers examine a videotape or audiotape of a lesson and try to recall their thought processes or decisions at different points in the lesson),
- Journal keeping (teachers make written records of their plans and describe the different decisions involved), and
- Comparisons between novice and expert teachers.

The nature of teachers' belief systems. A primary source for teachers' classroom practices is teachers' belief systems—the information, attitudes, values, theories, and assumptions about teaching and learning that teachers build up over time and bring with them to the classroom. Shavelson and Stern (1981) suggest that what teachers do is governed by what they think and that teachers' theories and beliefs serve as a filter through which a host of instructional judgments and decisions are made. Teacher beliefs form a structured set of principles that are derived from experience, school practice, personality, educational theory, reading, and other sources. For example, in a questionnaire study of the beliefs of English teachers in Hong Kong schools, Richards, Tung, and Ng (1992) found that the 249 teachers sampled held a relatively consistent set of beliefs relating to such issues as the nature of the ESL curriculum in Hong Kong, their views of the role of English in society, differences between English and Chinese, the relevance of theory to practice, the role of textbooks, and their own role in the classroom. Differences in their beliefs, however, resulted from the amount of teaching experience they had and whether they subscribed to a primarily functional or grammar-based orientation to teaching. A number of studies have also sought to investigate the extent to which teachers' theoretical beliefs influence their classroom practices.

Johnson (1991), in a study of this kind, used three measures to identify ESL teachers' beliefs: a descriptive account of what teachers believe to constitute an ideal ESL classroom context, a lesson plan analysis task, and a Beliefs Inventory. In the sample of teachers studied, she identified three different methodological positions: a skills-based approach that views language as consisting of four discrete language skills, a rules-based approach that views language as a process of rule-governed creativity, and a function-based approach that focuses on the use of authentic language within situational contexts and that seeks to provide opportunities for functional and communicative language use in the classroom.

The majority of the teachers in the sample held clearly defined beliefs that consistently reflected one of these three methodological approaches. Teachers representing each theoretical orientation were then observed while teaching and the majority of their lessons were found to be consistent with their theoretical orientation. A teacher who expressed a skill-based theoretical orientation generally presented lessons in which the focus was primarily on skill acquisition. A teacher with the rule-based orientation tended to employ more activities and exercises that served to reinforce knowledge of grammatical structures; she constantly referred to grammar even during reading and writing activities, for example by asking her students to identify a key grammatical structure and to explain the rule that governed its use. The function-based teachers, on the other hand, selected activities that typically involved the learners' personal expression, such as teaching word meaning and usage through a meaningful context, reading activities that focused on the concepts or ideas within the text, and context rich writing activities where students were encouraged to express their ideas without attention to grammatical correctness.

In exploring the relationship between teachers' beliefs and classroom practices, Wood (1991) carried out a longitudinal study of two teachers with different theoretical orientations, teaching the same ESL course in a Canadian University. He summarizes these two teachers as representing two different views of teaching: One he called a "curriculum-based" view of teaching, and the other a "student-based" view. A curriculum-based view of teaching implies that decisions related to the implementation of classroom activities are based primarily on what is preplanned according to the curriculum. Student-based teaching, on the other hand, implies that decisions are based primarily on factors related to the particular group of students in the classroom at that particular moment. Wood (1991: 4) found that for each teacher, there was strong evidence that:

(1) The decisions made in planning and carrying out the course were internally consistent, and consistent with deeper underlying assumptions and beliefs about language, learning and teaching; yet
(2) Each teacher's decisions and beliefs differed dramatically from the other along a number of specifiable dimensions.

For example, the teacher with the "curricular" view of teaching explained her goals and evaluated her teaching in terms of planned curricular content. Although she often mentioned the students in talking about her lessons, they were not typically for her a starting point in making instructional decisions. She tended to evaluate her teaching in terms of how successfully she had accomplished what she had set out to do according to the curriculum. When there was a choice between following up something that developed in the course of a lesson as opposed to keeping to her plan, she invariably followed her plan. The second teacher, on the other hand, was guided much more by student responses. He was much more prepared to modify and reinterpret the curriculum based on what the students wanted.

Smith (in press), in another Canadian study of ESL teachers in postsecondary ESL classes, found that teachers' instructional decisions were highly consistent with expressed beliefs and that personal belief systems influenced how teachers ranked their institutions' explicit course objectives for the courses they were assigned to teach. Among teachers teaching on the same course, teachers with a structured grammar-based view of language selected different goals for the course from teachers holding a function-based view of language.

In each of the studies described above, the teachers were relatively free to put their beliefs into practice. However, there are also well-documented accounts of situations where there is not a high degree of correspondence between teachers' expressed beliefs and their classroom practices. Duffy and Anderson (1988) studied eight reading teachers and found that only four of them consistently employed practices that directly reflected their beliefs. Factors cited as likely to prevent teachers from teaching according to their beliefs include the need to follow a prescribed curriculum, a lack of suitable resources, and the students' ability levels. Hoffman and Kugle (1982) found no significant relationship between teachers' beliefs about reading and the kinds of verbal feedback teachers gave during reading lessons. Yim (1993), studying ESL teachers in Singapore, likewise found that while they were able to articulate beliefs about the role of grammar teaching from a communicative orientation, these beliefs were not evident in their classroom practices, which were driven more by exam-based structured grammar activities of a noncommunicative kind.

Teachers' belief systems have also been studied in terms of how they influence the thinking and practice of novice teachers. The belief systems of novice teachers as they enter teaching often serve as a lens through which they view both the content of the teacher development program and their language teaching experiences. For example, Almarza (in press) studied a group of four student teachers in a foreign language teacher education program in the U.K. and examined how the relationship between the teachers' internalized models of teaching, often acquired informally through their experience as foreign language learners, interacted with the models of teaching they were introduced to in their teacher education (TE) program. The teachers responded quite differently to the method they were being trained to use in their TE program—a kind of modified direct method approach. For one teacher, the structure introduced by the method was something she welcomed. It provided her with a tool to manage her teaching and gave her confidence. She measured her own success in terms of how closely she was able to follow the method. For her the method superseded any instinctive views she had about the nature of teaching.

> Now having applied it [the model] with ... both classes and private students, I can see why it's been called the "miracle" method! Even my least confident students have been speaking the language with good pronunciation and without making mistakes and I know they'll never forget what they've learned ... With this method they never hear an incorrect version—so, of course, they don't make mistakes.
>
> The method was without question the decisive factor in my carrying out TP successfully. It gave me absolute confidence and it had a positive attitude on the pupils towards French or Spanish and towards me, as it allowed me, for the first time, to really achieve something in the language and feel that they had achieved something. (Almarza in press)

By contrast, other teachers rejected the method because it conflicted with their own theories of teaching. One teacher said she could not believe in a methodology that did not consider the learner as the center of the learning process.

> I feel first that it is not respecting the students' intelligence, in a way. Students may not have the word in the foreign language for a book or a chair, but they know very well that it is a book and a chair and to have to spend 10 minutes arguing or not arguing, but deciding that this is a book and this is a chair, seems is to insult the students ... the students may not be very motivated by that kind of presentation, firstly ... why should the student want to learn, I mean, to learn those items in the first place? ... I am just wondering to what extent, where is the balance on that scale, where can you sort of exerpt your knowledge as a teacher in order to choose the right kind of input, to guide the students to look into, lets say, certain texts, or certain whatever, but at the same time keeping up motivation in the student ..., I just feel I don't like to say: "right this is an orange, you have to learn this." (Almarza in press)

Almarza's study shows that while a teacher education program might be built around a well-articulated model of teaching, the model is interpreted in different ways by individual trainee teachers as they deconstruct it in the light of their teaching experiences and reconstruct it drawing on their own beliefs and assumptions about themselves, language, teaching learners, and learning.

The ways teachers' personal theories of teaching influence their perception and evaluation of their own teaching was further illustrated in a study of a group of novice teachers completing an introductory teacher preparation program in Hong Kong (the UCLES/RSA Certificate in TEFLA) (Richards, Ho, and Giblin in press). One of the issues that was studied was the theories of teaching held by each of the teachers in the program. Data was provided by written reports of the teachers' planning, interactive and evaluation decisions, and recordings of discussions with their supervisors. The individual differences in the way the five teachers planned, monitored, and described their own teaching suggested different ways they conceptualized teaching. These differences can be summarized in a series of perspectives.

A *teacher-centered perspective* sees the key features of a lesson primarily in terms of teacher factors, such as classroom management, teacher's explanations, teacher's questioning skills, teacher's presence, voice quality, manner, and so on. This view of a lesson sees it as a performance by the teacher. A different view of a lesson, which can be termed the *curriculum-centered perspective,* sees a lesson in terms of a segment of instruction. Relevant foci include lesson goals, structuring, transitions, materials, task types, and content flow and development. A third perspective on a lesson can be called the *learner-centered perspective*. This views the lesson in terms of its effect on learners and refers to such factors as student participation, interest, and learning outcomes. These different perspectives on a lesson are summarized in Table 1.

Table 1. Different Perspectives on a Lesson

Teacher-centered focus	The teacher is the primary focus, including teacher's role, classroom-management skills, questioning skills, presence, voice quality, manner, quality of teacher's explanations, and instructions.
Curriculum-centered focus	The lesson as an instructional unit is the primary focus, including lesson goals, opening, structuring, task-types, flow, and development and pacing.
Learner-centered focus	The learners are the primary focus, including the degree to which the lesson engages them, participation patterns, and extent of language use.

Any lesson can be conceptualized in terms of any or all of these perspectives. In the study, although each of the teachers (Teachers A, B, C, D, and E) referred to all three aspects of lessons in describing their teaching, Teacher A's focus of awareness was more consistently on teacher factors than on other dimensions of her lessons. Teacher B included all three perspectives in her discussions of her lessons and moved throughout from one perspective to another, though the role of the teacher was a recurring focus. For Teacher C, the learner perspective had priority. For Teacher D and Teacher E, lessons were discussed more frequently from the teacher's point of view and in terms of the design of the lesson.

In discussing each other's teaching in group sessions, these different perspectives often emerged. For example, Teacher B, commenting on one of Teacher A's lessons, described it from the "curriculum" perspective: "You did a good job on building it up, starting with revision. You didn't waste any time on setting up the lesson. It flowed through beautifully." Teacher A herself, however, commented on her lesson from the "teacher" perspective: "I thought the lesson deteriorated as it got to the end. I wasn't happy with the drilling. I didn't give myself enough time to do it properly." Teacher C commented on the same lesson from the "learners" perspective: "I liked the way your lesson went at the end. The students were being expressive. They put feeling into it." The differences in the individual teachers' views of a successful lesson can be seen by listing the three different perspectives according to the priority of each teacher (Table 2).

Table 2. Priorities for each teacher according to primary focus of concern

Teacher A	1 teacher	2 curriculum	3 learners
Teacher B	1 teacher and learners		2 curriculum
Teacher C	1 learners	2 curriculum	3 teacher
Teacher D	1 curriculum	2 teacher	3 learners
Teacher E	1 teacher	2 curriculum	3 learners

Teachers' preactive decisions. An issue that has long been of interest in understanding how teachers conceptualize their work has been the question of teacher planning. The planning of a lesson is a complex problem-solving task, involving thinking about the subject matter, the students, the classroom, and the curriculum, during which the teacher transforms and modifies an aspect of the curriculum to fit the unique circumstances of his or her class (Clark and Peterson 1986). But how does this process occur and what kinds of thinking are involved? And do experienced and novice teachers differ in the thinking they bring to this process?

In an influential paper, Shulman (1987) characterized these processes as pedagogical reasoning. Shulman describes the process in these terms:

> I begin with the assumption that most teaching is initiated by some form of "text": a textbook, a syllabus, or an actual piece of material the teacher or student wishes to have understood. The text many be a vehicle for the accomplishment of other educational purposes, but some sort of teaching material is almost always involved.
>
> Given a text, educational purposes, and/or a set of ideas, pedagogical reasoning and action involve a cycle through the activities of comprehension, transformation, instruction, evaluation, and reflection. (Shulman 1987: 14)

Shulman describes transformation as central to this process.

> Comprehended ideas must be transformed in some manner if they are to be taught. To reason one's way through an act of teaching is to think one's way from the subject matter as understood by the teacher into the minds and motivations of learners. Transformations, therefore, require some combination or ordering of the following processes, each of which employs a kind of repertoire: (1) preparation (of the given text materials) including the process of critical interpretation, (2) representation of the ideas in the form of new analogies, metaphors, and so forth, (3) instructional selections from among an array of teaching methods and models, and (4) adaptation of these representations to the general characteristics of the children to be taught, as well as (5) tailoring the adaptations to the specific youngsters in the classroom. These forms of transformation, these aspects of the process wherein one moves from personal comprehension to preparing for the comprehension of others, are the essence of the act of pedagogical reasoning, of teaching as thinking, and of planning—whether explicitly or implicitly—the performance of teaching. (Shulman 1987: 16)

One approach to exploring teachers' pedagogical reasoning is to give teachers with different degrees of experience and expertise identical tasks to perform, and then to examine differences in how they go about completing the tasks (Berliner 1987). For example, I recently compared two groups of teachers—a group of student teachers in the second year of a preservice TESL degree and a group of experienced teachers who had several years teaching experience and master's degrees in TESL. Their task was to plan a reading lesson for an ESL class at the lower secondary level around a short story called "Puppet on a String". The story is about a mentally retarded fourteen-year-old boy traveling on a bus for the first time. A passenger on the bus persuades the boy to get off the bus and drop off a package to someone en route. The boy decides to hand in the package at the police station:

> Presently Paul was climbing a flight of stone steps towards an impressive pair of blue doors with the word POLICE emblazoned above them. He was soon telling a policeman all that had happened. He apologized for not having completely succeeded in doing what he had been told. The police officer opened the box and was in conversation with the Chief Inspector within seconds.
>
> "... That's right, sir. Looks like heroin to me. Must be worth a bomb ... Yes ... Claims he was told to make the drop by a plain clothes officer ... If you ask me, sir, it's a load of rubbish ... No, I don't know why he should give himself up. Fit of remorse, maybe, and I reckon he's putting on an act of being nuts or something so he can get off lightly ... Yes, we have a cell free ... No, I understand—no maltreatment. Yes ... just so—not a leg to stand on in court. Borstal, I should think ... a touch of the short, sharp shock, eh? That's right—make decent citizens of them ... Bye." The policeman put the phone down.
>
> "Can I go home?" asked Paul.
>
> "Look, you can stop your act now, lad. You're in the proverbial hands of the law. This way."

In examining the lesson plans prepared by the two groups, those produced by the student teachers devoted much of the lesson plan to trying to communicate the linguistic content of the text to the students. These plans were time-consuming to produce, taking up to one and a half hours to prepare. A typical approach adopted was: "I would concentrate on the structure, the sentence patterns, and the organization of the text and analyze these with the students."

Many used a model format for a reading lesson studied in a methodology class—with a sequence of prereading, reading, and postreading activities built around the story. The main problems the student teachers anticipated had to do with the vocabulary load of the story: "My main concern was the vocabulary. Since it's the first time the students read the story, the only thing I can do is to teach the vocabulary through the context."

The experienced teachers offered a much greater variety of approaches to developing a lesson around the text. These included dividing the text in sections and having students predict outcomes, working from titles and headings to anticipate the story before reading it, small group discussion of issues in the story, and writing different versions of the conclusion of the story. Many of the experienced teachers moved quickly beyond the text to explore issues it raised.

Several of the teachers focused on the issue of being handicapped or of "mental retardation" to put the story into context and to make the students more sympathetic to the boy in the story. For example, one teacher wrote:

> The point that I'm trying to get them to see is all of us have disabilities, that the handicapped are not so different. They have a greater degree of disability. So I start out looking at students who wear glasses, and ask them why they need to wear them, and note that someone with eye disabilities may need help. I'll have a picture of someone with a hearing aid and talk about the possible problems that people might have in that area. And I'll invite a short student to come out to the board and write something at the top of the blackboard and the person will not be able to do it. So I'll ask a taller one. So they can see that being short is a problem or so is being tall. I'll give them an example of my own experience when I hit my head because I'm tall. And my mother is too short to reach the cupboard. So each one of us has some area that could be classified as disabilities. Then I would try to bridge the gap and begin talking about the problem that Paul had. Then I divide the group into listening teams and have them listen for certain specific information in a role play, e.g. one group might look at Paul and think about what characteristics he has that show or would give evidence that he's a bit slow. Another group might look at the wrong information or attitudes that the police officer had. And the other group might look at the way people take advantage of Paul. I would give them the text a week before the lesson. I'm not very fond of having kids read out loud a lot in class. I'm not sure if it's worth the time. Often the English is rather stilted. You have a tendency when you're reading out loud to give equal weight to each word and that's not the way we talk. Anyway, I'll then have students do a role play and I'll have prearranged that with some simple visuals like the seater, sign that says police station or police bus, and try to get quite a number of students involved in that role play. Other kids are involved as listening teams to take notes. Then I would get teams to answer the basic questions that have been given to each of them, and try to discover the bits as a whole.

The experienced teachers saw a much greater variety of issues and problems that the text posed for students and how these needed to be addressed. Some of these issues and problems were, for example, how the students would see the characters in the story, what the author was trying to communicate, and getting students engaged in the moral conflicts the story poses. The experienced teachers dealt with the text at the level of social meaning rather than at the level of linguistic meaning.

The differences between the two groups of teachers is in line with findings of a body of research on differences between the knowledge, thinking, and actions of experts and novices. Experts and novices have been found to differ in the way they understand and represent problems and in the strategies they choose to solve them (Livingston and Borko 1989). Novices have less fully developed schemata. In this context, schemata are described as abstract knowledge structures that summarize information about many particular cases and the relationships among them (Anderson 1984). Studies of expert teachers have shown that they are able to move through the agendas of a lesson in a cohesive and flexible way, compared to the more fragmented efforts of novice teachers:

> The cognitive schemata of experts typically are more elaborate, more complex, more interconnected, and more easily accessible than those of novices. Therefore expert teachers have larger, better-integrated stores of facts, principles, and experiences to draw upon as they engage in planning, interactive teaching, and reflection. (Livingston and Borko 1989: 36)

Experienced teachers hence have well-developed mental representations of typical students, of typical tasks, and of expected problems and solutions. As Calderhead points out, experienced teachers

> seemed to know the kinds of home backgrounds of students, they knew what to expect in the way of knowledge and skills in their classrooms, they had an image of the likely number of students who would need help, they had an image of the types of behaviors and discipline problems that could be expected. They knew what the students might possess in the way of previous experience, skills, and knowledge ... This kind of pedagogical knowledge is learned from thousands of hours' instruction, and tens of thousands of interactions with students. It is knowledge that influences classroom organization and management and is the basis for intercepting the curriculum. (Quoted in Berliner 1987: 64)

Teachers' interactive decisions. A parallel line of inquiry in the study of teachers' thinking has investigated the interactive decisions teachers employ while they teach. A metaphor used to describe this dimension of teaching is teaching as improvisational performance. During the process of teaching, the teacher fills out and adapts his or her lesson outline based on how the students respond to the lesson. While the teachers' planning decisions provide a framework with which he or she approaches a lesson, in the course of teaching the lesson that framework may be substantially revised as the teacher responds to students' understanding and participation and redirects the lesson in midstream.

How does this reshaping and redirection come about? Shavelson and Stern (1981) introduced the metaphor of "routines" to describe how teachers manage many of the moment-to-moment processes of teaching. Teachers monitor instruction looking for cues that the students are following the lesson satisfactorily. They teach using well-established routines. Berliner has commented on "the enormously important role played by mental scripts and behavioural routines in the performance of expert teachers" (1987: 72).

> These routines are the shared, scripted, virtually automated pieces of action that constitute so much of our daily lives [as teachers]. In classrooms, routines often allow students and teachers to devote their attention to other, perhaps more important matters inherent in the lesson. In [a study] of how an opening homework review is conducted, an expert teacher was found to be brief, taking about one third less time than a novice. She was able to pick up information about attendance, and about who did or did not do the homework, and identified who was going to get help in the subsequent lesson. She was able to get all the homework corrected, and elicited mostly correct answers throughout the activity. And she did so at a brisk pace and without ever losing control of the lesson. Routines were used to record attendance, to handle choral responding during the homework checks, and for hand raising to get attention. The expert used clear signals to start and finish lesson segments. Interviews with the expert revealed how the goals for the lesson, the time constraints, and the curriculum itself were blended to direct the activity. The expert appeared to have a script in mind throughout the lesson, and she followed that script very closely. (Berliner 1987: 72)

Novice teachers by comparison lack a repertoire of routine and scripts, and mastering their use occupies a major portion of their time during teaching (Fogerty, Wang, and Creek 1983). In my study of teachers completing the RSA Certificate program for example, a recurring concern of the teachers was the use of such basic techniques as eliciting, drilling, concept checking (i.e. checking that students understood new teaching points), monitoring (i.e. attending to student performance and giving feedback on errors), and how to use the overhead transparency and the white board. Discussion of how to carry out these procedures effectively occupied a substantial portion of time in group feedback sessions with their tutors.

Experienced teachers, on the other hand, have a better-developed schematic knowledge of teaching and access to a variety of familiar routines. Livingston and Borko (1989), studying differences between the improvisational performance of novice and expert teachers, observe:

> In the lessons we observed, the success of the experts' improvisation seemed to depend upon their ability to provide examples quickly and to draw connections between students' comments or questions and the lesson's objectives. In terms of cognitive structure, successful improvisational

> teaching requires that the teacher have an extensive network of interconnected, easily accessible schemata and be able to select particular strategies, routines, and information from these schemata during actual teaching and learning interactions based on specific classroom occurrences. (Livingston and Borko 1989)

Decision-making models of teaching propose that when problems arise in teaching, a teacher may call up an alternative routine or react interactively to the situation, redirecting the lesson based on his or her understanding of the nature of the problem and how best to address it. This process has begun to be examined in the context of second language teaching.

Nunan (1992) studied the interactive decisions of nine ESL teachers in Australia by examining with teachers a transcription of a lesson they had taught and discussing it with each teacher. Nunan found that the majority of the interactive decisions made by the teachers related to classroom management and organization, but also that the teachers' prior planning decisions provided a structure and framework for the teachers' interactive decisions. Johnson (1992) studied six preservice ESL teachers using videotaped recordings of lessons they taught and stimulated recall reports of the instructional decisions and prior knowledge that influenced their teaching. Johnson found that teachers most frequently recalled making interactive decisions in order to promote student understanding, (37% of all interactive decisions made) or to promote student motivation and involvement (17%). Reasons for other interactive decisions reported are shown in Table 3. Johnson comments:

Table 3. Reasons for interactive decisions.

Student understanding	37%
Student motivation and involvement	17%
Instructional management	15%
Curriculum integration	9%
Subject matter content	8%
Students language skill and ability	8%
Students' affective needs	6%

Source: Johnson 1992: 127

> These findings confirm previously held characterisations of preservice teachers' instructional decisions as being strongly influenced by student behaviour. In addition these findings support the notion that preservice teachers rely on a limited number of instructional routines and are overwhelmingly concerned with inappropriate student responses and maintaining the flow of instructional activity. (Johnson 1992: 129)

Ulichny (in press) describes a case study of an ESL teacher presenting a classroom activity to an ESL class. In her study, Ulichny uses a detailed microanalysis of the discourse of the event together with the teacher's own reflections and interpretations of the classroom talk. The teacher in Ulichny's study was an ESL teacher in an American university ESL program. The teaching moment Ulichny examines was an ESL reading class for incoming students. The teacher had a well-developed schema for teaching a reading lesson in this situation. The course was content-based and included a close reading of a chapter from a sociology textbook. The teacher planned to lead the students through the chapter, section by section, helping the students grasp the meaning of the text. She assigned part of the chapter to be read for homework.

> She has given them a simplified lecture that restated the five main points about why, according to the book, nuclear families are more functional in industrialized societies, and she is planning to have the students locate those five points in the words of the author in the text. (Ulichny in press)

However, once she began her lesson, she discovered that the students' comprehension of her lecture was unclear and she could not elicit the ideas she was looking for, and so she rethought her plan and began trying to build up their comprehension of the points of her lecture. Ulichny traces the teacher's thinking through a series of steps that started with discovering a problem, assessing the problem, and unsuccessfully attempting to elicit what she is looking for from the students. Then the teacher took over and did the work for the students, modeling and scaffolding the content of the text—a task she had originally planned for the students themselves to do. From her longitudinal analysis of the teacher's evolution of her teaching methodology through interactive interaction with the students, Ulichny concludes:

> Teaching is a constant mediation between enacted planned activities and addressing students' understandings, abilities and motivation to carry out the activity. How a teacher determines which activities to engage the class in, how she assesses the students' participation in the task and what she determines are reasons and remedies for lack of adequate participation are the basic units of the teaching moment. The particular construction or sense-making of the moment is a product of an individual teacher's past learning and teaching experiences, beliefs about teaching and learning—from both professional training as well as folk wisdom gleaned from fellow teachers, and her particular personality. (Ulichny in press)

Implications for SLTE practice. The metaphor of the teacher as thinker provides a conceptual framework that offers a rich alternative to behaviorally oriented views of teaching and one that also provides a useful research agenda. As Freeman observes:

> It focuses research on the teacher and recognizes the central importance of her cognitive world. It also provides a methodologically accessible architecture that can lend itself to both qualitative and quantitative study. (Freeman in press a)

Freeman also points out the limitations inherent in this framework, which he ascribes to

> The rigidity of decision-making as an a priori construct, the lack of attention to the context of decision, and the potential distraction from language as both the substance and the research vehicle of decision-making. (Freeman in press a)

Notwithstanding these limitations, the analysis of teaching as an activity that is grounded in the teacher's belief systems and cognitive world offers several important implications for the practice of second language teacher education, and I would like to conclude by examining some of these implications as I understand them.

Modeling the cognitive skills of expert teachers. An important goal of preservice experiences for language teachers is to expose novice teachers to the thinking skills of expert teachers in order to help them develop the pedagogic reasoning skills they need when they begin teaching. While many current resource books in SLTE make extensive use of tasks that student teachers carry out at their own level of pedagogical expertise, the value of these activities can be enhanced if they are followed by presentation of expert teachers' solutions of the same tasks, together with the thinking that accompanied them. For example, in my methodology classes with preservice teachers, after assigning students a planning task such as planning a reading lesson around a short text, feedback on their efforts includes not only peer and instructor responses to their lesson plans but a think aloud "walk through" of the same planning task, during which I try to model the thinking that an experienced teacher would bring to the task. This strategy is also appropriate for cooperating teachers.

> To promote knowledge development in student teachers, we believe that cooperating teachers should be able and willing to explicate the routines and strategies they use, provide systematic and constructive feedback, and engage with the student teacher in joint problem solving about pedagogical issues. They should also model pedagogical thinking to student teachers by

demonstrating and then explaining how they transform subject matter into pedagogically powerful forms. By making their thinking explicit, they reveal the connection between their actions and their knowledge structures. (Livingston and Borko 1984: 41)

Using case studies. Case materials, including both written and videotaped cases, also provide another rich vehicle for helping student teachers develop the capacity to analyze situations, to explore how teachers in different settings arrive at lesson goals and teaching strategies, and to understand how expert teachers draw on pedagogical schemas and routines in the process of teaching. Case-based approaches are widely used in other professions such as business, law, and medicine, but they have only recently begun to be used more generally in teacher education (Shulman 1992). Case reports can reveal ways of thinking about a significant teaching incident, and when accompanied by "deconstruction" through questioning and critical interpretation, they can help reveal how the teacher's beliefs, knowledge, personality, and pedagogical reasoning shapes a particular event.

A number of advantages have been suggested for using case studies in this way in teacher education (Kleinfeld 1992).

- Students are provided with vicarious teaching problems that present real issues in context;
- Students can learn how to identify issues and frame problems;
- Cases can be used to model the processes of analysis and inquiry in teaching;
- Students can acquire an enlarged repertoire and understanding of educational strategies;
- Cases help stimulate the habit of reflective inquiry.

The building up of a collection of case reports that can be effectively used in this way is a priority in the inservice MATESL program in the City University of Hong Kong, since case methods offer a potentially useful complement to other procedures used in the program, such as journal writing and other forms of reflective inquiry. At present, however, there are few case reports of this kind available as a resource in SLTE programs.

Providing focused field experiences. The inclusion of goals related to the cognitive and interpretive domain of teaching also suggests a different focus for field experiences such as practice teaching and classroom observation. In practice teaching for example, providing student teachers with multiple opportunities to teach the same content enables them to develop their schematic knowledge of teaching and to appreciate the effect of context on their understanding of teaching incidents.

> The opportunity to repeat and fine tune instructional strategies and explanations increases the likelihood that novices will incorporate these elements into their cognitive schemata. Similarly, critically analyzing performance and revising it for another session helps novices to elaborate and connect existing knowledge structures. This revision process contributes to the development of pedagogical content knowledge and pedagogical reasoning skills. (Livingston and Borko 1984: 40)

Such experiences can also be linked with the preparation of case reports for use as part of the on-campus program.

The concept of pedagogical reasoning skills also provides a rationale for a different focus to classroom observation. During observations, student teachers can be engaged in watching how an experienced teacher uses routines and scripts in teaching and how the teacher's improvisational performance helps resolve problems that occur during a lesson. Such activities can help novice teachers understand the interpretive nature of teaching and realize the conceptual basis for such interpretation.

Conclusions. While a focus on cognitive processes is not new in applied linguistics and TESOL, as seen in a growing literature on learning strategies and the cognitive processes employed by L2 writers and readers, interest in the cognitive processes employed by second language teachers is more recent. At present, the conceptual framework for such research has been borrowed wholesale from parallel research in general education, and only recently have attempts been made to incorporate a language or discourse orientation into that framework (see Freeman in press b). The cognitive analysis of second language teaching is, however, central to our understanding both of how teachers teach as well as how novice teachers develop teaching expertise. There is an important message in this research that can be expressed (with slight overstatment) in the following way: "There is no such thing as good teaching. There are only good teachers."

In other words, *teaching* is realized only in *teachers*; it has no independent existence. Teacher education is hence less involved with transmitting models of effective teaching practice and more concerned with providing experiences that facilitate the development of cognitive and interpretive skills that are used uniquely by every teacher.

REFERENCES

Almarza, Gloria. in press. "Student foreign language teachers' knowledge growth." In Donald Freeman and Jack C. Richards (eds.), *Learning to teach: A second language perspective.* New York: Cambridge University Press.

Anderson, Richard C. 1984. "Some reflections on the acquisition of knowledge." *Educational Researcher* 13(10): 5-10.

Berliner, David C. 1987. "Ways of thinking about students and classrooms by more and less experienced teachers." In James Calderhead (ed.), *Exploring teachers' thinking*. London: Cassell Educational Limited. 60-83

Calderhead, James (ed.). 1987. *Exploring teachers' thinking*. London: Cassell.

Clark, Christopher and Penelope Peterson. 1986. "Teachers' thought processes." In Merlin Wittrock (ed.), *Handbook of research on teaching, Third edition*. New York: Macmillan. 255-296

Duffy, Gerald and L. Anderson. 1986. "Teachers' theoretical orientations and the real classroom." *Reading Psychology* 5(2): 97-104.

Fogerty, Joan L., Margaret C. Wang, and Roy Creek. 1983. "A descriptive study of experienced and novice teachers' interactive thoughts and actions." *Journal of Educational Research* 77: 22-32.

Freeman, Donald. in press a. "The unstudied problem: Research on learning to teach second languages." In Donald Freeman and Jack C. Richards (eds.), *Learning to teach: A second language perspective*. New York: Cambridge University Press.

Freeman, Donald. in press b. "Renaming experience/reconstructing practice: Developing new understandings of teaching." In Donald Freeman and Jack C. Richards (eds.), *Learning to teach: A second language perspective*. New York: Cambridge University Press.

Freeman, Donald and Jack C. Richards. 1993. "Conceptions of teaching and the education of second language teachers." *TESOL Quarterly* 27(2): 193-216.

Hoffman, J.V. and C.L. Kugle. 1982. "A study of the theoretical orientation to reading and its relationship to teacher verbal feedback during reading instruction." *Journal of Classroom Interaction* 18(1): 2-7.

Johnson, Karen E. 1991. "The relationship between teachers' beliefs and practices during literacy instruction for non-native speakers of English." *Journal of Reasing Behaviour* 24: 83-108.

Johnson, Karen E. 1992. "The instructional decisions of pre-service English as a second language teachers: New directions for teacher preparation programs." In John Flowerdew, Mark Brock, and Sophie Hsia (eds.), *Perspectives on second language teacher education*. Hong Kong: City Polytechnic of Hong Kong. 115-134

Kleinfeld, Judith. 1992. "Learning to think like a teacher." In Judith Shulman (ed.), *Case methods in teacher education*. New York: Teachers' College Press.

Livingston, Carol and Hilda Borko. 1989. "Expert-novice differences in teaching: A cognitive analysis and implications." *Journal of Teacher Education* 40(4): 36-42.

Nunan, David. 1992. "The teacher as decision maker." In John Flowerdew, Mark Brock, and Sophie Hsia (eds.), *Perspectives on second language teacher education*. Hong Kong: City Polytechnic of Hong Kong. 135-165.

Richards, Jack C., Belinda Ho and Karen Giblin. in press. "Learning how to teach: A case study of teachers in the RSA Cert." In Donald Freeman and Jack C. Richards (eds.), *Learning to teach: A second language perspective*. New York: Cambridge University Press.

Richards, Jack C., Peter Tung and Peggy Ng. 1992. "The culture of the English language teacher: A Hong Kong example." *RELC Journal* 23(1): 81-103.

Shavelson, Richard J. and Paula Stern. 1981. "Research on teachers' pedagogical thoughts, judgements, decisions, and behavior." *Review of Educational Research* 51: 455-498.

Shulman, Lee. 1987. "Knowledge and teaching: Foundations of the new reform." *Harvard Educational Review* 57(1): 1-21.

Shulman, Judith (ed.). 1992. *Case methods in teacher education*. New York: Teachers' College Press.

Smith, Debbie. in press. "Teacher decision-making in the adult ESL classroom." In Donald Freeman and Jack C. Richards (eds.), *Learning to teach: A second language perspective*. New York: Cambridge University Press.

Ulichny, Polly. in press. "What's in a methodology?" In Donald Freeman and Jack C. Richards (eds.), *Learning to teach; A second language perspective*. New York: Cambridge University Press.

Woods, Devon. 1991. "Teachers' interpretations of second language teaching curricula." *RELC Journal* 22(2): 1–19.

Yim, Lai Wah. 1993. "Relating teachers' perceptions of the place of grammar to their teaching practices." MA dissertation. National University of Singapore.

www.ingramcontent.com/pod-product-compliance
Lightning Source LLC
LaVergne TN
LVHW090800070826
844660LV00022B/1047

* 9 7 8 0 8 7 8 4 0 1 2 9 1 *